The Greek and Persian Wars

John R. Hale, Ph.D.

PUBLISHED BY:

THE GREAT COURSES
Corporate Headquarters
4840 Westfields Boulevard, Suite 500
Chantilly, Virginia 20151-2299
Phone: 1-800-832-2412
Fax: 703-378-3819
www.thegreatcourses.com

Copyright © The Teaching Company, 2008

Printed in the United States of America

This book is in copyright. All rights reserved.

Without limiting the rights under copyright reserved above,
no part of this publication may be reproduced, stored in
or introduced into a retrieval system, or transmitted,
in any form, or by any means
(electronic, mechanical, photocopying, recording, or otherwise),
without the prior written permission of
The Teaching Company.

John R. Hale, Ph.D.

Director of Liberal Studies, University of Louisville

John R. Hale, Director of Liberal Studies at the University of Louisville in Kentucky, is an archaeologist with fieldwork experience in England, Scandinavia, Portugal, Greece, Turkey, and the Ohio River Valley. At the University of Louisville, Dr. Hale teaches introductory courses on archaeology and specialized courses on the Bronze Age, the ancient Greeks, the Roman world, Celtic cultures, Vikings, and nautical and underwater archaeology.

Archaeology has been the focus of Dr. Hale's career from his B.A. studies at Yale University to his doctoral research at the University of Cambridge, where he received his Ph.D. The subject of his dissertation was the Bronze Age ancestry of the Viking longship, a study that involved field surveys of ship designs in prehistoric rock art in southern Norway and Sweden. During more than 30 years of archaeological work, Dr. Hale has excavated at a Romano-British town in Lincolnshire, England, as well as at a Roman villa in Portugal; has carried out interdisciplinary studies of ancient oracle sites in Greece and Turkey, including the famed Delphic Oracle; and has participated in an undersea search in Greek waters for lost fleets from the Greek and Persian wars. In addition, Dr. Hale is a member of a scientific team developing and refining a method for dating mortar, concrete, and plaster from ancient buildings—a method that employs radiocarbon analysis with an accelerator mass spectrometer.

Dr. Hale has published his work in *Antiquity*, *Journal of Roman Archaeology*, *The Classical Bulletin*, and *Scientific American*. Most of Dr. Hale's work is interdisciplinary and involves collaborations with geologists, chemists, nuclear physicists, historians, zoologists, botanists, physical anthropologists, geographers, and art historians.

Dr. Hale has received numerous awards for his distinguished teaching, including the Panhellenic Teacher of the Year Award and the Delphi Center Award. He has toured the United States and Canada as a lecturer for the Archaeological Institute of America and has presented lecture series at museums and universities in Finland, South Africa, Australia, and New Zealand.

Dr. Hale is the instructor of another Teaching Company course, *Classical Archaeology of Ancient Greece and Rome*.

Table of Contents
The Greek and Persian Wars

Professor Biography		 i
Course Scope		 1
Lecture One	The First Encounter	 3
Lecture Two	Empire Builders—The Persians	 18
Lecture Three	Intrepid Voyagers—The Greeks	 33
Lecture Four	The Ionian Revolt	 47
Lecture Five	From Mount Athos to Marathon	 62
Lecture Six	Xerxes Prepares for War	 77
Lecture Seven	The Athenians Build a Fleet	 92
Lecture Eight	Heroes at the Pass	 107
Lecture Nine	Battle in the Straits	 123
Lecture Ten	The Freedom Fighters	 138
Lecture Eleven	Commemorating the Great War	 153
Lecture Twelve	Campaigns of the Delian League	 168
Lecture Thirteen	Launching a Golden Age	 184
Lecture Fourteen	Herodotus Invents History	 199
Lecture Fifteen	Engineering the Fall of Athens	 214
Lecture Sixteen	Cyrus, Xenophon, and the Ten Thousand	 229
Lecture Seventeen	The March to the Sea	 243
Lecture Eighteen	Strange Bedfellows	 259
Lecture Nineteen	The Panhellenic Dream	 273
Lecture Twenty	The Rise of Macedon	 287
Lecture Twenty-One	Father and Son	 301
Lecture Twenty-Two	Liberating the Greeks of Asia	 315
Lecture Twenty-Three	Who Is the Great King?	 330
Lecture Twenty-Four	When East Met West	 345

Table of Contents
The Greek and Persian Wars

Maps	360
Overview of Major Phases	379
Timeline	381
Glossary	390
Biographical Notes	394
Bibliography	402

The Greek and Persian Wars

Scope:

This course presents a rare opportunity to survey the entirety of the two-centuries-long conflict between the Greeks and the Persians: the greatest military contest in antiquity and one that forever changed the patterns of human history. Ruled by such Great Kings as Cyrus II (known as Cyrus the Great), Darius III, and Xerxes, the Persian Empire's extraordinary military might, bottomless treasury, and innovative engineering skills made it seem almost inconceivable that any nation could long resist conquest. Resilient opposition, however, came from the Greeks—first from the Ionian cities of Asia Minor, then from the leagues of city-states led by Sparta and Athens, and finally, from the kingdom of Macedon under its fabled rulers King Philip II and his son Alexander III (better known as Alexander the Great).

Beginning with the first Persian capture of Greek cities in the mid-6th century B.C. and concluding with the burning of the Persian royal city of Persepolis in 331 B.C., this tumultuous period was punctuated with some of history's most dramatic battles: the violent clash of soldiers on the plains at Marathon, the defiant last stand of 300 Spartans at Thermopylae, the crucial naval battle in the straits of Salamis, the march of the Ten Thousand under Xenophon, and the astonishing victories of Alexander at Granicus River, Issos, and Gaugamela that finally brought the wars to an end.

The story of the Greek and Persian wars, however, involves far more than epic battles; tales of heroism, treason, and martyrdom; decisive (and indecisive) rulers; and strategic military tactics. The wars proved integral to the cultural and political development of much of the ancient world. Among the most important of these developments was the creation of a concrete historical record based on eyewitness accounts that led to the writing of definitive historical texts, such as Herodotus's *Histories*, Thucydides's *History of the Peloponnesian War*, and Xenophon's *Anabasis*. Political developments abounded as well; the leagues of city-states and the spirit of democracy that matured during Greece's Golden Age were direct results of the region's opposition to imperial Persia. The period also provided a stimulus for cultural exchange between two seemingly disparate civilizations, creating a global market that stretched from China to Britain and from central Africa to the Baltic Sea. The wars also inspired great art, ranging from such works as Aeschylus's *Persians* and Phrynicus's *The Phoenician Women* (both dealing with the accounts and ramifications of the

Battle of Salamis) to oratorical masterpieces, including Isocrates's "Panegyricus" (a key inspiration for the Panhellenic dream of a united Greece).

Ultimately, this period set the stage not only for the immediate future of the Classical age but for the perpetual collision between East and West; many subsequent clashes—between Rome and Parthia, Christian Crusaders and Muslim Saracens, Byzantines and Ottomans—have been fought along this same fundamental fault line. A comprehensive study of the Greek and Persian wars, one that takes into account a view of the hostilities from both sides and augments the historical narrative with explorations of emergent cultural and political traditions, remains crucial to understanding the complex issues that still beset our modern world.

Lecture One
The First Encounter

Scope: The two centuries of hostilities that encompass the Greek and Persian wars saw numerous political, social, economic, and cultural developments. More importantly, however, this archetypal war between East and West prefigured all later conflicts along the cultural fault line running through the eastern Mediterranean. The first encounter between these two disparate civilizations occurred around 546 B.C., with King Croesus of Lydia's preemptive attack against the emerging Persian Empire and its ruler, King Cyrus II (known as Cyrus the Great). With the aid of Greek hoplite mercenaries from the Peloponnese, Croesus crossed the Halys River and fought the Persians to a standstill, until a lightning-like attack turned the battle in favor of the Persian Empire. The Lydians' subsequent defeat cemented Cyrus's role as the new lord of Asia Minor and alerted mainland Greece to the Persian menace. Thus was a spark ignited that would, in the time of Cyrus's successors, be fanned into a conflagration.

Outline

I. These 24 lectures are devoted to the Greek and Persian wars: one of the epic conflicts of world history.
   A. The chronological span runs from the emergence of Cyrus II (known as Cyrus the Great) around 560 B.C. to the time of Alexander the Great around 320 B.C.
   B. The geographical span reaches from Persia to the central Mediterranean.
   C. This period saw the development of military history and the world's first global market.
   D. The period also witnessed a conflict between Persian monotheism and the Greek polytheistic tradition, as well as tension between the political philosophies of Greek democracy and Persian monarchy.
   E. The period we will explore in these lectures was a time of "firsts."
      1. The Greek and Persian wars inspired Herodotus to write his *Histories*, the first formal written history in the world.

  2. The battles of this period inspired the first surviving play: Aeschylus's *Persians.*
- **F.** The roots of our contemporary world lie in this period—above all, in the great split between East and West that still dominates today's world affairs.
- **G.** Both the Greek and Persian sources have their own axes to grind in relating the events of the wars.
    - **1.** In general, the Greek sources misconceive much about the Persians; it is difficult to separate truth from Greek imagination.
    - **2.** On the Persian side, there was no known historical writing outside of the Persian court, leading to little objectivity.
    - **3.** These 24 lectures will highlight the amazing archaeological discoveries that have been made over the last 200 years and will use these discoveries to give a fair share of time, attention, and respect to both the Greeks and the Persians.

II. The Greek and Persian wars began around 546 B.C. with the arrival at Delphi of envoys from King Croesus of Lydia.
- **A.** Croesus was the fifth king of a dynasty that had ruled Lydia for about a century. His kingdom had grown within his own lifetime and had taken over Greek cities in Asia Minor, including Miletus and Ephesus.
- **B.** When Croesus learned of a Persian threat on his eastern frontier at the Halys River, he consulted the Delphic Oracle to decide whether or not he should challenge the invaders before they reached him.
    - **1.** The oracle responded, "Go tell the king if he crosses the river, he will destroy a great empire."
    - **2.** Believing that the empire in question was that of Cyrus II of Persia, Croesus made plans to attack.
- **C.** The Ionian Greeks under Croesus's command were obligated as vassals to follow the king wherever he went.
    - **1.** The Greek cities in Asia resented the fact that they had lost their freedom to the king of Lydia.
    - **2.** Eurybates of Ephesus was sent to recruit a mercenary army of Greek warriors to augment the Lydian cavalry; instead, he sent messages to the Persians offering help as a means of removing King Croesus.

3. Miletus, the greatest of the Greek cities in Asia, also sent secret messages to the Persians offering support.

III. The Persian civilization had been almost unknown to the people of the Mediterranean.
   A. In just under 15 years, with the leadership of Cyrus, the Persians took over the great kingdom of their neighbors, the Medes, and set out to conquer the world.
   B. Persian society was composed mostly of farming and nomadic tribes.
   C. What the Greeks called "the laws of the Medes and the Persians" unified the two kingdoms under the upstart Persians rather than the Medes.

IV. Cyrus may have meant to honor peace at the Halys River, but Croesus, by crossing the river, guaranteed war.
   A. Both parties met in central Turkey (Asia Minor) and fought to a standstill.
   B. Satisfied that he had stopped Cyrus and reasserted the boundary at the Halys River, Croesus returned home.
   C. But the Persians were relentless in their drive to conquer the world. Cyrus did not give up but instead decided to overtake the Lydians on their march homeward.
   D. Cyrus defeated Croesus's army before it returned home and subsequently captured the city of Sardis. At this point, Cyrus became the overlord of some of the Greek cities.

V. Though Miletus had capitulated to the Persians, other Greek cities, including Ephesus and Colophon, were averse to becoming part of the Persian Empire.
   A. These cities, believing that they were not strong enough to fight Cyrus on their own, asked the Spartans to help maintain their liberty.
   B. The Spartans sent a herald (with diplomatic immunity) to Sardis to ask Cyrus not to harm the Greeks of Asia.
   C. Cyrus told the herald that he was unafraid of the Greeks and advised the Spartans to think of their own safety.

D. When the herald returned with Cyrus's reply, it became clear that a lasting peace between this new empire in the East and the Greeks would be impossible.

Recommended Reading:

Allen, *The Persian Empire.*

Herodotus, *The Histories.*

Questions to Consider:

1. What would you consider to be the most important development that arose from the Greek and Persian wars? Why?
2. How do you think history would have changed if King Croesus had not decided preemptively to attack the Persians?

Lecture One—Transcript
The First Encounter

Hello and welcome to a course on the Greek and Persian wars. I'm John Hale, archaeologist at the University of Louisville, or as we say in Kentucky, "Louaville." In these 24 lectures, I will be introducing you to one of the epic conflicts of world history.

Our chronological span will begin with Cyrus the Great of Persia, a conqueror who emerged around 560 B.C., and we will then run more than two centuries through wars, through battles, through various times of troubled peace, all the way down to the time of Alexander the Great in the 320s B.C.

Our geographical span will reach all the way from Persia itself, in the far south of southern Iran, all the way into the central Mediterranean and the time when the Greeks and the Persians are fighting it out for control of that important body of water.

In addition to military history—although that is certainly one of our focuses—we're also going to be experiencing the economic growing pains of the world's first "global market." I always like to remind my students that when Socrates bit into his daily bread in the streets of Athens, that wheat in the bread was grown in Russia or Egypt, not in Athens.

We'll also be looking at a conflict between religions, with monotheism on the side of the Persians, worshiping the great god Ahura Mazda, and a great polytheistic tradition on the side of the Greeks, with many gods, like Zeus and Athena.

We will be looking also at a clash of political philosophies: freedom, city-states, democracy on the Greek side and, on the Persian side, one realm, one king, one ruler over all.

It's a time of "firsts." The first formal history ever written in the world was by Herodotus of Halicarnassus, who was inspired by this very conflict to invent the science that would go back, do researches, and collect information from both sides to explain to you a great event in human affairs. We will see the world's first drama. The first surviving play in world dramatic history is, in fact, *The Persians* by Aeschylus, a man who was a veteran of the battles of Marathon and Salamis and who actually wrote a play in which the Battle of Salamis between the Greeks and the Persians is described as the key scene of the play.

We will see firsts in the development of medicine, in the development of democracy as a functioning political system, and many others, and we will encounter some of the greatest leaders in world history. In fact, the Persian wars are sort of a lesson in leadership and all of its various styles.

Most of all, I hope you will come to feel that you are looking at a very modern story. The roots of our contemporary world lie in this period, in the 6th to the 4th centuries B.C., and above all, that great split between East and West—which still dominates world affairs today and which we probably associate most with matters of oil and conflicting religious creeds—is already there. In fact, it is formed in the 540s B.C. when Cyrus the Persian first encounters Greeks as he carries the western frontier of the Persian Empire into Asia Minor—that is, modern Turkey—and encounters Greek cities on the seacoast of Asia.

That created a fault line running through the Bosporus and the Hellespont—those narrow channels of water that separate Asia from Europe—down the coast of Turkey, across the eastern Mediterranean, right through the center of the island of Cyprus—which was at that time a divided island between Asia and Europe, as it is today—and then down somewhere around Egypt.

To end where do we find today's conflicts? Right along that line. Where did the Romans come to grief? Up against Parthia on the far side of that line. The Byzantines and the Sassanids of Persia, the Crusaders combating the forces of Islam, the modern Europeans against the Ottoman Turks, and finally, our own world today still see that great fault in human history. This course is exploring how it came to be and what were the first great conflicts fought along either side of it.

It's customary to think of this as a historical exercise, and certainly when you're dealing with great sources like Herodotus and Xenophon and when you can supplement them with the Persian records—and, as we'll see, the Persians themselves can now speak to us directly, thanks to an amazing decipherment of cuneiform characters and of the Old Persian language that took place back in the 19th century—we can hear the Persian kings in their own words proclaiming their victories and their greatness. But both sides on this historical issue have their own axes to grind. Herodotus is trying to be very fair; he's trying to tell you as much about the Persians as he does about their Greek opponents. He grew up in the city of Halicarnassus, which was a Greek city that had been taken over by the Persians, so he has a uniquely bipartisan kind of perspective. But in general, the Greek sources misconceive a lot about the Persians—they cover Persian history with legends, myths, folklore, and fables, and it's very hard for us to separate out truth from this gloss of Greek imagination.

On the Persian side, of course, there was no historical writing that we know about outside the court, outside the function of words to glorify the Great King himself and to make it clear to everyone that the great god Ahura Mazda had placed Cyrus, or Cambyses, or Darius, or Xerxes on the throne—that they were the god-appointed leaders of the Earth. This is not a place you're going to find objective history.

So we turn then to my field, archaeology. I hope that one of the features of these 24 lectures will be to give you a sense of the amazing discoveries that have been made over the last 200 years that have brought to light the lost cities of the Persian Empire, have even explored some of the battlefields and found relics of those great conflicts at the very place where the Greeks and Persians died, each fighting for their own side.

In addition, I want to make it clear that we are trying to give due weight to both sides. Since the histories were written by the Greeks, there's a great tendency in the part of modern accounts to emphasize the Greek point of view. I hope to use, as much as possible, archaeology to address that balance—and to give a fair share of our time, and attention, and respect to the Persians, whose ambition to conquer the world set the whole thing in motion.

As an archaeologist, I've had the good fortune to work in this part of the world. In fact, I've been involved recently in a groundbreaking effort—*groundbreaking* is the wrong word for something underwater—but in an effort to get under the waters of the Aegean Sea and look for the remains of the fleets that were sent by the great Persian kings Darius and Xerxes to invade Greece.

Those fleets of ships encountered storms, and they encountered sea battles with the Greeks—and in both cases, ships went to the bottom. No one had ever looked for these until I joined a team led by Shelley Wachsmann of the Institute of Nautical Archaeology, and together with the Greek government and a host of other scientists, we got out on a research vessel and combed the waters from Mount Athos in the north all the way down to the central Aegean, visiting the spots where the historian Herodotus said, "Disaster struck the Persian fleets and ships went to the bottom." I will be telling you about those searches as we come to that point in our story.

I've also had the good luck to work in Greece at the site of the Delphic Oracle, a place that was the heart of the Greek world, a place that was their most important shrine, a place where the gods themselves—Zeus, speaking through his son Apollo, the god of prophecy, and Apollo, speaking through the mouth of a mortal woman—they would direct human affairs. Delphi was so important that it wasn't only patronized by Greeks—whose leaders and whose common people would go to Delphi and ask questions, ask guidance as they had difficult choices to make—but even foreign rulers would send to Delphi, this very prestigious shrine, and ask for the gods' advice.

That's where we begin our story of the Greek and Persian wars. It's a day probably in the year 546 B.C. We can't be too sure to within a few years of when this happened. But it happened that in Delphi, envoys arrived from King Croesus of Lydia, the richest man in the world. His kingdom, Lydia, was the place where money was invented. The first coins were struck at Lydia. It was a kingdom in the western part of modern Turkey, what the Greeks called Asia Minor, and it had its capital at a city called Sardis.

King Croesus was the fifth king of the dynasty that had been ruling Lydia for about a century, and he and his forebears had invented coins. First, they used what's called *electrum*—silver and gold that they took out of the Pactolus River that ran through Sardis. But then, under Croesus, his metallurgical experts figured out how to refine that dust so that they could separate the gold and silver. Herodotus, the historian, tells us Croesus was the first king to mint coins of pure gold and pure silver, thus creating our monetary standard of the modern world. Croesus became proverbial for his wealth, and we still have a saying in English, "rich as Croesus," after this 6th-century-B.C. Lydian monarch.

His kingdom had grown in his own lifetime, carrying on the conquering habits of his fore-predecessors in the dynasty. They had taken over Greek cities in Asia. It will be our job in Lecture Three to talk about why there were Greek cities in Asia; how did it happen that Greeks migrated out of their homeland, crossed the Aegean, and settled down on that coast? But for now, just take it from me, some of the most important Greek cities were places like Miletus and Ephesus in Asia Minor, and they were now tributary and vassal to King Croesus up there at his citadel in the wonderfully rich city of Sardis.

When Croesus, who had taken a great interest in his Greek subjects—who was interested in their religion and in their culture—when Croesus learned that there was a threat to him on his eastern frontier—the river Halys, which runs through the center of Asia Minor and exits into the Black Sea—he decided not only to consult his own diviners but to send to the place that these Greeks thought was the source of knowledge about the future—this Delphic Oracle in central Greece. So he appointed some envoys, and they carried his question to the Delphic Oracle.

Croesus, of course, had the classic puzzle that confronts people who feel threatened: Is the best thing to be pacific about it—to sit back and assume with good will that all will be well, in which case, you may be subject to an invasion, and caught off guard, and fighting on the defensive, and go under to hostile outsiders? Or is it better to, as Shakespeare says, "Take arms against a sea of troubles,/and by opposing, end them"? In other words, should Croesus cross that river and challenge these people he is afraid are going to invade his kingdom before they ever get to him?

This was his dilemma—realizing, of course, that if he does cross the river, he may, in fact, precipitate the very war that he hopes to avoid. With that question, the envoys got in their ships, sailed across the Aegean Sea, and made their way to the southern slope of the holy mountain—Mount Parnassus, home of Apollo and the Muses—there to put their question.

It was a very impressive thing to come to Delphi. You had to purify yourself at shrines lower down on the mountain. You had to pay a vast sum of money. For an ordinary person, it was 10 days' pay. For a king, it would be gifts in proportion to his wealth, and since Croesus was the richest man in the world, he lavished golden bowls and other gifts of gold on the sanctuary at Delphi to show Apollo how much he desired the god's favor.

All these were given to the priests. Delphi's a little mountain village that started off as just a collection of herdsmen's huts. The Delphians admitted they'd be the poorest people in the world if it weren't for that oracle, and the oracle was there because—as we now know today and as the Greeks said themselves—of a geological accident. There was a fault that ran through the southern slope of Mount Parnassus. Out of that crack in the ground came mildly intoxicating vapors, and a woman, seated on a tripod over that fault, would have a trance triggered by inhaling the *pneuma*—the gas or breath that came out of the fault.

Her own consciousness would flee away, and she would become a medium for the god who spoke through her mouth while she was in this trance. So the envoys made their way up the switchback trail, they got to the temple, and they saw on the temple the famous slogan that hung there or was carved there: "*Gnothi seauton*"—"Know thyself."

Obviously, they couldn't read Greek or they would have paid a little more attention to what that implies: This isn't going to be a simple answer—you have to know your own self in order to interpret it correctly.

At any rate, they entered, and they went down the long ramp, past the sacred, ever-burning flame, into the crypt of the temple. There, in what felt like a cave-like sort of gloom, off to their left in a little inset in the temple foundations was the chamber where that woman of Delphi sat on her tripod above the crack in the mountainside, breathing in those fumes, ready to give answers in Apollo's voice to any questions that were put to her.

She had in one hand a little branch of Apollo's sacred bay leaves, the laurels, and she had in the other a flat dish—a *phiale*—filled with holy water from the sacred spring, which also bubbled up through that crack in the Earth.

So the envoys put the question: "King Croesus of Lydia asks should he cross the river Halys and attack these enemies, the Persians?" The oracle responded in that harsh voice that suggested someone else was speaking through the woman: "Go tell the king if he crosses the river, he will destroy a great empire." That sounded good to them. They took the word back to Asia Minor, and they climbed the hill to Sardis and reported to King Croesus what the oracle had said—and based on this belief that that had to be the empire of Cyrus, he made his plans to attack.

He asked the Greeks to help him in this upcoming war. It was part of their job as vassals to follow their lord and master wherever he went. In fact, being a part of an ancient empire is something that we need to talk about for a moment. In the time of the Romans, if you were part of the Roman Empire, you were caught up in a Roman lifestyle. You lived in a town that now had a forum that looked like Rome. There were temples to the Roman gods, you worshiped the emperor, you used coins with the emperor's head upon the coin, you obeyed Roman laws, and you were part of a great common culture.

Pre-Roman empires weren't like that. They were big engines for generating wealth in which previously autonomous kingdoms and city-states and peoples were drawn into the imperial net, and from that time on, they had to pay an annual tribute, or tax, to their imperial masters. But if they did that, they were, in general, free to go on living their own customary lives and, even within a given city-state, might have an independent government of the form of a democracy, say.

So these Greek cities in Asia hated the fact that they had lost their freedom to the king of Lydia, in spite of the fact that it was a very mild burden—all they had to do was pay that annual tax and give him young men when he wanted to make war. Still, they weren't free, and for Greeks, that was a terrible thing not to be free. The man that was asked by King Croesus to get some troops for him was a Greek named Eurybates in the great city of Ephesus.

He was told to send across the sea to the motherland of Greece to offer Lydian gold and silver coins. They had made a coin, the *stater*, which was calculated to be one month's pay for a mercenary soldier. Eurybates was supposed to recruit a mercenary army of these heavily armored, shield-bearing, phalanx-fighting Greek warriors to come over and add to the Lydian cavalry—the Lydians themselves were famous as horsemen, and they carried lances—and the two together would create a very formidable force to cross the river and pass eastward into Asia.

Eurybates did not do that. He sent messages to the invader, to the Persians, offering to help them, because the Greeks were looking for any way they could find to get rid of this royal taskmaster to whom they had to pay their tribute—Croesus of Lydia—and thought that once they got rid of him, they would have their independence back. Little did they know.

Second, the greatest of the Greek cities in Asia, Miletus—a city that was the center of science, of experimentation, and all sorts of things, like history writing. Wonderful philosophers lived there. They were a very rich Greek city, perhaps the richest of all. They colonized all the way up into the Black Sea. They sent secret messengers to the Persians offering to go over to the Persian side rather than remain loyal to their master, King Croesus of Lydia.

Who were these Persians that the Greeks were approaching? They were a people almost unknown previously to the folk of the Mediterranean. They came from an upland valley in the far south of Iran, very near the Persian Gulf, and in just under 15 years, under the charismatic leadership of a young king called Cyrus—*Kourosh* in Iranian—they had fought their way out of their mountain valleys; taken over the great kingdom of their neighbors, the Medes; and made the Medes partners with them—so after that, the Greeks called them the Medes and the Persians, although the Medes were very subordinate partners—and they had decided to conquer the world.

They were not people who had traditionally lived in cities; there were some farming tribes among the Persians in that upland valley, the center of what's called Anshan country, and there were tribes that were nomads who just bred horses and cattle; they were continually on the move. These were the new world conquerors, all thanks to the charismatic leadership of this one young man, Cyrus.

Cyrus was known for his justice, for his fairness, for his truthfulness, for his directness—you could count on Cyrus. Some people actually, as the Milesians did, as that Eurybates of Ephesus did, dealt with him directly, seeming to offer their submission to him because he looked so good. Later on, we'll find that the Babylonians think he has been sent by their gods to rule them. The Jews of the Old Testament look upon Cyrus as someone sent by Jehovah to straighten out the world and give the Jews back their liberty from the Babylonians and send them home.

So he's a man of a unique character, and we have to feel that some of their explosive taking over of the ancient world is very much due to this young Cyrus. He is the one who is now rampaging through the Median Empire that he took over. It had existed for little more than a century. Cyrus took it over. He was the grandson of the former king of the Medes, Astyages.

So when they put together what the Greeks like to call the "laws of the Medes and the Persians"—in other words, those immutable laws that the Greeks so admired—it was two people actually simply unifying themselves, who had long been neighbors and were certainly close cousins, but unifying themselves now under what everybody thought was the impoverished, poor, mountainous branch of the population—the Persians—rather than the former world rulers, the Medes.

Cyrus knew all about Lydia, that kingdom with its gold and its silver up there on his western frontier. After all, his grandfather, Astyages, the king of the Medes, was the brother-in-law of King Croesus. So it's almost a family affair. Cyrus must have some sense that he has a claim on that kingdom, because Media, the kingdom of the Medes, had almost captured Lydia in a great war from the time of Cyrus's childhood, and there was a total eclipse of the Sun when the fighting stopped between the Medes and the people of Lydia, and they agreed they would not carry on further—that the gods had shown they should remain at peace.

It may be that Cyrus meant to honor that peace and honor the river Halys as the frontier, but Croesus—inspired by his interpretation of the Delphic

Oracle—by crossing the river, guaranteed a war between himself and this young Cyrus.

They met somewhere in what is today central Turkey, probably near those old capital cities of the Hittites, a long-gone empire of Asia Minor. There had been many. There, the lancers of Lydia with their mercenaries fought the horsemen and spearmen of Cyrus to a standstill. Cyrus had some camels among his forces. The Greeks like to say that the Lydian horses were very disturbed by the smell of the camels and were unmanageable. That's probably another one of those Greek myths and fables to give colorful vivacity to one of these battle scenes.

At any rate, Croesus was satisfied that he had won—that he had stopped Cyrus. Croesus had shown Cyrus that Lydia was not to be trifled with and had reasserted the Halys as the boundary. So he crossed back over and headed home.

Cyrus had no intention of giving up. One of the things that I hope you come to realize about the Persians is they are relentless in pursuit of their purpose, and no number of defeats and setbacks will ever turn them away from the pursuits of anything they have set out to do.

Cyrus had decided to conquer Lydia, and he followed quickly and secretly in Croesus's path and caught him before he had returned all the way to his city but at a point where Croesus had disbanded his mercenary forces and was now a much-reduced shell of his former army. Cyrus attacked him, defeated him completely, marched on to Sardis, and captured Sardis as well.

At this point, Cyrus is the new king of Lydia, as well as king of the Medes and the king of the Persians. This inevitably made him overlord of some of the Greek cities. Miletus had already capitulated secretly, so he showed great favor to them. The Milesians responded. They had a little oracle in their own territory at a place called Didyma—another oracle of Apollo, founded from Delphi centuries earlier. The oracle of Apollo at Didyma produced an oracle for Cyrus telling him that it was his destiny to succeed in all of his ventures. That's what you got from an oracle if the gods were on your side.

But the other Greek cities, like Ephesus, the others up and down the coast—Colophon and others—didn't want to become part of a Persian Empire. The ones that had been halfhearted about supporting Croesus had been doing so not in hope of changing one master for another but of getting their freedom—their *eleutheria*—that quality of liberty that was more important to a Greek than anything else in this world.

Feeling that they weren't strong enough to fight Cyrus on their own, they sent across the sea to the motherland—the homeland—in what is still today Greece and, in fact, to the area called Lakedaimonia and the city of Sparta, where the greatest, toughest warriors lived. They asked the Spartans to come and help them maintain their liberty against Cyrus.

The Spartans convened to consider this request. They decided not to send an army across. The Spartans didn't like to go across the sea, and they didn't like to venture far from home, but they did decide that they would send a herald.

Now, what's a herald? A herald is a person with diplomatic immunity. You can't have international relations if these countries don't dare communicate with each other. So they told their Spartan herald to take his staff of office—his wand—and to go across the sea and go the 60 miles up from the coast to Ephesus, across the hills to Sardis, and confront this conqueror and give him word from the Spartans.

So the herald went. He crossed the hills, he arrived at Sardis, and he had his audience with Cyrus. Through the interpreter, he said, "The Spartans bid you not to harm the Greeks of Asia." Cyrus looked at him for a while and said, through the interpreters, "Tell this man to tell the Spartans I have no fear of men 'who meet in marketplaces to make speeches and cheat one another.' My advice to the Spartans is to think of their own safety. They will soon have enough to worry about in their own homeland."

With that reply, the herald returned to Sparta. Two great forces had met in that audience chamber: the expanding Persian Empire, which at that point seemed absolutely unstoppable, and this resistant force of Greeks, very warlike—a wonderful tradition as these highly desired, heavily armored infantrymen but also with a burning love of freedom—a love of freedom that made it very difficult for them to combine, because each city-state and each people of the Greeks valued their own freedom above all.

Here, we see that first collision between these peoples. When the herald returned home and told the Spartans what Cyrus had said, it became plain that there would not be peace for long between this new empire in the East and between the Greeks in the Aegean. Everything that happened after that flowed from that first encounter.

As a general reflection on the Spartans, nothing could have been more unjust than Cyrus's remark about the marketplaces, the free speech, and the cheating each other. The Spartans were, in fact, a lot like the Persians: They didn't like buying and selling and dealing, and they didn't have elaborate marketplaces—*agoras* as the Greeks called them—they didn't cut into free speech except within the assembly, where each warrior could speak his mind, and they certainly did not cheat each other. But this was the Persian view of the Ionian Greeks: great merchants, great speechmakers, great orators, great philosophers—thinkers, talkers. We will see in this conflict between the Persians and the Greeks a conflict between two extraordinarily different mindsets and ways of life, as well as a conflict between two peoples.

Now that we have seen our opening clash, it's time to get to know a little better the two sets of people behind this confrontation, and we will begin next time with the Persians.

Lecture Two
Empire Builders—The Persians

Scope: Modern scholars have learned about the Persians in their own language thanks largely to the translation of the inscription at Behistun rock by Henry Rawlinson in the 1830s. That inscription tells the story of the accession of King Darius to the throne of the Persian Empire. Other Old Persian texts give us a sense of what the Persians were like both before and after they became the dominant power in the ancient world. It was Cyrus who initiated the drive to dominance, uniting the formerly tribal Persian people and leading them to expansion through the conquest of Media, Lydia, and other Greek city-states. Cyrus's son Cambyses organized the ever-widening empire into provinces and continued the tradition of engineering projects begun by his father. One such project, the Royal Road, typifies the qualities of relentlessness, duty, and achievement that made the Persian Empire a force to be reckoned with.

Outline

I. Modern scholars owe much of their understanding of the Persians to Henry Rawlinson's translation of an inscription on a cliff at Behistun.

  A. The Behistun rock is a 1,700-foot-high cliff with a relief carving and hundreds of lines of inscription written in "cuneiform"—the script developed in Mesopotamia and originally written on tablets of moist clay with a stylus.

  B. Observers had different theories about the figures depicted on the Behistun rock: a victorious Queen Semiramis of Assyria; Jesus and his Apostles; or Shalmaneser, the king of Assyria, in front of captive Jews.

  C. In 1835, Henry Rawlinson, a British military officer, realized that there were three inscriptions on the Behistun rock. We now know that the languages of these inscriptions were Old Persian, Elamite (an unrelated language of the territory of Elam), and Babylonian (the lingua franca of Mesopotamia).

  D. Rawlinson learned that the relief carving depicted a story behind the accession of King Darius.

1. When Smerdis, the rightful heir to the throne of Cambyses, died, the Achaemenid warrior Darius decided to make himself king.
2. The carving was a declaration of Darius's legitimacy as a descendant of the Achaemenid dynasty, named after its original founder, Achaemenes.

II. Samples of Old Persian text provide a sense of the Persians both in their time of glory (when their rulers had become kings of the world) and as they were before.

   A. Modern scholars describe the Zoroastrian Persians of this era as henotheists: monotheists who are willing to tolerate and accept the polytheistic religions of others. Their holy book was the Avesta.
   B. The idea of "the good" (associated with truth and light) is an essential part of the Zoroastrian religion, which sees the universe as a battleground between the forces of light and darkness.
   C. The Persians were the cousins of the Greeks; both cultures descended from the Indo-Europeans.
      1. The Indo-Europeans were a community that spoke related languages and lived along the Caucasus Mountains.
      2. One important element of Indo-European life was horseback riding.
      3. The Indo-Europeans gradually overtook the world that had been ruled by the Semitic peoples (e.g., Babylonians, Assyrians).
   D. The Persians maintained much of the traditional Indo-European way of life.
      1. Persian culture was not an urban culture at the start; rather, it consisted primarily of farmers and nomads.
      2. The essence of Persian male education was: ride hard, shoot straight, and tell the truth.
   E. The Greeks, who loved to tell stories, wove myths around the Persians.

III. Cyrus projected the Persians out of their traditional homeland and onto the world stage.

   A. The Greeks told many myths about Cyrus's boyhood.
      1. They said that his grandfather, the Median king Astyages, had a dream in which he saw his grandson engulfing the world.

2. Perceiving a threat to his rule, King Astyages ordered a minister to kill the infant.
  3. Instead, the minister ensured that the child was raised to become the leader of the Persians.
 B. Cyrus motivated and united the formerly tribal Persian people.
  1. He infused them with a vision—that they had the right way of life, that they were the toughest people on Earth, and that it was their right to rule over others.
  2. He confronted the neighboring Medes, who had spent more than a century conquering the central part of the ancient world, and combined them with the Persians.
  3. Afterward, he began to expand the Persian Empire by conquering Lydia and other Greek city-states.
 C. Cyrus instigated another element that is part of the unique Persian culture: enormous works of engineering. He diverted the Euphrates River where it passed through the city of Babylon and sent some of his men along the dry riverbed to get inside and open the city gates.
IV. When Cyrus died, he passed on the great empire he had cultivated to his son Cambyses, who developed a system to rule the ever-expanding kingdom.
 A. The Persian Empire was divided into provinces; often, these were the old kingdoms.
 B. Old royal capitals were used as provincial capitals called "satrapies."
 C. Each satrapy was ruled by a satrap: a Persian who was almost always a member of the Achaemenid line.
 D. The Persian Empire guaranteed peace within its borders as long as its citizens paid their tribute.
 E. The Persian Empire was kept together through the engineering of royal roads.
  1. Royal roads were limited-access highways along which travelers presented papers at way stations to pass through checkpoints.
  2. A "pony express" carried the king's messages from station to station; the one most familiar to the Greeks extended 1,600 miles from Sardis to Susa.

V. The Persians were a people to be feared, but above all, a people to be respected and marveled at. One can see the Persians' extraordinary characteristics at work as they set out to deal with the Greeks on their western borders.

Recommended Reading:
Kuhrt, *The Persian Empire: A Corpus of Sources from the Achaemenid Period.*
Lyle, *The Search for the Royal Road.*

Questions to Consider:
1. What characteristics do you think made King Cyrus, instead of his predecessors or descendants, the perfect individual to unite the Persian Empire?
2. What were some potential problems associated with the system of satraps and satrapies in the Persian Empire?

Lecture Two—Transcript
Empire Builders—The Persians

Welcome back. As you remember from last time, it's our mission today to try to get to know the Persians—to get to know them on their own terms and even in their own language. This is something we've only been able to do over the past couple of centuries, and it's thanks to the translation of a remarkable document of ancient Persian that was made by a young English adventurer named Henry Rawlinson, who first saw this inscription in the 1830s, when he was just 25 years old and a soldier in the East India Company.

The inscription is at a place called Behistun (B-E-H-I-S-T-U-N), the Behistun rock. If you start at Baghdad or ancient Babylon, which lies near it, and take the road eastward toward the old summer capital of the kings of the Medes, Ecbatana, where the road rises up into the hills, there are immense cliffs. The last of these great cliffs, 1,700 feet high, has on it—for the last 2,500 years—a sort of a Mount Rushmore–type relief carving, but unlike Mount Rushmore, it also has an inscription. People down on the road below for centuries have looked up 300 feet and seen this high, polished rock, these figures carved on it, something floating in the air above, and then all those hundreds of lines of inscription, and what they could tell, even from way down there, is a script called "cuneiform."

Cuneus is the Latin word for a "wedge," and cuneiform is the kind of script that was developed in Mesopotamia, where writing was done on little tablets of moist clay with a stylus that had a thin, triangular-shaped point. The scribes would punch those little triangles—those wedge shapes—into the tablets, and put them in different configurations, and use them as we use the alphabet. So cuneiform is a script in which you can write many languages.

As they looked up there, they could see all those things, but you couldn't get up and look closely because the stone cutters who made it, when they finished and as they came down the cliff, they chiseled away the steps by which they had used to go up and make the inscription and show the relief. So within a few centuries of being created in the time of the Great Kings of Persia, the identity of the figures was lost and what the inscription said was forgotten.

There were different theories about it. One was that it was Queen Semiramis of Assyria shown as a triumphal victor. Another was that it dated from Christian times—that it was the Twelve Apostles talking to Jesus, because there was a row of small figures in front of a big one. A third idea was that it was the king of Assyria—Shalmaneser—shown in front of the captive Jews. He had conquered the Israelites of the northern kingdom and carried them off into an Assyrian captivity long before the Babylonians conquered Jerusalem and carried the Judean Jews away to Babylon to captivity. This was supposed to be, by people who had a very bibliocentric view of the past, that act represented on the Behistun rock.

In 1835, this young Englishman, Henry Rawlinson—not a scholar, not an academic, had not had a brilliant career at school, but he'd had one thing, a gift for languages, and he'd had a second thing, he'd been great at games—he was a very athletic young fellow. He joined the British East India Company at a time when they were trying to establish land route connections from the Mediterranean—which had become a sort of lake for the British Navy after Admiral Nelson's victory at the Nile over the French—across the central part of the Near East and Middle East to India, which at that time was controlled by the British East India Company, but everyone could see the time when it would be absorbed into a proper British Empire.

So Henry Rawlinson is an empire builder, and he came to this place on this great road, and he looked up and he saw the cliff, and it instantly entered his mind: People who have been trying to crack the code of this lost cuneiform writing system have only had tiny inscriptions—individual tablets, strips of metal, a bit of cuneiform on a pot. Here are hundreds of lines, and he could see that it was in three zones. This immediately put him in mind of the famous Rosetta Stone.

It had been in his lifetime that a French scholar, Champollion, had taken the Rosetta Stone (found by Napoleon's troops in the delta of the Nile River) and seeing that the top was Egyptian hieroglyphs, the middle register was Egyptian demotic script, and the bottom was Greek—that half the officers in the French army could read at sight—they realized that the Greek would provide the clue to interpreting or cracking the code of the other two scripts.

This is what Rawlinson thought, and he knew from his linguistic studies that fairly recently documents of a language called Old Persian—that went all the way back to Cyrus and Darius and Xerxes, the great conquering kings—had been found in the Middle East as the holy book—the Avesta (A-V-E-S-T-A)—of the Zoroastrian religion.

Zoroaster was a great prophet. We're not sure exactly when he lived. He may have lived just shortly before Cyrus the king embarked on his career of conquest. He may be a mythical character—we don't know—but he left behind this book about the one god, the one true god—Ahura Mazda—the fact that you don't build temples to him or make statues of him—he's everywhere. He's in the air, his element is fire, his altars are portable, and fire burns atop them.

Magi (an individual is a "magus," and in the plural, they are "magi") are his priests, and they carry the fire altars around. They read the heavens. The magi who show up in the Gospel of Matthew in the Christian tradition are Persian. They're not kings at all, as they become called the three kings of the Epiphany story. They are Persian wise men who interpret the heavens and have seen this star in the Bible story. They go all the way back 500 years to this time of Darius and Cyrus.

Now, this Avesta had provided a gold mine of the Old Persian language. It was now quite well known. It had close relations to modern Iranian tongues, and so Henry Rawlinson immediately thought: "With that much script and some idea of what might be in the inscription itself, I may be able to crack this code." He knew that other scholars in other countries were working on it, that proposals had been made, and that nobody had been able to prove anything or convince everyone else. He made it his mission in life to crack cuneiform and read Persian.

He got up there, he did some free climbing, and he got up that sheer rock face. He realized that there were, as on the Rosetta Stone, three inscriptions. We now know that there was Old Persian; Elamite, which is an unrelated language of the territory of Elam, a kingdom that included the great city of Susa, which became the Persian capital; and at the bottom was Babylonian, which was a sort of lingua franca of Mesopotamia.

He made a transcription of the whole thing, line by line by line, character by character—very tough to do when you don't know what the characters actually mean. He could tell that the languages were quite different because it didn't need nearly as many lines and characters in one language as in another to express the same thought.

Over the next set of years, he began to work with his transcriptions of these remarkable documents. He was helped by the fact that it was a royal Persian inscription, and the kings of Persia were very vainglorious and very proud of their titles. A typical inscription would read—and he knew this from reading his Herodotus because Herodotus records inscriptions and proclamations by the kings of Persia—a typical one would read: "Darius, Great King, king of kings, successor of Cyrus, Great King, king of kings and Achaemenid. ..." And this royal house, this clan of kings of Persia, all claimed to descend from this original forebear Achaemenid, so they called themselves the Achaemenid kings.

He realized that if it is a Persian royal inscription, and he thought it was, then if there was a short word that was repeated five, six, seven times in the opening preamble, that word was *king*, and he knew what the word was in Old Persian. It was a word related to *shah*. It has more of a "shach" kind of a sound to it. The Hs are sort of guttural. It's still around in the word *checkmate*, which was *shâh mât*, which means "the king is dead." It's sometimes thought that chess itself might be a Persian game that got transmitted to India.

At any rate, he had no trouble at all in seeing that in the opening of one of these things that he had decided was Old Persian, there was that short word again, and again, and again. Now he says, "Which king is it?" Because that word immediately gave him the phonetic equivalence for a short set of the cuneiform signs. He said, "Which king am I dealing with?"

Well, Kourosh—Cyrus—and his son, Cambyses, and his father, Cambyses—it all begins with the same letter, the Greek *kappa* (K). Well, whoever this king was, he had a different name from his father, because he knew that they always start with themselves and then go on to their father, so it can't be Cyrus or Cambyses. The logical next one was Darius—*Daryavaush*. So in this way, he was able to get more and more letters and ultimately translate the whole inscription.

What he learned was it was a picture in relief of the Great King Darius, shown gigantic, holding his bow in his left hand, as a proper Persian warrior would, with his foot on the neck of a fallen enemy and nine enemies strung out in front of him in a long line, the last one wearing a funny sort of dunce's cap. It was a scene of the story behind the accession of Darius.

Great King Cyrus, whom we met last time and whom we'll be reverting to to learn his story, was not a founder of a dynasty; he was simply the one who propelled his dynasty down to the world stage. He had a legitimate son, Cambyses, who followed him, and just as Cyrus had conquered the Medes, had conquered Lydia, as we saw last time, had conquered Babylonia, and died trying to conquer central Asia, his son, Cambyses, was also a great conquering king. He brought Egypt, one of the richest kingdoms of the ancient world, into the Persian Empire. But when Cambyses died, there was a sudden hiatus.

The claim was made that the rightful king had been killed, the rightful heir had died—a young man named Smerdis—and this warrior from the same family, the Achaemenid family, named Daryavaush—Darius—decided to make himself king. Well, it was a time of chaos. There were many claimants, and he had to overcome the armies of those other nine and get them to swear fealty to him as the new king. That was what the rock at Behistun showed. It was sort of the declaration of legitimacy of the new Great King, who was not a descendant of Cyrus, but he was a descendant of that original forebear, Achaemenid, and that was his claim, and that is what is up there for all to see.

The stonemasons had chiseled away the steps so nobody could ever get at his monument and deface it. Whenever you put up a proclamation in the ancient world, you're always worried that someone is going to chisel it away as, for instance, was done to the Pharaoh Hatshepsut in Egypt when she left such a bad name behind her that her successors actually made sure that her name was chiseled off the monument. Darius made it impossible for that to happen.

I want to read you a little bit of this Old Persian to give us a sense of these people, both in their time of glory, when their rulers had become kings of the world, and then as they were before that happened, because that was a great shift in their personality at that time. Let's start with the kind of thing that Darius would have said himself, apparently on any and all occasions. That strange thing floating in the air in the scene on the rock is, in fact, the god Ahura Mazda in a Sun disk with wings, floating above the scene to give legitimacy to his appointed ruler on Earth, Great King Darius.

From that Zoroastrian book, the Avesta, we know a lot about Ahura Mazda and his worship, and we know it was a monotheistic religion in a way. But to deal with the Persians, who were very tolerant of other religions, modern scholars of religion have had to invent a new word, "henotheism" (H-E-N-O-theism), for monotheists who are nonetheless willing to tolerate and accept the polytheistic religions of others.

I mentioned last time that Cyrus is the king who was so beloved of the Jews because when he conquered Babylon, he freed the Jews from their captivity and sent them home. He did more than that. He gave orders that the Persian treasury should pay for the rebuilding of the temple in Jerusalem. Well, that's not the act of someone who thinks my god is the only god and only those are right who are worshiping him.

Here is the voice of Darius: "Great Ahura Mazda, greatest of gods, he created Darius the king, he bestowed upon him the good kingdom, possessed of good charioteers, of good horses, of good men." This idea of the good, the truthful, the light, is an essential part of the Zoroastrian religion, which sees the universe as a place of battle—of warfare—between the forces of light and the forces of darkness.

That flowed into a later cult of a god named Mithras, took the Roman Empire by storm, and became very popular with its legionnaires, who liked the feeling that you could be a soldier on a religious front, fighting for light against the powers of darkness. Let's face it, it's still with us today. Christianity has a hard time keeping this Zoroastrian idea out because in a world where there's an absolutely supreme God, darkness really shouldn't have any particular chance to threaten him.

So this idea, this grandeur, this pride, this clankity-clank proclaiming voice that we hear in most Persian inscriptions is a great contrast to the oldest parts of the Avesta, which seem to us to go back to a time before Cyrus, to a time when the Persians were a nomadic, farming people in those upland valleys—living in a hard land, leading a hard life among their tribes.

This is one of the early passages from the Avesta:

> To what land shall I flee? Where bend my steps? I am thrust out from family and tribe. I have no favor from the village to which I belong nor from the wicked rulers of the country. How then, O Lord, shall I obtain Thy favor? I know, O Wise One, why I am powerless, my cattle are few, I have few men.

This could be a psalm of David at the time when he was on the outs with King Saul of Israel and trying to make his way in the wilderness. It is a voice we will not meet again in the Achaemenid inscriptions—the Great Kings quickly become wrapped around with ceremony as super human beings, but it's important to get back to it and remember the kind of people the Persians were when they embarked upon their rampage of conquest.

They were, in fact, cousins of the Greeks. When Cyrus, the king of Persia, stood in Sardis in his audience hall and talked to that Spartan herald who had come over to demand that Cyrus leave the Greeks of Asia in peace, it was cousin speaking to cousin.

One or two thousand years before that meeting, their ancestors had been together in central Asia, in the land between the Black Sea and the Caspian Sea—the Caucasus Mountains. They were the Indo-Europeans—a family of people speaking common languages that have really only been known about since the 18th century, when the British in India realized that Sanskrit sounded an awful lot like German and the whole idea of evolving languages and splitting into new languages from a common root became part of our view of history.

The Indo-European languages have many different branches. Greek is a strange and anomalous one—a small group who got down through the Balkans and into modern Greece. We're going to be talking about them next time.

The Persians were part of the mainstream. The great Iranian family ran all the way from the Ukraine and Russia—where the Scythians spoke a form of Iranian—all the way to central Asia and the high plateaus that border the western side of the Himalayas. That's all the province of this one language, and the Persians probably could make themselves understood to most of the people whom they met. The Medes, their neighbors, also spoke one of these Iranian tongues.

The basis of Indo-European life was horseback riding and the idea that, as a mounted warrior, you could go wherever you wanted on these oceans of grass that were the steppes of central Eurasia. This carried over into almost all of their descendants. All of these people believe that warriors are cavalry—horsemen, knights—and they give an aristocratic kind of respect to a horseman. Of course, this made them very formidable conquerors as they came sweeping down—very mobile, very hard to predict where they would hit next.

They gradually took over the world that had been colonized and ruled for so long by the Semitic peoples, like the Babylonians and the Assyrians; the older people, like the Sumerians and the Egyptians—these new Indo-Europeans, led by folks like the Hittites and the Mitanni, become forces in the world with their horses.

So the Greeks had forgotten that they had much in common with the Persians, but in fact, they had a lot in common, and the Persians, living down in their highland valley, down near the Persian Gulf, had maintained a lot of that traditional Indo-European way of life.

It was not an urban culture from the beginning; it was a countryside kind of culture—some farming but mainly nomadism, with these herds of cattle and horses, as I said last time, and a great respect for these military leaders, these chiefs, because tribe was always against tribe. Family was against family, just as we heard in that little passage from the Avesta.

Boys were brought up in the Persian way in a very simple system: You learned three things—ride hard, shoot straight, and tell the truth. That was the essence of Persian education, and they were somewhat anti-intellectual. As you can see, their religion is quite simple and straightforward also: God is there, and he is to be worshiped. There is not an elaborate, confusing theology, and the ceremonials are simple. There is no temple. There is no elaborate statue of a god. All of this gave a certain clarity, and simplicity, and beauty to the Persian way of life that the Greeks and other subject peoples were very impressed by.

The fact that they were so fast in those early generations, that Cyrus could be down in his little corner of Anshan country by the Persian Gulf in one year and then, shortly thereafter, be knocking at the gates of Sardis, half a world away—almost 2,000 miles away in the western parts of Asia Minor—this made them seem like supermen, and it was part of their mystique.

It also is a little hurtful to us, as we try to understand them, because the Greeks—who loved to tell stories—would weave myths around the Persians. Cyrus himself became a character we see more through myth than we do through history. We're going to encounter midway through the course a man named Xenophon, an Athenian who led a group of 10,000 mercenary soldiers in the wake of a Persian prince—coincidentally, also named Cyrus—all the way to the heart of the empire to make that Persian prince the next king.

Xenophon worshiped the Persians. He wrote the world's first historical romance on the boyhood of Cyrus, the *Cyropaedia of Cyrus*, to describe in his imagination how you would create the perfect ruler. He took a little bit of authentic Persian tradition, a mass of folklore and mythology and added it to that.

So it's going to be our job now to try to strip away the myths and see the Persians as they were and talk about Cyrus, the man who projects them out of their traditional homeland and onto the world stage.

The Greeks told a lot of myths about Cyrus's boyhood. He reminds me of George Washington. More people know the cherry-tree myth than they do any of the authentic stories about his actual upbringing. Cyrus was like that. He seemed larger than life, so they gave him a larger-than-life background. They said that his grandfather, the king of the Medes, Astyages, had a dream in which he saw that his daughter, who had married a Persian, was going to bear a son who would flow from her and engulf the world. His interpreters told Astyages, king of the Medes: "This means you are in danger from the son that will be born to your daughter."

So just as in the Oedipus myth and probably with no more historical foundation, he ordered the infant baby to be taken from the young mother, his own daughter, and given to a minister with orders to kill the child so that it couldn't grow up and threaten him.

Well, of course, just as in Oedipus, you can't trust people to carry out this kind of inhuman demand, and in fact, the minister ensured that the baby was brought up—that Cyrus did, in fact, grow up to become the leader of his own people, the Persians, having a mother who was one of the Medes and a family line going back to Achaemenid in his own valley.

What Cyrus did do—and this is probably historical—he motivated and united the Persians. One of the problems that they'd always had is the problem that tribal people inevitably have, of divisiveness—they have a little bit of that love of freedom and liberty and "no one will tell me what to do" that we talked about last time for the Greeks.

Cyrus somehow overcame that. He infused them with a feeling of vision—that somehow they had the right way of life, they were the toughest people, and it was right that they should rule over others. It was a short step from that to confronting their neighbors, the Medes, who had spent a century and a quarter conquering the central part of the ancient world—what the Greeks called the empire of Upper Asia—reaching from the Halys River in Asia Minor all the way to beyond Mesopotamia.

Once they had combined with the Medes—and, remember, he's the grandson of the king of the Medes, so Cyrus has royal Median blood, which makes it easy for people to shift their allegiance to his line—he then begins to expand on that empire: first going up to Lydia and conquering it and, of course, getting those Greek city-states into his empire that are going to be the source of all the trouble to come. But then he goes down to Babylon, and here, we see a new element that's a part of the unique Persian nature—enormous engineering works.

How to get into Babylon? Towering walls, tremendous supplies of food inside. The Babylonians would come up on the walls of the city and shout and laugh at Cyrus outside, who was trying to take their city. Engineering—a former queen, Nitocris, had created a great reservoir above Babylon where the Euphrates River flowed through the city. He diverted the river into the reservoir and sent in some of his men on the dry riverbed to get inside and open the gates. This was the famous occasion recorded in the Old Testament—the Hebrew scriptures—where the prophet Daniel is inside—one of the captive Jews—and he tells Belshazzar, the ruler in Babylon, that he can interpret the handwriting on the wall at Belshazzar's feast and that it says, "You have been weighed in the balance and found wanting." And at those very moments, the Persians are coming into the city to take it over.

Many Babylonians were glad that the Persians came—they had a reputation for justice. The Babylonians said, "Our god Marduk has appointed this Cyrus to rule us." Cyrus put a lot of money into refurbishing the temples in Babylon and then headed eastward. He died trying to conquer another people like the Persians—horse lords of central Asia called the Massagetai, who had a famous queen named Tomyris. Some of these mounted women warriors are probably those behind the legends of the Amazon in ancient Greek mythology.

But he passed on to his son Cambyses this great empire. How to rule it? Well, they divided it up into provinces. Often, these were the old kingdoms. They used the old royal capitals now to be their provincial capitals, and they called each one a "satrapy." Now, ruling each satrapy in the name of the Great King is a Persian, almost always, sometimes a Persian of the royal house, of the Achaemenid line, who is the satrap. We will be encountering these satraps again and again as we go along with our story, and their loyalty is always something the Great King has to think about, because he has basically given to each one a kingdom: satrap of Egypt, satrap of Lydia, satrap of Babylon.

It's their job to keep those places peaceful, and this is, of course, what is the great benefit to anybody being drawn into the Persian Empire: You don't have to worry about your neighbors anymore. You don't have to worry that an army is going to come out of nowhere and besiege your town and kill you, take away your family into slavery. The Persians guarantee peace within their borders. You are safe; you are secure. All you need to do is pay your taxes—pay your tribute—and all will be well.

How do you keep this vast area together? More engineering: the royal roads. These were limited-access highways where people had to present passports at the way stations all along the way, where there were guards to check everybody's papers. If you were an ambassador, if you were a special envoy, if you were an army on the move, if you were anyone sent by the Great King or on the Great King's business, you had a right to be on that Royal Road. The ordinary caravan routes went elsewhere. These were not sort of mass trunk roads with all kinds of traffic on them.

There was a "pony express" that carried the king's messages from way station to way station along the great road. The one most familiar to the Greeks was the road from Sardis—the old capital of Lydia—all the way to Susa, 1,600 miles away. Herodotus—who records for us the way stations along the road and how long it was—marveled at these riders who made their way along that with a speed unknown to anything else that moved on the surface of the Earth, carrying the king's dispatches to his satraps in those distant capitals.

It's a fascinating thing that the motto of these riders of the king on the Royal Road is still with us today. I'd like to end with that today because I think it sort of sums up that quality of relentlessness, that quality of simplicity, of duty and pride and achievement that is the essence of these Persians that we've come to know today. You can see it engraved on any U.S. Post Office because it has become the motto of our postal service also: "Neither snow, nor rain, nor heat, nor dark of night shall stay these couriers from the swift completion of their appointed rounds."

There you have in a nutshell everything that made the Persians what they were—a people to be feared, but above all, a people to be respected and marveled at—people who could seem to overcome time and space, people to whom the challenges of nature were simply obstacles to be overcome. As they begin to set out to deal with these Greeks on their western borders, Greeks whom we will get to know in our next lecture, we can see all of those extraordinary characteristics at work.

Lecture Three
Intrepid Voyagers—The Greeks

Scope: Though the Greeks did not leave exact historical records about the Bronze Age period in which their culture and civilization developed, the myths and epics they left behind offer key insights into their origin and their establishment of great cities along the coast of Asia. By the end of the Bronze Age, Mycenaean Greeks were using their knowledge of shipbuilding and navigation to launch expeditions into Asia. As more Greeks headed east, they used Athens as a starting point for the foundation of such cities as Ephesus and Miletus; Rhodes and Halicarnassus were colonized by Dorian Greeks related to the Spartans. In time, these colonies far outshone their mother country in terms of population and cultural advancement. These Ionian Greeks were heavily influenced by the older cultures of Asia and Egypt, but they added their own distinctive skeptical rationalism to the mix. It was this unique world that Cyrus encountered as a result of his conquest of Lydia.

Outline

I. The Greeks are a branch of the Indo-European family that went west from the Caucasus Mountains and migrated down into modern-day Greece.

II. The Greeks did not leave exact historical records about the Bronze Age period, but their myths and epics suggest that as soon as the Greeks became seafarers, they began to develop connections with Asia.

   A. The myth of Jason and the search for the Golden Fleece at the far end of the Black Sea tells us that the Mycenaean Greeks (the Greeks of the Bronze Age) were already in contact with the people of Asia.

   B. The Trojan War represented an attempt by the Mycenaean Greeks to take over a city with a key location in the northwest corner of Asia Minor.

   C. Classical archaeology reveals that the city of Miletus was founded not by the Ionians but by earlier Bronze Age Mycenaean heroes from across the Aegean Sea, sometime before 1200 B.C.

- **D.** The great colonizing expansion of the Greeks toward Italy and Sicily during the Iron Age of the 7th century B.C. followed in the footsteps of the heroic Mycenaeans from classic songs and stories.
- **III.** The Mycenaean world ended around 1200 B.C. in a great calamity that is not fully understood. This period marked the collapse of the Bronze Age.
  - **A.** For about a century, Greece was virtually depopulated.
  - **B.** The people of these fallen kingdoms embarked on a great eastward movement.
    1. Many Greeks followed trade routes and routes of conquest into Asia and became caught up with the Sea Peoples (a confederacy of sea raiders).
    2. Some Mycenaean Greeks settled on the coast of the Levant, south of Lebanon, in the area known as Palestine.
  - **C.** A group of refugees from mainland Greece remained unconquered and re-founded great cities, including Miletus, Ephesus, and Priene; these refugees were the ancestors of the Ionians.
    1. Athens became the mother city for the group of colonies surfacing in Asia Minor.
    2. The Ionians remained the most populous and most adventurous Greeks and inherited from the Mycenaeans the idea of the bronze-clad warrior.
  - **D.** Scholar Martin Bernal sparked a debate with his thesis that Greek civilization owes its roots to what it borrowed from the people of Egypt and the Near East.
- **IV.** Ionia (used broadly to mean the Greek realm in Asia Minor) became the core of Greek cultural values, while mainland Greece (the area that included Athens and Sparta) became a backwater.
  - **A.** One of the tragedies of these Greek cities in Asia is that they never recovered from the Persian conquest; thus, the balance in the Greek world eventually shifted away from Ionia, to which it owed so much.
  - **B.** Homer is the most famous and earliest writer from this area.
    1. Sometime around the 8th century B.C., he pulled together traditional stories into two great epics: the *Iliad* (about the Trojan War) and the *Odyssey* (about the return of a Greek hero from Asia).
    2. The Greeks revered Homer.

3. The similes used by Homer to describe the Bronze Age world of the *Iliad* and the *Odyssey* offer pictures of his own Iron Age world, depicting Ionia as a place of competing city-states.
- **C.** Homer was followed by a flood of lyric poets, including Sappho, who wrote about her brother's adventures in Egypt as a trader bringing Egyptian wealth home to Ionia.
- **D.** Other great poets could be found up and down the coast, along with philosophers, scientists, and the first Greek geographers.
- **E.** The Ionians were great borrowers and travelers. They saw the world and brought back to Ionia ideas on art, architecture, engineering, mathematics, science, and religion.
- **F.** The unique contribution of the Ionians to world civilization is the idea of knowledge for its own sake—pure intellectual speculation about human life, politics, and the universe. Their love of the counterintuitive is exemplified by Aesop's fables.
- **G.** The Ionian poet and philosopher Xenophon challenged traditional ideas about religion. His scientific and philosophical approach to the subject reflects the beginnings of comparative religion.

Recommended Reading:

Camp and Fisher, *The World of the Ancient Greeks.*

Hanson, *The Western Way of War: Infantry Battle in Classical Greece.*

Questions to Consider:

1. Where do you weigh in on the debate about whether Greek civilization owes its roots to what it borrowed from the people of Egypt and the Near East?
2. Can you point out a particular passage in the *Odyssey* that might illustrate the experience of living in the Ionian world of Homer? If so, which one and why?

Lecture Three—Transcript
Intrepid Voyagers—The Greeks

Welcome back. Last time, we got to know the Persians and their traditions about their origins, and now it's the turn of the Greeks.

Up until 1950 or so, most scholars believed that the Greeks who were mentioned in the epic poems, like the *Iliad* and the *Odyssey*, and in the myths about Jason and the Argonauts, who went to the ends of the Black Sea, that those were not, in fact, the Greeks of classical times or their ancestors and that they weren't speaking the Greek language.

It wasn't until a young Englishman named Michael Ventris repeated Henry Rawlinson's great translation feat—but in this case, for a script called *Linear B*, which had been found on the island of Crete and in some of the Mycenaean centers in the Peloponnese at places like Mycenae and Pylos—that people realized that that script, Linear B—which is called linear because the clay tablets had lines drawn on them so that the scribes could keep between the lines, like children in primary school today—was a form of Greek, and all those palace accounts had been written in Greek by Greek scribes using a Greek language.

That tied the Bronze Age civilizations to a Greek people. *Linear A*, the earlier form of the script used by the scribes at places like Knossos in Crete, turned out to be a pre-Greek language. So just from that one decipherment that was published in the early 50s, it became clear that the Greeks entered a literate world of kingdoms and palaces and very civilized people that preceded them in the Aegean area. Those same Greeks could trace their line back to the Neolithic farmers who came down through the Balkans with their cattle herds, and their crops, and their habit for building little hilltop villages—which are the ancestors of the Acropolis of the classical world—thousands of years before the time of classical Greece, and the age of Pericles, and the building of the Parthenon.

We associate the Greeks with Europe. They are a branch of the Indo-European family that went west from the homeland in the Caucasus between the Black Sea and the Caspian Sea, and then they drifted down through the Balkan Mountains, and they entered what is today the country of Greece.

The question for us is: How did they become the builders of Greek cities in Asia, which is what Cyrus the Persian encountered them as? And, second, what are the unique features of the civilization that they created as they began to interact, first, with the pre-Greek peoples in Greece on the Aegean and on the island of Crete and, second, with a wider realm, as they learned from those pre-Greeks—like the Minoans of Crete—how to build ships, how to navigate over great distances, and acquired a taste for seafaring and adventure?

The Greeks themselves did not leave exact historical records about that Bronze Age period, but they left myths and epics. Those myths and epics make it plain that already in the Bronze Age, as soon as the Greeks became seafarers, they began to have connections with Asia.

We know the myth about Jason and the Golden Fleece, which is represented on some pottery vessels—drinking cups where the Greeks would show their mythical stories. They would show the monstrous dragon of Asia at the far end of the Black Sea at a place called Colchis, where you could get these magic fleeces, the fleece of a ram impregnated with gold. It was hung on a sacred tree. Jason and his Argonauts went all the way to the ends of the Black Sea to steal that Golden Fleece and bring it back to Greece with the help of the gods.

That was one of the myths that shows us that the Mycenaean Greeks as they are called—the Greeks of the Bronze Age—were already in contact with the peoples of Asia. An even more famous epic, myth, involves the Trojan War. This is very well known in modern times thanks to all sorts of retellings in books and in cinema, but it was also well known to the Greeks. In fact, just as the education of a typical Persian was to learn to ride and shoot and tell the truth, the education of a typical Greek for centuries before the classical era was also to learn to ride and to hunt and to know Homer and the story of the Trojan War and of the return of the heroes that was told in that second epic, the *Odyssey*.

So they would also create images that showed scenes—in a way, sort of cartoon-like scenes—of the Trojan War's episodes—scenes such as Achilles, the great undefeatable hero, tending the wounds of his dear friend Patroclus on the plains of Troy.

The Trojan War represented an attempt by the Mycenaean Greeks to take over a city that had a key location. It's a city of Asia (Troy is in the northwest corner of Asia Minor), and it's right by the Hellespont, that narrow channel of water through which the waters of the Black Sea flow out into the broader Aegean and Mediterranean. That was one of the great trade routes. We already know from the story of Jason and the quest for the

Golden Fleece that the treasures of the Black Sea area could be reached by the Mycenaean Greeks and brought back home to enrich their kings and their heroes.

The Trojan War, if it had an economic basis, is probably on the same footing—an attempt to seize a little beachhead in Asia so that they can monitor that trade and foster their own Mycenaean trade up into the Black Sea. But we also know from archaeology something that's not so plain from the myths: that city of Miletus—the largest city of classical Ionia, the one that we encountered already surrendering to Cyrus in order to get out from under the yoke of the Lydian kings—when archaeologists excavated there, turned out to have been founded not by the classical Ionians but earlier, by Bronze Age Mycenaean heroes coming across the Aegean Sea from their homeland in the heartland of Greece sometime before about the year 1200 B.C. and founding a city in Asia.

We also know that the Mycenaeans went west toward Italy and Sicily—so, in fact, the great colonizing expansion of the Greeks during the Archaic period of the Iron Age—of the 700s, of the 600s B.C.—was simply following in the footsteps of the heroic Mycenaeans of song and story who led the way centuries before those later migrations.

This grand Mycenaean world ended in a great calamity that we can't fully understand yet. We call it the collapse of the Bronze Age. It was a time around the year 1200 B.C., when these ancient citadels—like Mycenae, like Pylos, like Tiryns—they all were destroyed and abandoned. Greece itself for a period of about a century was virtually depopulated. Here had been one of the richest, most progressive areas in the Mediterranean, trading with peoples in Asia and North Africa, suddenly put out as if someone turned off a light.

We know that there was a great movement of peoples—refugees from these fallen kingdoms. The Greeks themselves say that this was a time when the sons of Heracles, whom they called the Dorian Greeks—the ancestors of the Spartans and other Greeks—came down into Greece and reclaimed their patrimony.

That's not the way we would guess that it happened from the archaeological record, but it's a complicated picture, and that was the Greek legendary story—the return of the sons of Heracles. They seemed to have pushed out other Greeks.

Where did those Greeks go? Many of them went east toward Asia. They followed those trade routes and those routes of conquest that the Mycenaeans had been going on for centuries. They went all the way to Cyprus looking for a safe haven from whatever chaos was happening at home. They became caught up in the group called the Sea Peoples, who sometime in the 1100s attacked Egypt and then, a great confederacy of ships, tried to find a safe haven for themselves there at the delta of the Nile. But a great pharaoh named Ramses—a descendant of the famous Ramses the Great—puts together an Egyptian fleet and holds off these invading Sea Peoples.

Some of them, though, were Greeks, were Mycenaean Greeks, and they settled down on the coast of the Levant, south of Lebanon, in an area that's still called Palestine today. That name comes from the Philistines, and those Philistines were Mycenaean Greeks—we know that from their pottery. They probably came through Cyprus, claimed that coast as a new safe haven, built five cities (like Gath and Ashkelon), and set up the Philistine way of life: Goliath of Gath who fights David in the biblical story is the descendant of one of these Mycenaean bronze-clad warriors.

There's suddenly a great Greek presence in Asia, but the ones that really interest us are from about a generation later than these Sea Peoples. They are a group of refugees from the chaos of mainland Greece who funnel themselves through Attica and that city of Athens, which alone remained unconquered by whatever force came through and put an end to Mycenaean Pylos and the other big centers.

These people are the ancestors of the Ionians of Asia Minor. They came through Athens, and they still had kings and chiefs. Some of their descendants could trace their lineages back to the heroes of Homer's time, and they flooded in ships across the Aegean Sea, through the Cyclades islands, to the coast of Asia Minor. There, they founded or re-founded great cities, like Miletus, Ephesus, and Priene. That was the central group—the ones who came to call themselves Ionians—and they always felt a kinship with the Ionians back home: the Athenians.

So we've got Athens as a mother city now and a group of colonies across the sea in Asia Minor who had gone east and founded cities in a place that seems more fertile, more safe, and closer to the centers of civilization—further from whatever wildness is going on in the mother country of Greece.

They are followed by other Greeks, not Ionians, but Dorians—cousins of the Spartans—who go across to the southern parts of Asia Minor, places like Halicarnassus or the island of Rhodes, and to the north, the island of Lesbos and places like Kyme on the mainland are colonized by the Aeolian Greeks. But the Ionians remain the center, the most populous, the most adventurous—the ones whose mercenaries are desired all over the Mediterranean because these Ionian Greeks inherited from the Mycenaeans the idea of the bronze-clad warrior.

There is an amazing find from a place called Dendra in the Peloponnese of a sort of Michelin Man in bronze. These were plates of armor that were buried with a Mycenaean warrior: great cylindrical rings of bronze to cover the man's chest, a boar's-tooth helmet, a big shield, and spear that would have been carried by this man. He's a Homeric hero, but he is, in fact, prefiguring those people we talked about earlier—the hoplites—the heavily armed infantry for which Greece was noted, who carried spears, swords, and daggers. Their main feature was this big, round shield and the fact that they fought lined up shield to shield in these phalanxes—these impenetrable walls of bronze, many men deep—that could move very steadily towards an enemy and mow them down.

All of Asiatic, all of Egyptian warfare was based on the idea of mobile troops: charioteers, cavalry, fast-moving infantry with bows and arrows and with spears, javelins, and slings. The Greeks were different. They trained hard to master this, and they trained hard to be able to fight and run in this heavy armor. The kings of southern Spain—there was a man called the King of the Silver Mountain, who brought a group from Phokaia in Ionia—Ionia now being Asia Minor and the Greek realm there—who lured these Phokaians all the way the length of the Mediterranean to southern Spain near Cadiz, and he hired them to fight his local wars for him and begged them to emigrate to Spain so that he could have them with him all the time. But no, these mercenary Ionian Greeks wanted to go home and spend their money back in the hometown.

We know that other Ionians went down to Egypt and fought for the pharaohs of Egypt and scribbled their names and graffiti on some of the ancient pharaonic monuments. So they're getting everywhere. What do these mercenaries bring home to Ionia? Wealth and ideas.

There's a great debate in the classical world today sparked by a couple of books (written by a scholar named Martin Bernal) that carried to its extremes a premise—the idea that Greek civilization owes its roots not so much to its European-Greek past but to what it borrowed from the people of Egypt and the Near East—from Asia and from Africa.

He has gotten many people angry with this claim, but the irony is the ancient Greeks would have been proud of exactly this, that their ancestors had borrowed so many great ideas—even Plato refers to this—so many great ideas from Asia and from Africa and welded into a new civilization. The idea of temples with long porticoes of columns is from Egypt; the idea of these upright statues, which start very stiffly in the Greek world, the *kouroi* (the young men stone statues), looking very like Egyptian statues, straight out of Egypt.

Their alphabet from the Canaanites, the seagoing Canaanites that they called the Phoenicians, lots and lots of their ideas of religion, of myth, of technology, of mathematics—all coming out of Egypt and the Near East, and they come to Ionia.

Ionia (used broadly to mean the Greek realm in Asia Minor) becomes the core of Greek cultural values, and the mainland of Greece, the Athens-Sparta area, which went through that horrific decline right after the collapse of the Bronze Age kingdoms, it becomes a backwater. It's the source of these populations, but it's being left in the dust by the achievements of its colonies in Asia Minor.

Later on, the motherland is going to send off new colonies westward, and they will colonize Sicily in southern Italy, places in Spain (like Ampurias), places in France (like Marseilles). These great colonies also will overshadow, for a time, the achievements of Athens, Sparta, Thebes, and Corinth—the cities in the motherland of Greece.

Why did they go back to Greece? They went there because, as colonists, they still had fond feelings and religious ties to the mother city, and because there were ceremonial centers—Panhellenic sanctuaries—at places like Olympia (for the famous Olympic Games, founded in the 8th century B.C.) and at the Oracle of Delphi (which we talked about in our first lecture, where King Croesus of Lydia sent his envoys to Delphi in central Greece to ask the advice of the Delphic Oracle about whether or not to attack Cyrus of Persia). That was a place that drew Greeks from all over the Greek world back to the motherland.

The action was in those seemingly peripheral zones and especially in Ionia. What I'd like to do is introduce you to this world of Ionia because we only know it in reflection through a few works that have survived, like the *Iliad* and the *Odyssey* of Homer, and then mentions of other works by equally important people—maybe not equally important as Homer but certainly very important Greek writers in many fields. I'd like to give you a sense of what Ionia was—what this amazing realm of the Greeks in Asia was like at the time that the Persians came in contact with it and conquered it. Because one of the tragedies for these Greek cities was that they never really recovered from the Persian conquest—that once Cyrus had brought them in under the Persian overlordship, they steadily lost their initiative. That great line of thinkers, writers, and energetic leaders petered out, and the balance in the Greek world shifted decisively away from Ionia, to which it owed so much.

Homer is the most famous and the earliest one that we can name. We're not sure where he was born. Many cities claimed him. The island of Keos said that he was from there, and the great Greek city of Smyrna on the mainland very near Keos—modern Turkish Izmir—also claimed Homer as a native son.

What did Homer do? Sometime—probably in the 8th century B.C., the same period when the Olympic Games were founded, the same period when the mainland Greeks started sending new colonists west to Sicily and Italy—Homer, an oral poet who had mastered by memory thousands of lines of traditional verse about the heroes of the Trojan War, seems to have decided to pull together all the stories that he could and tie them up into two great epics, one of which would show you the Trojan War and its essential conflict focused around one hero: this angry young man, Achilles. Achilles is the leader of a tribe from mainland Greece—the Myrmidons—who come from that area around the Gulf of Volos that was also the source of Jason and his Argonauts, the starting point for their voyage.

Achilles is the center of the *Iliad*. It's his anger at the Great King Agamemnon (who rules the Greeks from Mycenae) and having booty (in the form of a girl) taken away from him that should have been his prize for an exploit in the Trojan War that set the *Iliad* in motion. It only covers a few days. It doesn't get all the way to the Trojan Horse and the taking of the city of Troy by the Greeks. But it is the tragedy of the death of the hero Hector that brings it to an end after Achilles swears to revenge the killing of his own friend Patroclus (by Hector) by catching Hector outside the walls of Troy and fighting him to the death. That's the story of the *Iliad*.

Into that basic framework, Homer has fitted seemingly the history of the world. The Greeks considered Homer their equivalent of the Bible. That's something that troubled thinkers like Plato, that anybody should look on this work—which portrays the gods and goddesses in such a strange and skeptical and sometimes satirical light, which is going to be typical of

Ionia—the way that they look at their gods; you shouldn't build a religion on something like the *Iliad*.

The *Odyssey* was the story of the return of the Greek heroes from Asia, where they had now destroyed the city of Troy after 10 years' siege thanks to Odysseus's stratagem of the hollow Trojan Horse packed with Greek warriors. They all come home. It takes Odysseus 10 years to get back. He has many adventures along the way, seemingly in North Africa and the western Mediterranean. But he finally makes it home to his island of Ithaca; his wife, Penelope; and his son, Telemachus, and he kills the suitors who have been eating him out of house and home in his absence and restores stability in his home kingdom.

Homer made a picture of that lost Bronze Age world of the Mycenaean palaces in the *Iliad* and the *Odyssey*. He brought it up-to-date showing us pictures of his own Iron Age, Ionian, Asiatic-Greek world in the similes: It was the time of day when a judge would sit down in the marketplace and listen to cases brought to him by the common people. "It was that time of day …"; well, that's a picture for us not of the Bronze Age but of Homer's own Ionia—a place of kings, a place of assemblies, a place of feastings, public weddings, and woodcutters going out into the hills to cut down trees to build ships. All that world of Homer is also in the *Iliad* as the similes—the examples of what something "other" is like. Poor Ajax—the hero hounded by Spartans—is like a mule surrounded by boys who are trying to beat him to get him to go in a certain direction—a picture of Ionia. So we have a double vision in Homer; the epic world of the past, the sagas (as it were) that are so much like those Viking sagas that were found on Iceland, recording the deeds of the very early Vikings. But Homer also gives us—time and again—little pictures of his own Ionian world. It was a world of war. Ionia was a place of competing city-states. The essence of the Greek world was still that hill crowned by a settlement that had been part of the tradition since the very beginning. Each hill seems to have been, in some ways, competing with all of its neighbors, so that there was a great disunity within the cultural unity of the Greek world—a great political disunity.

Homer describes that for us in the similes. There's a very beautiful one that sticks in my mind. Achilles has discovered that his friend Patroclus has been killed. He's to blame because he let Patroclus borrow his armor—Achilles's famous armor—while Achilles himself was withdrawn from the fighting. Patroclus went out and, because he was in Achilles's armor, became the target for the Trojans, and Hector killed Patroclus.

Achilles, in his rage, no armor now to wear, goes to the trench that separates the Greek camp from the plain where they're fighting, and he stands on the edge of the trench, and he yells with his grief and with his fury, yells so loudly that it terrifies all the Trojan horses, and they retreat. Athena, the goddess, puts a ring of fire around Achilles's head to show that the gods are with him. Homer says this is as when an island far out at sea is beset by enemies coming in ships, and the islanders go to the top of their mountain, and they light beacon fires at night so that there will be a blaze to show their neighbors on distant islands that they are imperiled and that their friends must come and help them.

That image of the blaze, the beacons on the mountains of Ionia, sending messages back and forth, I think is a beautiful glimpse for us of that lost world of the Greeks of Asia Minor.

Homer is the first, but he is soon followed by a flood of lyric poets—for example, Sappho, the great female poet of the island of Lesbos, who lived near a city called Mytilene on Lesbos. She is supposed to have had unconventional love affairs with girls, and the word *lesbian* comes from this idea of erotic love between woman and woman that is celebrated, or at least hinted at, in some of Sappho's poems. But she also wrote about her brother going off to Egypt as a trader and going down to the Ionian version of Hong Kong, which was a Greek city planted in the Nile delta, so that those Ionian Greeks could get down to Egypt, trade with the Egyptians, and bring the wealth back home to Ionia. Sappho's own brother was involved in this trade and, therefore, a man of the world—a cosmopolitan.

There were other great poets up and down the coast, and there were also philosophers, scientists, and the first geography. We're going to encounter a map in our next session that was created by an early geographer, a Greek geographer in the city of Miletus. There were philosophers who began to speculate about the universe in a way that nobody else had, and here's the point: These Ionian Greeks were great borrowers. They were travelers; they saw the world; they brought back to Ionia the ideas of art, architecture, engineering, mathematics, and all kinds of science that they found elsewhere and some religious ideas, too—some myths and some cults that they encountered on their travels.

They made them part of Greek civilization, and those things, in turn, flowed back into the mainland, the heartland of Greece from Ionia. The unique contribution of the Ionians to world civilization to come is an idea of knowledge for its own sake—pure intellectual speculation about human life, about politics, and about the universe. These Asiatic Greeks loved the counterintuitive. This is the world that *Aesop's Fables* comes out of. We don't take them very seriously today, but the Greeks certainly did. Aesop was a Phrygian slave who lived on the Ionian Greek island of Samos. He was probably alive at the time that Cyrus the Persian came and added the Ionian Greeks to his empire.

Aesop took homely little tales about a plodding tortoise that can win the race over a very rapid but rather lazy hare (or rabbit); about a fox that grumbles because he can't get the grapes hanging too high and says, "Well, they must be sour anyway"; about a dog who sees his own reflection in the water and drops the bone in his mouth to go after the much-bigger-seeming bone that's down there in the water and, therefore, loses both. All of these different stories, especially the animal fables, come to us through Aesop, who seems to have collected them and probably created some of his own.

We think of them as children's literature—just little stories to be illustrated, one page after another, in a child's book. The Greeks didn't see them that way. They were used by orators in the public assemblies of Ionia—and, remember, this is something that Cyrus scorned about the Ionian Greeks: "They meet together in marketplaces, they make speeches, and they cheat each other." That was the essence of the Ionian—talking things over, exchanging goods and ideas, enriching everyone by this talk, and things like Aesop's fables were used to illustrate the counterintuitive.

The race is not always to the swift. The fight is not always to the strong. Don't give up a small thing that you have just to grab at something that looks bigger and better that's down there in the water. You may be going after an illusion. This is the kind of thinking—the kind of mental gymnastics—that these Greeks like to get into and that lies at the basis of Greek philosophy. Let's never forget that Socrates in his prison, more than a century later in Athens, spent his last days turning the fables of Aesop into verse—into poems—so they'd be easier to memorize.

From this bedrock came speculation. I'd like to end with a remarkable poet and philosopher named Xenophon of Ionia. Xenophon was a great challenger of traditional ideas about religion. In the Near East, science served religion through astrology, or science served the king through great applied scientific things, like irrigation that enlarged the king's realm and tax base. In Ionia, people argued and speculated about religion. Xenophon said, you know, the Ethiopians say that god, or their gods, have black skins and short noses. The Thracians—people of the north of the Greek world, modern Bulgaria—say that their gods are blue-eyed and redheaded. Well, I believe that if horses could draw, they would show us gods that looked like horses. Truly, each makes their gods after their own image.

This is a scientific, a philosophical approach to religion—the beginnings of comparative religion—bringing the intellect rather than faith to bear on the question of religion in human affairs, and it starts in Ionia.

It seems right to stick with Xenophon for our closing quote from one of these great Ionians. He lived at the time of the Persian invasion. He seems to have been one of the Greeks who may have fled westward to get away from the heavy hand of Persian authority that brought an end to Ionia as a great independent center of energy and innovation in the Greek world. He left a little fragment behind which says, the right things to talk about on those wonderful occasions when it's winter time, you're by the fire, reclining on your couch, sharing a dinner with friends, drinking the sweet wine after the meal—the things to talk about are these: Who are you? Who are your parents? Where are your lands? And how old were you when the Persians came?

This was the great watershed of Ionian history. This was the dark line of demarcation that separated that world of light and creativity from the troubled times that were to follow, and that will be the subject of our next lecture: the Ionian revolt.

Lecture Four
The Ionian Revolt

Scope: By about 500 B.C., the Greeks of Ionia decided to revolt from Persian rule and regain their freedom. Aristagoras, an emissary from Miletus, appealed to the democratic assembly of the Athenians for help in the wake of a Spartan refusal for aid. Landing at Ephesus, an Athenian army joined the rebellious Ionians and took the city of Sardis by surprise, burning it to the ground and destroying a temple of the goddess Cybele. Suffering a defeat after their withdrawal from Sardis, the Athenians refused to involve themselves further in the Ionian revolt. One by one, the Persians recaptured the rebellious Ionian cities, and the revolt ended with the Battle of Lade. King Darius, learning of the Athenian complicity in the burning of Sardis, vowed revenge for what the Persian Empire considered an act of unprovoked terror.

Outline

I. After Cyrus conquered Lydia, he left his subordinate officers behind to bring the Greek cities formally into his kingdom. He went eastward into central Asia and died trying to add the central Asiatic plateau to the empire he had built during his lifetime.

II. Cyrus had always wanted the Persians to remain true to their roots and their country.

  A. During his lifetime, he created the Persian capital city of Pasargadae, a paradise of palaces dotted around a park.

  B. Cyrus's successors, Cambyses and, after Cambyses, Darius, realized that their realm could not be governed from a small upland valley. They chose the old Elamite city of Susa as the administrative capital for the new empire.

  C. At Parsa, King Darius and his successor, Xerxes, built the city of Persepolis.

   1. Persepolis was meant to be the emotional and spiritual center of the realm, not its administrative heart.

   2. The city was created to host ceremonies, such as the annual new year festivities that brought together representatives from every tribe, nation, and kingdom within the Persian Empire.

3. In reliefs throughout the city, the Medes, Ionians, and other nationalities were shown coming to Persepolis to honor the king.

III. By about 500 B.C., the Ionians decided to rebel against the Persians and liberate themselves in what became known as the Ionian revolt.
  A. The Ionians knew they would need help and looked across the sea to Sparta for assistance.
    1. Aristagoras, the leader of Miletus, traveled to Sparta to meet with the city's kings.
    2. Unlike most mainland Greek city-states, Sparta was still nominally a kingdom, ruled by two kings from different royal houses. The kings, however, were what we might think of as generals for life and ceremonial leaders. Real power lay with the council of five *ephors* and, ultimately, the assembly of Spartan warriors.
    3. Aristagoras tried to bribe one of the Spartan kings, Cleomenes, with promises of treasure if he induced his countrymen to join the revolt, but Aristagoras was turned away.
  B. Aristagoras then went to the Athenians, who agreed to send some ships and men to support the revolt that was to liberate Ionia from the Persian yoke.
  C. Twenty Athenian ships and six Eretrian ships landed at Ephesus, came down onto Sardis, and captured the lower city.
    1. The Persian garrison and the Persian governor held out on the high citadel of Sardis.
    2. Either by accident or design, a fire burned Sardis to the ground.
    3. A temple of the mother goddess Cybele burned as well—a desecration that the Persians never forgave.
  D. Finding that they could not capture the Persians up in the citadel, the Greeks made their way back to Ephesus but were caught by a Persian counterattack. Badly beaten, the Athenians barely escaped and resolved to have nothing more to do with the Ionians.
  E. Though the Athenians and Eretrians pulled out of the Ionian revolt, the Greek cities in Asia Minor rose up in rebellion and threw out their Persian rulers.
    1. These Persian rulers were *quislings*: local Greeks in the pay of the Persians to govern their fellow Greeks.

      2. The rebellion spread all the way to Cyprus, an island divided between Greeks and Asiatics.

  F. The Persians ultimately sent armies and navies to Ionia to end the revolt. Up to this time, the Persians had not been a seafaring people; thus, they used ships from conquered maritime cities and nations to bring the Ionians back into their empire.

IV. The Ionian cities contributed large numbers of ships to face the approaching armada of 600 Persian vessels. In charge of the Phokaian contingent of three ships was a strong-willed organizational genius named Dionysius.

  A. Even though Dionysius was the leader of the smallest group of ships, he was given command of the whole fleet. Some of these ships may have been triremes, large vessels about 120 feet long with oars at three levels that carried more than 200 men.

  B. Dionysius held the Ionians to a strict training regimen.
      1. His aim was to transform the fleet into a superior force of rowers, pilots, and lookouts who could use their ships as missiles.
      2. The men practiced the *diekplous* maneuver, in which a ship breaks through the enemy line, turns around, and aims its bronze ram, mounted on the prow, at its target.
      3. On the eighth day of training, the tired Ionians revolted against Dionysius.

V. As the Persians came into view, the two fleets collided at the Battle of Lade.

  A. Some of the individual contingents of the Ionian fleet panicked and pulled out to save themselves.

  B. Some of the Samians and others remained in the battle, but once the pullouts began, the outcome was inevitable. The fleeing contingents shattered the dream of Ionian independence.

  C. The Battle of Lade was the last hurrah of the Ionian revolt.
      1. When Darius received word that the Ionian navies had been defeated, he knew that the Ionian rebellion was essentially over.
      2. Darius also swore an oath that he would punish the Athenians for the burning of Sardis.

Recommended Reading:

Miller, *Bridge to Asia: The Greeks in the Eastern Mediterranean.*
Stark, *Ionia: A Quest.*

Questions to Consider:
1. Do you think the Ionian revolt was an eventuality, or could it have been staved off by the Persian Empire? If it could have been avoided, how?
2. Imagine the Battle of Lade played out with a modern-day navy. In what ways would the battle differ from the one fought with ancient military strategy?

Lecture Four—Transcript

The Ionian Revolt

Welcome back. Now that we have gotten to know the protagonists of our epic, the Persians and the Greeks, it's time to return to Sardis, the old capital of the Lydian kingdom, now in the hands of Cyrus the Conqueror at that moment when he has found that by conquering Lydia he has brought some of the Greek cities into his realm.

Cyrus had so little regard for the Greeks that he didn't even stay around to conquer them himself. He left behind some of his subordinate officers to bring the Greek cities formally into his kingdom. He went rampaging off eastward, like a flame, like just a restless source of energy, settling nowhere, capturing Babylon, and moving on then into central Asia to try to bring those horse people into his great kingdom. That's where he died, trying to add the central Asiatic plateau to the empire that he had built up in just a single lifetime.

He had always wanted the Persians to remain, as we would say, true to their roots and true to that country—Parsa (or Persia)—down in the southern part of modern Iran. There was a time in his own life where his fellow Persians wanted him to move the population out of that upland plateau, that harsh land, down onto the plains, where all the rich cities were and all the beautiful life, and live like conquerors.

Cyrus was well aware of where that would lead. He knew what had become of the Assyrians, and the Babylonians, and the Acadians, and all the ones before who had gone the way of empire and soon become soft. So he said to these Persians: "You know, rough country breeds rough men and hard men. Soft countries breed soft men. Which do you want to be? Do you want to live in a hard country and rule others or live in a soft land and be ruled yourself?"

When he put it that way, they all agreed. So there was no move out of Persia, the traditional homeland, in Cyrus's lifetime. Instead, he created an odd sort of capital city called Pasargadae up there in the original plateau, and that was a place where he had little palaces dotted around a park—what the Persians called a *paradeisos*. That's the origin of the word *paradise* in the Bible. Paradise, we should remember, is a cultivated piece of land with trees growing in it, wild animals for the king to hunt, vast tracks of grassland, a wall around it or some sort of delimitation, and the idea that people are in there tending it.

We should never forget that in the book of Genesis that *paradeisos*, which is the Garden of Eden, is a place where Adam is put to work it and to be looking after God's *paradeisos*.

Cyrus created a beautiful *paradeisos*, and he inculcated in his line of Achaemenid kings a great love for trees. One of the images that the kings of Persia liked to use of themselves is: "We are the gardeners of our realm. We make things grow." So *paradeisos* meant that Pasargadae was more about growing things than about the little palaces and houses that were dotted around in it.

When Cyrus died, his body was brought back to Pasargadae. They built, up on a flight of stone steps, a pedestal of stone steps, a little thing that looks like a wooden cabin turned into stone with a gabled roof, no elaborate inscriptions, no beautiful reliefs, and there in that humble place, the body of the first and greatest of the conquering Persian kings was laid to rest.

It was up to his successors to deal with the great empire that this restless, fiery person—Cyrus—had created. His son Cambyses, who conquered Egypt, and Cambyses's successor, Darius—who then added India, or at least Pakistan and the Indus Valley of northwest India, to the empire on the east and who added Scythia, parts of Russia, the Ukraine, and eastern Europe on the west—realized that they were in charge of administering a realm that could not be governed from a small upland valley. So they chose the old Elamite city of Susa, one of the great metropoles of Asia, as their administrative capital for their new empire. But they wanted to be true to Cyrus's vision of the homeland—the place called Parsa, which gives us both the word *Persian* in English and, in the Indo-European languages that went further east, *Farsi* in India, which was the designation for the Persians who'd crossed down into the Indian subcontinent.

Parsa was a place they wanted to commemorate. So at a place that they called Parsa and that the Greeks called Persepolis—"city of the Persians"— they built, under Darius and Xerxes, a great ceremonial center—what we call Persepolis.

Persepolis was a capital of sorts, but it was a capital that was meant to be the emotional, spiritual heart of the realm, not the administrative governing heart of the realm. So at Persepolis, Darius and then his son Xerxes brought together from all parts of the empire building materials and craftsmen. As far away as Ionia, Greeks were recruited or forced into labor groups to come to that high upland plateau and, at Persepolis, create the most magnificent palace anyone had ever seen.

The columns soared up to the sky. They were crowned with capitals that, instead of being little floral motifs, were capitals like pairs of bulls yoked together at the midriff or strange lions. They decorated the walls, and the Ionians clearly did a lot of the artwork, but they were joined by the Lydians, and the Phoenicians sent cedar of Lebanon for the roof beams. The whole empire was involved. But the artists created on the walls images of the Persians and their subject peoples.

For instance, you could see Persian spearmen with their light, round shields; their spears; and those distinctive upright crown-like helmets or hats that the Persians wore into battle. Elsewhere, and dominating the art of Persepolis, you saw images in stone of the ceremonies that Persepolis was created in order to enshrine. Those ceremonies seem to have been the annual new year festivities, where the kings of Persia would summon to Persepolis, that remote place, representatives of every tribe, every nation, and every kingdom within their empire. Those peoples would come, and they would bring tribute and gifts to the Great King.

We talked in the first lecture about Cyrus and his initial conquest of the Medes and their kingdom of Media. The Medes had been civilized much longer than the Persians had, and those Median officials were shown with sort of rounded hats or turbans and always—like the Persians themselves—wearing trousers (something that the Greeks considered truly barbaric) for riding, sometimes with kilts also. They were shown all over the reliefs of Persepolis, these Medes, leading—sometimes leading by the hand like schoolchildren in a queue—the representatives of the subject nations through the passageways, along the corridors, up the flights of steps, stone versions of the living people who were walking by them once a year.

The Medes were shown carrying flowers—another symbol of the gardening that went on in the Persian Empire. They passed between little trees that look like Christmas trees to us, and they are leading people who are bringing camels, horses. The Ionians are shown bringing wool cloth, and they are wearing the trailing garments for which they were famous. All of these people are shown coming to Persepolis to worship the king.

It was in this way that the Ionian Greeks got to know the heartland of the Persian Empire. Some of their important people, their important leaders, became attached to the court of King Darius, were among his advisors. Many of their craftsmen had been taken out of their homes, forced to march almost 2,000 miles to that high valley to create this beautiful palace—and each year, some Ionians would participate in that great ceremony.

You would have thought that the message they got from all this was: These people are kings of the world. No puny little group like us Greeks could hope to challenge them. But it didn't work out that way. Somehow, by about the year 500 B.C., 22 years after King Darius began to reign and began to get to know the Greeks of Ionia very well, the Ionians decided to rebel from the Persians, to stage a revolt, break away, and liberate themselves.

They knew that they couldn't do it alone. They would need help. After all, the Persians were watching them at all times. There was a very heavy security system imposed upon you when you became part of the Persian Empire. They looked across the Aegean Sea to the old mother country of Greece and to the great hoplite phalanx of Sparta—that heavily armed infantry that was the most famous in the Greek world—to come across the sea and save them.

The leader of that Ionian city of Miletus, a man named Aristagoras, relying on that great scientific revolution that had happened in his city, took one of the city's treasures—a bronze map of the world that showed Greece, and the Aegean, and the Persian Empire. He took it onboard a ship, and he had himself rowed or sailed across the Aegean Sea to the Peloponnese, and he made his way to Sparta. There, in front of the kings of Sparta—Sparta, unlike most of the Greek city-states of the mainland, was still nominally a kingdom. It had two kings from two different royal houses, but they were really just generals for life and ceremonial leaders. This was not a monarchy, not an autocracy like the Persian Empire. The Spartan kings were not even politically the most powerful force within the land. That was a little council of five *ephors* and, ultimately, the assembly of the Spartan warriors.

Aristagoras talked to one of the kings, a man named Cleomenes, and he showed him the bronze map. He traced for Cleomenes on the sheet of bronze what the Ionians had learned about this great Persian Empire. "Here," he said, pointing with his finger, "here is Ionia beside the sea. Next to Ionia is Lydia, that fabulously wealthy kingdom. Next to Lydia, as you go toward the rising Sun (toward the east), is Phrygia, a land famous for its cattle and its crops. Next to Phrygia, Cappadocia. Next to Cappadocia, Cilicia. Next to Cilicia, Armenia." As he's in Armenia, he's starting to move into the mountainous area that lies north of the headwaters of the Tigris and Euphrates Rivers. "Next to Armenia, Mitanni," and now he's coming down into Mesopotamia, the land between the rivers. He's gotten to the far side of the Tigris. And finally, he said, "

Cassia, or Cissia, and in Cissia is the great city of Susa at the end of this great road. And in Susa lives the Great King of the Persians, and there is all of his treasure. Zeus himself would not be more rich than you would be if you would go to Susa, conquer the Persians, and capture their treasure.

Cleomenes, the Spartan king, said to Aristagoras, the Milesian, "How long is this trip?" We talked about the Royal Road two lectures ago when we talked about the Persian Empire, this great unpaved but carefully leveled highway on which the king's messengers, his riders who relayed his letters and orders, and his armies would pass. Aristagoras had probably been on that road, and he said, "Well, from Ionia to Susa, it takes three months." The king of Sparta said, "Get out. It is a very bad thing to ask Spartans to march three months away from the sea. I will listen to you no more."

Aristagoras tried to bribe him, and there's a charming addition to the tale that Herodotus tells. Cleomenes had a little daughter named Gorgo, and she saw the stranger—Aristagoras—approaching her father again, and she said, "Send him away father, or he will corrupt you." No Spartan ever wants to be corrupted by filthy lucre, so Aristagoras was sent packing.

He went to Athens, which at that time was a second-rate power, but it was the mother city of the Ionians, and he expected a better hearing. As Herodotus says, it proved easier to fool 30,000 or 40,000 Athenians in their democratic assembly than it had been to fool one Spartan king. Herodotus thought the whole Ionian revolt was a terrible idea.

At any rate, Aristagoras repeated the show with the map, and he convinced the Athenians they should try it, and they agreed to send him some ships and some men to support the revolt that would liberate, as they hoped, Ionia from the Persian yoke.

These Athenians marshaled in 20 ships, open galleys that were the descendants of the Argo that had taken Jason in quest of the Golden Fleece, possibly ships in which the warriors themselves pulled the oars and rowed as they would have done back in the old heroic days—possibly the trireme, the larger ships on three tiers (we'll learn more about them in a little bit) that were originally troop ships and transport ships.

At any rate, 20 ships carried several hundred or perhaps a few thousand Athenian warriors across the sea from Athens eastward to Ionia. They were accompanied by six ships of another central Greek city-state, Eretria, on the island of Euboea, just north of Athens—they also went along. These were the only supporters in the old Greek heartland for the Ionian rebellion.

Twenty Athenian ships and six Eretrian ships also. They landed at Ephesus, and the Persians did not know they'd arrived. They crossed over the hills. The 60 miles to Sardis probably took them on a march that would get them to Sardis on the third day. They came down on Sardis—a completely unsuspecting city—at dawn, and they captured the lower city. The Persian garrison and the Persian governor fled up to the high pinnacle of the hill by the city where the acropolis was—the citadel—and held out there. Somehow, either by accident or by design, a fire was lit in Sardis, and the city burned to the ground—the greatest city that the Persians held among their administrative capitals in Asia Minor.

A terrible blow, and to the horror of the local people, the temple of the mother goddess Cybele (C-Y-B-E-L-E) burned, too. The burning of a temple was a terrible desecration in the ancient world, and those people of Asia never forgot or forgave the Ionians and their Athenian accomplices for having destroyed that temple.

The Greeks, finding that they couldn't capture the Persians up in the citadel, decided to make their way back to Ephesus, but they were caught on the way by a counterattack of the Persians, and they were very badly beaten in a battle. The Athenians barely got away with their ships and their lives, and they resolved to have no more to do with the Ionians. Something that had happened in that initial attempt had convinced the Athenians that went that: (a) The Ionians were not to be relied on as allies, and (b) they had been sold a bill of goods. Persia was not this easy pushover of a place that a few men and a few ships could hope to topple.

So the mainlanders withdrew. The people of the motherland—the Athenians and the Eretrians—pulled out of the Ionian revolt, but the cities of the Greeks in Asia Minor all rose up in rebellion and threw out their Persian rulers. The Persian rulers, by the way, were mainly *quislings*—local Greeks who were in the pay of the Persians to govern their fellow Greeks. These were run out, and the whole of Ionia, for six years, was independent. The rebellion spread all the way to Cyprus, which was then also a divided island between Greeks and Asiatics. The Greeks there also rebelled, but the Persians are relentless. They may be slow to get things together, but when they do, there's no stopping them.

They sent armies and navies up to Ionia in order to end the Ionian revolt. The big problem for the Persians was they had not, up to this time, been a seafaring people. There is one story that said that the Great King himself should not go to sea—that that was not an element where the Persians should be. Nonetheless, if they were going to safeguard their western frontier, which now was on the coast of the Aegean, they had to have ships.

Fortunately, just as the Romans, centuries later, conquered the Greek cities of southern Italy and added these naval allies—as they called them—to their growing empire, the Persians had also conquered maritime cities and nations. Cambyses had conquered Egypt. The Egyptians had a fleet. The Phoenicians of modern Lebanon—those seagoing Canaanites from their centers like Tyre, and Sidon, and Byblos—had hundreds of warships—great triremes—triple-tiered ships in which they had circumnavigated Africa, in which they had planted colonies way to the west at Carthage. They had hundreds of these ships to now answer the king's call, and ships elsewhere in Asia Minor, like Cilicia, a famous nest of pirates. They were added to the ship roll.

In this way, King Darius put together a fleet of 600 warships, according to Herodotus, and sent them west to bring the Ionians back into the empire. The Ionian cities were either on islands—like Lesbos, and Keos, and Samos—or they were on the mainland but connected to the sea, so that as long as they had their walls and a connection to the sea, their friends from the islands could supply them with food, and you could never take those cities by starving them out.

So Darius realized, "I've got to beat them at sea. I must destroy their naval power." The Ionians learned that this great armada of 600 ships or so was coming at them with the core of that navy the fearsome Phoenicians, who were very well known for their seagoing exploits but perhaps not so well known for their fighting at sea. At any rate, just in terms of sheer numbers, it was a terrifying prospect because the Ionians could only muster 353 ships to face this horde almost double that size.

The Ionians had great islands like Keos that contributed 100 ships; other cities, the Ephesians, the city of Miletus, the island of Samos also contributed ships. Lesbos contributed ships. So we go from a 100-ship contingent on the island of Keos down to the smallest contingent of all, three ships from that little city-state of Phokaia that was part of Ionia on the mainland of Asia. But there was in charge of the Phokaian contingent of just three ships a superman of strong will and organizational genius named Dionysius.

Even though his contingent was the smallest, he stood up in the council—and, remember, these are Ionians; they're all going to debate everything rather than having a king to tell them what they're going to do and give them their orders. They gather together, they take votes on what to do, and Dionysius stands up and says, "If you are willing to undergo toil, trouble, hardship, and privation to train yourselves for this battle that is to come, you can win. It's a short time of effort and denial of comforts that will lead to everlasting freedom."

Well, who's going to resist that? Certainly not the Ionians. So even though Dionysius was the leader of the smallest group, he was put in charge of the whole fleet. He said, "We are going to train."

They were off Miletus, which was the greatest of the Ionian cities and the one that had the most to lose in terms of having started the whole thing by sending their leader, Aristagoras, to Greece to recruit the Athenian help. They were in the sixth year now of their revolt, and everything obviously rested on the success of this battle.

There were sort of wars of nerves that were going on at the same time. King Darius had all of the former leaders who had been ruling the Ionian cities on his behalf—the Ionian leaders he'd appointed—now send messages to the different people, saying, "If you would just come back into the Persian fold, you will be spared. If you do not, you will be destroyed." So they're trying to get at people's morale and work it away.

At the same time, Dionysius is making them train. These ships that they're in—these triremes—are about 120 feet long, and they have oars at three levels, probably 170 oars in each ship, so that's 170 men and 30 or 40 who are additional sailors, and marines, and pilots, and lookouts. They do have a sail, but the sail doesn't matter in battles. They take out the mast and the sail and leave it on shore and just row. All those oars are like an engine, and each ship is, in essence—if you want it to be—a torpedo, because it has at its beak a bronze ram that can punch through, sink, and destroy an enemy ship.

This was what Dionysius wanted them to do. The old-fashioned way of fighting at sea is the same way the Vikings fought at sea: You bring a whole lot of ships side to side, and then the armed men drop their oars, grab their weapons, and just slug it out on floating wooden platforms—very primitive, very unscientific, and requires no skill on the part of the pilots or the rowers.

Dionysius wanted to train them to be a super-force of rowers, pilots, and lookouts who could turn their ships into missiles. Remember, one stroke from a ram can eliminate a couple of hundred of the enemy at a blow, whereas an individual archer shooting from a deck or throwing his spear from a deck—one weapon, one kill. It just wasn't an effective way to fight, especially when you're outnumbered.

So every day, those ships were taken away from shore. They spent the whole day at sea. He did not allow the Ionians to go ashore and have their midday meal as they normally did. Triremes were amphibious ships that were always drawn up on shore at night and went back out to sea during the day. They had very shallow drafts.

From dawn to dusk, day after day, seven days in a row, Dionysius kept them at it, and the maneuver they were learning was called the *diekplous*. *Dia* is the Greek for "through," *ek* is "out," and *plous* is what a ship does in the water. We have to say ships "sail" in the water, because our English language is very deficient in words for ships moving at sea. We still say even things like the *Queen Mary* sail. I've even seen people talking about submarines or stern-wheel paddle ships having sailing dates. The Greeks were better—they've got that word *plous* for "ships moving in the water through and out." What are they moving through and then out of? The enemy line.

He was teaching the crews of rowers, the Ionians and their pilots, to break through an enemy line, come out the other side, and turn and then come back, and aim their rams at targets. This was very scientific. It took a lot of skill, a lot of focus, discipline, concentration, hard work, no heavy dinners in the middle of the day, and on the eighth day, the Ionians staged another revolt. They revolted against Dionysius the Phokaian. They said, "This is worse than being the slaves of the Persians. We never dreamed that this would happen to us when we put our defense into the hands of this madman. Why should we suffer this way? We can win the battle without this; let us go sit in the shade," and that's what they did.

Dionysius found he had a mutiny on his hands, and he realized that now the cards were stacked against them. So the Phoenicians came into view; the fleet of the Greeks—the Ionians—scrambled to its places and faced them, but they were a group who had now mutinied against discipline, failed to complete their training, and had been assaulted individually by messages from their former pro-Persian leaders urging them to come back in the fold. It was a fleet already rife with division—weakened by disunity.

This probably is what Herodotus, the descendant of the Greeks of Halicarnassus, had against the Ionians: They just couldn't seem to unite for anything. They seemed infirm of purpose where discipline and self-denial were involved. This was the time that called for it, and they proved lacking.

As the Persians came into view, the two sets of ships, the two fleets, came together and collided. The Phoenician ships, fighting for the Persians, had enough that they could actually start to wrap around the ends of the Greek line. Seemingly as this happened, as I would read the description in Herodotus, some of the individual contingents of the Greek fleet—the Ionian fleet—panicked and decided to save themselves.

Remember, they are a temporary alliance of otherwise disunified cities—they're not one national fleet—and so starting with the islanders of Samos, followed by the islanders of Lesbos, the contingents pull out. The core of the fleet (the 100 ships from the island of Keos) remains true. To their great honor—there are about a dozen, I think, maybe nine of the Samian ships—those great Samian triremes remained in their place because their captains refused to retreat with their countrymen and save their own skins at the expense of the common effort.

Long afterwards, monuments were put up in the marketplace on the island of Samos to these men who had remained true to their station, had captained their ships right on through the battle, suffered defeat, but had kept the honor of the island strong.

However, once the pullouts began, the outcome of this battle was inevitable. It's called the Battle of Lade (L-A-D-E) because the Greek headquarters had been on the little island of Lade, right by the city of Miletus. If you go to Miletus today, you will look in vain for Lade. The sediments from the streams on the coast have spread a delta—a sheet of land—out into the sea and have captured that island, so it's just a little hill. But I urge you to look for the hill, stand upon it, look around you, and imagine that sea filled with the ships of the first great sea battle between the Greeks and the people they called "the barbarians"—those who spoke a non-Greek tongue—and imagine those fleeing contingents, the Phoenicians taking off after them, and the shattering of the dream of Ionian independence at Lade.

That was the last hurrah of the Ionian revolt. King Darius—when he got the word from his messengers that the Ionian navies had been defeated, that the Ionian revolts shortly after that had collapsed—he was happy, and he knew that he had punished the Ionians for their rebellion, but there was something on his mind. Six years earlier, Athenians had crossed over in 20 ships and had helped burn Sardis in an act of unprovoked terror that must have loomed in his mind, not unlike 9/11 in the American consciousness: People out of nowhere coming and burning a great city near the coast.

The Athenians love to tell the story that when Darius got news of the burning of Sardis in about the year 499 or 498 B.C., he took an arrow, fitted it to his bow, shot it into the air, and swore a great oath—that he would punish Athens. He told his cupbearer, the young man who poured his wine at dinner: "At every meal, remind me, remind me three times, 'Sire, remember the Athenians.'"

The Ionian revolt was over, and it was indeed time for the Great King to "remember Athens."

Lecture Five
From Mount Athos to Marathon

Scope: Seeking revenge against Athens, the Persian Empire made two attempts to reach the city, which was separated from the Great King's territories by the wide moat of the Aegean Sea. The first attempt involved a massive Persian fleet traveling parallel to a troop march around the northern end of the Aegean; the ships were caught by a violent gale and wrecked on the coast of the Mount Athos peninsula. The second involved the dispatch of a large fleet directly across the Aegean, which landed at Marathon in 490 B.C. and clashed with the Athenians in one of the most famous battles in history. The confrontation resulted in the resounding defeat of the Great King's seemingly invincible army and the death of the Persian mystique; the Greeks must have believed that the threat had been averted, but they could not have been more wrong.

Outline

I. When the Ionian revolt ended around 494 B.C., Darius set about planning the punishment of Athens and the addition of mainland Greece to his realm.
   - **A.** The Persians considered the Greek armies to be all that stood between them and a domain that would reach the Atlantic Ocean.
   - **B.** Darius ordered the Persian army to march around the north end of the Aegean Sea through Thrace while the Persian fleet of about 300 ships paralleled the army just along the coast.
   - **C.** The Persians sought first to capture the famous gold and silver mines on the island of Thasos and the mountain of Pangaea on the mainland to pay for the campaign.
   - **D.** A kinsman of Darius, Mardonius, sent heralds to city-states in Greece asking for tokens of submission to the Persian king. At this point, the Greeks realized that all of their cities were targets.
   - **E.** All the way up to Macedon, tribes and cities capitulated to Darius's invasion.
   - **F.** In 493 B.C. or 492 B.C., a north wind came down on the Persian fleet at Mount Athos and put an end to the invasion.
       1. Thousands of men perished and the entire fleet was lost.

      2. Returning home, the army left garrisons and administrators behind to take control of the newly submitted lands that were now part of the Persian realm.
II. I have been lucky enough to be part of a scientific expedition to Mount Athos that searched for the remains of those Persian ships.
    A. My colleagues and I used side-scan sonar to identify potential shipwrecks.
    B. We found modern shipwrecks and learned that many ships over the centuries since Darius's disaster had been lost in the waters off Mount Athos.
    C. On the last day of the expedition, we found what could be a relic of the lost Persian fleet: a *sauroter* ("lizard killer") that had served as a butt-spike on the end of a spear shaft.
III. In 490 B.C., a few years after the disaster at Mount Athos, Darius tried a second invasion route.
    A. The Mede Datis and the Persian Artaphernes transported the Persian army straight across the Aegean. Along the way, islands that never dreamed they would see Persian troops on their shores immediately submitted to the Great King.
    B. The fleet made its way unopposed across the Aegean and went first to Eretria, conquering the town and deporting the Eretrians to Persia.
    C. From Eretria, Darius's forces went south to the coast of Attica and landed at Marathon.
      1. Decades before the Persian landing at Marathon, the Athenians had expelled the last of their tyrants, a man named Hippias.
      2. Hippias was now traveling with the Persians as a puppet who would be returned to power in Athens should the Persians conquer the city.
      3. The Persians also counted on Hippias for strategic advice and for his friends inside the city, who would open the gates to the invaders.
    D. An Athenian of great military genius and inspiring presence, Miltiades, had experience fighting with the Persians.
      1. In his role as tyrant of the Thracian Chersonesus, Miltiades had become a vassal of the Great King.

- **2.** He later participated in the Ionian revolt and had fled to Athens after the Battle of Lade.
- **3.** Miltiades called for the Athenians to take the offensive and march to Marathon to confront the Persians.
- **4.** Miltiades led the Athenian hoplites from Athens to Marathon. These hoplites were heavy infantry troops drawn from the ranks of upper-middle-class men; at about 10,000 strong, they constituted a substantial portion of the Athenian population.
- **E.** The battlefield was constricted at Marathon, and the Persians were pinned by Miltiades and his Athenians, whose entrenched position was protected from the Persian cavalry by a rocky slope.
- **F.** The Athenians sent to the other Greeks for help, but the only response came in the form of an army of 1,000 men from Plataea, a village just outside Athenian territory.

IV. Miltiades held his position at Marathon before finally deciding to launch an attack.
- **A.** The attack may have been precipitated by a signal flashed to the Athenians by the Ionians: *chorís híppeís* ("the horse are away"), meaning that the Persian cavalry had been loaded onto ships and moved in an effort to attack Athens from its own shore.
- **B.** When the Persian and Athenian forces collided, Miltiades's expectations were fulfilled: The Athenian center gave way, but the wings of the army, along with the Plataean allies, pushed in and forced the Persians into chaotic retreat.
- **C.** Along with a reported 6,400 Persians, 192 Athenians died on the field at Marathon.
- **D.** Miltiades left one of the 10 Athenian tribal regiments under the command of Aristides the Just to guard the booty and led the others on a march back to Athens to array themselves on the beach where the Persian ships intended to land.

V. The victory at Marathon was the greatest battle in Athenian history for the morale of the citizens.
- **A.** The Athenians had faced the Persians virtually alone and had won.
- **B.** The Athenians never forgot the assistance of their Plataean allies or the failure of the Spartans to come to their aid.

C. From the Persian point of view, the Battle of Marathon was merely a test to see how the enemy would respond and to learn for the next attack.

Recommended Reading:

Pritchett, *Marathon.*

Time-Life Books, *Persians: Masters of Empire.*

Questions to Consider:

1. Is there any way that Xerxes's forces could have planned for the north wind that destroyed the Persian fleet at Mount Athos? If not, what does this say about the role of geography in warfare?
2. If the Battle of Marathon was indeed just a test from the Persian perspective, what lessons do you think the Persian Empire learned?

Lecture Five—Transcript
From Mount Athos to Marathon

Welcome back. News of the great Persian victory—that Phoenician fleet—over the rebel Ionians at the Battle of Lade spread like wildfire through the Aegean and the Mediterranean. Some of the news was carried by survivors of the battle, and one of those survivors was that Phokaian leader, Dionysius, who had tried in vain to persuade his Ionian confederates to train seriously for this battle and, thus, have a hope of winning.

When the battle was lost, Dionysius led his three ships back to shore, loaded their gear and their masts and sails onboard, and headed not for safety but into the heart of Persian-controlled waters, knowing that every warship the Great King had had been deployed at Lade and that the ports of the Persians were now stripped of defenses. He sailed all the way to Phoenicia, attacked Persian merchant shipping, loaded his ships with loot, and then sailed to the other end of the Mediterranean—all the way to Sicily, where he set himself up as a pirate. From then on, for the rest of his life, he preyed on the shipping of Etruscans, of Phoenicians, of Carthaginians, but never on his fellow Greeks. Such was the end of Dionysius of Phokaia.

Meanwhile, Darius had resolved to "remember the Athenians." They had, in fact, done him a favor. Empires must grow, but even the most brutal autocracy needs excuses and pretexts for its wars. The Athenians had handed him a wonderful pretext. Here they were outside his empire, and he had never injured them, and they had sent men across to participate in about the year 499–498 B.C. in the burning of his provincial capital at Sardis. Now it was time to punish them.

The Ionians had been defeated at Lade. The great Ionian revolt was over, probably in about 494 B.C. He set about planning the punishment of Athens but also adding all of mainland Greece to his realm. He had, in fact, had a Greek doctor named Democedes, who was from a western Greek city, who had helped Darius get through the recovery from an injury. He had had that doctor take him on a Phoenician ship with Persian guards through the Greek world already, to show the Persians the harbors and cities—scout out the coasts and the sea routes—preparatory for a takeover of all of the Greek world—a takeover that would have carried him right into what is today southern France.

The Persians, we know, considered that the Greeks were all that really stood between them and a dominion that would reach the Atlantic Ocean, because the Greek armies were the last really strong resistance—Greek armies and Greek fleets—that the Persians felt they would have to face in their bid to take over Europe. So it was a grand campaign but a small announced target—Athens and its neighboring city Eretria—who were now going to be punished for participating in the Ionian revolt.

The Persians still didn't like the idea of trusting their troops to ships, so they decided that the army would march around the north end of the Aegean Sea, through what was called Thrace, while the fleet—that Phoenician fleet, now augmented by the Ionians who had been brought back to the fold and had their own naval contingents to serve the Great King—another fleet, this time about 300 ships, would parallel the army, just along the coast.

These triremes, as I said, went ashore every night so that the crews could spill onto shore, sleep, have their evening meal, and then get back onboard ship. These aren't like British men-of-war that are at sea for months or even more than a year without letting the men onto land.

So this was the idea: a fleet and an army in parallel around the north end of the Aegean, and halfway along, in Thrace, they would come to the famous gold mines on the island of Thasos. On the mainland in Thrace, by the river Strymon, was a mountain called Pangaea—"all the Earth"—that seemed to have great ores of gold and silver in it and was the source of a lot of the wealth of the northern Aegean—if that could be captured by the Persians, it would pay for the whole campaign.

A kinsman of Darius (whom we shall meet several times in the future) named Mardonius—a Persian prince who was of the royal family—had the dream of becoming the satrap of Greece once Greece was conquered and brought into the Persian world. He was very happy when his kinsman, King Darius, sent heralds from the Persians into Thrace, into Macedonia—which is north of the main part of Greece—and into Greece itself, going to every city-state and asking for those tokens of submission to the Great King: earth and water. This was the point at which it became plain to all the Greeks that they were targets, too.

Darius launched his invasion. The army marched without incident along the northern shore of the Aegean, and the fleet kept pace with it. All along the way, tribes and cities surrendered to them. In fact, all the way up to Macedon (Macedonia is the region; Macedon is the kingdom), everyone capitulated. The Great King's western frontier now extended into the Balkans. It had already been a success when a terrible natural disaster put an end to this invasion, which took place probably in 493 or 492 B.C., a year after the great victory over the Ionian fleet at Lade.

This time it was a force of nature, as I said, that brought the Great King's ambition low. His fleet had to navigate a great cape that sticks out into the northern Aegean. On the southern tip of that cape is a mountain more than a mile high—Mount Athos—today, the holy mountain of the Greek Orthodox religion, studded with monasteries, but in that time, a formidable hazard to navigation because Mount Athos brews at its tall summit storms. It catches clouds; katabatic winds sweep down its slopes, and hit the sea, and spread out in ship-killing waves. It was one of these great winds—a north wind—that came down on the fleet of Darius, 300 ships strong, as it was trying to get past the cape of Mount Athos. That great wind destroyed them all.

Herodotus (who gives us the story) says that the men spilled into the sea, that as they swam over to the land, they were confronted by sheer cliffs and couldn't get up onto the shore, that they were eaten by monsters—we believe these are probably sharks that are eating these hapless mariners from half a world away, it would seem, the sunny coasts of Phoenicia. Thousands upon thousands of men perished. The entire fleet was lost—a terrible setback. The army returned home, having left garrisons here and there and administrators to take control of the newly submitted lands that were now part of the Great King's realm.

Darius then set his mind to other approaches and decided on a straight-across attack through the islands of the Cyclades. But before we follow him there, I would like to tell you that I have been lucky enough to be part of a scientific expedition to go to Mount Athos and look under the sea for remains of those famous ships of King Darius that were lost in that great storm.

My colleagues and I—Greek, Canadian, American—we were all together on the Greek research vessel *Aigaio*. We went up there and spent weeks off Mount Athos, using side-scan sonar to identify hundreds of bumps on the sea floor—each of which could have been a shipwreck—then sending down robots on tethers and going down ourselves in a little two-person submersible called the *Thetis*, named after the sea goddess who was the mother of the famous hero Achilles. (One of the robots, by the way, as sort of a joke, was named Achilles, himself a smaller version of the big mother ship.)

In that little submersible was room for a navy pilot and an archaeologist. We would pick the side-scan sonar targets that looked best and then go down on the sea floor and see if one of them wasn't a shipwreck. We were very sorry to find that erosion of Mount Athos, which is now a bare cone of rock, has spilled, over the years since Greece was deforested, the topsoil into the sea. The skirts of that peninsula under the water are now cloaked with sediments that used to be on the land, and it's very hard to find a spot where you can see anything ancient.

But down there amongst the coral reefs and the sponges, we did find modern wrecks. We knew that it was a place where ships, for many centuries after King Darius's disaster, did continue to go to the bottom. We were lucky enough to encounter a local fisherman who had dragged up in his nets from 300 feet down, just off the point of the cape, a helmet—a Corinthian helmet of early Greek style that he showed us a picture of (he'd already turned it over to the antiquities authority)—and he offered to take us back to the spot where he hauled up that bronze helmet.

It was the last day of the expedition. It's always an axiom in the archaeological world that the big finds are made on the last day, usually after lunch. We took our fisherman onboard, and I think he felt he'd been brought onto the Starship *Enterprise* when he found himself on the bridge of this research vessel with all of its space-age equipment. But he took us to the place; he pointed exactly to the spot in the water and said, "It was there." We put down one of the robots on the spot, and as we checked our charts, we found he had pointed us to our side-scan sonar target number 1 of the 250 that we had encountered, so we were being brought back to our beginning. We had not yet checked it.

As the robot got to the bottom and turned on its lights and fired up its camera, there—transmitted to us up the cable from the video camera on the floor, within a few yards of where it had hit the bottom—was a great pot on its side, and glinting in the mouth of the pot was something green. We could even tell that underwater. Green is the color to which bronze oxidizes, and so we were very excited, immediately thinking that we had found another relic of this lost fleet.

The little Achilles maneuvered itself over to the pot. Young Angelos, who was the man at the controls up on the bridge of the ship, was the youngest member of the team. He had misspent his teen years in video arcades, but he alone had the gift of maneuvering all those joysticks so that the titanium grab arm, the camera lens, the lights, the engines, and thrusters of the little Achilles to take it up and down or forward and back could all be maneuvered at once. He had the arm reach in, grab that green thing, and bring it up to the surface.

It turned out to be, we believe, a relic of that lost fleet of King Darius. It was a weapon about a foot long, made of bronze. It was from a spear but not from the working end of a spear—the weapon end—that would have been an iron or steel blade. This bronze thing was the butt-spike so that you could thrust your spear into the ground at night by your bivouac, and if there was an alarm, you could leap up, grab the spear—ready for action—and charge off into the battle.

Also, if your spear broke, you could use that butt end as a subsidiary weapon. It has not yet been dated, but we believe it will be soon because inside that hollow bronze weapon, called a *sauroter* (a "lizard-killer"), was the wood of the original spear shaft, at least 2,000 years old. We hope that through radiocarbon dating it will be possible to determine whether or not this remarkable weapon found alongside that helmet that the fisherman had already discovered does date, in fact, as a relic of this great disaster that carried the Persian hopes of an easy attack on Athens to the bottom of the sea.

In the year 490 B.C., a couple of years after the Mount Athos disaster, King Darius tried again. He sent a Mede this time. We don't often read about those people—the Medes and the Persians—that the Medes get a leading role. But there was a Mede who was considered a very good military leader named Datis, and Darius sent along with him a Persian named Artaphernes. The two of them loaded an army and horses into these ships that they had converted to troop carriers and horse carriers and transported the Persian army—this time straight across the Aegean, island-hopping their way, places like Naxos and Delos, all the islands submitting to the Persians as they came. These islanders, who had never dreamed they would see Persian troops on their shores, immediately submitted to the Great King.

In this way, the fleet made its way unopposed across the Aegean in the fair summer weather and went first to Eretria, up there on the island of Euboea. After a short siege, they conquered that town, deported the Eretrians to Persia—just as the Syrians and Babylonians had deported Jews from Israel and other peoples from their homelands—and resettled them at a place as a sort of semi-enslaved working community. They were still there half a century later when Herodotus came through and met the descendants of those Eretrians, those deported people.

So these masses of people on the move as a result of warfare and so on, they're not just a function of our modern chaotic world, they go back to the ancient world as well. It's a tool of terror, a tool of kings and conquerors having one more threat to hold over the heads of people who are resisting.

From Eretria, that force that Darius had put together got back in their ships and went the short distance south to the coast of Attica, the territory of Athens. The place they chose to land was Marathon. They were led there by an Athenian—an Athenian turncoat who was traveling with them. This is one way that great powers conquer. They don't just line up on the frontiers of the country that they want to beat and launch an attack; they find someone inside the gates who will collaborate with them, who will bring over to them certain disaffected minorities in the population and make it easy for them to get inside and to win—to get the people fighting for them and undermining the resistance within their enemy's own citadel.

That's what happened at Athens. A couple of decades before the Persians landed at Marathon—22 years, in fact, in about 512 B.C.—the Athenians had thrown out the last of their tyrants, those dictatorial nobles who had seized power and kept it all in the dynasty of one family called the Pisistratids. The last of these tyrants was a man named Hippias. As you can tell from his name—Hippias—the family liked horses and horseracing.

Hippias had then gone away from Greece in exile and had been absorbed into the Persian realm, and he was now traveling with the Persians as a puppet who would be placed back in charge of Athens should they win— and whom the Persians were counting on, both for strategic advice and for friends of his inside the city to undermine unity and open the gates.

The Athenians were aware of this. They knew that Hippias, their old tyrant, was with the Persians, and when they came to Marathon, there was a great debate in Athens: Should they go out and meet the Persians on the field? Nobody had beaten the Persians in a pitched battle at this point. The best that anybody had done was King Croesus of Lydia fighting Cyrus to a standstill. Here was tiny Athens—the total military force was only about 10,000—up against a Great King who could muster more than a million people to throw at them. Should they not rather stay within their city, sit tight, guard their gates, and hope that they could withstand a siege, and eventually the Persians would go home frustrated?

There was at this time in Athens, almost by chance, an Athenian of great military genius and inspiring presence named Miltiades, or as a Greek would have called him, "Milthiades." Miltiades was of an Athenian family, but he knew the Persians because he had fought not against them but with them. Among those waves of adventurers who had been spreading out from the motherland of Greece over the past decades—mercenaries, and explorers, and soldiers of fortune—this Miltiades belonged to a family that had been in the forefront. They had established a little private fiefdom for their noble house on the north shore of the Hellespont—that long peninsula that borders the Hellespont and looks across to Troy. That had been their family's domain, and from there, they had enriched themselves by preying upon or levying tolls on the shipping that came out of the Black Sea into the Aegean.

In this role as tyrant of the Thracian Chersonesus—this little neck of land—Miltiades had become a vassal of the Great King. He'd been absorbed into the empire, along with the Greeks of Asia. When King Darius (some years before) had led an army into Europe, crossed the Danube River over a quickly built bridge, and led an army up into the land of the Scythians—what would be in the area around Romania, and the Ukraine, and Russia—on a vast campaign of conquest, Miltiades was appointed to guard the bridge. This was how much the Great King trusted him.

He did guard that bridge, but later on, he participated in the Ionian revolt, and he had to flee for his life after the Battle of Lade, when the Great King was after all those who had resisted him—all those rebel leaders who had dared to rise in rebellion. This had brought Miltiades back to Athens—the one man who really knew the king, who had talked with Darius, who had been a friend of his, and it carried tremendous weight with the Athenians when Miltiades said to them, "We should take the offensive. We should march to Marathon and meet them there."

Marathon lies, as you are probably already guessing, about 26 miles away from Athens. The distance is, in fact, the basis of the modern race, the marathon. It's actually only about 25 and some miles. The marathon got changed when the Olympics were held in London in the 1920s and the reviewing platform for the royal family turned out to be about half a mile further on than the proper end of the race, which was 25-point-something miles. So they've all been 26-point-something since.

At any rate, Miltiades led the full levy of Athenian hoplites. These are men of the upper-middle class; they're landowners, and they are the sort of yeoman stock—not quite a majority of the Athenian population of 30,000 or 40,000, but at 10,000 a very substantial portion of it. Most of the Athenians were, in fact, un-landed, poor workers and laborers—craftsmen. These hoplites put on their helmets, their breastplates—or, actually, handed them to their slaves (each man had a slave to carry the 60 pounds of armor)—and they marched off across the hills—it's rugged terrain—from Athens to Marathon, where the Persians had landed.

The Persians had set up camp there. The field did not look as it looks today. A colleague of mine, a great geologist named Rick Dunn, whom I once worked with in Portugal on a project—we were trying to locate Phoenician harbors around the coast of Portugal through remote sensing and through geological coring. Rick Dunn, in 1996–97, when he was attached to the American School of Classical Studies in Athens and working at the Wiener Laboratory, went out and did coring all over the plain of Marathon and showed that this vast expanse of dry land that is there today was, in fact, featuring a large freshwater lake, a stream that ran from the lake into the sea, and marshes all around the lake.

So there was a very constricted area for a battlefield—you don't realize that when you go today—and the Greeks set themselves up on a slope above one edge of this rather difficult piece of terrain and guarded the pass to Athens. No matter how big an army you are, you don't dare leave an enemy behind you, or they will get you in the rear or in the flank.

The Persians were now pinned at Marathon by Miltiades and his Athenians, and though they had all their ships there, and their horses, and so on, they couldn't attack the Athenian positions with the cavalry, because the horses couldn't charge up the rocky slope at the entrenched Athenian position.

The Athenians sent to the other Greeks for help. They had allies. They sent a runner named Phidippides all the way to Sparta. In those days, there were day runners in Athens—that means a runner who can run all day long—a *hemerodromos*; he can run all day long—and it's only in the late 20th century that people have been able to duplicate the exploits of these great runners of antiquity. He ran all the away to Sparta, not stopping day and night, got to Sparta, told them that the Persians had arrived, asked for help, and was told by the Spartans: "We are in the middle of a religious festival. It's the festival of the Carnea, and until the full moon is past, we cannot assist you."

So Phidippides had to run all the way back to Athens with this terrible news. The only people who came were the townsmen of a little village just outside Athenian territory, a place called Plataea that we will meet again because it's going to be the site of another confrontation between Greeks and Persians. But these Plataeans put together their little army of 1,000 and joined the Athenians. So now we've got 10,000 troops facing allegedly—according to Herodotus—hundreds of thousands out there on the plain of Marathon. What are they going to do?

Well, the Persians were being frustrated in their expectation that they would get a message that Athens had opened its gates. What could have been more favorable? All the Athenian soldiers are out of the city—wouldn't the traitors open the gates? This is part of Miltiades's genius: The would-be traitors are probably part of the army, so they are with him under his eye, and the loyal people are back home guarding the city, which is now emptied of its army.

The days went by. Miltiades, who was just one among many generals—and, in fact, there was a *polemarchos*, "a war leader" of the Athenians, who should have been in charge, but because Miltiades knew the Great King, because of his charisma, he was given the leading role. He finally decided, "We need to attack them."

What seems to have precipitated the attack is a detail that doesn't exist for us in the old account of Herodotus—the earliest one we have. The Persians, of course, never wrote about this at all. Persian history does not record its defeats. It's meant to glorify the Great King. Herodotus simply tells us that on a given day, Miltiades ordered a charge. But from 1,500 years later, from a little dictionary of the ancient world that existed in Byzantium—it's called the *Suda* (S-U-D-A)—there is an entry for a popular saying called *chorís hippeís* , "the horse are away."

There's an explanation that the Ionians—who were perforce fighting with King Darius's troops against the Athenians and were there on the plain of Marathon—flashed a signal to the Athenians with Miltiades up on the slope above the plain, saying *chorís hippeís*—"the horse are away"—in some sort of Morse code. What this meant was that the fearsome Persian cavalry had been loaded the night before into the transports, and those ships had slipped away in the darkness—they were going to try to get around the point of Attica and attack Athens from its own shore, leaving the army helpless and unknowing, pinned down at Marathon.

True or not, it explains what happened. Miltiades said, "Arm yourselves; we will attack." He lined up his phalanx—his shield-to-shield array of men—several men deep, strong on the wings, weak on the center, so he could spread it wide. He headed them down and along the plain to a narrow place near the lake and the marshes, where the Persians, on seeing him come, started to muster to meet him. He led them at a run.

They ran a mile—each man wearing 50 to 60 pounds of armor—to confront the Persians. For a long time, it was doubted by modern historians that this was even possible. "Who could run a mile? Certainly not me," said all these soft professors like myself. Then in 1976, at Pennsylvania State University, the classicists asked the physical education majors if they would please put on 60 pounds of equipment and run a mile, and they asked them at the end, "Do you think you could fight?" To which they said, "Of course we could."

To make the point even more clearly, Peter Krentz, a great classics professor at Davidson, has recently interviewed lots and lots of people in the American military and found that, for crying out loud, it's part of basic training to be able to carry that kind of a pack at a dead run for a considerable distance and still be combat-ready when you arrive.

So there's no reason to doubt that there was that charge, that extraordinary run at an opponent that had never known defeat and seemed unbeatable. When they collided, what Miltiades expected happened: He'd weakened the center, so he had a long line. The center gave way, but the wings of his Athenian army with the Plataean allies pushed in and brought the Persians in retreat, into chaos behind their own center. The center had won but was now isolated. The Greeks turned on them, and pushing and pushing, they ran the remnant of the Persian army into the marsh. There, they were butchered as they floundered around among the yellow water lilies on that plain of Marathon—lots of herbs and wildflowers at Marathon. The name of the place means "fennel."

They finally got them out of the marsh and onto the beach, and as they're trying to get up onto their ships, the Athenians pursue them even there, fully armed onto the ships, grabbing onto the railings themselves and hoisting themselves up. The battle continued on the decks as the Persians tried to escape. The brother of a famous Athenian, a poet named Aeschylus, whom we will meet again—he's going to write a play about the Persian wars—this brother was grabbing a railing to hoist himself up, and a Persian took an axe and cut off that Athenian's hand, and he bled to death.

One hundred and ninety-two Athenians died on the field at Marathon. They took a tally, and it's just hard to know whether to believe it or not: 6,400 of the enemy died, as well. It's certainly true that in very well attested battles, ancient and modern, you do get that kind of incredible disparity once a rout has begun; once the enemy, even if they are larger, have thrown down their weapons and have begun to run, the butchery can be terrifying.

The Athenians under Miltiades then send a runner back to Athens, and that's the origin of the original marathon run—that young man who raced through the hills to carry the word to Athens, not only to shout, "*Nike! Nike!*" ("Victory!") but to warn them that the fleet was coming around and they must be prepared for the horsemen to appear off their coast.

Miltiades, not content with this, left one of the tribal armies; there are 10 tribes in Athens. They divide the population in these 10 groups. One of the 10 was left under the command of a young man named Aristides the Just to guard the loot and the prisoners. The others did a quick march across the hills, back to Athens, and they arrived in Athens in time to be arrayed along the beach when the Persian ships came up over the horizon, intending to land, but finding, as if by a nightmare, there was the Athenian army they'd left behind at Marathon now waiting for them on the plain.

That was the victory at Marathon. It was one of the greatest battles. It was certainly the greatest battle in Athenian history for Athenian morale. They had faced the Persians virtually alone and won. They never forgot their Plataean allies who had helped them. They also never forgot the Spartan failure to come when called. The Spartans came a few days later, and toured the battlefield, and offered their congratulations, but they had taken no part in helping the Athenians repulse this initial invasion.

From the Persian point of view, maybe even though they lost the 6,400 men, it's just a test, after all. You're throwing a little advance force out there, and you're seeing how the enemy responds; you're learning about the enemy, and you're learning for next time. The relentlessness of the Persians will now shift into focus.

Miltiades offered his helmet in the sanctuary of Zeus at Olympia. It has been discovered there by the German archaeologist who worked there in the 19th century. You can see it in the archaeological museum at Olympia, the very helmet that he wore on the battlefield at Marathon 2,500 years ago. Next to it in another case is a helmet from a Persian or Median warrior—a shining bronze helmet, sort of a skullcap with a little peak. That one says, "From the Athenians to Zeus."

Miltiades's helmet has on the cheek piece inscribed the words: "Miltiades dedicates this to Zeus." It was his thank offering for the supreme moment of his own life, a chance to lead a small city-state against the invading force of one of the greatest nations ever seen in the ancient world. That was the victory at Marathon—that was the first Greek success as they confronted the Persians in this epic struggle that we call the Greek and Persian wars.

Lecture Six
Xerxes Prepares for War

Scope: Darius died before he could complete his mission to punish Athens, and the task fell to his son and successor, Xerxes. For his invasion of Greece, Xerxes planned a strategy of shock and awe that would harness the enormous power and resources of the Persian king to terrify the Greeks into submission. In 483 B.C., Xerxes used his empire's engineering skills to dig a canal across the Mount Athos peninsula and build pontoon bridges across the Hellespont so that his grand armada could enter Greek waters without having to round the peninsula's dangerous tip. To the Greeks, such re-engineering of nature was an act of hubris, violent arrogance, for which the Persians would earn the enmity of the gods. In 481 B.C., accompanied by an army of men from every satrapy in the Persian Empire—the largest force ever assembled in the ancient world—Xerxes set out for Sardis.

Outline

I. After the victory at Marathon, the Athenians honored their fallen soldiers in a way they had never done before and would never do again: They buried them on the field of battle.

    A. Customarily, the remains of fallen Athenian soldiers were returned to their families as ashes or were buried on the Sacred Way that ran from the city gates to the Academy.

    B. The great mound (Soros) that the Athenians created at Marathon still survives and was excavated in the 1890s by archaeologists.

II. Darius died before he could assemble another invasion force; his mission to punish Athens fell to his son Xerxes.

    A. Xerxes was more accustomed to administration and diplomacy than actual fighting. Pressured by Mardonius, however, he decided to invade Greece.

    B. In order to conquer Greece, Xerxes relied on a war of shock and awe, with amazing engineering feats that would show the power of the Persians over nature and frighten the Greeks into surrendering.

- C. In 483 B.C., Xerxes set his engineers to two great tasks.
    1. The first was to cut a canal through the neck of the Mount Athos peninsula so that Persian ships could enter Greek waters without circumnavigating the dangerous cape where Darius's fleet had met disaster.
    2. The second was to bridge the Hellespont so that the Persian army could march across from Asia into Europe.
    3. These projects were not strictly necessary for the invasion but carried the message that the Great King could do anything he wished.
III. While Xerxes gathered his enormous army and fleet, construction began on the canal through Mount Athos.
    - A. Xerxes's cousin Artachaees was put in charge of the digging.
    - B. The challenge was to dig a canal about 1.25 miles long through the neck of the peninsula (which rose to a height of almost 50 feet above sea level in the middle) and to make the canal wide enough so that two triremes could row through it side by side.
    - C. Artachaees used the usual Persian work levy: a group of men recruited from different satrapies within the empire. Confusion among the polyglot work teams, however, prolonged the project.
    - D. Even classical historians doubted that Xerxes managed to cut a canal through the neck of Mount Athos.
        1. That skepticism grew stronger in the intervening centuries; by the 20th century, historians thought of the canal as a legend.
        2. All doubt was put to rest by a geological team that found the remains of a vast cutting, 80 to 100 feet wide, buried under the neck of Mount Athos.
IV. More spectacular to the Greeks than the canal was the bridging of the Hellespont.
    - A. The Hellespont is the mile-wide, slightly twisting channel of water that comes from the Sea of Marmara down to the Aegean and is part of a complex of waterways that drain the waters of the Black Sea into the world's oceans.
    - B. Xerxes's engineers came up with a way to bridge the Hellespont by constructing a "suspension bridge" based not on pilings set down into the sea floor but on warships used as pontoons on which the roadway could be set.

1. Xerxes gave the engineers permission to requisition more than 600 hulls of triremes and *pentekontors* (50-oared galleys).
2. Once the hulls were in place, the engineers brought in gigantic cables made of papyrus and esparto grass and attached them to wooden posts set on the coast; the cables were then stretched across the lines of anchored ships.
3. Wicker screens were erected on either side of the passage so that the horses and pack animals would not see the water and panic.
4. Gaps in the lines of ships were left in a few places so that merchant ships and warships could pass through.

C. Shortly before Xerxes and his forces planned to march across, a storm tore up the cables and swept away the bridges. In record time, the bridge was reconstructed.

V. The Greeks had a double image of the Persians as both warriors with pure ideals and barbarians (*barbaroi*).

A. To the Greeks, Xerxes's engineering efforts were marked by hubris (violent arrogance) against nature.

B. Consequently, the Greeks met the arrival of the Persians with both fear and scorn.

VI. To cap off the preparations for his invasion, Xerxes assembled a Grand Army in 481 B.C.

A. No one can definitely say exactly how many soldiers and followers Xerxes brought with him, but his army is known as the largest ever assembled in antiquity, bringing together troops from every part of the Persian Empire.

B. Xerxes had no intention of hurrying the invasion. His slow approach was calculated to engender panic in the Greeks and separate them, making them easier to conquer.

C. As the Grand Army left Susa, an eclipse of the Sun was interpreted by the Persians as a sign that the Persian Empire would block out the light of the Greek world and guarantee a Persian victory.

D. One of the reasons for the extended march of this enormous army was to strip the empire of militias that could rise up against Xerxes while he was away on campaign.

E. We'll pick up the story of Xerxes's march to the sea in the next lecture; we end this lecture with the image of Xerxes worshiping a large sycamore tree placed in his path, true to the tradition of the gardener kings of Persia.

Recommended Reading:

Burn, *Persia and the Greeks: The Defense of the West, c. 546–478 B.C.*
Farrokh, *Shadows in the Desert: Ancient Persia at War.*

Questions to Consider:

1. Which of Xerxes's two engineering feats do you think was the more impressive: the canal through Mount Athos or the bridging of the Hellespont? Why?
2. Why do you think natural events (such as the eclipse as the Grand Army left Susa) played such an important role in interpreting the outcome of a particular battle?

Lecture Six—Transcript
Xerxes Prepares for War

Welcome back. After that amazing victory at Marathon, the Athenians did something to honor those 192 fallen soldiers that they had never done before and that they would never do again. They allowed them to be buried on the field of battle itself, where they had won their great victory.

Customarily in Athens, if you fell fighting for your city, you were either given back to your family as incinerated ashes in an urn following a cremation (and your family would place your remains in the little family burying plot outside the walls of the city) or, if you were considered to have been a great benefactor of the state, you would be buried on the Sacred Way that ran from the city gates out to the grove of olive trees called the Academy.

But in this case, we know what they did. We know that because the great mound—the Soros—that the Athenians created at Marathon for their honored dead still survives and was excavated in the 1890s by archaeologists. What the archaeologists found was that the Athenians had gone out to the battlefield and first dug a trench about 30 feet long and 3 feet wide. Into that trench, they had placed the burned bodies of sacrificial animals—offerings to the gods and heroes who had assured this victory.

There had been a shrine nearby where the Athenians were encamped at Marathon to their hero Heracles. He probably was represented in the sacrifices. There was another shrine nearby to their old hero Theseus, the slayer of the Minotaur, the liberator of the Athenians from Cretan domination. He would have been represented and, of course, their own goddess, Athena, who was the patron goddess of their city, and gods like Poseidon, who was very dear to the Athenians—all of these gods were probably honored in that trench at Marathon.

Miltiades himself had a cult of the goddess Artemis, and he had promised her a lot of goats, so they may also have been sacrificed among those burned animal bones that they found in the narrow trench. But above that trench was an enormous rectangle, 85 feet long, 30 feet wide, filled with the cremated remains—bones and ashes—of those 192 men and of a special kind of Athenian vase that was offered in graves.

It's called a *lekythos*, and it had other purposes, too. It would have unguents or perfumes in it, but it was sometimes placed on tombs. There was a tradition that you would go out and shed a tear into the vase and replace it on the tomb to let the dead soul of the person there below know you were still thinking of them, still grieving for them.

Among the remains were these *lekythoi*—these little upright jugs—and also remains of other vases, some of them dating right from the time of the Persian war, sometimes older ones. Apparently there were so many dead they had to ransack other cemeteries to get older vases for the occasion. Also, one big urn with the cremated remains of a single individual. We think that was perhaps one of the 10 generals.

Each tribe was headed by a general. The Athenians called them a *strategos* or multiple *strategoi*, who are the leaders of the tribal regiments and, together, lead the army of Athens. One of them probably was killed. Hoplite warfare had its generals on the front rank, and they were subject to a very short life expectancy if battles were at all frequent.

So with this monument—this Soros—at Marathon, the Athenians marked forever the site of this amazing victory.

Meanwhile, Darius received word of the disaster. The fleet returned to the coast of Asia Minor, the messengers set out from Sardis on their horses (one after the other) carrying the word back to Susa, and Darius decided he would try again. But before he could assemble another invasion force, he died.

He was buried, not up at Pasargadae with Cyrus, but at a new place that was to become the sort of Valley of the Kings of the Great Kings of Persia, Naqsh-i-Rustam We still can see Darius's tomb today, like that carving at Behistun rock—a sort of Mount Rushmore effect carved into the living cliff—lots of figures, inscriptions, and his epitaph. It's so interesting to me that he was most proud of being a warrior, a man who fought his own battles. He says, "I was a good spearman on foot and on horseback. I was good with the bow and arrow on foot and on horseback." It will be a long time before we encounter another Persian king who is fighting in the front ranks of his army as they confront their enemies.

Darius passed the grudge against the Greeks and the mission to punish Athens as an inheritance onto his son Xerxes. Xerxes is one of the first Persian kings to grow up entirely wrapped, during his childhood, in the enormously elaborate, civilized, and intricate ceremonials of the court—ceremonial procedures of the court at Susa—and to grow up in a world dominated by the harem, by the women, by his own mother, Darius's widow, Atossa, who remains a major figure in his reign.

He is a Great King used to palaces, to ceremonies and receptions, and to administration and diplomacy much less than he is to actual fighting. This is going to put a mark on his reign and make it ironic that it was into his hands that this mission to conquer the Greeks was ultimately entrusted.

Xerxes, however, did decide—partly because his father would have wanted it, I'm sure, and partly because that Persian noble Mardonius—that kinsman of the royal house who had led the invasion around the northern end of the Aegean after the Battle of Lade at the time when Darius lost his fleet to the big storm off Mount Athos. Mardonius was still at court. Mardonius was still pressuring the Great King to invade Greece, to punish those Greeks, to set up a satrapy, and to make him, Mardonius, the ruler of it.

Xerxes finally agreed. He was delayed, like Darius, by other business. The Persians, by this time, unlike Cyrus, did not rush into things. The energy had settled into a much more monumental sort of movement. In order to conquer Greece, Xerxes relied not on lightning-like attacks, as his predecessor Cyrus had done, or on marshaling these great armies and getting these allies together and venturing into unknown territory. He was going to rely on a war of shock and awe, with amazing engineering feats that would show the power of the Persians over nature so that the Greeks would, he hoped, simply surrender. Just to back that up, Xerxes had decided to assemble the largest army and the largest navy the world had ever seen to conquer Greece.

Surely in this way, he could guarantee his own safety, the safety of the Persians themselves and of his realm, and of the god-assured success of his mission. Three years before he actually planned to attack (we're now in the year 483 B.C.), Xerxes set his engineers to two great tasks. One was to cut a canal through the neck of the Mount Athos peninsula so that his fleet, unlike his father's, could row through the canal ship by ship, get to the other side, and enter Greek waters without ever having to circumnavigate that very dangerous cape where his father's fleet had come to grief. The other great task was to bridge the Hellespont so that his army could walk or march across from Asia into Europe.

These were not strictly necessary for the invasion effort, but they sure carried a message: The Great King can do anything he wishes. If he wants to have his ships sail or row through dry land, they will do so. If he wants his army to walk on water, it shall be done.

Meanwhile, while these were in progress, these two great engineering feats that we will look at in detail in just a moment, Xerxes was gathering that enormous army and fleet. Let's look first at the Mount Athos canal. He put a cousin of his, the tallest Persian known, way over six feet, a great giant of a man with a huge voice—Xerxes put this man, Artachaees, in charge of the digging of the Mount Athos canal.

The chief geniuses behind it all seem to have been the Phoenicians, who had created various works around their own harbors. They were transported, along with lots and lots of workmen, up into this inhospitable area. There weren't markets and cities close by, so they had to ship the men in relays off to a place where they could have some R&R and get well fed, and then they'd bring them back to the isolated little peninsula for the canal digging.

The challenge was enormous. They had to dig a canal about a mile and a quarter long through the neck of a peninsula that rose from the level of the sea, at the beach on either side, to a height of almost 50 feet in the middle. They had to do this in three years, and they had to have it big enough so that two triremes—each ship was about 20 feet wide, and with their oars extended, they were taking up about 40 feet of space, so you're talking 80 to 100 feet of space—so that they could pass each other or row side by side through this canal from the sea toward Asia into the sea on the European side.

Well, Artachaees set his workmen to it. What he did was he'd gotten the usual Persian work levy: A group of workmen are recruited from many different satrapies within the Persian Empire—so you get these polyglot, or many-languaged, work teams, just as the Persian armies tend to be many-languaged. This can be kind of like the Tower of Babel situation, where people don't understand each other very well.

Certainly, the Phoenicians failed to convey to the others the right way to do it. The Phoenicians were given the central section, where the land rose highest. They knew that they had to dig it very wide if it was going to be the proper depth at the bottom. So they started wide, and they cut it down through the soil, sloping in toward the middle, and at the bottom, it was the proper width for the water to be let in and the triremes—those great galleys—to be rowed through.

The other nations, each with their own segment, they weren't so smart: They dug it to the prescribed width at the top and went straight down, and of course, the sides fell in, and they had to do the whole thing all over again.

So the Persian overseers were very disgusted with them. The job stretched out for a long time.

It wasn't until the actual year of the invasion that they were finally getting around to putting the breakwaters at either end that would keep the sea from bringing sand immediately into the canal and filling it up, and the watch towers on the end of each breakwater.

Those are still out there somewhere under the sea. We went up during our Mount Athos expedition to see if we couldn't find the remains of the Persian breakwaters. No luck, but I'm sure they're down there. But we did have a chance, since we were there, to walk the line of Xerxes's famous canal.

It was doubted even in antiquity by some historians that Xerxes had really managed to have his men cut a canal through that neck of Mount Athos. It had only been used once after all and never heard of again, and the Persians were used to boasting about their achievements, so people doubted it.

That doubt grew stronger and stronger as the centuries went by until there were many scholars in the 20th century who said flat out: "This is just a legend. This is something the Persians said they did, but it doesn't make sense that they really could have." Well, those doubts were put to rest by a British and Greek geological team who, with some fancy geophysical seismic survey techniques, went up to Mount Athos and found the narrowest neck of this isthmus that connected Mount Athos itself to the mainland. They took their sensing tools over that hump of land and found that there was buried under the modern surface the remains of a vast cutting, 80 to 100 feet wide at its top, tapering to the bottom, and getting down below sea level, exactly as Herodotus had said that the canal really was.

They found that original ideas that it would have run into great masses of bedrock and they couldn't have dug through it were wrong. The canal builders had, in fact, chosen a path so that they only had to work with compacted sand, clay, and gravel. So there was obviously a good deal of advanced study and coring of those pieces of terrain that they were going to dig the canal through to make sure that the thing would be practical.

So we know that it happened; the remains of it are there, buried under the ground. The most of it that I saw was a little dip in the ground near one end, with some cattle lapping fresh rainwater out of a puddle that had formed.

That was all that I saw of Xerxes's great canal, but the ability of modern geophysics to look under the surface assures us it is still there.

Even more spectacular to the Greeks than the canal was the bridging of the Hellespont. The Hellespont is that mile-wide, slightly twisting channel of water that comes from the Sea of Marmara down to the Aegean. It's part of a complex of waterways that drain the waters of the Black Sea out into the main oceans of the world.

The Black Sea is, of course, filled up with the waters from Russia and the surrounding territories, through rivers like the Don and the Dnieper. The Danube flows into the Black Sea. All that fresh water gets out through the Bosphorus, a little channel up near Byzantium, or modern Istanbul; then gets into a sort of "valve" with a heart in the middle of it, a large inland sea called the Sea of Marmara, so-called because of the marble that is found on its island; and then out through a second narrow channel, the Hellespont; and into the Aegean.

Xerxes did not want to have his men ferried across the Hellespont. It's not entirely clear why, but partly it must have been that idea of showing the Greeks: "I can do anything. Surrender while you have the chance. I am a man who can cast bridges across arms of the sea."

His engineers came up with a wonderful way to bridge the Hellespont. In a way, it was a kind of a "suspension bridge," but the basis was not pilings set down into the sea floor; the basis was boats, warships used as floating supports—pontoons—on which the roadway would be set.

So Xerxes—wanting, in fact, not one but two bridges so that the main army could cross on one and all of the pack animals and supplies and baggage could cross on the other—gave the engineers permission to requisition more than 600 hulls of triremes and the smaller galleys called *pentekontors*—the 50-oared galleys, as opposed to the triremes, which had 170 oars at three different levels. These ships were brought to the Hellespont. Each one of those ships had anchors on long cables. Their crews would row them out into the stream, and the anchors would be thrown over from stern and from bow, and the ships were then anchored facing into the oncoming water. The water rushed around them, and they were held in their places, and eventually a line of ships was created—more than 300 in one, more than 300 in the other—from the Asiatic shore across to the European shore.

These anchored ships were to be the basis for Xerxes's bridge. Once they were in place, the engineers brought gigantic cables. Many of these cables had been plaited in Egypt out of papyrus, and some were made of esparto grass, but they were brought from Xerxes's empire and then attached to gigantic posts that were set on the coast facing out toward the line of ships. Tied to those posts—I believe there were winches so that they could be tightened—and then the cables were laid across the lines of ships—across their decks—from ship to ship to ship, and then attached to the ships. That's the sort of suspension part.

The ships held up these long suspended cables, and then, on top of the cables, a roadway was built. Brushwood was laid down, earth was put down on top of the brushwood to give firm footing for the animals that were going to go across, and finally, wicker screens were erected on either side—upstream and downstream—so that the horses and the other pack animals wouldn't see the water (the rushing water that they were passing over), panic, and bolt off the bridge.

In a few places, gaps were left in the long line of ships that ran from shore to shore, so that merchant shipping and warships could get up and down through those gaps. So it was an amazingly sophisticated piece of engineering.

The engineer who was in charge of the first thing put up a little plaque. He was a Greek from Ionia, taking credit for having bridged the Hellespont. Maybe he shouldn't have been so boastful. Shortly before Xerxes was actually planning to have his troops walk across, a huge storm blew down the Hellespont, tore up the cables, and the bridges that had taken so long to build were swept away. In record time—the original engineering team having been beheaded—a new set was found to do the job again, get the bridge put up, and be ready for Xerxes and his "Grand Army" to cross.

There are stories that the Greeks like to tell. They had very ambivalent feelings—not just about the Persians but about Xerxes himself. I guess this is the moment to talk about the Greek double image of these Persians. On the one hand, they have tremendous respect and admiration for the Persians. The Persians occupy that elite little circle that the Spartans are in, of warrior people whose ideals are pure.

The Greeks may not have understood the concept of Ahura Mazda and the battle of light and darkness, but there was something about the purity of the Persian purpose in their wars—the idea that it was a war of right, and justice, and light against darkness and chaos—that came across. It also came across to them—the Greeks had a great admiration for success. The Persians were so successful as administrators, as builders, and so on, and they lived in this lifestyle of great achievement and great refinement—beautiful civilization, palaces, great feasts. All of this was on the good side.

But the Greeks still classed them as *barbaroi* ("barbarians"). I mentioned that word before. It means to a Greek, on the one hand, simply someone who doesn't speak Greek. What do they speak instead? "Bar-bar-bar-bar-bar." We can't really put a name to it; it's just a non-Greek language and, therefore, not worth classifying.

By the way, the shift from R to L, which is common in all languages of the world, means that that word "bar-bar-bar" is the same as our "blah-blah-blah." It's the way of expressing that someone talks in a way you can't understand. They're not real words.

You will sometimes read that barbarian was not originally to the Greeks a derogatory term. Don't you believe it. The attitude that people who don't speak Greek are just making noise has its own derogatory insult built right into it. In time, the Persians and their cousins, the Medes, became the barbarian, and if you see a Greek monument that says, "These arms were taken from the barbarian," never doubt that that is the Persians.

So it is a double image. One thing that increased the barbarian side of it—the not-proper-Greek side of it—was exactly what Xerxes had done in expending all this money, all this effort, all this manpower on bridging the Hellespont and cutting that canal through Athos—he was showing something that the Greeks knew and despised, called hubris.

Hubris is violent arrogance, and Xerxes was showing violent arrogance against nature in yoking two continents together with his cables of papyrus suspended on his bridge of ships. He was showing hubris, and arrogance, and violence against nature in cutting through what the gods had meant to be dry land so that his ships could easily pass. He even—according to Herodotus, just to show the peak of his mad hubris—sent some of his men out into the Hellespont with whips to beat the water for having been so unruly as to break up Great King Xerxes's first bridge.

So in this way, the Greeks saw the arrival of the Persians both with fear and yet, in a strange way, with scorn. These are people behaving unnaturally, and it is inevitable that the gods will be on our side and not on theirs.

We've already encountered the great storm that happened to Darius's fleet. The Greeks put a theological spin on such natural disasters. The Delphic Oracle had told the Greeks, or was going to tell them, "Pray to the winds," and the Greeks believed that the winds were, in fact, fighting for them as forces of the nature that the Persians had violated. Xerxes, too, will find his fleet on a couple of occasions struck by violent storms to which the Greeks gave all the credit to the gods for punishing this madman and his hubristic ambition.

Xerxes, to cap off all the rest of the preparations, decided to assemble this great army. People have doubted that there were really 1.7 million who were marching with him, and that's, I think, just the combatants. Herodotus says the full force was 4 million. Some German logistical scholars have studied the terrain that this Grand Army would have had to pass through, and they say, "There's not enough water. You can't support that many people living off the land."

That's a strong argument, but not 100 percent strong. One of the things that Xerxes had his quartermasters do was establish supply depots all along the path of advance years in advance, with imperishable foods heaped up and stockpiled, ready for the army to come. We know that the Persians did that with water also. We have Herodotus's statement that in Egypt, all of the wine jars that were imported from Greece with wine into Egypt during the Persian reign were emptied of their wine and sent out in the desert to Persian forts filled with water, so that you could stockpile water for troops in areas where nature did not supply it.

So we're not yet at a point where we can definitely say exactly how many people the Great King could have brought with him, but we do know it was the biggest army ever put together, that he brought together troops from every part of his empire—all the way from the Indus River Valley beyond the Khyber Pass, from Arabia, from the steppes of Russia, the Phoenicians, the Egyptians—they were all summoned to come to Susa, the capital of the Persian Empire, in the late spring of the year we call 481 B.C., two years after the work had begun on the canal, and they marched with the Great King to conquer Greece.

Herodotus gives wonderful descriptions of all of the different clothing, all of the different uniforms, the armor and the weaponry and the customs of all these different people, brought together in this gigantic host—this nation on the move.

Xerxes, of course, had no intention of hurrying. He wanted the slowness of his approach to give time for the Greeks to panic, to divide and separate, as the Ionians had done in the Battle of Lade, and ultimately, because they would be divided, be easy to conquer.

He himself traveled slowly. He had his chariot. He had his women with him in their covered carts, and they couldn't move faster than the pace of the magi—the holy men of the Zoroastrian religion—who were carrying the portable altars with the fire on them, walking along with the army to, as they hoped, a victory assured by Ahura Mazda.

As the army left Susa in April of 481 B.C., there was an eclipse of the Sun. The Persians, like other people, set great store by this kind of celestial phenomenon, and there were among the Persian troops, as I said, magi who could interpret all these star signs and sky signs. Xerxes immediately asked them, "What does it mean that there should be an eclipse of the Sun?" These experts on astronomy knew what caused the eclipse. They knew that it was the disc of the Moon passing over the Sun, and they said, "Great King, the Sun represents the Greeks, just as the Moon represents the Persians. Your force is being seen to block out the light of the Greek world. Your victory is guaranteed."

This was exactly what Xerxes wanted to hear. I'm sure he would have been very embarrassed if they'd said the other way around. What's he going to do—disband the largest army the world has ever seen? So he set off on the march.

We need to remember that one of his reasons for being on the march with all these troops from all over the empire is to strip the empire of local armies—militias—that could rise up against him while he's away with the main force of Persians attacking Greece. So there was military method to what the Greeks saw as madness.

On the way to Sardis, he passed a sycamore tree. We're going to end here. We will pick up the king's approach to the sea next time. But this is such a beautiful story in Herodotus, and it reminds us of that quality of the Persian kings as creators of the parks, the paradises, the gardener kings.

There was a tree called a plain tree, a sycamore, or cousin of the American sycamore tree. It grew to great height, and its branches were enormous, and it was there by the road from Susa to Sardis, by the Great Road. The king saw it, and it was the most beautiful tree he had ever seen. True to that strain of the Persian kings, that they were the gardener kings, he had the army stop so that he could have the tree decked with ornaments and could worship it as this great force of nature placed in his path to be honored as if it was something divine.

If you have ever heard the beautiful piece of music by Georg Frideric Handel that's called the "Largo," it is from an opera called *Xerxes*. It opens with this scene of the young king glorying in the beauty of this lovely tree, singing that immortal melody and capturing (in the 18th century of our era, in that Baroque stage work) the beautiful side, the nature-loving side of these Persian kings—a world that was about to be violated and broken by this extraordinary invasion of Greece and all of the bloodshed, all of the battles, and all of the disasters that lay ahead.

Lecture Seven
The Athenians Build a Fleet

Scope: Well aware that they were Xerxes's prime target, the Athenians (persuaded by a farsighted citizen named Themistocles) created a Greek navy of 200 triremes. In the autumn of 481 B.C., a Greek city-state convention at the Isthmus of Corinth sent spies to Sardis to uncover the Persian army's strength. Themistocles, who proved to be the most persuasive voice at the convention, convinced his fellow Athenians to evacuate their families to offshore islands or to the Peloponnese and urged the delegates to confront Xerxes as far forward as possible to slow his progress into central Greece. When the Greeks learned of Xerxes's success crossing into Europe, they took Themistocles's advice and set out to bar the Great King's path.

Outline

I. At the end of the last lecture, we left Xerxes on the Royal Road from Susa, his capital, marching to Sardis, at the western end of his empire, with an immense army, aimed at invading Greece.

   A. No one in the classical world fought during the wintertime; summer was the time for warfare. When Xerxes arrived at Sardis in the autumn of 481 B.C., he went into winter quarters.

   B. Messengers announced the arrival of Xerxes in Sardis, and in response, the Spartans convened an assembly, in the sanctuary of Poseidon at the Isthmus of Corinth, of those Greeks who were willing to stand up to the Persians and resist invasion.

   1. The Spartans asked for votes on what course of action to take in preparing to resist the Persians.

   2. In the end, only 31 Greek cities proved willing to stand up against the Persians; among these was Athens.

   3. It was agreed that spies should be sent to Sardis to gather intelligence on the enemy.

   4. The Persians apprehended the spies, showed them the Grand Army, explained their war preparations, and sent them back to the conference to report their observations.

II. One theory of history holds that events of the past are shaped by monumental movements of people, that great men do not make history. The man who subscribed least to this theory was the Athenian Themistocles.
   A. Themistocles had led the city of Athens as archon (chief magistrate) for a year, but he had no autocratic powers and could only help persuade his fellow citizens at the convention.
   B. Themistocles possessed a high degree of *metis*, cunning intelligence, which guided him through his public career in Athens.
   C. Themistocles took advantage of a chance discovery of silver ore in the hills outside Athens to suggest to the democratic assembly that it should build a navy of 200 ships to become the most superior naval power in the Greek world. The Athenians agreed and became the masters of the greatest fleet of all the Greek city-states.
III. When the Athenians learned that Xerxes was planning to take his army across the Hellespont and into Europe, they sent envoys to the Delphic Oracle to seek advice.
   A. The envoys asked the oracle how Athens should face the impending Persian invasion. The oracle told them to leave the city and save themselves because Athens would be destroyed.
   B. Unable to take this response back to the convention, the envoys did what no one else had done: They appealed to the oracle for a second prophecy. This time, they were told that a wooden wall would preserve the citizens of Athens.
      1. The conservative element in Athens thought that the wall was the palisade of wood around the Acropolis and suggested waiting out the invasion there.
      2. Other Athenians wanted to abandon the city altogether and found a new city in a safer place.
      3. Themistocles suggested that the wooden walls were the hulls of the ships Athens had recently constructed and that the oracle was advising them to face the Persians at sea.
      4. Themistocles was so persuasive that his motion carried the day.
IV. In the spring of 480 B.C., Themistocles went back to the Isthmus of Corinth to tell the Spartans and the other Greeks that Athens planned to fight the Persians at sea.

- **A.** Themistocles was a rough contemporary of Sun Tzu and subscribed to two of the Chinese military thinker's principal ideas: Attack the enemy's weakness and know the terrain.
    1. Posting themselves on the beach at Artemision would enable the Athenians and other Greek naval contingents to block the progress of the Persian armada.
    2. If the Athenians could stop the fleet, Xerxes's land army would be forced to wait and would be trapped in Greece without proper supplies.
- **B.** Themistocles saw the Persians as completely inexperienced at sea.
    1. Xerxes had appointed six family members as admirals of his fleet.
    2. The Persian navy's one strength was its core of Phoenician ships, but the Phoenicians were not known as warriors at sea—they were great explorers.
    3. The Persian fleet was a jumble of contingents from many nations, including the Ionian Greeks who were fighting on Xerxes's behalf with, Themistocles guessed, mixed emotions.
- **C.** Themistocles saw the resistance to Xerxes as an opportunity to catapult Athens out of the rank of second-class Greek cities and make it the leader of the Greek world.

V. The Spartans were recognized already as leaders of the Greek resistance on land. Despite the Athenians' hope of taking the lead at sea, the Spartans accepted the majority decision and agreed to lead the naval force, as well.
- **A.** Due west of the Artemision Channel was Thermopylae ("Hot Gates"), where the path into Greece narrowed to a road so constricted that only two carts could pass through it side by side.
- **B.** The Spartans sent a force to hold the pass at Thermopylae while the Greek fleet held the Artemision Channel.
- **C.** The Spartan commander at sea was a man named Eurybiades, and the Spartan chosen to hold the pass at Thermopylae (until the main army was mobilized after the conclusion of the Olympic festival) was King Leonidas.
- **D.** The 300 Spartans who held the pass at Thermopylae (known as the Three Hundred) were the core of an army of 7,000 troops: 4,000 from the Peloponnese and 3,000 from central Greece.

Recommended Reading:

Lazenby, *The Defence of Greece, 490–479 B.C.*

Lenardon, *The Saga of Themistocles.*

Questions to Consider:

1. What are some advantages and disadvantages of having a stronger navy than an army?
2. What made Themistocles such a crucial figure in the development of a Greek response to the impending Persian invasion?

Lecture Seven—Transcript
The Athenians Build a Fleet

Welcome back. Last time, we followed the preparations of the Persian king Xerxes over a space of three years for a massive invasion of the Greek world.

We left Xerxes on the road, the Royal Road from Susa, his capital, going to Sardis at the western end of his empire, in western Asia Minor, and leading an immense army, drawn from all the satrapies of his empire, for the invasion of Greece.

When Xerxes got to Sardis, it was the autumn of the year 481 B.C. He went into winter quarters there because in the classical world, in that world of the Aegean, Anatolia, western Asia, nobody fought in the wintertime. That was the season of rainy weather, storms, muddy roads, difficult mountain passes that were sometimes blocked with snow, and above all, an army could not bivouac in the open. So you couldn't have these men camping out in their thousands as you could in the dry, warm summer months.

Summer is the time for warfare, and autumn and winter are the time for getting yourself under cover and waiting for spring. We'll find that this has important strategic implications for the whole campaign as the Greeks turn this to their advantage.

Xerxes and his arrival at Sardis were announced in the Greek world by messengers. The Spartans convened an assembly of those Greeks who were willing to stand up to the Persians and try to resist the invasion. They called that "convention of the resistance" at the Isthmus of Corinth—the place in the center of Greece where Greece narrows down to a little, tiny neck of land between north-central Greece, where you find Athens, and Thebes, and Mount Olympus, and the Delphic Oracle, and southern Greece, called the Peloponnesus, where you find Sparta, and Corinth, and the site of the Olympic Games.

At this narrow isthmus, sacred to the sea god and Earth-shaker of Poseidon, they met in the sanctuary of Poseidon, under his sacred pine trees, and the Spartans asked for votes on what people thought the course should be for preparing to resist the Persians. In the end, out of all the hundreds of islands and cities of the Greek world, only 31 proved willing to stand up to the Persians. Among these was the city of Athens.

The Athenians had chosen to send to the isthmus one of their citizens as their counsel or their representative—a man named Themistocles. As they conferred, they all agreed that they should send spies across the sea to Sardis to count the Persian forces and give the Greeks some idea of what they were up against. So three Greeks were dispatched in a boat across the Aegean. They made their way to Sardis. I think they probably felt confident that among so many other Greeks—since Xerxes had lots of eastern Greeks fighting for him in his army—that they, those three spies from the mainland of Greece, could escape detection. But they didn't.

They were apprehended. They were about on the point of being executed when Xerxes learned that there were three spies from Greece in his camp. He sent a messenger saying, "Do not kill these men. Show them everything they want to see, and give them a full count of the army, and send them home." So that's what they did. The Persians conducted them around the camp, and they showed them the tens of thousands, hundreds of thousands, of men, of cavalry, of pack animals. They explained all the preparations, and they gave them a count of the ships, and they sent them home.

This was the terrifying report, then, that reached the Greeks in their conference at the Isthmus of Corinth that probably also led to the huge figures we have in histories like that of Herodotus, which put Xerxes's forces at 1.7 million and his fleet of ships at 1,200—more than Agamemnon was supposed to have taken to Troy for the Trojan War. This probably came from Xerxes's war of nerves and propaganda, where he's trying to convince the Greeks he's just too big to be resisted.

There's a certain theory of history that states that history is all about monumental movements of people—mass movements of people. This was first articulated, as far as I know, in the 1860s by Leo Tolstoy in his work *War and Peace*, which chronicles Napoleon's invasion of Russia in 1812. If you think of parallels for Xerxes's invasion of Greece, that invasion of 1812 seems the closest in all of human history. A whole continent, the continent of Europe, marshaled together by Napoleon under the banner of France and on the move to conquer a distant land.

Tolstoy drew from that epic the lesson for history—that history is all about the movements of people. Great men don't make history; great men are just the labels that history puts upon events, and like all labels, they have very little to do with the real events. Napoleon didn't invade Russia; Europe invaded Russia and took Napoleon with it.

In this theory of history, this comforting theory to which I'm sure Xerxes himself would have subscribed—the idea that it's all just great forces of destiny, unstoppable by any individual—is a very comforting thing for all of us, because it allows us to be off the hook. No individual can stop the great train of historical events. It's an illusion to think that you can, and so we are all somehow blameless for the things that go on in this world.

The Greeks never bought that idea, and it's one of the things that separates the Greek mind and approach from the mindset that was very common in the Asiatic world and revived in our modern times by Tolstoy. It became the basis for the social sciences approach to history in the 20th and 21st centuries—the idea that history is just mass movements of faceless populations, and individuals may appear to be leading the way, but they don't really.

The man who subscribed least to this theory was Themistocles. It's such an extraordinary thing to think that Xerxes, the Great King, king of kings, king of the world, sitting there in Sardis, surrounded by the biggest army that the human race had ever seen, was about to be opposed by one man—a man named Themistocles, a citizen of Athens, who, even though he'd been elected general sometimes and had led the city as archon—or chief magistrate—for a year, had no autocratic powers whatsoever; could do nothing except persuade his fellow citizens in their democratic assembly to take one course or another; who lived in a city street with his wife, Archippe, and a brood of boys and girls—their children that they were bringing up; a man who had inherited from his father a very modest fortune; who didn't stand high in the aristocracy of Athens. This was the man who was convinced that he could defeat Xerxes—this single citizen of a small democratic city.

Themistocles was laughed at by the aristocrats of Athens because he'd never bothered to learn the accomplishments of an Athenian gentleman. He told them: "It's true; I cannot play a lyre or tune a harp, but I know how to make a small city great." What quality would enable a man to say this? It's a quality that the Greeks prized and that the Persians despised. If we think back to Cyrus in his first confrontation with the Greeks, telling them that he can't respect them or fear them—they're just men who make speeches and cheat each other—that cheating each other, that use of craft and cunning, was the essence of the Greek approach to life.

We talked about Aesop being part of the great Ionian tradition. Aesop is all about the counterintuitive, the fact that you can find a way around the obvious conclusion to events if you're willing to put your mind to it. The quality is called *metis* (M-E-T-I-S). *Metis* is something we don't have a word for in English. It means something like cunning intelligence. It's looking for points of leverage in a situation, where you can shift enormous forces one way or the other, just through art or craft.

One of the examples the Athenians had for it, as well as the other Greeks, was what happens on a ship, a trireme. Here are 200 men, 200 men, 170 at the oars, others working the ship and ready to fight; who determines what happens to that ship—its fate, its potential for winning a battle? One man, the man at the steering oars. With the leverage that he exerts, he can direct that ship and the forces and labors of all those 200 to his purpose.

This was Themistocles's view. He got it as he grew up also from Homer. There is a beautiful passage toward the end of the *Iliad* on how to win a chariot race when your horses aren't the fastest horses. It's spoken by old King Nestor, who is the giver of advice to the Greeks, and he's here giving advice to his son, who is trying to win this race. I'll give it to you in Alexander Pope's translation where *metis* is represented by the word *art*. But we need to remember that *art* here is as in our adjective *artful*—crafty, thinking things through.

> It is not strength, but art, that wins the prize,
> For to be strong is less than to be wise.
> 'Tis more by art than force of numerous strokes
> That dexterous woodman shapes the stubborn oaks;
> By art the pilot, through the boiling deep
> And howling tempest, steers the well-built ship;
> And 'tis the artist wins the glorious course;
> Not those who trust in chariot and in horse.

This was the philosophy of Themistocles, and this is what had guided him through his public career in Athens as he sought to make Athens the greatest city in the Greek world and himself the greatest and first man in that city. He was an ambitious man, and his ambition served his patriotism and his desire to help save Athens and Greece from the invasion of Xerxes.

Themistocles had already exerted himself three years earlier. In that same year when Xerxes's engineers were digging the canal through Mount Athos, Themistocles took advantage of a chance discovery in the hills outside Athens of an immense vein of silver ore. The mines of Mount Laurion had been worked for generations, but just before the Persian wars, in one of the great coincidences of world history, the Athenian miners, burrowing down in their tunnels hundreds of feet below the surface, suddenly hit this vast reef of silver ore.

They brought it up—bag after bag, bucket after bucket—to the surface. It was pounded, washed, refined, and turned into those beautiful silver coins called *owls*—the owls of Athens—with Athena's head on one side, her helmet to show she was always ready for war, and on the other side, her owl, the bird that is the symbol of wisdom.

It was proposed that the Athenians simply divide among themselves all this windfall of silver, so every citizen would receive 10 drachmas, and there were 30,000 to 40,000 citizens. Themistocles had stood up in the summer of 483 B.C. and said in the democratic assembly: "Don't divide the money. Let's keep it all together and let us build a navy—a fleet of 100 triremes this year—and add to it, every year more and more, until we will have a fleet of 200 ships and are the greatest naval power in the Greek world."

He pointed out that he wasn't even talking about the Persians then; he picked a closer target that was an island near Athens—the island of Aegina—that was a rival to Athenian shipping. He pointed to those troublesome neighbors and said, "This will at last give us the upper hand here at home." He was a good psychologist, as well as everything else.

The Athenians agreed. They voted to build those ships. They had spent now three years in building up this navy, and now they were the masters of the greatest fleet in the entire world of the Greek city-states.

Now it was time that they learned that Xerxes was in Sardis, that he was headed for the Hellespont—he was going to take his great army across into Europe, crossing those pontoon bridges. Now it was time to seek the advice of the Delphic Oracle about what the Athenians should do. They knew they were the targets of Xerxes's invasion—the ostensible targets—they were the pretext for invading Greece, and they were fearful, and it was also right and pious if you were a religious Greek—and all Greeks were religious except for a few philosophers—to go and consult the oracle of Apollo at Delphi.

We started at the Delphic Oracle in our very first lecture. We were there when King Croesus of Lydia inquired of the god through his envoys: "Should I attack the Persians, or should I wait and let them attack me?" He had been told: "If you cross the river, you will destroy a great empire." He did cross the river, and he did destroy a great empire; it just turned out to be his own. Despite this kind of ambiguous answer and the mixed record of those who tried to follow Delphic oracular pronouncements, Greeks still thought it was the right thing to do—to go and ask.

So envoys from Athens were sent on the journey to Delphi. They climbed up the mountainside, and they got in line on that day, the seventh day after the new moon, and they went down into the crypt of the temple, and they asked their question: "What should Athens do?" The woman seated on her tripod in the heart of the temple, with her little dish of holy water from the spring underneath her in one hand, her branch of the sacred bay of Apollo—the laurel leaves—in the other hand, and seated over that crack in the Earth, breathing in those fumes, she said to them: "Fly. Leave your city. Nothing can save you. Athens will be destroyed. I see the temples with blood on them. I see the gods weeping. Save yourselves."

They went back out into the light of day, these envoys, appalled. There was nothing cryptic or riddling about this response, and in their despair, they sat down and they shared their feelings with their friend in Delphi, who was the Athenian representative and who had conducted them down into the temple. He said, "Try again. Get back in line. Go through and ask the god one more time. You don't want to take that message home." So they did get back in line—no one had ever done this—and they went down a second time. She only prophesied once a month.

They asked her again, and she said: "Zeus cannot save Athens, but he will grant to Athena—the goddess of Athens—a wooden wall which will stand and not fall—a wooden wall to preserve the Athenians." There was a ray of hope, so they took it home, and it was debated in the assembly.

The conservative element in Athens thought that the wooden wall was the palisade of wood around the Acropolis—that high rock in the middle of Athens that had the temples on top. So they were all for just going up on the top of the rock and waiting out the invasion there, maybe under siege, but with some sort of guarantee that the wooden wall would not fall.

There were probably others who wanted to abandon Athens altogether, load their wives and children and their belongings in their ships, and sail off to the far west of the Mediterranean—get out of the path of this juggernaut of the Persian invasion and found a new city in a safe place. Other Greeks had already done this. The Greeks from Phokaia in Asia Minor had gone off and founded Marseilles in southern France. They called it Marsalia. So the idea of getting away and founding a new city, moving a whole population, was not a novel one.

It was at this point that Themistocles stood up and said: "I believe I understand the meaning of this oracle. The wooden walls are the hulls of our ships, of this navy that we have just built. The god is telling us to face the Persians at sea—to leave our land, to carry our wives and children to safety on the islands or on the Peloponnese, but for all of us Athenian men, whether we are riders, or hoplite infantry, or ordinary citizens, to get in those ships, man those oars, and fight it out on the water."

He's saying this to the group of people who could still remember 10 years earlier how they or their fathers had beaten the Persians on land in the battle at Marathon. So persuasive was he that he carried the day. The vote was with Themistocles's interpretation of the wooden-walls oracle, and he was able to go back to the Isthmus of Corinth, in the summer of the year 480 B.C.—after Xerxes had crossed the Hellespont, after Xerxes was already headed down into central Greece with his huge army and his fleet of 1,200 ships paralleling his motion along the coast—and tell the Spartans, the Corinthians, all those other Greeks, that Athens was going to fight at sea.

Why did he think this? Why was this his strategy? Themistocles was a rough contemporary with a famous Chinese military thinker named Sun Tzu. Sun Tzu had a golden rule: Do not attack the enemy's strength; attack the enemy's weakness. He had another golden rule: Know the terrain. Themistocles subscribed to both of these. He knew the terrain. He knew the course that the fleet of Xerxes was going to have to follow if it wanted to get down into Greek waters around Athens. He knew there was a place they would have to pass through a narrow channel of water between north-central Greece and the northern tip of the island of Euboea, at a place called Artemision, sacred to the goddess Artemis.

Through that channel, Xerxes's ships would have to pass. He would not be with them, and if the Greeks could post themselves there, on the beach at Artemision, they would be able to block the progress, in Themistocles's view, of the Persian armada. For Themistocles, that's a great victory, because if they can stop the fleet from coming in, Xerxes's land army will wait for the fleet, and the whole invasion will be delayed. If they can hold it up for a month or six weeks, the winter storms will arrive, the fleet will have to go home, and the army will be stuck in Greece without proper supplies. The great invasion will probably peter out—die of its own weight—lose momentum, and the battle will be won.

This was the strategy of Themistocles: Meet the Persians as far forward as possible, block their advance, slow them down, delay the entry into Greece, and do it at sea. Why did he think the sea was the place? He'd heard the reports on the Grand Army of Xerxes; he knew that with that immense cavalry, any time they caught the Greeks out in the open, they could simply surround them and crush the Greeks on land by sheer force of numbers. Also, the Persian cavalry and their ability to shoot those arrows from horseback at a full gallop—that was something the Greeks didn't know how to do. It meant that a cavalry could surround and pepper with arrows any infantry force if they could get them on flat land and ultimately overwhelm them.

The navy was very different. Yes, it was huge: 1,200 ships, supposedly. Even with the non-Athenians added on—the people from Corinth, and Aegina, and the other freedom-fighting Greek states that had ships—the Greeks could only muster about 300 of these big triple-tiered triremes. Xerxes had four times that number, but this was his Achilles's heel, in Themistocles's view.

Themistocles looked at the forces that were headed for them, and he saw on land a great army, not only led by Xerxes but with a core that was pure Persian—the most fearsome fighting force in the world—mobile, tough, big, successful, except for Marathon—a little battle won by the Athenians back in 490 B.C.—no record of defeat. The navy was different. The Persians were completely inexperienced at sea.

It turned out that Xerxes had appointed six admirals for his fleet—six! What do you do with a divided command at sea? Who's going to be making the decisions? Who were these six? Were they experienced Persian seafarers? There was no such thing. They were just members of Xerxes's own family that through a process of nepotism, he had given the title of admiral to, so that they would have this nice title to carry with them as they marched on Greece.

Some of them weren't even with the fleet. They were marching with Xerxes on land, and they were part of his great court. They would sit with Xerxes in his immense pavilion—this gigantic tent that was his field headquarters that was set up every night—and there they would be, feasting and drinking with their kinsman, the king. They didn't know anything about the ships, and if you looked at the navy itself, it had one strength: Its core was a group of Phoenician ships. But the Phoenicians did not have a great track record as fighters at sea—they were great explorers at sea. They were great traders and merchants.

As I've said, they had circumnavigated Africa in their triremes, but they hadn't won many battles, so even the core element of the fleet looked vulnerable to Themistocles. When he added in the consideration that the fleet was this jumble of contingents from many nations—Egypt, Phoenicia, Cyprus, Cilicia, and those Ionian Greeks who were fighting on Xerxes's behalf with (as Themistocles guessed) very mixed emotions—this is why Themistocles thought if you are going to attack the enemy's weakness, attack Xerxes at sea.

He went back to the isthmus, and he explained what Athens intended to do to the Spartans. I'm sure he didn't say it to the Spartans, but we have to realize this was part of Themistocles's other plan—this man of *metis*—he not only wants to beat Xerxes and save Athens, he wants to use this crisis as an opportunity to catapult Athens out of the rank of second-class Greek cities and make it the leader of the Greek world.

Yes, times of danger are times of danger. Things can go terribly wrong. You can lose everything. But if you're willing to take the risks—the big risks—the rewards can be far greater than you will ever get through small increments of progress in times of stability and peace. Themistocles knew that, and he was staking everything on Athens's behalf on being able to lift his city up and make that small city, as he liked to say, a great city—the greatest in all the Greek world.

At the Isthmus of Corinth, this pronouncement was thrown in with all of the others: that the Athenians were going to meet the "barbarian"—as they called the Persians—at sea and that they were going to go far north to Artemision to do it, having evacuated their wives and children so that they wouldn't be leaving potential hostages behind them if the Persians got around and marched on Athens.

The Spartans are now left with a dilemma: They want to be the leaders of the whole Greek resistance. They feel that they should be the prime hegemon—the sort of leading force, chief state—within this alliance, this league of cities and islands who are trying to keep out the Persians. So the Athenians have, in a way, thrown down the gauntlet. They are saying, "We are taking the lead at sea; what are you going to do?"

The majority of the Peloponnesians, if you had taken a head count, were quite willing to vote to leave all of north and central Greece to the Persians, to build a great wall across the Isthmus of Corinth—in fact, they'd already started building that wall—and sit behind it on this semi-island of land, which was only approachable through this narrow neck—the isthmus itself.

They didn't think this through, and they didn't really stop to think that if Xerxes commands the sea, he can go to any part of the Peloponnesian coast and land. But that was their plan, and it was with some difficulty that the Spartans made their allies agree that if the fleet is going north, the land force should go north with them.

The Artemision Channel is at the north end of the island of Euboea. Due west of it, on the mainland, was a narrow pass called Thermopylae—that means the "Hot Gates." Sulfurous springs of hot, bubbling water come to the surface at Thermopylae. It's a place where the mountains come down to the sea, and the path into Greece narrows to a road of such constricted span that only two carts could pass along it. Xerxes was bringing, allegedly, 1 million and 700,000 men into Greece, but they would have to go through the pass at Thermopylae—maybe 10 abreast.

His great advantage in numbers would be negated at the pass at Thermopylae in the same way that Themistocles had seen the huge numbers of the fleet would be negated in the narrow channels of Artemision—just to the east of Thermopylae, out at sea.

So the Spartans decreed that in spite of the fact that, yes, there's another festival going on—the Olympic festival—and in spite of the fact that we really need to stay here in Peloponnese and see it out for the honor of Zeus and the other gods, we will send a force to hold the pass at Thermopylae at the same time that the Athenians and the other naval powers go up and hold the channel at Artemision, and they said, allegedly in response to demands from the non-Athenians in the alliance, "We will send a Spartan to command the fleet as well"—so that it would be a Spartan command both at sea and on land.

The Spartan chosen to command at sea was a man named Eurybiades, and the Spartan chosen to hold the pass at Thermopylae until the main army was mobilized at the end of the Olympic festival and sent north, that Spartan was a king named Leonidas.

So it was that at the end of summer 480 B.C., as Xerxes is leading his great army south past Mount Olympus, as his fleet is preparing to come down and meet him somewhere near Thermopylae—they will be separated for awhile by the mountains of Greece—two contingents of freedom fighters on what looked like the most forlorn of all possible hopes went north to meet them: the fleet, going to Artemision, and that little army, going to Thermopylae.

We mustn't over-exaggerate the size of the army that went to Thermopylae in terms of how small it was. It's popular to call it "the 300 Spartans" ("the Three Hundred"). Well, the Three Hundred was the core of an army of 7,000—4,000 troops from the Peloponnese, 3,000 from central Greece—plenty to hold the pass, one would think. But it will be our task in our next time together to follow these forces northward—this bold attempt to stop the greatest military force in history from getting into Greece, both on land and at sea, and both with the same policy: Use the terrain, know your enemy, fight hard, and see if you cannot change the course of history with a little courage and a little cunning.

Lecture Eight
Heroes at the Pass

Scope: Because the other Greeks refused to follow the Athenians, the Spartans organized the forces designed to resist the Persian advance. The Spartan officer Eurybiades was sent to the Artemision Channel to lead the Greek naval forces; we will look at the sea battles in the next lecture. On land, the Spartan king Leonidas led 300 Spartan hoplites and several thousand Greek allied troops to hold the pass at Thermopylae against Xerxes's army. When the Persian army negotiated a hidden mountain track around the pass, Leonidas and his 300 hoplites defended the pass to the last man. Though the way into Greece was now open to Xerxes, the Greek resistance had found both its first martyr and an inspirational story of defiant opposition.

Outline

I. August of 480 B.C. is a point of crisis not only in the history of Greece but in the history of the world.

    A. Xerxes was making his way south with his immense army toward the pass at Thermopylae. His fleet, meanwhile, was waiting at the port of modern-day Thessaloniki to follow Xerxes through the Artemision Channel after his army passed Thermopylae.

    B. The Greeks were moving northward from the Isthmus of Corinth to face the immense invasion and try to save their homelands and their freedom.

        1. Under Athenian inspiration, a naval arm of the resistance, led by the Spartan Eurybiades but masterminded by Themistocles, rowed northward toward the Artemision Channel.

        2. The land enterprise, under the leadership of the Spartan king Leonidas, traveled toward Thermopylae, where they would guard the pass against the Persian army.

        3. Leonidas also posted a small scout ship to watch the events at Thermopylae from the sea; the ship would then carry word of the outcome of the battle eastward to the fleet.

II. The Spartans are an anomaly among the Greek peoples.
   A. The Spartans were the Dorian nation of Greeks who had settled in the southern and eastern quadrants of the Peloponnese after the Dorian invasion around 1200 B.C.
   B. A few hundred years before the Persian wars, the Spartans conquered their western neighbors, the Messenians, and became militaristic overlords.
   C. The bulk of the population in Sparta was made up of workers known as "helots."
      1. Helots had slave status in Spartan society and were bound to the land.
      2. The Spartan citizens were full-time warriors; the helots did all other work.
   D. The Spartans used a method of upbringing that was admired by aristocratic Greeks in other cities.
      1. Young Spartan children were raised by women before being taken away.
      2. Boys and girls alike trained in athletics.
      3. Boys eventually were sent to "boot camps," where they learned to live like warriors.
      4. Boys graduated into manhood through an initiation called the *Kryptaia* (the "hidden thing"), during which they lived apart from Spartan society in a test of their survival skills.
   E. Spartans looked to their two kings—each descended from Heracles through different lineages—for leadership in the field.
III. In the late summer of 480 B.C., the Spartan mission to Thermopylae was led by King Leonidas.
   A. King Leonidas was the half-brother of King Cleomenes. He had been catapulted into the kingship after Cleomenes's mysterious death.
   B. Until 480 B.C., Leonidas had accomplished nothing of note; however, he was chosen to lead the 300 Spartan warriors north to Thermopylae and hold the pass until the rest of the Spartan army came north after the conclusion of the Olympic festival.
   C. His contingent marched through the plains of Boeotia, where the heralds of Xerxes had undermined the mood of Greek resistance.

1. A wall was being built across the Isthmus of Corinth because the Peloponnesians only halfheartedly believed they could save central Greece.
2. Many Greeks were "Medizing"—going over to the Persian side, submitting, and fighting for the Great King.

IV. Leonidas did not go to Thermopylae thinking it would be his last stand; rather, he believed he was the vanguard of a great army. That army, however, never materialized because the Spartans at home assumed that Xerxes's forces would not move so fast.

   A. Thermopylae in 480 B.C. was not a pass between two mountains the way one often thinks of a pass.
      1. The precipitous mountains of central Greece came down almost to the water's edge. A narrow, flat road wound around the foot of the mountains.
      2. The hot springs bubbled up along the road, making progress difficult and treacherous.
      3. On the other side of the road, the cliffs fell sharply to the sea.
   B. Leonidas posted 1,000 men on the high pass to guard the trail against a Persian attack from behind.
   C. Leonidas planted himself in the pass, expecting to be able to hold off the Persians until the main Spartan army arrived.
   D. Xerxes marshaled his troops and began to throw his forces at the pass to test the Spartan resistance.
      1. Xerxes first sent the Medes, who were beaten back.
      2. He then sent some of his Persians, who met the same fate.
   E. The Spartans stood firm in the "phalanx" formation, a row of soldiers in tight array with overlapping shields.
      1. The survival of a phalanx depends on the cohesion of the shield line.
      2. The spears of the soldiers in the Spartan phalanx were longer than those of the Persians.
      3. Those fighting on the Spartan side spelled one another on the front, so that the front line of the phalanx was always fresh.
   F. The Spartans used a strategy in which they would pretend to retreat, then suddenly turn and butcher the headlong and disorganized Persian pursuit.
   G. With the aid of the Greek traitor Ephialtes, Xerxes sent his Immortals around the pass to attack the Spartans from behind.

- **H.** Receiving word of this strategy, Leonidas sent most of his troops away and fought with his remaining soldiers to the death.
- **V.** With the Spartan defeat at Thermopylae, the way to central Greece lay open. Xerxes had won his first great victory.

Recommended Reading:
Cartledge, *Thermopylae: The Battle That Changed the World.*
Fitzhardinge, *The Spartans.*

Questions to Consider:
1. What do you consider to be some advantages or disadvantages of a warrior society, such as Sparta?
2. Do you consider Leonidas to be a courageous warrior or a foolish strategist? How does his subsequent martyrdom at Thermopylae affect your view?

Lecture Eight—Transcript
Heroes at the Pass

Welcome back. We have reached a point of crisis not only in the history of Greece but in the history of the world and of the Persian Empire, as well. It is late summer of the year 480 B.C.—our month of August. Xerxes is making his way south with his immense army, his engineers in front as they pass through the range that includes Mount Olympus in northern Greece. His engineers are straightening and smoothing the roads so that the horses and the men can get through this mountainous region on their way to the pass at Thermopylae.

His fleet, meanwhile, is giving him a few days' lead. They are waiting up there in the port of what is today modern Thessaloniki, and they are going to follow Xerxes, then, southward—they, going down the coast of Magnesia, passing through the Artemision Channel, as they hope, and having a rendezvous with their lord and master, the Great King Xerxes, after he has gone through the pass at Thermopylae.

The Greeks, meanwhile, have gone northward from the Isthmus at Corinth, where the Spartans have convened and are heading a Hellenic League—a league of freedom-fighting Greeks who, a couple of dozen strong, have decided that against all odds, they will face this immense invasion and try to save their homelands and their freedom.

They have now divided themselves in two. Under Athenian inspiration, there is now a naval arm rowing northward, headed for the Artemision Channel to try to block the advance of Xerxes's armada at sea. Although that is led by a Spartan, Eurybiades, the mastermind of that policy and the man who is really directing the strategy of that fleet is the Athenian Themistocles. Almost two-thirds of the fleet are the 200 Athenian triremes that the Athenians have recently built to transform themselves—sort of pulling themselves up by their own bootstraps—into this great naval power.

But our focus at first will be on the land enterprise, which is under the leadership of a Spartan king—a very famous man today, a very famous man ever since the events that happened in that narrow pass of Thermopylae, a man named Leonidas. He has attached to his army of 7,000 as they go north, one little scout ship, a 30-oared vessel, an Athenian vessel with a commander named Abronichus. That scout ship will watch the events at Thermopylae in the pass from the sea and then carry word eastward to the navy to let the men in the fleet—to let Eurybiades, the Spartan commander or admiral, and Themistocles, the Athenian commander—know how Leonidas and the men are faring in the pass at Thermopylae. So, whatever goes on at Thermopylae will be reported by this little scout ship to the Greeks, off to the east, holding the pass at sea.

It's time to talk a little bit about the Spartans and about the kind of man that Leonidas was. Let's start with Leonidas himself. The Spartans are an anomaly among Greek peoples. They have gone a different path, certainly very different from that of the Athenians and the Ionians, who are expansive, adventuresome, experimental, talkative, love to thrash things out, love to explore all possibilities, like to cross new horizons, believers in entrepreneurship, free enterprise, and privatization of all kinds of things—building up of great fortunes. That's the world of the Ionian Greeks and the Athenians, the Corinthians, and many other Greeks. It was that world that created the explosive diaspora of the Greeks that carried Greek colonists to the Black Sea, to the coast of Asia, and to Sicily, Italy, France, and even Spain and North Africa.

The Spartans had a grand total of one colony—that was Tarentum in Italy. They didn't take part in all of this "adventuresomeness." The Spartans had gone a different path. They were the Dorian nation of Greeks who had settled down in the southern and eastern quadrant of that landmass the Peloponnese. They had dug in there after the so-called return of the sons of Heracles—the Dorian invasion around 1200 B.C.—and for generations, they had been living there, working their farms—sort of ordinary Greeks.

But then a few hundred years before the Persian wars and the invasion of King Xerxes, the Spartans conquered their neighbors to the west, their close cousins, the Messenians, and took over their territory. Suddenly, they had a little empire. Their two Spartan kings, as I said before, are really just generals for life. They're military leaders, ceremonial leaders. They're not monarchs in the autocratic sense of running the country.

Their two kings, their little group of five *ephors* or elder counselors, and their assembly of warriors are now governing both Sparta and this conquered realm of Messenia, which included the kingdom of old King Nestor, whom I quoted last time from Homer's *Iliad*—that Homeric king who ruled at Pylos in the southwest corner of the Peloponnese.

So they are masters of the southern half or almost the southern two-thirds of the Peloponnese. There are still people that hold out against their power in the Peloponnese—the people of Argos to the north and east of them are fiercely independent of the Spartans—but the Spartans themselves now have a country that they must police, and watch, and keep under their authority. They've already militarized themselves for the running war between the Messenians and themselves, which took so many years to win, and now they remain in active service permanently.

For other Greeks, being a soldier was something to be taken up temporarily. You're a young man, you become a soldier of fortune, you go off to the ends of the Mediterranean, and you fight for a foreign power and bring the wealth home. Or your city-state is suddenly threatened by an invasion from your neighbor, and you go out and fight a battle on a summer day and then go home and put the shield in the corner of the room and lay down your helmet. Maybe spiders come and weave their webs over your shield, and a beehive gets made in your helmet, and everything is peaceful. It's not like that in Sparta.

From the time they conquered Messenia, the Spartans become, in a sense, imperialists. They got a little empire—it's there in the Peloponnese—and their great goal in life is to hold onto it, to keep things stable. They are, in fact, a tiny minority in their own country, because they have the Messenians to their west, whom they rule, and within Lacedaemon, the Spartan home territory—Sparta itself was technically just the capital city—within Lacedaemon or Laconia, their home territory, the main bulk of the population are people called "helots" (H-E-L-O-T-S).

These are the workers—the serfs—almost with the status of slaves—people bound to the land, people who do not have wealth of their own—not that any Spartan is after wealth in this life; this resentful population of people are doing all the work. This isn't like a typical Greek city-state where the hoplite warrior puts away his armor and goes out and helps with the olive harvest or supervises the getting in of the grain. No, the Spartans are full-time warriors. It's the helots who do the work, and the helots are always (or almost always) looking for opportunities to regain their freedom and get rid of these pesky Spartans.

One can understand some of the resentment that the helots and the Messenians feel when you consider how the Spartans are brought up. It's a method of upbringing that the aristocrats of other Greek cities really admired. If they could, they got young Spartan girls to Sicily or to Athens to be nursemaids for aristocratic babies because they wanted that toughness bred into their children.

Spartans had their children brought up by the women for a while, but then taken away. Boys and girls alike trained in athletics, in the arts of warfare, in toughness. Girls were not expected to fight, but girls were expected to grow up and bear strong Spartan boys who would be the next generation of warriors. So they, too, had to be fit, and strong, and competitive.

The boys are sent off to school. They are not learning philosophy; they are not learning mathematics; they're certainly not learning anything about trade. No Spartan sullied his hands with anything mercantile. The gold that various people brought to Sparta to try to bribe the Spartans into helping out with various wars was often sent away in disgust. The Spartans were interested in honor; the Spartans were interested in a pure military society. And so the boys graduated from these sort of boot camps for children, where they learned to be tough, to fight, to endure, to hide their hunger, and to hide their ordinary human feelings. They graduated into manhood through a frightening sort of active initiation called the *Kryptaia*—the "hidden thing"—where they would go out and live off the land for awhile, stealing, killing to survive, and the test was: Can you do it without being caught? One of the elements of the *Kryptaia* was to hunt down and kill a helot without being caught.

So it was a brutal life, and it was turning men into fighting machines, but fighting machines that still had a thought in their head, and that thought was honor: "I must never dishonor myself." It wasn't so much for foreign wars. Sparta was not trying to expand. Sparta was simply trying to maintain mastery of its homelands and of its conquered realm of Messenia on the other side of Mount Taygetus, and to do that, they became militarized as no other Greek people had ever been militarized.

They looked to their two kings, who were each descended from Heracles by different genealogies—two separate royal houses and royal lines—they looked to their two kings, typically, for leadership in the field. When they went away to war, they were a little like the Persians. They carried their altars with them, and they prayed to the gods. They sacrificed before battle. War was a great ceremony for them—a religious experience. All of this in the service of maintaining that permanent hold on their land.

As an adult male, you did not live at home with your wife. You were in your mess tent. Even the king was in the mess tent with his fellows, sharing the black bread, the black broth, the simple water or rough wine there with his fellows in the mess tent. Not surprisingly, Spartan population was a bit of a problem. They were always seemingly in decline; fewer and fewer Spartans. Ultimately, the state of Sparta had to offer bonuses to couples that would actually produce children.

Nonetheless, it was a way of life that was intensely admired by other Greeks, as I said, especially aristocrats, especially Athenian aristocrats, who looked south and saw in Sparta some sort of ideal. Well, the Spartans certainly thought of themselves as the ideal also. They respected themselves and nobody else, and they were wonderful people in a crisis because you knew they would never back down. They would never surrender. They would always be willing to hold their post.

Not typically the most imaginative of military strategists, not people who used a lot of cunning or art—as the Athenian Themistocles had done as he worked out how he thought the Persians could actually be beaten—but certainly in the right place—and the pass at Thermopylae showed every indication of being the right place—they would be the people who you wanted on the spot.

They were led on this occasion, in late summer of 480 B.C., by a man who grew up never expecting to be king. He was the half-brother of that King Cleomenes who had been visited in the year 499 B.C.—19 years before this invasion of Xerxes—by Aristagoras of Miletus, that Ionian who crossed the sea with his bronze map, and showed the Spartans the Persian Empire, and asked them to come across the sea and liberate the Greeks of Asia and conquer the Persians.

Cleomenes had sent Aristagoras away once he found that the capital of the Persian Empire was three months from the sea. No Spartan would ever be that far from home, and now you understand why. They've got a threat, permanently, at home—these disaffected peoples that they must keep down.

Cleomenes had died unexpectedly in very complicated and mysterious circumstances. He had become a man who was so convinced of his own talents that he wanted to be a real king and rule. He had many enemies within Sparta. It's not entirely clear exactly how he met his end, but suddenly, his half-brother, Leonidas, which means something like "son of the lion," was catapulted into the kingship.

The lion is a symbol of Sparta. Leonidas, Leotychides—we're going to meet a lot of Spartans with that *leo* ("lion") in their names. There really were lions in Greece at this time. Xerxes had discovered to his sorrow that the mountain lions of northern Greece developed a taste for camels, and they would attack his baggage train as he marched along with his great army, from the Hellespont into the mountains of northern Greece.

Lions symbolize for the Greeks (as you can see from *Aesop's Fables*) strength, majesty, toughness, large-mindedness, big-heartedness, and ferociousness. All of this was what it was to be a lion, and in turn, all of this is what it was to be a Spartan. We have a few works of art from the Archaic period in Sparta, where they created lions, and when they buried their dead on the battlefields, they would often erect a lion over the mass tomb of Spartan warriors to show that here lies a set of men who were lions' sons.

Leonidas had not accomplished anything of note by the summer of 480 B.C. He'd been king for several years, succeeding his half-brother, but he was chosen—he didn't volunteer, and it was certainly not his policy—he was chosen by the Spartan assembly of warriors, led by the five *ephors*—the magistrates—to be the king who would break the Olympic truce (they were holding the Olympic Games in 480 B.C.), and he would lead this little contingent of 300 Spartan warriors north while the rest of the Spartans stayed home and completed the festivals for Zeus. He would also be the leader of a larger allied contingent on land: 4,000 hoplite, heavily armed warriors from the Peloponnese, 3,000 from central Greece, but minus the Athenians (remember?), who are all in their ships with the fleet, committed completely to holding Xerxes back at sea.

They marched through the plains of Boeotia, past the city of Thebes, and they became aware that all around them there was a sort of a rot in central Greece, as the heralds of Xerxes (who had been south, asking people to give earth and water to the king to show their submission and save themselves) had undermined the feeling of resistance.

The Greeks in the center part of Greece were well aware that a wall was being built across the Isthmus of Corinth—that the Peloponnesians only halfheartedly believed that they could save central Greece. Attica, remember, had already been evacuated by the Athenians, who took the bold step of sending their wives and children away, so that even if Xerxes broke through, he would find only an empty city.

A lot of Greeks were doing what was called in that year "Medizing." Remember the group of Asiatics whom the Greeks had encountered first (of the Medes and the Persians) were the Medes. They often called them the "barbarian" or the "Mede" when they were properly speaking to Persians. It was just a shift in nomenclature that they'd gotten in the habit of. So they invented this word "Medizing" for any Greek who went over to the Persian side, submitted, and then fought for the Great King.

Well, there were Medizers all over, and a lot of the people in the great city of Thebes, Oedipus's old city, had decided to Medize. So Leonidas did not get a full levy of soldiers as he had expected from central Greece, and he was always thinking that the main Spartan army was just a few days behind him and was going to come up and commit to the defense of Greece at that narrow pass at Thermopylae.

When he arrived at Thermopylae, he had 7,000 men. That was enough to hold the pass. In fact, deploying more would have been a problem. Remember, as I said last time, the cart road that ran through the pass at Thermopylae, the only way into central Greece for an army—certainly an army with wheeled vehicles—it wasn't even as wide as a two-lane blacktop. And to have a million and a half men trying to get through it, as Xerxes allegedly had, it didn't matter how many there were—they could still be plugged and prevented from going further by a small force in the pass.

Nonetheless, Leonidas did not go north thinking he was going to a last stand or a forlorn hope; he thought he was the vanguard of a great army. As we'll see, that great army never materialized as the Spartans changed their minds—not thinking Xerxes would move so fast—and they left Leonidas out there alone to figure out how to hold that pass.

When he got to Thermopylae, he found a very different place from what you see today if you visit Thermopylae. Thermopylae today is the main four-lane divided highway that comes down from the north into central Greece. Eighteen-wheelers are barreling along, and they go past a nice monument to the Spartans and to Leonidas there. But if you stand there on the hills and on the Spartan burial mound on one side of the highway and look, you can barely see the waters of the gulf—of the sea. The Spercheios River has come down with all of its sediments, filled up the land, and created a vast plain. So you get no sense of the narrow pass that was there.

It's not a pass between two mountains as we often think of a pass being—instead, the mountains (the precipitous mountains of central Greece) came down almost to the water's edge. There was a tiny flat space, a little winding road at the foot of the mountains. The hot springs of Thermopylae, the "Hot Gates" with their sulfurous waters and their steam, bubbled up along that road, making progress even more treacherous and difficult. On the other side of the road, the cliffs fell down into the sea—cliffs that are no longer there. The bubbling travertine, the calcites from the bubbling springs, have flowed over the cliffs and created this smooth descent down to the plain. So we don't see Thermopylae as they did then. We don't realize that this was truly a place where a few men could hold off a gigantic army.

Leonidas knew that there was a weakness at Thermopylae—there was a way around it. It wasn't a way that Xerxes could take his whole army. He couldn't take the cavalry and the wheeled carts up there, but it was a way that you could get a small contingent to circumvent the road through the pass, go up in the hills, and get around. He knew it was there, and he had 1,000 men with him from the territory of Phocis nearby. He posted them up on that high pass, telling them to guard the trail so that the Persians wouldn't be able to get there, get behind him. He then planted himself in the pass itself, expecting to be able to hold off the Persians until the main army came, and then it would be the job of the main army to hold Xerxes there until winter came and the whole thing had to be given up for that year and, as the Greeks all hoped then, given up for good.

There was, by the way, a precedent for this. You may remember when we talked about Miltiades of Athens and our run up to the Battle of Marathon, Miltiades of Athens had been along as a vassal of King Darius when King Darius tried to invade the land of the Scythians. He finally had to give up that attempt (King Darius) because the Scythians refused him a pitched battle. They just kept retreating. They were nomads, and when he sent them a message saying, "Stand still and fight," they said, "Well, we're just going about our normal nomadic business. We move from place to place. Catch us if you can."

So he'd never gotten the decisive battle he wanted, and it was certainly the initial strategy of the Greeks not to give him a decisive battle but to delay him so that he couldn't get down to the open waters of central Greece, or to the open plains of central Greece, where his army or his navy could have been deployed in full force and beaten the tiny forces of the Greeks who were in place to resist him.

Remember also that we've got our little Athenian guard ship out there, watching from beyond the bubbling mudflats, the whole thing as if it were a scene at a play. Xerxes arrived, coming over the mountains of the north, around the corner of that gulf, crossing the Spercheios River, and his scouts informed him the pass was held against him. He surely expected this, that the Greeks would be there. There was, in fact, an old wall that the Spartans had repaired because this was a traditional place to keep northerners out of central Greece.

He settled down, and he got his whole army together. It took him a couple of days in order to marshal the troops in this new place and scout it out, and then he began to throw his forces at the pass to test the resistance. The first day, he picked the Medes—those partners of the Spartans whose empire the Spartans had conquered—and sent them in.

Remember, these are not heavily armored men, like the Spartans in the pass and the other Greeks that the Spartans are leading; these Medes are lightly armored. Their shields may have been just made of wicker. They're very mobile, and they're much faster, but if you're not on an open plain, then speed counts for nothing. So the Medes had a lot of trouble. They were beaten, and they had to go back. Xerxes next tried some of his Persians. They met with the same fate—they couldn't break through that shield wall.

The Spartans were standing in the phalanx. There's a reason our fingers are called *phalanges*—that comes from the word "phalanx." It's a row of things in tight array, very powerful together, but very weak if you spread them out. That's what a phalanx is. So the phalanx was like the nailed fist of the Greek fighting machine: warrior after warrior after warrior, shield to shield to shield—each man's shield on his left forearm, protecting not himself but the man to his left. So the phalanx depends for its survival on the cohesion of the shield line, and every man depends on his fellow. That was the Spartan mentality: to never let down another warrior—another Spartan.

So they would stand in position, the lines of their national poet Tyrtaeus, who was the great hoplite poet of more than a century back, as he wrote: "Plant your feet, spread your legs, stand firm, hold that shield, never give into the enemy." Their spears are then pointed forward, and they have one big advantage: Their spears are longer than those of the Persians. Remember, if you want to be mobile, you don't want to be encumbered with a nine-foot spear. But here, coming out of the wall of shields were those nine-foot spears.

The Medes first, then the Persians—they couldn't get through. The next day, Xerxes tried again, sending in these groups of men. The Spartans, according to Herodotus, behaved slightly differently on the second day. The pass was actually a corridor. It would open up here and there into slightly wider places. It had very narrow places. For one thing, on the second day, the Spartans were clearly alternating who was on the front. So they not only spelled each other off, they would let the others come up—the other Peloponnesians, the people of central Greece—to take their turn at the front. So the front line was always fresh. It's a day-long battle, and this way, everybody had time to sit down, have their meal, and then come back to the front and take their turn—a very sensible way to do it. One feels that Leonidas is learning on the job.

They also worked out a stratagem—very surprising for the Spartans. They would pretend to stand firm and then suddenly they would retreat. Well, hallelujah! The Persians immediately would be off on the attack, running into the narrows of the pass, heedless of their own danger because they thought they now had the enemy in flight, and then at a signal, the Spartans (or whoever was on the front line) would wheel around, form that shield wall again, and march forward. Now having trapped some of the enemy in the narrows, they would butcher them all.

Xerxes saw contingent after contingent killed in this way, and he realized, "This could go on until I've got nobody left." The Spartans were losing very few; the Persians were losing large numbers because each Spartan was like an armored tank, sheathed in bronze: bronze greaves, which are shin guards; bronze body armor, a sort of cuirass for the chest area, or sometimes a sort of bulletproof-vest idea—padded linen, very densely woven, over the breast; the great bronze shield, which was really a wooden shield with a bronze cover; the bronze helmet over their heads—that classical Corinthian-style helmet that we met before, which Miltiades of Athens also wore, with this great fearsome crest—often dyed scarlet—of horsehair along the top. Then the weaponry: the spear, the sword, often a dagger for close-in fighting in the final stages of the fight. All of this was the panoply of the hoplite warrior.

You could pick out the Spartans because they had on their shields the Greek letter *lambda*, or L, which stood for Lacedaemon or Laconia. So here they are, and they fight through the day, and they make it to the end of the day, and all this time, of course, the scouts and the translators of Xerxes's force—and he has many Greeks with him, remember. He has all those Ionian Greek subjects. He had some Greeks with him; most of the Ionians are with the fleet—they are scouting for people who know the area.

They finally find a local Greek of a place called Malis, who Herodotus says in hopes for pay, he became a great traitor to Greece, and so he was demonized. His name, Ephialtes, ironically means "nightmare." He told them about the way around the pass, and Xerxes decided, in the night after the second day's fighting, to send his best troops—the Greeks call them "the Immortals"—his spearmen, his own personal bodyguard, up that mountain track to get around behind Leonidas and trap him in the pass.

They went up by night. As dawn was breaking, the men of Phocis, those 1,000 men up in the pass, heard down in the oak woods that led up to their protected positions the rustling of leaves, as if a great wind were passing through the dry leaves on the ground, but there was no wind. This terrifying sound of an army rustling through the leaves alerted them. They got up, and they seized their spears and their shields, and out of the wood came that fearsome fighting force: Xerxes's Immortals. They could recognize them by the silver pomegranates that were on the tips of their spears right under the blade.

They turned and ran. They thought they were the target. For all they knew, Thermopylae had already fallen down there in the pass, and they ran for a high place that they knew they could defend themselves on and left the pass open. The Immortals paid no more attention to the men of Phocis; they filed as quickly as they could over the summit to the ridge and down the other side.

The little scout ship then, out there at sea, saw in the early morning light—off on the down-end of the pass, the one toward central Greece—the Immortals coming down out of the heights, ready to trap Leonidas and his men, and Xerxes preparing to invade from the northern side.

Leonidas got word of this, and he sent most of his troops away. He probably sent 6,000 men out of the 7,000 south to save themselves—to fight another day. This is where he turns from a man who was somewhat out-generaled into a true hero. He himself stayed in the pass, and he fought it out that day with his 300 Spartans, the 700 men from Thespiae, and several hundred other men who'd come up from Sparta, possibly even helots who had been given armor. They fought through the barrage of arrows, and they did not surrender, which he could have. Xerxes would have been thrilled to have a captive Spartan king in his train.

Instead, they fought until their spears had been broken, and they pulled their swords and fought on with the swords, close at hand to the crush of Persian warriors. Leonidas fell during the sword fight. His men would not surrender. They fought on without him until they were finally using their hands and their teeth, and when the last was killed, Xerxes knew he had taken the pass.

Thermopylae had fallen, the way to central Greece lay open, and Xerxes had won his first great victory. The Athenian guard ship out at sea saw the disaster and, appalled, headed eastward to carry the news to the fleet. We will follow them next time as the news of Thermopylae spreads through the world of the defenders, and they make one last stand at a place called Salamis, against this gigantic invading force, under the greatest king the world had ever seen, now ruling an empire even bigger than that of his father—Xerxes himself.

Lecture Nine
Battle in the Straits

Scope: While the Spartans and other Greeks fought valiantly at the pass at Thermopylae, the Greek fleet held the Persian line of ships at Artemision. On the third day of fighting, battered but victorious, the Greek fleet escaped in the night, the island of Salamis their ultimate destination. At the same time, Xerxes led his army through Greece and into the evacuated city of Athens; there, he burned the old temples on the Acropolis, finally avenging the Athenian destruction of Sardis two decades earlier. Meanwhile, the Persian armada and the Greek fleets met in the straits of Salamis for what would prove to be the most crucial battle in the entire epic of the Greek and Persian wars. Many Greeks believed the straits to be a deathtrap, but the Athenians were convinced the Persians could be defeated. Though the Persians outnumbered the Greeks three to one, the constricted fighting space (as at Thermopylae) negated the Persian advantage of numbers. Thanks to recorded eyewitness accounts of the battle, it is possible to follow the course of this day-long battle—from the first clash of the fleets at dawn to the final Greek massacre of stranded Persian troops in the evening light.

Outline

I. Before the Persian victory at Thermopylae, the Greeks had been successful at preventing the Persian armada of 1,200 ships from getting through to Greece.

A. As Xerxes's armada came south from Thessaloniki, a great wind from the Hellespont destroyed hundreds of ships and reduced the armada by the time it reached Artemision.

B. The Persian subjects in the ships—the Phoenicians, the Cyprians, the Ionian Greeks—did not fight with the same fervor that the Medes and Persians did at Thermopylae.

C. On the first day of fighting at sea, the Greeks waited until late afternoon before going out into the open channel and assembling into a *kyklos* ("wheel") formation.

1. This formation offered no way for the Persians to surround or get behind the Greeks.
2. In trying to encircle the Greeks, the Persians turned their triremes broadside to the Greek rams and split up their own line.
3. To the amazement of Xerxes's captains, the Greeks suddenly charged, expanding their circle and ramming the Persian ships.

D. On the second day of fighting, the main Persian fleet hoped to stay at their scattered stations on the north side of the Artemision Channel, but the Greeks crossed over, dared a Cilician contingent to come out, and cut them to pieces.

E. On the third day of fighting, Xerxes's armada approached the Greeks. With their own shore behind them, the Greeks could not be encircled; the Greeks managed to hold their own and remain masters of the sea.

F. After scouts brought news of the fall of Thermopylae, the Greeks got back into their ships and rowed homeward under cover of night.

II. Xerxes moved south to the empty territory of Athens, where both his army and his navy were reunited.

A. Xerxes managed to take the Acropolis from the few troops holding onto it and burned the Athenian temples to pay the Athenians back for destroying Sardis during the Ionian revolt.

B. The main mission of the Persian invasion was now accomplished: Athens was punished and in the hands of the Persian Empire.

III. As the Greek fleet retreated, Themistocles had persuaded Eurybiades to take the fleet to Salamis, where the elders of Athens were now in exile.

A. Many Peloponnesians feared that the Persians would use their ships to block both ends of the Salamis Channel and hold the Greek fleet there while the Persian army destroyed their fellows on land at the Isthmus of Corinth.

B. Themistocles used the threat of abandoning the Peloponnesians to the wrath of Xerxes in order to make them stay.

C. Themistocles did not want to wait for Xerxes's fleet to cross back to Asia during the winter; he wanted to bring on a battle.

1. He believed that if he could lure the Persian fleet into the straits of Salamis, the narrow fighting room would offer the Greeks a chance at victory.
2. For the glory of the new Athens he saw emerging after the wars, Themistocles wanted the city to have to its credit a great victory at sea.
3. Themistocles sent a false message to Xerxes through his sons' tutor, Sicinnus, stating that the Greek fleet planned to disband during the night and abandon Athens to its fate.

D. Planning to close off the exits of the Salamis Channel and destroy the whole Greek fleet, Xerxes moved his armada into the channel.
1. Artemisia, the female commander of the small fleet from Halicarnassus, advised Xerxes against going into the straits.
2. Xerxes himself planned to watch the battle from a knoll opposite the harbor at Salamis.

IV. At dawn, the Greek fleet gave the signal to charge, and the Persians realized they had been fooled.

A. The Greeks fanned out so that their 300 ships had room to fight, placing themselves against the rocky coast of Salamis so that the Persians could not get behind them.

B. The rear Persian lines, fearing that Xerxes would think they were holding back, crushed forward and prevented the front lines (now pinned against the Greeks) from maneuvering.

C. The Athenians, after a hard struggle, swung around the western end of the Persian formation and pushed the Persian fleet out of the straits of Salamis.

V. The battle was a crucial victory for the Greeks and an example of the use of stratagem, wits, and courage to defeat the largest naval force the world had ever seen.

Recommended Reading:

Green, *The Year of Salamis, 480–479 B.C.*

Morrison, Coates, and Rankov, *The Athenian Trireme: The History and Reconstruction of an Ancient Greek Warship.*

Questions to Consider:
1. Does Artemisia's crucial role in the Persian navy (despite the small size of her fleet) surprise you? Why or why not?
2. Do stratagem, wits, and courage really outmatch superior size and strength when it comes to military battles? Why or why not?

Lecture Nine—Transcript
Battle in the Straits

Welcome back. It was evening on the day that the Spartans and the other Greeks were killed in the pass at Thermopylae that the Greeks with the fleet at Artemision saw, over to the west, a little boat rowing at high speed toward them. It was the Athenian guard ship, commanded by the Athenian citizen Abronichus, who'd been the observer off Thermopylae and had seen from their observation point out in the water the disaster as Leonidas, his Spartans, and the hoplites from Thespiae were caught in the pass by the Immortals from one side and Xerxes's main force from the other and, after hours of fighting, had finally all been killed.

Then the Athenians had sprinted away to carry the news of the disaster to the fleet. This horrifying revelation came to a group of Greeks who had been winning for three days at sea and had been carrying out that original plan of Themistocles to hold the line far forward from Greece, with the ships of the Greek states centered around the 200 triremes and the new Athenian fleet, and prevent Xerxes's grand armada of 1,200 ships from getting through. They had been successful.

They were still holding the pass there—the channel of the Artemision waters that flowed past the beach at Artemision where they'd made their camp, and they had been aided by the weather. You may remember there was a Delphic Oracle that said, "Pray to the winds." Well, the winds had been fighting for Greece. As Xerxes's armada came south along that rocky Magnesian coast, they'd gone in for the night, and they'd had to anchor offshore instead of drawing their ships up on the beach because the beach was too narrow. They were eight-deep strung out from the beach, anchor to anchor to anchor, and a great wind came up in the morning out of the Hellespont to the northeast, and the whole sea was on the boil, and the ships of Xerxes were dashed up against the rocks. They lost hundreds of ships.

So the armada was reduced by the time it got to Artemision, and in three days of fighting, the Greeks had showed the Persians that they did not intend to let them pass. The Persians (it's actually a misnomer to call it "Persian," this fleet), the Persian subjects—the Phoenicians, the Cyprians, the Ionian Greeks who were in the fleet—didn't fight with the same fervor that Xerxes's Medes and Persians were fighting with over in the pass at Thermopylae. They were just trying to do enough of their duty so they wouldn't be blamed afterwards and suffer the consequences.

On the first day of fighting at sea, the Greeks had done a novel formation. They'd waited—remember, it's all about *metis*, that cunning intelligence that was the Odyssean quality that the Greeks liked in Themistocles—he waited until almost sundown so that it couldn't be a very long fight—you can't fight a naval battle in the dark—and he knew that it couldn't be a decisive defeat, even if worst came to worst. He let out, really under Eurybiades's—the Spartan admiral's—command, the Greek ships into the open channel, and they formed a hedgehog formation, in a circle, with all their rams pointing out. So there was no way to surround or get behind the Greek formation—it was all this great *kyklos* (or "wheel"), as they called it.

The fleet of Xerxes came out, saw this novel formation, and sort of spread themselves around it in a way that if you had circled the wagons in a wagon train, your mounted opponents might be circling around you. In the circling motion, the enemy turned their triremes broadside to the Greek rams, and they also split up their own line. Triremes were a little like hoplites in a phalanx: They were formidable at the front where their bronze ram was, but the long sides of those 120-foot-long galleys bristling with oars were just wood and completely defenseless, as was the stern, where the steering oars hung down into the water. So all of trireme tactics, ship to ship, was an attempt to get behind your enemy or get on the enemy's flank, where you could deliver a torpedo-like strike with the bronze ram, punch a hole, and sink the entire ship.

The Greeks had been waiting for this surrounding motion, and to the amazement of Xerxes's captains, the Greeks suddenly broke from that in an explosive charge. The circle expanded, and each Greek *trierarch*, or trireme captain, picked the target among the enemy, hit them hard, and rammed and destroyed those ships. The fight began but very quickly turned into a rout as the armada of Xerxes, already battered by the storm, headed back for their beaches. The Athenians and the other Greeks were able to tow off vessels that had been damaged, pick up survivors, and make some wonderful captives. Important people who had been with the fleet were now in their hands, and maybe they'll be questioned, and put in chains, and sent off to the isthmus, to the high command, for more questioning.

The second day, the main fleet, the Persian fleet, tried to stay on their scattered stations on the north side of the Artemision Channel, but the Greeks crossed over and dared them to come out. One little contingent of Cilicians came out. The Athenians cut them to pieces.

Finally, on the third day, the day when Leonidas was killed in the pass of Thermopylae, they had stayed on their own shore. Xerxes's armada had come over, and the Greeks—with their own shore behind them, could not be encircled by the Persians, who still outnumbered them—had managed to hold their own, remain masters of the sea. How do you remain masters of a battlefield either at sea or on land in the ancient world? If you are the one who can go out onto the battlefield and pick up your dead after the battle without asking permission from the other side, you have won.

The Greeks were able to do that, and they towed home their shattered wrecks; they picked up their survivors and the corpses from the water. They had won that day, although they'd suffered terribly and were losing ships all the time. Many of the Athenian ships were now out of commission from damage during the ramming strikes because ramming was very hard on your own ship.

It was to this group on the beach after three days of fighting that the guard ship from Thermopylae came and told the news. This was disastrous. They had hoped to hold Thermopylae for a long time. It had fallen after three days. The only bright spot was the sort of heroic nature of the last stand. The Greek resistance had been somewhat divided, somewhat troubled. There was a lot of contentious rivalry, like the rivalry between the Athenians and the Spartans, for the Athenians hoped for control of the naval defense.

What Leonidas died for was to set an example to the other Greeks—to give them a martyr, a hero—and that happened simply by standing his ground until he was cut down; he had fired the Greek resistance as nothing else could have done. With that image before them of the Spartans and the others dying in the pass, the Greeks got into their ships by night. Themistocles said, "Build up the fires on the beach here, so the Persian scouts looking across from the other side will assume we're still here at our stations," and they headed back home in the moonlight, rowing as quietly as they could.

As they rounded the corner, the western end of the island of Euboea, they were quite close to Thermopylae, only 20 miles away over the sheet of water, and they could see the victory fires—the bonfires, the sacrificial flames, the fire altars of the magi—as the Persians there with King Xerxes were celebrating their first great victory. Somewhere there amidst all of the revelry, standing on a pike, was the head of Leonidas, which had been cut from his body and stuck up there as a trophy to be gloried over and mocked by the Persians, who had finally broken through.

The Greek fleet got home. They were spotted by a man in the darkness—a Greek on the island of Euboea, who rode across and told the Persian "admirals" that he had seen the Greeks retreating in the moonlight. They didn't believe him because they could still see the campfires. By the time they had sent their own scout ships over and discovered the ruse of the Greeks to make them convinced that the Greeks were still in their place, it was too late. The Greeks had escaped.

So Xerxes, on land with the army, came south to Athens, and the fleet came around to Faliron Bay—the beach that served Athens as its little harbor on the south side of Attica—and army and navy were reunited at Athens. The city of Athens was empty; there were a few troops holding onto the Acropolis. After a long time, Xerxes managed to take the Acropolis, and the defenders threw themselves to their death, over the edge of the rocky precipice, rather than be prisoners of the Persians, and Athens was his.

Xerxes burned the temples of the Athenians up on the top of the Acropolis to pay them back for that outrage 18 years earlier when they had burned the temple of the mother goddess in Sardis in their attack on the western edge of the Persian Empire that started the Ionian revolt.

The main mission, the ostensible mission, of the great Persian invasion had now been accomplished: Athens was punished; Athens was in the hands of the Persians. He sent a rider off along those immensities of distance and down the Royal Road to Susa to carry the news home to the court that he had been victorious over the Athenians and that he had killed a Spartan king.

It was well that he was celebrating because there was still trouble for him. It was almost the autumn equinox; the season was almost over, but he had not beaten the Greek fleet, and it was very nearby. Off the Attic coast, almost within sight of Athens itself, well within sight of the Acropolis, was a great island called Salamis. In the days of the *Iliad*, this had been the home island of Ajax, the great hero who fought at Troy for the Greeks, the biggest and strongest of the Greeks. He'd been king of Salamis. In later centuries, it had become Athenian territory.

As the Greek fleet was retreating, falling back after Leonidas was killed at Thermopylae, Themistocles persuaded Eurybiades, the Spartan admiral, not to go all the way back to the Isthmus of Corinth and rejoin the army there but to go to Salamis, where the old men of Athens—the men too old to fight—had moved the city treasury and all of the files, and papers, and the ceremonial regalia. Athens was now in exile on Salamis. They had reconvened their little city there with the elders. They created a station, and to that station Themistocles was able to persuade Eurybiades to go and take the whole fleet—with additions, now still about 300 triremes strong.

Eurybiades agreed, but many of the Peloponnesians in the fleet of ships didn't think this was right. Between the island of Salamis and the coast of Attica ran a narrow channel of water, less than a mile wide. They were afraid they were now in a trap, that the Persians—or Xerxes—would now use their ships to block up both ends of the Salamis Channel and hold the Greek fleet there while the main army went down and destroyed their fellows at the isthmus on land.

So the Greeks were now united together—the navy—all together there at Salamis—but divided in their ideas of what should be done. It was all that Themistocles could do to argue and argue and keep them there. Finally, he had to use the threat: "If you do not stay here at Salamis and help us defend Attica and defend this last little corner of the soil of Attica—Salamis Island—we will get in our ships, and we will collect our wives and children from the islands and from the city of Troysan in the Peloponnese (where they are now refugees), and we will all go away to southern Italy and found a new Athens in the west, and you will be left to face Xerxes alone."

They all knew that without the Athenian navy to protect their coasts, Xerxes could land. Even on the Peloponnese, there was a great city, Argos, that had Medized—that had gone over to the Persian side and submitted to the Great King. He could have taken his fleet to their harbor, unloaded his army, and attacked the Spartans on land in their own territory. So they did not dare let the Athenians leave, and they agreed to stay.

So it was that they saw one day, smoke rising from the top of the Acropolis, and they realized the Acropolis had fallen; the last mainland stronghold north of the isthmus was now in Xerxes's hands. Here, too, they had hoped, I am sure, that it would hold out for a long time. They're almost up to the equinox, and they're almost up to the rising of the star Arcturus, which shows that the winter storms are about to begin and everybody needs to haul their ships out of the water. They know it's just a matter of time; if they can just hold on long enough, Xerxes will have to disband his fleet, and they will be safe until spring, and maybe the whole thing will just evaporate.

Themistocles didn't want that to happen. He wanted to bring on a battle. He believed that if he could lure the vast Persian armada—which probably still outnumbered the Greeks three to one in terms of ships—if he could lure them into the straits of Salamis, that the same thing would happen there that had happened at Thermopylae: In the constricted space, the vast superiority of the Persians in sheer numbers would be negated by the narrow fighting room, and the Greeks would have a chance to actually win a victory.

He was firmly of the belief that however you run a war, wars are ultimately won by victories—not by stratagems, or holding off, or anything else. For the glory of Athens and that new Athens he saw emerging after the Persian wars, he wanted Athens to have to its credit a great victory at sea.

Perhaps with the connivance and the knowledge of the Spartan admiral Eurybiades, Themistocles embarked on his most famous stratagem. He decided that he would send a false message to Xerxes that would bring him by night with his ships into the narrows—the channel of Salamis—and allow the Greeks to fight there in the narrows. How did he do it?

I mentioned that he was the father of a big family. His oldest son had died. His oldest son was named Neocles. He died when he was bitten by a horse as a boy, and he died of that accident. But he still had many children. Some of his political aspirations were apparent in the names of the girls: Italia was one girl; Asia was another girl. He had a brood of boys also, and the boys had a tutor, a very capable man named Sicinnus, a Greek, who was the *paedagogos* for these children—*pedagogue*—and that means, in ancient Greek, he is the servant who accompanies the boys to classes and also gives them tutorials himself.

He apparently spoke many languages, and he was a very trusted servant of Themistocles. Themistocles told him: "Go to the Persian camp; we'll put you in a small boat. Tell the captains of the fleet that you have a message from me, Themistocles, the leader of the Athenians. Tell them that the Greeks are about to disband—that in the night, they are going to board their ships and each contingent will fly away, seeking their own safety, abandoning Athens and Attica to its fate, and that we Athenians are so angry about this that we will fight for the Great King. But if he will bring his fleet into the channel tonight, he will close off the exits, catch the whole Greek fleet at once, and destroy them all."

So Sicinnus took this message by night to the camp by the sea where Xerxes's naval commanders were. Probably from his boat, because he did manage to get away afterwards, he called out the message from the water.

When he was sure it had been heard, he vanished away into the night. The message was then carried to Xerxes.

Xerxes convened his naval arm—those admirals, the contingents of the fleet, the kings of Tyre and Sidon who traveled with the Phoenician contingent. They all agreed to enter the channel. There was only one holdout. There was a Greek city in Asia Minor called Halicarnassus—it's going to be famous to us as the hometown of the historian Herodotus, who will write down the chronicle of this war. Halicarnassus also had a ruler who would come along with the navy in charge of the contingent of ships from that city. This ruler was a woman—the only woman among the hundreds of thousands of men fighting for Xerxes. She was the leader of the little fleet from Halicarnassus. Her name was Artemisia.

Artemisia told the king: "This is not a good plan. Think of these naval forces of yours, how little account they are. Think of how they failed to break through at Artemision. Do not go into the straits." Xerxes—to the surprise of all those who disliked Artemisia and hoped that she would come a cropper over this untimely advice—expressed his thanks to her for speaking her mind. But he said, "Nonetheless, I agree with the majority. We shall go into the straits."

During that next day, the Persians put to sea, and by arraying themselves at sea, they both challenged the Greeks to come out and prevented them from leaving their anchorage, because the Persians are thinking now they're going to break away. And if it seems to us a little naïve that they should have fallen for this, let's remember something that is almost never mentioned: It had happened before. After Artemision, when the Greek camp was aglow with fires, these captains of the Persian fleet had received a messenger coming in the dark from the Greek side, saying, "The Greeks have all fled away, and if you act now, you can catch them."

They had disbelieved this messenger, they had waited too long, and the Greeks had escaped. The message had been true. They were not going to be fooled a second time. So they decided when the Sun went down—and the crews had been at the oar all day—to bring them onshore, give them their dinners there on the Attic coast, and then as the Sun went down, all those thousands and thousands of rowers got back in the ships. They had left their oars with the loops securing them to the thole pins. They got back on the ships, and they pushed off from shore. The fighting men were loaded onboard the triremes—a special set of fighting men were sent out to a little island called Psyttaleia, which lay between the mainland and Salamis—and they were going to kill any Greeks that washed up on the island.

As the Moon rose about midnight, that great armada began to flow like a river of ships, three abreast, because they outnumbered the Greeks three to one. They flowed into the Salamis strait, and they stayed close to the Attic shore, because now that's Persian—that's part of the Persian Empire—it's the safe shore. They know there won't be enemies there—archers or people throwing missiles—so that's the safe shore for them to cling to as they flow into the straits.

Xerxes wanted to watch this battle. He thought the reason that his ships had performed badly at Artemision was because he was not there to watch them. There was a little knoll, and it's still there—a conical hill just opposite the harbor of Salamis town. The double harbors of Salamis were the place where the Greek triremes were over on the island. All the time Xerxes had been in Attica, which is about a month now, the scouts of his army must have stood on top of that knoll to watch the Greeks—keep an eye on their ships, watch the Athenians repairing their ships, new people arriving from the islands.

That was where Xerxes went in the hours before dawn. He went in his chariot. They took him as far as they could up the slope. He went the rest of the way. They put up a throne for him so he could watch the whole thing like a spectator at a play. He had his scribes along, and they had their writing materials and their styluses. They were going to mark down all of those commanders who distinguished themselves in the battle and deserved to be rewarded and all of those who played the coward and deserved to be killed.

A complete record would be kept for the Persian files of this great and glorious victory, where the Greeks would be trapped in the straits, and they would be divided and destroyed, and the naval resistance to Xerxes's invasion would be over. He knew once the fleet was gone that he could land anywhere he liked—the war would be won.

He knew it was a risk, but it seemed a risk worth taking. Xerxes was now on his hilltop. The Persian armada had flowed in three deep and lined the shores at his feet. It was a line of ships several miles long because there were somewhere between 600, 800, and 1,200 ships in that line. One end, the western end, was over facing or close to the sacred town of Eleusis, where the Athenians practiced, on exactly these days every fall, the Eleusinian mysteries in honor of the goddess Demeter and her daughter

Persephone—fittingly enough, a ceremony of rebirth, where people entered a dark hall as initiates, and the priestesses showed the miracle of new grains sprouting up from dead seeds.

Over on the left, to the east, the far-left wing (or they called it the "horn" of the position), the great fleet was over toward the Piraeus promontory, not yet a great harbor. Over on the other side—a mile away in the shadowy gloom of predawn (hidden from view)—were the Greeks.

The message, of course, had been a lie. The Greeks were not disunited, and they were going to fight, and Themistocles was hand in glove with Eurybiades, the Spartan commander, about how they were going to operate. As soon as it was light enough for the steersmen to see, they brought the crews down to the shore. Each commander gave a speech, probably just to the fighting men on deck—the few marines, maybe as few as 10 in number for each ship—that would have been in each contingent.

Themistocles was the one who gave the speech to the Athenians, and he told them that: "In this life, we are continually faced with choices. Today, choose the better course, not the worst. Fight and die for your country; do not run away."

They all got onto their ships. They spread gently out of these two harbors at Salamis, and as it got lighter, they prepared themselves to fan out very quickly along the shore because they wanted to be at a full battle line by the time the Persians got across and hit them.

Eurybiades had a trumpeter with him. This was the way they gave signals to the fleet. You've seen the Corinthian helmets that the hoplites wore, and you can tell they couldn't hear many commands during a battle, and that's why hoplite battles were, in general, so simple—just stand and hold your ground. But at sea it was a matter of complicated maneuvers, and they were signaled by these Greek trumpeters—the Greek trumpeter was called a *salpinktes*, and his instrument was a *salpinx*—in the same way that we use bugle calls on a military field today.

As it got to be dawn light, an hour before actual sunup and light enough that he knew these steersmen could see, Eurybiades, on his Spartan flagship—over on the right wing, facing across to the Ionian Greeks—gave the trumpeter the signal to blow the charge.

As the signal sounded, not only the Greeks, but the Persians on the other side heard it, too, and they realized they had been fooled. They had been drawn in to what they were told was a disunited, unsuspecting group of

Greek ships that would be easy prey. Instead, here was a battle call coming. At the same time, they heard the singing of the Greek marines onboard the ship as they sang the *paian* (P-A-I-A-N), the battle hymn sacred to the god Apollo, with which every Greek force went into combat.

The Greeks immediately fanned out quickly from their positions as they got to the full extent of the line, so that all of their 300 ships now had room to fight. They turned to face the enemy and had the crews backwater, away from the Persians, so that they would be right up against the rocky coast of Salamis, and just as at Artemision, on the last day, the Persians—even though they outnumbered them—could not get behind.

It was daylight now. The Persians surged across. The Phoenicians—the best of the Persian armada—were facing the Athenians on the westerly wing; the Spartans, the Aeginetans, and the others were facing the Ionian Greeks on the east wing; the Corinthians and others in the middle were facing the Egyptians, and the Cilicians, and so on.

They collided. Three deep, the Persians had come across. Nobody had held back. They all knew that their royal master was up on that hilltop watching. They were much more afraid of him than they were of the Greeks, and their great fear was that Xerxes would see them as someone who had held back, mark their name down on the little tablets, and that they would suffer after the battle. So those at the rear crushed forward and prevented any maneuvering on the part of the front line of Xerxes's ships, now pinned up against the Greeks.

So it began. When there was still a little bit of room, one Athenian ship on the left wing had darted forward, done a quick swerve, and had actually sheared off the stern section—the rear section with the steering oars—of one of the Phoenician ships. At about the same time, on the right wing, an Aeginetan ship had attacked an Ionian ship. As they became locked in combat, their fellow Greeks moved forward to assist them, and the battle was joined.

The Sun came up, and Xerxes saw this amazing sight. Four triremes deep, miles long—this long line—most of the battleships in the Mediterranean there spread out before him as they fought and fluctuated back and forth in this immense wooden snake of ships. But his undoing was the fact that he was there and his rear ships would not back off and let his forward ships actually maneuver. One by one, they were destroyed by the Greek rams. Their oars were broken. They tried to escape and limp home. A seepage began toward the exit to the strait, so they could get back to their headquarters.

The Athenians under Themistocles, seeing this, swung around the far western end of the Persian formation and began to push and push and push them out of the strait, destroying more and more as they went. As they were pushed to the east, the Aeginetans—those islanders from the rival island of Aegina—began to take them in the flank as they tried to escape. They pushed them out of the channel by end of daylight. They made a great attempt to catch Artemisia because they didn't like it that a woman had come against them, but she managed to evade them. In fact, she did so by ramming one of her own allied ships, but Xerxes, seeing her do it, assumed she'd rammed a Greek enemy and said, "My men fight like women, but my women fight like men."

At the end of the day, from his hilltop, Xerxes had the mortification of seeing the channel cleared of his grand armada, strewn with the wrecks of his ships and the corpses of his men. Those prime Persian troops that had been landed on the island of Psyttaleia in darkness in the hope that they would be killing shipwrecked Greeks were destroyed by a mass of Greeks, led by the Athenian Aristides the Just, who had guarded the treasure at Marathon 10 years earlier. They got onto the island, and they rounded up the Persians, and they killed them all. It was a gigantic victory for the Greeks, and Xerxes tore his robe in a gesture of grief and mourning, got back into his chariot, and went back to his camp.

Some time after the battle, a Greek went up the hill where he had been sitting and found that a little golden footstool had been left behind—the footstool on which the king's foot had rested as he climbed back up into his chariot. This became the first trophy for the Greeks of the Battle of Salamis, but it was only the first of many.

The tide had turned there in the channel on that September day in 480 B.C. Against all odds, a small group of Greeks, using stratagem, using their wits, but also fighting with tremendous courage, had managed to defeat the biggest naval force the world had ever seen. Truly, it was a new ballgame. Xerxes was now on the run, and the tide was about to turn.

Lecture Ten
The Freedom Fighters

Scope: Having captured Athens and having burned the temples on the Acropolis, Xerxes returned to Asia a conqueror of sorts and left subsequent operations to his general, Mardonius. Despite the Persian departure, the Greeks remained somewhat divided among themselves. The next spring opened with the Greeks aware of two campaigns ahead of them: The Spartan king Leotychidas mustered the Greek fleet to guard the seaways around Greece, while the Athenians (led by Aristides the Just) sent the bulk of their forces to join the main allied army opposing Mardonius. Under the leadership of the Spartan regent Pausanias, the Greek land army defeated Mardonius near the town of Plataea in a tense battle, thanks in part to the cunning of Pausanias. News of the victory soon reached the Greek naval forces, which had sailed to the island of Samos and were preparing to confront the Persian fleet that had drawn up onto the Asiatic coast of Mount Mycale.

Outline

I. Although the immediate result of the Battle of Salamis was some confusion on the side of the Greeks as to who had won, it quickly became apparent that this battle had set a limit to the Persian expansion into Greece.

   A. The Persians' loss can be attributed to a number of factors.
   1. They should not have fought on the enemy's terms by entering the straits.
   2. The exhausted Persian rowers did not have the power to organize maneuvers that would have brought about victory.
   3. The various national contingents of the Persian fleet exhibited disunity of purpose.

   B. For once, the Greek forces had cooperated and were able to accomplish miracles at the Battle of Salamis.

   C. Despite apparent Persian plans to prepare for a new phase of battle, Xerxes decided to return home.

        1. Artemisia rationalized that Xerxes could leave with honor because he had taken Athens, burned the Acropolis, and punished the Athenians for the burning of Sardis.
        2. Xerxes left Mardonius in charge of a core of the Persian army.
II. After the Persian departure, the Greeks returned home, somewhat divided among themselves.
    A. The Greeks honored Themistocles with a second-place prize for valor.
        1. The Spartans treated him like a hero.
        2. His standing was less than good among the Athenians, his countrymen, some of whom had been his political rivals and were now returned from exile.
    B. Although Athens was vacated by the Persians for the winter, the Athenians were afraid that the enemy would return again soon.
    C. A message from Mardonius stated that the Persians would restore Athens to the Athenians if they submitted to the empire's rule.
        1. The Athenians felt betrayed by their allies; Themistocles had been passed over for the first prize of valor and their immense force of 200 triremes had been passed over in favor of a few ships that had been on the right wing next to the Spartans during battle.
        2. The majority of Athenians voted not to accept Xerxes's offer.
    D. The next spring opened with the Greeks aware of two campaigns ahead of them: tackling the Persian army that remained in Greece and dealing with the menace of the Persian fleet.
        1. The Spartan regent Pausanias would lead the Greek land forces.
        2. King Leotychidas of Sparta went to Aegina and amassed a small naval force that would make sure the Persian fleet did not invade again.
III. The movement of Pausanias and his land army led to a conflict with Mardonius's Persian army known as the Battle of Plataea.
    A. Early in the summer, the Persians had returned to Athens and destroyed the city.
    B. The Persians, seeking a place to meet the Greeks, crossed into the Medized city of Thebes and built a palisade next to a vast plain, where Mardonius felt confident of beating the Greeks.

- **C.** Pausanias brought north an army ultimately numbering 38,700 Greek hoplites. Most of the Athenian hoplites were there with the main force (not with the fleet) and were under the command of Aristides the Just.
- **D.** Mardonius had to bring on a battle because another year without a decisive Persian victory was unthinkable.
    - **1.** He attacked the Athenians with his Persian horsemen, who were quickly cut down by Athenian archers.
    - **2.** The Athenians managed to retrieve the body of the fallen Persian commander Megistias and treated his corpse as the first great trophy of an eventual victory.
- **E.** In a cunning move, Pausanias ordered his army to divide, giving the Persians the illusion that they were pulling back.
    - **1.** When Mardonius launched his cavalry attack, he discovered a Spartan and Athenian phalanx that was impossible to break.
    - **2.** Gradually, the Greek hoplites forged their way down the slope and defeated the Persians.
    - **3.** With the death of Mardonius in battle, the Athenians stormed the Persian stockade and led the other Greeks inside.
- **F.** The Greeks looted the Persian treasure, setting aside one-tenth to make statues and victory monuments dedicated to the gods and using the rest to reimburse the states for some of the costs they had suffered during the war.

IV. Word of the victory on land reached the Greek fleet, which had arrived at the island of Samos. There, the Greeks prepared to meet the Persian fleet, which had drawn up on the coast of Asia Minor at Mount Mycale.

Recommended Reading:

How and Wells, *A Commentary on Herodotus.*

Warry, *Warfare in the Classical World.*

Questions to Consider:

1. What do you think would have happened had Xerxes decided to stay in Greece instead of leaving Mardonius in charge?
2. Was there any way the Persian Empire could have won the Battle of Plataea? If so, how?

Lecture Ten—Transcript
The Freedom Fighters

Welcome back. More than 2,000 years after that autumn day in 480 B.C., when a small Greek fleet defeated the great armada of King Xerxes in the straits of Salamis, a young English poet named George Gordon Byron, whom we know as Lord Byron, set out to write a poem that he titled "The Isles of Greece," that would sum up all the heroic past of the Greeks and serve as a rallying cry—not just to the Greeks but to his own fellow Englishmen—to try to liberate Greece, which at that time was dominated by the Ottoman Empire.

One of the stanzas in "The Isles of Greece" was inspired by the Battle of Salamis—the battle that we have just lived through. It goes like this:

> A king sat on the rocky brow
> That looks on sea-born Salamis;
> And ships, in thousands, lay below,
> And men in nations;—all were his!
> He counted them at break of day—
> And when the sun set, where were they?

In these few lines, Byron summed up the drama of that day. He meant it to be an example—a beautiful statement of a cause: the idea of liberty for Greece against a foreign invader, but it was more than that, that victory at Salamis.

It was one of the hinges of history. It was one of the places where a great movement was checked, where this empire that seemed unstoppable found its limit. On that September day, the world changed, and people at the time were aware of that. Although the immediate result of the Battle of Salamis was some confusion on the Greek side as to whether they had really won, it quickly became apparent that this had set the limit to the Persian expansion into Greece.

Marathon had been a victory more cherished by the Athenians because they won it basically all on their own, and Salamis was a collaborative effort. But seen with hindsight, we can understand that when Themistocles—through his guile, his cunning, his exercise of *metis*—managed to draw the Persians into the straits in the same way that his spiritual ancestor Odysseus had managed to fool the Trojans with the famous Trojan Horse, he had set in motion forces that would suddenly alter the balance of the great powers, would catapult Athens to a position of leadership among the Greeks, and open up a new era in the history of the ancient world.

However, it's time to get back to the day itself. Xerxes left his high perch and went back to his beautiful pavilion in his main camp on the field outside Athens. There must have been some interesting postmortems on the Persian side following the battle. We need to remember, though the Greeks must have been sky high to have pushed the Persian fleet out and to have destroyed so many ships, most of the Persian armada had survived. Most were still alive to fight another day. They had failed to rout the Greeks out of their little position of hiding there in the straits—their safe corner—but they hadn't lost any ground themselves, and although the Greeks were still entrenched, they, the Persians, were still masters of the sea.

It may not have seemed initially the debacle that it seems today to us looking back on it. Why did they lose? There were a number of factors. They shouldn't have entered the straits. It's clear with hindsight that to fight on the enemy's terms is to break one of the cardinal rules of warfare. You want to make the enemy fight on your terms, in territory to your advantage, which would have been, for the Persians, the open sea. Did they need to go into the channel? They may have thought so, in that bypassing Salamis to take the ships all the way to the isthmus would have left this unbeaten Greek navy at their rear or on their flank. But they outnumbered the Greeks. They could have left a small pair of contingents to bottle up each end of the Salamis straits and hold the Greeks in there indefinitely. That would have been using one's mind—that would have been using *metis* in the Greek way. They just didn't consider that possibility.

On the day of the battle itself, a terrible error had been made. Themistocles's plan ensured that the Persians—now intending to slip into the straits by night—would have their rowers at the oars the previous day, all night long—in other words, almost 24 hours—before the battle began, and the battle itself was to last all day. The rowers—the engines that propelled the Persian ships—were exhausted from the beginning. So no matter how skillful their steersmen may have been—and they were no match for the Greeks—they simply didn't have the power at the oars to do the kinds of maneuvers and charges that might have brought them some victory.

Finally, there was the disunity of the Persian fleet, not just among the national contingents but the disunity of purpose—all those commanders not thinking: "What can I do to win this battle?" but "What can I do to shine more than the people on either side of me in those other ships before the eyes of the Great King who is watching me?"

This is no way to win a battle. All these things contributed to creating a situation in which Greek determination, superior Greek seamanship, and for once, a Greek unity of purpose—the incredible millennial sight of Athenians on one end of the line cooperating with their ancient enemies, the islanders of Aegina, on the other end of the line. The Athenians pushed the Persians out to sea—the Aeginetans taking them from the flank as they went by. For once, the Greeks united together at sea, able to accomplish miracles.

There must have been some doubt, though, among the Greeks the next morning because they had to see, with a sinking feeling, Phoenician merchantmen—those big freighters that transported grain and wine—being brought into the far end of the straits and tethered to the far shore—the mainland shore by the Persians—with the realization: "Oh my gosh, they're going to try to build another bridge of ships to Salamis." Or, as they saw people bringing loads of rock down to the edge of the shore: "They're going to build a mole"—a sort of jetty of rock extending out into the channel, which would ultimately reach over and allow Xerxes to get his troops onto the island on dry land.

Here is where the psychological force of Xerxes's tradition came into play: The Persians were known for their relentlessness. They never gave up. They never stopped. Setbacks were only temporary with the Persians. And so it must have been with a great sinking feeling that Themistocles, Eurybiades, all the Greeks who had just fought all day long to push the Persians out of the straits at Salamis saw that the Persians had not folded their tends and gone away but seemed to be prepared for an entire new phase of the battle.

It was only a ruse. Xerxes had decided to go home. Who helped him to his decision? Artemisia. She was now regarded, of course, as one of the chiefs among his counselors since she had given the correct advice before the Salamis battle: "Don't go into the straits." He trusted her a great deal, and she handed him the rationalization that allowed him to leave Greece with honor. "Great King," said Artemisia, "you should go home. You have accomplished your purpose. Athens is yours; you have burned the great high citadel of the Athenians; you have punished them as you said you would for burning the city of Sardis in your father's time. You have accomplished something your father could not do"—something I'm sure she also pointed out to him. "It's time for you to leave the end of this campaign to your servants, and above all, to your servant Mardonius, who wanted to bring the invasion to Greece in the first place. Leave some of the army with him. He can finish up, and since he and everyone else in your army, they are only your slaves, if they should fail without you, well, it was just a matter of those slaves unable to do your bidding. No discredit will be held to your account."

This was exactly what Xerxes wanted to hear, although Herodotus has a humorous passage in which he says he believes that if the entire Persian army had laid down in his path and begged him to stay in Greece, he still would have left.

At any rate, he left Mardonius in charge of a core of the Persian army, including some of the picked troops. He himself headed north. The fleet went home. It would have been insane for the Persians to try to pay to supply all those rowers—tens of thousands of rowers—who were doing nothing between October and probably April or May, except eat two or three meals a day. How are you going to do that? Even the Great King didn't have that kind of wealth.

They left under an odd circumstance: Herodotus says that the Phoenicians of Tyre and Sidon, led by their kings, left without the king's permission, slipping away the day after the battle. It seems odd to us that vassal kings would dare to defy their overlord by doing this. But there may have been an extenuating circumstance. You remember those scribes who stood behind Xerxes, noting down who performed well and who performed badly during the battle? Xerxes was under the impression the Phoenicians had performed badly.

What had happened was this: As the Athenians pushed some of the Persian ships up against the shore of Attica, their crews spilled out, they waded to shore, and their captains—their *trierarchs*—came up the hilltop to talk to Xerxes. The Phoenicians came up and said, "O, Great King, we are losing this battle because of the Ionian Greeks who are fighting in your fleet. They are betraying us. They are fighting in a cowardly way. They are impeding us." It's maybe true that as the Phoenicians were trying to escape from their position on the right wing, far up the channel, they were being impeded in their escape as their ships were disabled by Ionians that got in the way.

At any rate, here was the complaint: "The Ionians are not fighting well for you." Xerxes at that moment looked down, and he saw an amazing feat. One of his Ionian ships rammed another ship. It was eastern Greeks from the island of Samothrace. They were javelineers. They rammed another ship, but then they were rammed in their turn by a Greek ship. What did they do? They were immobilized because their ram was stuck in the first ship, and so they grabbed their javelins, they poured onto the ship that had just rammed them—the Greek ship—cleared its decks with their weapons, took possession of it as their own prize, backed out of their now-sinking original ship from Samothrace, and continued to fight for Xerxes.

Xerxes said, "You see how my Ionians serve me? Off with their heads." According to Herodotus, who actually knows by name some of the Persians that were around Xerxes and implies that he has firsthand information here—eyewitness accounts—they were beheaded. So it may have been that the kings of Tyre and Sidon, angered by this treatment of their sea captains, had taken the fleets from Phoenicia back home and were willing to suffer the consequences.

At any rate, a few days after the Battle of Salamis, the scouts of the Greeks on Salamis, who had been able to see nothing—they could be looked at all the time from the hills on the mainland, but they couldn't see anything except the narrow stretch of water themselves—they finally learned that the Persian fleet was gone. All of this bridge-building or mole-building—it was a fake to hold them there, and they poured out of the Salamis channel in their ships and set off in pursuit, hoping to catch the Persian fleet before it escaped from Greek waters.

They rowed past the vast plain in front of the city of Athens. They saw for the first time the king's pavilion and that whole mass of men and nations, as Byron says, on the plain before them. They raced south to the point at the tip of Attica, where the temple of Poseidon stands on its rocky headland. It, too, like the temples on the Acropolis, had been burned and destroyed. Beyond it lay the open sea—not a sail, not a ship—the Persian fleet had escaped. But they knew for sure in that moment Salamis had been a great victory after all.

They headed home—now somewhat divided among themselves—into what is often called their "winter of discontent." The fleet went to the isthmus to report to the high command there of the Hellenic League (led by the Spartans) what had happened at Salamis. During this campaign—it happened seemingly first at Artemision—the Greeks had decided to start voting on who was the most brave in each of their battles. It's sort of like treating them as if they were athletic competitions. The Greeks, of course, loved an *agon*—a competition, a contest—and they always liked prizes.

Unlike that bit in Lewis Carroll's *Alice in Wonderland*—"All have won and all must receive prizes"—no, no, no. There's only one winner, and that person must receive the prize for valor. So they took a vote. Herodotus says that they voted on the altar of Poseidon, casting their ballots—all the commanders of the fleet that had beaten Xerxes's armada at Salamis. Who deserved the prize for valor?

Every man's honor, everybody who had been a commander in the fleet, his honor required that he vote for himself first. But they had voted for a second place, and every one of them named Themistocles as the second place. He'd fought with valor during the battle, but that vote was really a tribute to him. They all knew that if three years earlier he had not persuaded the Athenians to forego a short-term profit, pool their resources from the amazing silver strike, and build the fleet of 200 triremes, that battle would never have been won.

They knew that if Themistocles had not urged them to hold the advance of the Persians at the north end of Euboea, at the Artemision straits, everything might have changed if Xerxes had been able to get down unchecked. They finally knew that if his guile, his cunning, had not lured the Persians into the straits, the battle would never have happened, and this great victory would never have occurred.

It was probably the high point of Themistocles's life, even though no prize was awarded, because nobody had the majority for first place. He had been recognized, and the Spartans treated him like a hero: feasting him, taking him down to Sparta. Young Spartans pulling the horses out of his chariot so they could tow the chariot behind them themselves—the kind of treatment only reserved for a divine hero or an Olympic victor.

With Themistocles's own Athenians, his standing was less good. Many Athenians who had been in exile, who had been his political rivals, were now back with the mass of Athenians returned from exile during the emergency of the Persian invasion, and the very fact that he was being so feted and lauded by the Spartans went to his head. He became arrogant himself. He built a little temple to the goddess Artemis on the street where he lived to thank her for helping him win this battle for the Greeks.

He'd always had kind of an itching palm. He was born to very moderate means. He meant to become rich, as well as powerful and famous, and now he got involved in bribes and corruption. So Salamis was his great moment. He will have one more great service to perform for the Greeks that we'll get to next time—or, specifically, for the Athenians—but it is other commanders who will now take the lead after this winter where the Greeks begin to feel that all the unity they had the previous year is starting to slip away.

For one thing, the line at the isthmus held. The Peloponnesians showed no sign of coming out of it, and although Athens was now vacated by the Persians, the Athenians were afraid they would come back again from the place where the Persians were encamped—they were spending the winter to the north—that it would all happen again the next year, and that finally— who knows?—maybe the Persians would win.

Into this time of doubt came a man from the north. He was the king of Macedon. His name was Alexander—not Alexander the Great but an ancestor of his, of the same Greek dynasty that ruled Macedonia in this classical age. He was now a servant—a vassal—of Xerxes. He brought a message from General Mardonius of the Persians, saying to the Athenians, "Xerxes knows that you are about to be abandoned by your fellow Greeks. They are leaving Athens to its fate, even though you have done so much for them. If you will submit, just submit to fight no more against the Great King and be his friends, he will restore Athens to you. He will let you govern yourselves in any way that you wish, and he will enrich you beyond your wildest dreams."

The Athenians were feeling a little bit betrayed by their fellow Greeks. They had been passed over—not only Themistocles being passed over for the prize for valor (the official prize as an individual), but they as a contingent of the fleet had had the mortification of seeing their immense force of 200 triremes passed over in favor of the few ships from the island of Aegina that had been on the right wing next to the Spartans. How just was that?

The Athenians felt snubbed. They felt embittered. Some of them probably considered maybe it would be best to accept the Great King's offer. Perhaps we're headed for a new world order; let's find a good place for Athens in it. But the majority said no. They told Alexander, king of Macedon: "Go back and tell the Persians no amount of gold will make the Athenians betray the Greek cause."

The next spring opened with the Greeks aware they had two campaigns yet ahead of them: Tackle this Persian army that had remained in Greece, and deal with the menace of the Persian fleet still outnumbering us, possibly ruling the Aegean.

The Spartans had now awakened fully to the importance of the naval side. They had appointed an admiral who was a Spartan the previous year—the famous year of 480 B.C., when Xerxes was in Greece. That was Eurybiades. Now they gave the assignment to a king—one of the two kings. They upgraded the naval arm. This king was Leotychidas. Leonidas, of course, was dead. The other king was so young that there was a regent in charge of that other branch of the dual Spartan kingship. His name was Pausanias. The Spartans had found in him a man a lot like Themistocles—very ambitious, very clever, very charismatic, and a man able to persuade people to forget their differences and unite in a common cause.

Pausanias, the regent of Sparta, would lead the forces on land. Leotychidas went to Aegina—Athens had even been stripped of the honor of being the headquarters of the fleet—and on the island of Aegina, he amassed a small force—only 50 or 60 triremes—that would be watching the waters of the Greek world to make sure that the Persian fleet did not reinvade.

Let's follow the fortunes of the land army first. It became plain that Mardonius and his Persians were uncertain about where to fight. They wanted a vast plain where they could deploy their cavalry. They still knew that the cavalry, with its lancers and bowmen, was their strongest arm. There was one plain near Athens—the plain of Eleusis, site of the shrine of the Eleusinian mysteries. They, in fact, came back to Athens, and this time, in their fury at the Athenians not surrendering, they destroyed the whole city.

So Athens became a vast disaster area. The only buildings left standing were Athenian houses where the Persian officers had billeted themselves. Everything else was gone. Everything was destroyed. The walls, if there were any, had been thrown down; the city was a smoking ruin.

As the Persians left and sought a place to meet the Greeks, they finally crossed over the hills, over Mount Cithaeron. Going north into the vast plains of Boeotia, the city of Thebes had Medized. It had surrendered to Xerxes. They built a vast palisaded camp. The palisade was supposed to be a great square, a mile on each side, of wooden uprights—a stockade that was made of the fruit trees of the Thebans. They had submitted to Xerxes, but that meant that everything they had was his, and so all of their orchards were cut down to make the uprights for this vast fence. Inside there was the army. Outside was an immense plain where Mardonius felt confident of beating the Greeks.

Pausanias summoned all of the allies, all of the resistance, and amazingly, even after the successes of 480 B.C. at sea and after the heroic death of Leonidas in the pass at Thermopylae, there were still people hanging back. Nonetheless, Pausanias brought north, over the passes of the mountains, an army that ultimately numbered 38,700 Greek hoplites.

This time, most of the Athenian hoplites were there with the main force. Pausanias wanted no more of this fighting at sea for Athens; they needed to be doing their contribution along with the other Greeks on land. So the Athenians joined the other Greeks. They were under the command of that man we've met before, Aristides—called "the Just" probably because he was a good arbiter. It was very common in the Greek world, if you had a difference, to settle it out of court. Certainly, between nations or two islands, they would find a non-interested—a disinterested—party and have that person come and be an arbiter. That's how he would get this nickname: Aristides the Just. He was universally respected, incorruptible, very honest, and he was at the lead of the Athenian hoplites at Plataea.

They came down over the mountain, over Mount Cithaeron. They came down onto its lower slopes. As they came over the pass, they could see Thebes, and they could see the great square of the palisaded camp of the Persians. They all knew this territory very well, and they realized as soon as they were off the mountain, beyond the little foothills at its base, they would be mowed down. So began a very strange battle. It led to a battle at a place called Plataea. Plataea was the town in Boeotia that had sent its men to Marathon to help the Athenians.

Near Plataea there were little hills, and there were springs of water, so that these tens of thousands of Greeks had a good water supply all night long, and carts were bringing food over the mountains from free Greece to the south to supply this huge army. Pausanias knew: "If I attack, they will destroy me. I must wait here until they attack us."

Mardonius, out on the plain, this Persian, knew equally: "If I go up on their territory, I am fighting in terrain where my horses will have trouble maneuvering." Nonetheless, he decided to take the first action. After all, his head was at stake. If he failed to conquer Greece for Xerxes, who knew what would happen? He had to bring on a battle. A year that ended without a decisive victory for the Persians—or at least an attempt at a battle—was unthinkable as far as Mardonius was concerned. So he began by sending up some of his famous Persian horsemen. They came up along the Athenian ranks, and they threw their javelins at the Athenians.

By a lucky shot and by a lucky chance, the Athenians had brought some archers. Archers were not well thought of among the Greeks. You'll all remember in the story of the Trojan War the archer Paris who shoots Achilles in the heel; that's considered a cowardly way to fight. Nonetheless, the Athenians had some archers. One of their archers managed to get an arrow into the horse of the commander of the Persian force—a man named Megistias. As the horse fell, so did the commander.

He was very conspicuous: He was wearing a plate of gold mail that looked like fish scales—gilded fish scales—and he had a scarlet cloak. The Persians had been running up, launching their missiles and then turning to retreat, and then coming back again. It was on one of those turns that Megistias's horse was hit. The other Persians didn't see it. They had already turned and were in their tactical retreat.

The Athenians surged forward, surrounded him, and killed him. Then, as the Persians, realizing what had happened, came to try to retrieve the body of their fallen leader, the Athenians managed to get him back to their lines and treated his corpse as a first great trophy of what they hoped would be the victory to come.

This made Mardonius more determined than ever to attack, and finally Pausanias realized: "If I'm going to do this, I'm going to have to do some of the same kind of luring that Themistocles did, only not with words but with actions." So Pausanias ordered, first of all, his army to divide. The Athenians on the left wing went off on their own, and he and the main force seemed to retreat behind the little range of hills where they'd been into an area where they couldn't be easily seen.

Mardonius, assuming that this was a sign of them pulling back altogether, thought: "There's no better way to catch an army of hoplites than in the rear, because they've got no armor on their backs. You can always catch them once they're on the retreat." So he launched the attack of his cavalry. They divided in order—some of them to take the Athenians and some of them to go after the main body. But as they came up and over the hill, they made the horrifying discovery that it had all been a very tactical retreat.

They found the Spartans and their allies in good order, and although they hurled themselves against that phalanx wall (the cavalry), the horses were daunted by the bristling spears of the phalanx; they were unable to break the formation with the Athenians also. There was no way to get them off their little slope and to defeat them. Gradually, the Greek hoplites—forging their way down onto the terrain more favorable to the horses, the cavalry of the Greeks—won the day.

Mardonius was hurt by the fact that his second-in-command, a royal Persian named Artabazus, was not heart and soul in this, resented Mardonius and his command, and actually left the battlefield at a time when he could have still been effectively fighting for the Persian side. He headed north. What he told the Great King later was apparently: "I saved as much as I could from the disaster at Plataea for your future campaigns," and he was well rewarded by Xerxes. But the fact was Mardonius was killed, and the great stockade was stormed, and the Athenians were the ones who had the sort of siege craft to get over the wall and lead all the Greek troops inside.

They found the bronze manger where Mardonius's white stallion had taken its grain. They got all kinds of treasure and loot from Plataea, and they all met there in the stockade after the battle was over. Beforehand, they had said, "We're going to swear an oath before we go down to Plataea." The oath was that they would fight to the death and never surrender and that at the end they would swear to dedicate to the gods who had helped them win the battle one-tenth of all of the loot that they found.

A tenth of it was set aside to make statues and victory monuments dedicated to the gods. The rest was shared out among the states, paying them back for some of the tremendous costs that they'd suffered in this war. They had the satisfaction of knowing that the remnant of the Persian army was now headed north as fast as it could go, trying to get out of Greece and back to safety.

The war on land had been won. When the news spread across the Aegean, it reached the Greek fleet. Leotychidas, the Spartan admiral, had been lured, himself, across to the Asiatic side by the Greeks of Asia, who'd heard about the successes at Salamis, who now felt that the time for their liberation was at hand, and who believed that this little Greek fleet could be the force that would finally destroy the remnants of Xerxes's naval force—as we know, the remnants of his armed force were being destroyed at Plataea—and that if they could only get Leotychidas, the Spartans, and the few Athenians who were with that fleet over to Ionia, the war at sea could be finally conclusively won there also.

The place they came to after stopping first on the island of Delos (halfway across) was the island of Samos. They learned—these Greeks in their ships—that the Persians had gone to Mount Mycale. The coasts of that large, dark mountain came almost up and touched the island of Samos.

They were told by scouts that the whole Persian fleet—all that was left of it—was drawn up there on the coasts of Mount Mycale. There, we must leave them, at Samos, laying their plans to forge ahead and see if they can finally destroy the last remaining element of Xerxes's great invasion force there at Mycale.

They later said that their battle at Mycale happened on the very day of the Battle of Plataea, and that, in fact, the Spartan king Leotychidas had been inspired to say to his men that a great battle had been won in Greece and they could add to the glory and the victory by winning a great battle here in Asia. Circumstances proved him to be speaking the truth when it was later learned that the two great conflicts were fought on the same day.

We've been today on land. We will go back to sea next time and explore the Greek victory over the Persians in the naval battle, the strangest one ever fought, at Mycale.

Lecture Eleven
Commemorating the Great War

Scope: With the victory over the Persian fleet at Mount Mycale, the Athenians, commanded by the aristocratic Xanthippus, took control of the Hellespont; the bonfire created from the hulls of Persian ships became a beacon that announced to the Ionian Greeks their freedom from Persian control. Victorious, Xanthippus and his army returned home to rebuild Athens and join in the celebrations taking place throughout the Greek world. Various monuments—the Spartan burial mound at Thermopylae, the dedication of triremes at Sounion, the construction of new temples to the gods—served to commemorate the fallen soldiers and memorialize the tremendous military achievements of the Persian wars. In addition, a new art form—tragedy—received a great impetus from such playwrights as Phrynichus and Aeschylus, whose respective plays *The Phoenician Women* and *The Persians* were inspired by the horrors of Salamis. These various forms of commemoration ensured that knowledge of the Greek victories would pass down to subsequent generations.

Outline

I. The battle at Mycale was the strangest naval battle in history.
   A. Leotychidas gathered together small contingents with the initial idea of guarding the seaward approaches to Greece against the possibility of Xerxes's return.
   B. Ionian ambassadors arrived at Aegina, an island in the Saronic Gulf within sight of Athens, where the Greek fleet was now located, and begged the Greeks to send ships across the sea to help the Ionians finally win their freedom.
      1. At first, Leotychidas did not want to be drawn into the unknown, but he soon agreed to go halfway across the Aegean Sea to the island of Delos.
      2. With the pleas of additional Ionian envoys, Leotychidas agreed to continue to Samos.
   C. The Greek fleet arrived to discover that the Persians had fled and sought refuge on the southern side of Mount Mycale.

- **D.** Xanthippus, the leader of the Athenians, urged an initial attack, even though the Greek forces would be venturing into the unknown to land on Asiatic soil.
    1. Arriving at Mount Mycale, the fleet discovered that the Persian navy had pulled their ships up on the shore.
    2. The Greek fleet went along the shore beyond the Persian position and assembled a small hoplite army of about 600 marines.
    3. Xanthippus was determined that the Athenians should not wait for the Spartans and attacked the barrier of Persian archers.
    4. The Spartans, who had circled the slopes above the camp, came down upon the Persians and helped win the battle.
- **E.** Not wanting the remaining Persian vessels to fall back into the hands of Xerxes, the Greeks made an enormous bonfire from the wooden ships. The flames signaled to the Ionian Greeks that they were finally free of their Persian masters.

II. The victories at Plataea and Mount Mycale marked the end of the war that had begun with Xerxes's invasion. Celebration broke out across the Greek world.
- **A.** The Greeks gave offerings to the gods in thanks for their victory.
    1. The cables from Xerxes's bridge across the Hellespont were cut up and dedicated in Greek temples.
    2. Phoenician triremes were placed in the sanctuary of Poseidon at Sounion as a memorial.
    3. A great funeral mound was built for the fallen Spartans at Thermopylae.
- **B.** No dead in history were honored more than the dead of Marathon, Thermopylae, and Salamis.
- **C.** The Greeks also used the treasure looted from the Persian palisade after the Battle of Plataea.
    1. The Athenians built an *odeon* (music hall) modeled after Xerxes's field pavilion.
    2. The tithe set aside to honor the gods was used to create a memorial at Delphi.
    3. Bronze from captured Persian armor was melted down to create the Serpent Column: a column of three coiled serpents topped by a golden tripod.

- **D.** The Greeks dedicated new temples to Boreas, the god of the North Wind, who was considered responsible for destroying part of Xerxes's armada, and to Pan, the god of wild places, to whom the success at Marathon was attributed.

III. The most wondrous of all the postwar celebrations was created by the Athenian poet Aeschylus, who was also a veteran of the wars.
- **A.** Aeschylus was among the first to develop the genre of tragedy.
- **B.** His contemporary, Phrynichus, wrote plays based on current history, including one about the capture of Miletus shortly after the Persians put down the Ionian revolt.
- **C.** Sponsored by Themistocles, Phrynichus wrote *The Phoenician Women*, a tragedy about the Battle of Salamis.
    1. The Phoenician women are the wives of mariners who fought and died for Xerxes at the Battle of Salamis.
    2. In part, the play mourns those Phoenicians who had fought for Xerxes.
- **D.** Aeschylus's *Persians* is the oldest surviving drama and was presented in 472 B.C.
    1. The play's chorus consists of the noble Persian elders who stayed at home in Susa during the wars.
    2. The play's central character is Atossa, the widow of Darius and the mother of Xerxes.
    3. The messenger speech is one of the longest speeches in any Greek play, retelling the entire Battle of Salamis as envisioned through Persian eyes.

Recommended Reading:

Aeschylus, *Prometheus Bound and Other Plays.*

Rosenbloom, *Aeschylus: Persians.*

Questions to Consider:

1. What are some examples of postwar celebrations over the last 100 years? How are they different or similar to those undertaken by the Greeks after their victory against Persia?
2. Why do you think Aeschylus chose to write tragedies about the wars from the Persian point of view instead of the Greek point of view?

Lecture Eleven—Transcript
Commemorating the Great War

Welcome back. There has never in human history been a war that was celebrated as long, as grandly, and as permanently as the war between the Greeks and the Persians that started with Darius's attempts to get across the Aegean and punish Athens back in the 490s B.C. and ended a little over a decade later, when the Greek army, under that great Spartan regent and general Pausanias, beat the remnant of Xerxes's army at Plataea and when the Greek navy crossed the Aegean and did the same thing to the remnant of Xerxes's grand armada.

We're going to start with that naval engagement. I said last time that it was the strangest naval battle in history, and it was. As you remember, at the time that the Greek armed forces were gathering from all corners of mainland Greece to form an army almost 40,000 strong and push the Persians out of Greece in 479 B.C., a very small fleet had mustered at the island of Aegina—maybe only about 60 ships—but also under the command of a Spartan, the Spartan king Leotychidas. Leotychidas had gathered together small contingents—apparently with nothing more than the idea, initially, that they would spend that summer guarding the seaward approaches to Greece from the possibility that Xerxes might send the big fleet back across and might be bringing reinforcements to his army.

But there they were at Aegina, a little island in the Saronic Gulf within sight of Athens, and to them came ambassadors from Ionia and from the islands, begging them to send those ships across the sea. The Persians were now demoralized. This was the chance of the mainland Greeks, finally, to help the Ionians win their freedom from their Persian overlords.

At first, Leotychidas, who was a typical Spartan, didn't want to get far from home, didn't want to be drawn away into the unknown; he was adamant about not going. But at last, he agreed to go as far as halfway across the Aegean to the holy island of Delos, which we will be visiting again next time. There he sat. He had a whole lot of steersmen in his Greek ships who had not routinely been beyond Delos. It had been a generation since Greek ships could freely navigate in those waters controlled by the Persians, and so the remembrance and the knowledge of the different ports, and seaways, and reefs, and hazards had grown dim.

There's a wide-open stretch of sea after you get to the end of the Cycladic archipelago, and they just weren't sure what lay beyond. As Herodotus says, "It seemed to them as far to Samos on the other side as it was to the Pillars of Hercules"—a great exaggeration, but it gives some idea of the trepidation they felt.

Nonetheless, they continued to receive these envoys, and finally, Leotychidas agreed—"Well, we'll go at least to Samos"—to this island within sight of the Asiatic mainland that had been held by Greeks for so long.

Arriving there, they discovered that the Persians, at their approach, had fled. The mystique of the Greek navy is now so great that the Persians, even when they outnumber them greatly, will not stand and face them. Remember, the Persians have never been a naval people, and they no longer trust their Phoenicians and their other subjects who are providing their ships for the Persian fleet. So they flee to the mainland, and scouts tell Leotychidas and the other Greeks that they're just around the corner of that mountain you can see from Samos. They are hiding on the southern slopes of Mount Mycale.

So Leotychidas conferred with his other commanders, because from each Greek city there were very few, if any, Spartan ships. These are ships from Aegina itself, from Athens, from Corinth. He confers about what they should do.

The leader of the Athenians is a remarkable man named Xanthippus. To give him the true tribal flavor of his name, that means "Yellow Horse," and he's one of those Athenians that was mad about horseracing. He is also famous to us as the father of the greatest of all Athenian leaders, Pericles, who was at that time a boy of about 14 and still at home with his mother—watching the battles from the heights of Salamis but not actually getting involved in them yet.

His father, Xanthippus, is the leader of this little naval contingent of Athens. Most of the Athenians now, of course, are on the battlefield at Plataea waiting for the great conflict to happen there. The fleet has been stripped of a lot of its manpower to fight the Persians on land.

Xanthippus also urges that they go ahead and attack—take the initiative, even though it's really venturing into the unknown to land on Asiatic soil. So they load boarding bridges onto the ships—these portable wooden contraptions with which you could span the distance between you and an enemy ship once you've rammed them or come alongside. And your marines, of whom there were very few on each trireme—triremes were designed for speed in these battles—but your 10 marines could run across and hope to capture the other ship.

With all this gear, they rode out of Samos harbor, around the corner of Mount Mycale, and toward the Persian position. When they got there, expecting that the Persians were going to come out in their hordes of ships and surround them—instead, there were no ships to be seen. They realized eventually that the enemy navy was on shore. So great was the fear of the Persians of the Greek fleet that they had drawn their triremes up out of the water. These great, big, 120-foot-long vessels with their shallow drafts were now up on land—a fleet on the shore, surrounded by a little palisade. They'd cut down all the fruit trees in the area and created a barrier around the ships, and they had all of their men inside as if they were in a fort filled with ships.

Leotychidas told his pilot—his steersman—"Take my flagship in close to shore." He told his herald—the Spartan herald—to shout into the Greek camp: "O, you Ionians who are fighting with the Persians, we are going to attack. This is your chance to win your freedom. Betray your Persian masters and fight with us." The watchword of the day was either "Hera," the goddess whose temple stood on Samos, or what it actually says in the text of Herodotus, "Hebe," another goddess. Her name means "youth." Every day in Greek military tradition, there is a watchword—a special code word for the day—and that was the one for that day, the name of one of these goddesses.

So Leotychidas, for once having a kind of a non-Spartan strategic bit of cunning in mind, is sure that this will either bring the Ionians over to their side and really split the Persian forces or—much more likely because the Ionians, in fact, had been, in general, pretty loyal to the Persians—it will sow seeds of suspicion in the Persian admirals' minds, and they won't trust the Ionians. That is what happened. The Ionians were either disarmed immediately by the Persians under suspicion that they were going to fight for the enemy or they were sent off out of the camp to guard mountain passes and to keep them out of the battle altogether.

The Greek fleet went along the shore to a position well beyond where the Persians had their ships, and they came to shore. This is a difficult maneuver for triremes. They've got to reverse themselves, because you can't run up on the beach ram-first or you'll break the keel of the ship, as well as hurting the ram. You've got to reverse; there's a smooth, up-curving stern to each ship, with the steering oars dropping into the water. The pilots then have to turn and look over their shoulders as the crews push the oars in reverse and reverse those ships into the beach. As soon as they had their upright sterns—their upward-curving sterns—hanging over the sand, the marines drop off onto the shore.

You can always make a little army out of the marines—10 strong, 14 strong—from any Greek fleet by getting them onshore and assembling them all together. So they had probably about 600 or a few more of their marines now standing onshore as hoplites, shield to shield, forming this little army.

It is an absolutely obligatory thing in Greek military tradition that the post of honor is the right wing. Well, the right wing, since they were facing back west toward the Persian palisade, the right wing going to the Spartans is inland and away from the water's edge, and the beach was very narrow. This meant that the Athenians—who were either on the center or the left— were on the open sand and were able to march right along toward the Persians. As they advanced toward the Persians, these Spartans got into rough terrain, were swallowed up in a ravine, and disappeared, and the rest of the Greeks were left alone on the beach, facing this barrage of Persian arrows from the stockade. The Persians had, in fact, come out and formed a little wicker-shield barrier and were shooting from behind it.

This is where Xanthippus took the lead. He was determined that the Athenians should not wait for the Spartans. They had, after all, faced these same Persians at Marathon about 11 years earlier, and they had charged them then, and he urged his fellow Greeks to pass the word along the line: "We're going to charge them now." The best way to get out of the range of a barrage of arrows is to close in quickly so that they can't shoot at you anymore, and that's what they did.

They ran at those wicker shields, and they broke through them. The Persians panicked and ran, and they climbed back over the barricade of hastily cut fruit-tree logs to get back in with the ships, but the Athenians were on their heels, burst into the enclosure, and fought it out hand-to-hand. As the whole battle hung in the balance, suddenly—like the cavalry arriving on the white horses—the Spartans arrived. They had, in fact, circled around the upper slopes, came down from above onto the enclosure, and helped win the battle.

A few of the Persians escaped to go back to Sardis, where Xerxes was, and carry him word of this final disaster to his fleet. The Greeks stripped the ships of their bronze rams and their treasure chests, because all fleets had to carry war chests with them to pay for the food for the crews, and bribe cities to open their gates, and so on. Once they'd done that, they looked at the ships, and they didn't have enough men to man them, and the last thing they wanted was that they would ever fall back into the hands of Xerxes.

So at the day's end, they lit the world's biggest bonfire, putting all of those ships, all that timber and pitch, to the torch. The resulting fire must have been visible 30 miles away to the south at Miletus. That was the beacon that told the Ionian Greeks: "You are free at last of your Persian masters."

It was shortly after that that the heralds arrived from Greece, saying, "On Greek soil also, the Persians have been beaten," and gave Leotychidas the report of Pausanias's great victory at Plataea. This was the end of the Persian wars. The only tailpiece was that Xanthippus the Athenian and the Ionians decided to go north to the Hellespont where the bridges had been— those pontoon bridges of boats and cables that Xerxes had created so he could march with his forces into Greece a year and a half earlier. They laid siege to the great fortress city of Sestos near the mouth of the Hellespont, on the other side from Troy, and they captured it—and inside the fortress, they found the great coils of the papyrus cables. They took those into their triremes and carried them back to Greece as trophies.

Now an incredible celebration broke out in many forms and many places all over the Greek world. The first thing to do was to give offerings to the gods in thanks for their victory, so they took the cables, cut them up in sections, and dedicated them in their temples—the Athenians did—so that those who visited them in ages to come would see these amazing sections of the cables of Xerxes's bridge and be reminded that, yes, this man was master of the world, but we Athenians helped to defeat him.

They took actual Phoenician triremes from the Persian fleet that fought at Salamis—intact ships—and hauled them up on land, and put them in the sanctuary of Poseidon at Sounion in Attic territory—that famous cape, crowned with its Doric temple of Poseidon—and then off to the Isthmus of Corinth—also sacred to Poseidon—where the Hellenic League had met, and they dedicated one there in the sanctuary, again, to be a memorial for generations yet unborn of this tremendous achievement.

They went back to Thermopylae, where no one had been since the disaster in August of 480 B.C. when Leonidas and his Three Hundred were overwhelmed by the Persians pushing their way through the pass at Thermopylae. They collected the bodies of the fallen Spartans, and they built a great funeral pyre and cremated them. They discovered, apparently, among the ashes and the bones of the cremated soldiers, that in a few cases—half a dozen or so—the Persian arrowheads and spear points that killed them were still in the remains and were now mixed up with the ashes.

In the 1930s, when the great Greek archaeologist Spiridon Marinatos excavated the Spartan funeral mound at Thermopylae, he found those Persian arrows interred along with the remains of the fallen Spartan heroes.

On the top of that funeral mound at Thermopylae they erected a lion, that emblem of Sparta that was also the animal whose name was enshrined in the name of the king who fell there—Leonidas, the lion's son. The greatest poets in Greece were asked to write epitaphs for the fallen. The most famous one of all was the couplet—the pair of lines does not rhyme in the original Greek, but they said of the Spartans who fell at Thermopylae: "Go tell the Spartans, passerby,/That here, at their commands, we lie."

It's said to be by Simonides. You'll often read that he was the most famous poet of the time. We don't actually have that ascription in the ancient sources, but it could be his work. Other poets were set to work commemorating people like the Corinthians who fought in the Battle of Salamis, and a beautiful turn of phrase was found for them. Their *cenotaph*—their empty memorial that looked like a tomb—was built overlooking the battle site on the island of Salamis. The bones of the men who died had actually been sent back to Corinth. But there was a lovely little poem on their tomb saying that these men had saved Greece when the affairs of Greece stood upon a razor's edge. That was how the Greeks saw it.

It was one of those moments in history where things could have gone either way at a touch of the slightest chance event, and somehow, because of all this patriotism and all this surge of willingness to risk one's life to fight the Persians, these people had triumphed. No dead in history were more honored than the dead of Marathon, the dead of Thermopylae, and the dead of Salamis.

You'll remember that after the Battle of Plataea, Pausanias, the Spartan regent, had had them collect all of the loot, all the booty, from the Persian camp. This included some interesting things. I mentioned the bronze manger out of which the Persian general Mardonius's horse—a big white stallion—had been fed. He ate his oats and hay out of a bronze manger. The people of Tegea, a little hoplite power from the Peloponnese, they got that as their trophy. The Athenians got the great, big field pavilion—the huge tent that Xerxes had left behind with Mardonius.

They took it back to Athens, and when they finally built an *odeon*—a music hall (*odeon* means "a place to hear things")—they used Xerxes's field pavilion translated into stone as the model for their new *odeon* to commemorate, again, the victory at Plataea. All of the loot, having been put together, a tenth of it—a tithe—had to be set aside for the gods, who had to be thanked for giving the Greeks the victory.

They took that tenth aside, they melted a lot of it down, and they created a remarkable memorial at Delphi, the site of the Delphic Oracle that had predicted the wooden walls would save Athens and had told the Greeks to pray to the winds—the Delphic Oracle that seemed so involved in so much. They took the bronze from all the captured Persian helmets and armor, they melted it down, and they created a column that was actually the bodies of three great serpents coiled together and rising up in the air, and then on top of the column was set a golden tripod.

On the coils of the column, under the rubric "These fought for Greece," were the names of the 31 cities and islands who had actually joined the freedom fighters, the Hellenic League meeting at the isthmus, and who had won that incredible victory. The 31st name had been added afterwards. It was the little, tiny island of Tenos out in the Aegean, and after they'd already inscribed the column, the people of Tenos, or maybe their friends in Athens, reminded the Spartans (who had directed the creation of the Serpent Column): "You need to put Tenos on there, too."

On the night before the Battle of Salamis, when the Persian armada was flowing in its triple line into the straits by moonlight and we Greeks were sitting in darkness on the other side of the channel on the island of Salamis—not sure whether there would be a battle the next day or not, not sure whether Themistocles's ruse of sending a messenger with a false message to Xerxes to bring them into the straits would work—there appeared out of the darkness one ship, one trireme, from the island of Tenos, that had learned about the plan. They had been part of Xerxes's fleet but realized that they might be joining the losing side and yet had broken ranks and had slipped away in the darkness. They came to us and gave us the message that assured us that when the Sun came up the next morning, we would see the Persians in the straits, and we would be ready for a fight. They need to be on this column, too. So Tenos is the last of those 31 names.

There were also new temples to new gods, especially at Athens. The Athenians declared Boreas, the North Wind, a god because he had come down out of the northern mountains, struck the sea, and destroyed so many

Persian ships—thus bringing down the numbers of Xerxes's grand fleet. A god that had been around for a long time but was never worshiped at Athens was the god Pan, whose name actually is in Greek "everything."

Pan is the god of wild places. When Phidippides, that Athenian runner, ran from Athens to Sparta before the Battle of Marathon, running day and night to carry the word that the Persians had landed and the Athenians needed help from their Spartan allies—help that they did not receive—as he ran back, no doubt kind of weakened from loss of sleep and the incredible rigors of running there and back in consecutive days, he had a vision. He saw the god Pan stop him over one of the mountain passes and say, "Phidippides, ask the Athenians why they do not pay me tribute and worship me. If they will pay me honors, I will help them beat the Persians."

The Athenians attributed their success at Marathon partly to Pan. His name is the root of our word *panic*, which is also a Greek word. The idea is that Pan, the god of wild places, will infect a mass of people with irrational fear. They will scatter in flight. That's what happened with the Persians at Marathon. So in thanks to Pan, a temple to him and a cult of Pan were created in Athens.

The most wondrous of all of the celebrations of the Persian wars was created eight years after the Battle of Salamis by a man who fought in that battle and who also fought at Marathon: the Athenian poet Aeschylus.

We know that one of the things we owe to Athens is the theater—drama, tragedy, and comedy. In the form that we know, those great forms of literature and cultural creativity—they are Athenian inventions, and Aeschylus is the man who really got tragedy started. He had a contemporary named Phrynichus who had had the idea of taking current history and turning it into plays. You'll remember back in the Ionian revolt, after the Battle of Lade at sea, when the Persian fleet managed to defeat the Ionians, they then mopped up on land by recapturing the rebellious Ionian cities. The greatest of these was Miletus.

Miletus was the city that was closest to the heart of the Athenians and was, in fact, in a sense, a colony from Athens. It was the capture of Miletus by the Persians that Phrynichus made the subject of a play shortly after the Persians put down the Ionian revolt and took those cities back into their empire. The Athenians wept all the way through the play as they saw the enactment of this recent history and were so angry at the playwright for making them cry that they fined him a huge amount of money.

Nothing daunted and after the great success at Salamis, he was sponsored by Themistocles—who was the Athenian commander at the time and took credit for the victory at Salamis—in putting on a new tragedy called *The Phoenician Women*, which was all about the battle at Salamis. These ancient Greek tragedies are often named for what their chorus was dressed up as. There are one, two, or three actors who will play the parts of the solo performers—the individuals—but there's always a chorus, which is a mass of people who sing, and who dance, and who really provide the show and the spectacle for the dramatic presentation. Their name, what they are, is often given as the name of the play.

The Phoenician women—who are they? They are the wives of the Phoenician mariners who fought at Salamis and who died in such huge numbers. So it was a mourning play—a play of grief on the part of these Phoenicians who had fought for Xerxes at Salamis. Although nothing of the play survives, we know that. We also know how it began. You're at the court in Susa waiting for news of Xerxes and his great fleet and his great army. It's the year 480 B.C., and there's a eunuch, a sort of subsidiary actor, with pillows, going around and placing them for the Persian counselors who are going to come in and get the news of the Battle of Salamis.

Themistocles sponsored that one. It was traditional in Athens that the dramas were competitions in honor of the great god Dionysus, and the leading citizens of Athens—the richest men—would take it in turns to be sponsors of these plays, put them on for the people's entertainment, but also for their education and their spiritual enrichment.

Young Pericles, the son of Xanthippus who had now come to manhood—his father had died shortly after the great successes at Mycale and Sestos—is now head of his household, owner of one of the great fortunes in the city of Athens. He takes money from the family coffers, even though he's only in his early 20s, and he works with this great poetic genius Aeschylus on a play that was a little like Phrynichus's *Phoenician Women* but far grander.

That play has survived—copies of it have survived. It's the oldest drama we know of still surviving in the world. It was presented in the year 472 B.C., sponsored by Pericles and written, and produced, and probably acted by Aeschylus. It had that same idea of taking you to the Persian court, but it's called *The Persians* because the chorus are the gorgeously clad elders of Persia—the princes and aristocrats who stayed home in Susa. The chief character is the queen mother, Atossa, the widow of King Darius and the mother of King Xerxes, who has all of a mother's anxiety and forebodings about her son.

Aeschylus started his play with the elders gathering at the court for yet another day of waiting for news of Xerxes and his expedition. They have every reason to be confident. They keep reciting those lists of the big battalions that were sent against Greece and saying, "How could they not succeed?" But they have forebodings, and when the queen comes in, she and the elders feed off each other's sense of dread. She recounts to them a terrifying dream she had where Xerxes is a charioteer and his two horses are Asia and Greece. Asia moves smoothly and proudly through its paces, whereas Greece is a rebellious horse—kicking and, ultimately, throwing the young charioteer out of the chariot and injuring him there on the ground.

She's terrified by this, and she asks for the elders to interpret her dream for her, but they, instead, bid her to call up the ghost of her dead husband, Darius, the earlier king, and ask him. So Darius is conjured up out of the stage—this is the second actor—and he hears all of what's going on. He's appalled at what Xerxes has done. They tell him about the bridge of boats across the Hellespont. He thinks, "What madness was this?" So they are left with even more terror than they felt before, and sure enough, hard on the heels of the apparition of King Darius comes the messenger from having run or ridden—that last messenger in the line who has come along the Royal Road—with the reports of the Battle of Salamis.

I shouldn't say the last messenger in the line—this is an exceptional case in Aeschylus's mind. This is a man who saw Salamis, saw the defeat of the Persians in the straits, and he has come now, himself, to give the word to Queen Atossa and the elders at home.

This is the longest speech in the play, and it's one of the longest speeches in any Greek play because it's the entire Battle of Salamis, envisioned from the Persian side and seen through Persian eyes. I've had the good luck to see *The Persians* performed at Loyola Marymount by students in California, and I've seen it performed in New York City by the national theater company of Greece. It's often described by scholars as a jingoistic play—a sort of rattling the standard and cheering on the part of the Athenians and rubbing it in the noses of the Persians that they lost. I went to see it in California with Larry Tritle, who is a great classicist and a Vietnam veteran, and he said to me, "Nobody who has ever been in combat thinks *The Persians* is a play that is glorying over the enemy. Instead, you are seeing the tragedy that befalls anybody who falls into the world of war."

There are great moments in *The Persians* where one feels that great sympathy that Aristotle said tragedy should evoke—the sense of catharsis and identification, and you feel it for the Persians. I certainly felt it in both of the productions that I saw once I was there and experiencing it not as a scholarly text on a page but as a theatrical drama on stage.

One of the great moments, of course, in the messenger speech is the charge of the Greeks. The messenger is describing the demon that came out of the night and gave Xerxes the false information that lured him into the straits. He then goes on to the movement of Xerxes's fleet into the straits by night, and then, with the breaking of day—"the horses of dawn leap into the sky"—they hear the trumpet, and they hear the singing of the Greeks, the war cry. They realize that they have been fooled, and then they hear the battle cry of the Greeks. It's an extraordinary moment, and the lines of the battle cry are: "Go sons of Greece; free your fatherland; free your children, wives, tombs of your forefathers, shrines of your ancestral gods. Fight now for all"—some of the most patriotic lines and images ever conceived and, probably, since Aeschylus was there, carrying for us—2,500 years later—the authentic battle cry that sounded over the waters at Salamis.

Earlier on, Aeschylus took the chance of having an exchange between the queen and the elders which tried to show how the Persians might look at Athens. I'd like to end with this. They are there on the stage, and the queen is questioning the elders about what they know about this distant city, this tiny place that has dared to challenge the great Persian Empire.

Atossa: Tell me, where does Athens lie?

Chorus: Far westward, where the sun god sinks his fainting fires.

Atossa: Why should my son yearn to make this town his prey?

Chorus: Athens once conquered, he is master of all Greece.

Atossa: Have they such a rich supply of fighting men?

Chorus: They have; soldiers who once struck Persian arms a fearful blow [a reference to Marathon].

Atossa: Besides their men, have they good store of wealth at home?

Chorus:	They have a spring of silver in the earth. [That's a reference to the discovery of the silver that built the ships that fought at Salamis.]
Atossa:	Are they skilled in archery?
Chorus:	No, not at all. They carry stout shields; they fight hand to hand with spears.
Atossa:	Who shepherds them? What master do their ranks obey?
Chorus:	Master? They are not called servants to any man.

And if that line did not get a cheer in the theater of Dionysus in Athens when it was premiered in 472 B.C., I would truly be amazed. There you have, in dramatic form, the Greeks' own view of what set them apart from the Persians. It was their love of freedom, it was their love of liberty and independence, that made them supermen in that hour, that enabled them to defy the forces of history and turn what seemed like an inevitable defeat into the most shining and glorious victory that the Greeks would ever know.

Lecture Twelve
Campaigns of the Delian League

Scope: Impressed by the honorable conduct of Aristides the Just, the Ionians formally allied themselves with Athens and vowed to maintain everlasting enmity with Persia. Under the leadership of Cimon, the Delian League began its operations with seasonal campaigns against Persian positions, proving wildly successful and ultimately enrolling some 150 cities and islands as members. The league's campaigns reached a high point in 466 B.C., when the Greeks squelched Persian hopes for recovery by defeating a large army and fleet at the Eurymedon River. Following the Battle of Salamis, the Ionian Greeks, those from Asia and the Aegean Islands, saw a chance to ensure their permanent freedom from the Persians with the sworn protection of the mainland Greeks. Rebuffed in this appeal by the Spartans, the Ionians turned to the Athenians, led by Aristides the Just, to serve as their hegemon. In 478 B.C., the Athenians and Ionians met on the island of Delos and created the Delian League. Under the leadership of Cimon, the league began its operations with seasonal campaigns against Persian positions, liberating Greek cities that remained in Persian hands and adding to its own treasury with captured booty. The campaigns of the league reached a high point in 466 B.C., when the Greeks squelched Persian hopes for recovery by defeating a large army and fleet at the Eurymedon River.

Outline

I. The fly in the ointment of Greek and Persian relations was the Ionian Greeks, who now saw a chance to ensure their permanent freedom from the Great King if only they could receive the sworn protection of the mainland Greeks.

  A. The Spartan king Leotychidas suggested that the Ionian Greeks move to the mainland and settle in cities such as Thebes that would be easier to defend.

  B. The Athenians sprang to the Ionian Greeks' defense, arguing that every effort should be made to allow these Greeks to stay in their traditional homelands.

- **C.** At Byzantium, the Ionians appealed to the Athenians, led by Aristides the Just, to serve as their "hegemon" ("war leader"). Knowing this role would elevate Athens to a position of equality with Sparta, Aristides agreed.

II. In 478 B.C., the Ionian Greeks and Athenians met at the island of Delos and created the Delian League, composed of the Athenians and their allies (those cities and islands that initially wanted protection from Athens against reconquest by the Persians).

- **A.** After Athens elevated itself to a first-rank naval power in the Greek world, a surge of Ionian interest grew in the idea of Athens as a leader.
- **B.** The reunion of distant Ionian clans in Asia Minor and in Athens allowed the Ionian Greeks to share a sense of common ancestry and, with the formation of the Delian League, a sense of common purpose.
- **C.** The league's mission was to punish Persia perpetually for daring to invade Greece, for burning the temples at Athens, and for enslaving the Ionian Greeks.
- **D.** To pay for their war, the league needed contributions from all its allies in the form of money, ships, or men. Many allies initially sent ships and men because they wanted to take an active part in the ongoing war against Persia.
- **E.** At the time of its creation, the Delian League did not include all of the eastern Greek cities, many of which were still in Persian hands. The liberation of these cities was part of the league's ongoing campaigns.
- **F.** Aristides the Just did not go on to lead the Delian League; instead, Cimon took his place. Meanwhile, Themistocles—who wanted to regain a position of prominence—took charge at home in Athens.
    1. He helped establish a new city at Piraeus and re-walled the city of Athens.
    2. He got rich through misappropriated funds, embezzlement, and bribes.
    3. Exiled from Athens, he surrendered to the Persian king Artaxerxes, who gave him three cities on the coast of Asia Minor to govern.

III. As Themistocles's star sank, Cimon, the son of Miltiades, emerged as a leader.

A. Cimon took charge in the very first campaigning season of the Delian League as its new general.
  1. The league's fleet sailed north to the river Strymon and attacked the town of Eion, still held by the Persians.
  2. Cimon took over the area's mining district as the property of Athens; colonists were sent out to create new communities there.

B. Cimon desired a religious sanction for the Athenian navy and the Delian League; thus, he took steps to appropriate the divine hero Theseus as patron of the navy.
  1. Cimon managed to find an oracle that advised him to recover the bones of Theseus from the island of Skyros.
  2. Cimon used this mission as a pretext to attack the island, take it over, and add it to the Delian League.
  3. When the recovered bones were taken to Athens, the citizens built a new temple to Theseus.

C. Cimon spent years "navalizing" all levels of Athenian society.
  1. Rich men in Athens took turns serving as captains of triremes.
  2. The lower classes pulled the oars of the triremes.

D. When he learned about Persian plans to repeat the invasion of 480 B.C. in response to continued harassment by Delian League allies, Cimon sent a fleet of 200 triremes to the city of Cnidus in southwestern Asia Minor.
  1. The league took the Persians by surprise at the Eurymedon River.
  2. Cimon captured the Persian navy and the Persian army on the same day—a double victory the likes of which had never been seen.
  3. This string of victories lent tremendous luster to Cimon's name and was the climax of his career.

Recommended Reading:

Bengtson, *The Greeks and the Persians: From the Sixth to the Fourth Centuries.*

Blamire, *Plutarch: Life of Kimon.*

Questions to Consider:

1. Why was religious sanction so important to Cimon's leadership of the Delian League?

2. Do you think, in some way, that this mission only perpetuated a conflict that could have ended after the victory at Mount Mycale? Why or why not?

Lecture Twelve—Transcript
Campaigns of the Delian League

Welcome back. We must return now to the years of fighting, the year 479 B.C., that year after Salamis when the Greeks finished their mopping-up operations on land and sea against the Persians, and when, by all rights, the great war should have been over, since Xerxes showed no signs of marshaling his vast forces again for another attempt to conquer Greece.

But the fly in the ointment of peace and stability were these Ionian Greeks—these Greeks of Asia and the Aegean Islands. They saw now a chance to ensure their permanent freedom from the Great King if only they could get the sworn protection of the mainland Greeks. Having been rebuffed by the Spartans initially at Mycale—Leotychidas telling them that they lived too far away to be protected by the Spartans; they should, in fact, pick up and move to Greece. The Spartan plan was to clear out some of the Medizing cities, like Thebes, and turn their territories over to these Ionian Greeks—just so they wouldn't be so far away and difficult to defend.

The Ionians did not like that idea, and Xanthippus the Athenian sprang to their defense and said it was wrong that they should have to abandon their cities; the war had been partly fought for their freedom. Every effort should be made so that they could stay where they belonged—their traditional homelands.

The Athenians began to shine as the great hope of the Ionians, and in the following year, 478 B.C., Aristides the Just—the Athenian hero who had led the Athenian troops at Plataea—came out with a fleet this time. He was at Byzantium. The Spartans are still very concerned that they may be losing their role as the great leaders of all the Greeks—they're a bit like Aesop's "Dog in the Manger"; they don't particularly want to be tied to distant campaigns, but they darn well don't want anyone else to have the prestige of being leaders in their place, least of all the Athenians. They have sent out Pausanias the regent, the man who masterminded the Greek victory at Plataea over Mardonius's army.

Away from Sparta, Pausanias goes bad. He is involved in corruption scandals; he's brutally tyrannical to the other allies—very high-handed and acting the part of almost an oriental potentate and not to be trusted. He scorns them—he does not let them into his confidence. Finally, there's an open break with the Spartans, and the Ionians go to Aristides the Just, who is there with the Athenian contingent of ships at Byzantium, and virtually force themselves on him as allies. They ask Athens to be to them what Sparta has been to the traditional Peloponnesian League and the Hellenic League that fought the Persians and met at the Isthmus of Corinth. They ask Athens to be what the Greeks called their "hegemon"—their war leader.

This will elevate Athens, which will now have a league of its own—to borrow our American phrase—elevate Athens to a position of equality with Sparta. Aristides, whose own incorruptibility of character, whose own reputation, whose own fairness and openness has, in part, brought the Ionians over to the Athenian side—he agrees.

So they go to the island of Delos. They meet there, and they create a new league that we in modern times call the Delian League, but they never called it that in ancient times. It was always the Athenians and their allies. Who were the allies? The cities and islands that initially wanted protection from reconquest by the Persians and who turned to Athens for help.

Athens itself had been elevated (just as Themistocles hoped it would be) from that second-class rank that it had occupied before the Persian wars—a city with no distinguished monuments, or creative artists, or philosophers, or geniuses of any kind—it had been elevated to a sort of first-rank position in the Greek world, thanks to its energy and thanks to its willingness to take risk. And now the payoff seemed to be this wonderful surge of interest in Athens as a leader on the part of these Ionians.

So Aristides met with the representatives of these cities and islands. They met on Delos, and they picked Delos because it was a traditional family reunion place of all the Ionian peoples. That included Athens on the west side of the Aegean, and all those cities on the Asiatic mainland, and the islands on the east side. They had traditionally, for centuries, every year, in earliest spring when the sea lanes opened again for navigation, these Ionians would meet on the island of Delos. They would celebrate their ancestral god Apollo, who was believed to be the father of the entire Ionian race of Greeks through his son Ion.

There's a wonderful picture of these Ionian family reunions on Delos. It comes to us from a hymn that the ancients said was written by Homer. Modern scholars think it was written by a follower of Homer. It's a hymn to Apollo, and I want to share with you a little passage from this, where this early poet—he's probably writing in the 7th century B.C.—is describing what it's like to be on Delos, when to this barren island, with its temple to Apollo and its sacred palm tree (it's supposed to be the island where Apollo and his sister Artemis were actually born), there suddenly come, as the sea lanes open and the winter is past, all these ships from East and West bearing the Ionians to the great festival.

> You, Apollo, you rejoice above everything else in your heart for Delos, where Ionians in their trailing robes gather with their children and their wives. They remember you; they gladden you with contests of boxing, singing, and dancing.

It's a very strange part of the Greek religious ethos that one way to worship the gods is to have a race or hold a competition, but this was part of that Homeric world also.

> Anyone who came upon this gathering of Ionians would liken them to immortal gods. He would see the happiness of them all, and he would delight at the sight of the men, the women with their beautiful girdles, the swift ships and the many possessions.

This lovely snapshot of an Ionian reunion was something that was held in the hearts of all these people as a beautiful annual ceremony that brought together distant clans, allowed them to share their feeling of common ancestry, and now, with the Delian League founded on Delos, a sense of common purpose.

What was the mission stated for this league, founded in the year 478 B.C.? The mission was to punish Persia perpetually for having dared to invade Greece and burn the temples at Athens—for having dared to enslave the Ionians of Asia. Persia would be a target forever. This was a war that would never end—a war of reprisal. They knew that they would collect booty and loot from that war and that they would have a treasury on the island of Delos, under the guardianship of the god Apollo. There, that treasure would be kept.

They knew that it would cost money to run the war, and this is a great difference between naval wars and hoplite infantry wars. On land, every hoplite is a man of property: He owns his own armor; he brings his own food for the campaign. It costs a city virtually nothing to put on a hoplite war. Navies are completely different. There is tremendous investment in the ships, and there's an even bigger ongoing cost of keeping the ships maintained.

There's a wretched little mollusk called the "teredo"—the teredo worm or "ship worm" we call them in English, but it's not really a worm—that in warm waters, like the Mediterranean, will burrow into the timber of ships and riddle them with holes, and after a very short time, they become unseaworthy unless they are very carefully maintained, cared for, drawn up out of the water, and loose or teredo-ridden planks pulled out and replaced by other planks. This costs money.

You also have to train your crews, and the navy can't be suddenly pulled together in the same way that the trumpeter standing in the marketplace can pull together a hoplite phalanx. There are maneuvers to practice, as we saw at Lade with that Phokaian leader Dionysius. You can't just stand in the line, be brave, and win a battle. So for all these reasons, they needed contributions from the allies, and the allies were all happy to contribute. They, after all, had been paying tribute to Persia, and Aristides commanded so much of their admiration that they agreed that he would set the tribute levels for every ally.

He basically took the Persian standard as his own, but he said, "You can pay your tribute in money, in ships, or in men." These are the three ways, and many of them initially sent contributions of ships and men. They wanted to take part actively in this ongoing war against Persia.

At the time that it began, the Delian League did not include all of the Greek cities of the East. Many of them were still in Persian hands, and it was going to be part of the ongoing campaigns, the campaigns every year, to liberate those cities. Nonetheless, a lot of the campaigns just looked like buccaneering pirate raids, where this amphibious expedition would set out in their ships, they'd come to an unsuspecting shore held by the Persians, spill off the ships onto the land, gather up all the loot that they could—everything from cattle to family treasures—and haul them off back to Delos, distribute them among the allies who had taken part, and add the surplus to the treasury on Delos.

Aristides did not himself go on to lead the league. I always think of him as sort of a Moses-like figure who had this vision of a unified Ionian world led by Athens but did not pass over into it as leader. Instead, the leadership was up for grabs. One of the men who's still around in Athens and wants to get back into a position of prominence is that great leader Themistocles, who was the one who originally had the idea of using the silver from the silver strike in about 483 B.C. to build the ships. He'd always had a naval policy. Even before the Battle of Marathon, he had told the Athenians they should turn to the sea—that line of his that I quoted before and that he quoted more than once. It was sort of his motto: "I do not know how to play a lyre or tune a harp, but I know how to make a small city great." That "knowing how" was naval power—that was what could make a city great.

Back in 493 B.C., when he was the archon—the chief magistrate of Athens—he'd used his prominence and his influence to get the Athenians to start to fortify and develop a promontory 4.5 miles from Athens (Athens is a slightly inland city), a promontory stretching out into the sea, called the Piraeus, which had three natural harbors. It was very rocky and waterless, so they hadn't built a city there previously, but he got them to build some walls. They'd given up after Marathon. Piraeus was sitting there as a half-finished fortification at the time that Xerxes came with his invasion, but now Themistocles got them back in the groove.

They finished the walls of Piraeus, and they hired the world's first-known city planner—a strange fellow named Hippodamus of Miletus, who reminds me very much of Frank Lloyd Wright. He dressed in an unusual way; he had wild and outlandish theories about relative Pythagorean ratios between the widths of alleys and side streets and main boulevards, how big the blocks should be. He believed that cities should be laid out on a grid—rationally, scientifically.

There were a lot of ancient people who thought this was a terrible way to lay out a city because it meant that if enemies got inside your walls, they could find their way around without getting lost. They preferred that old, winding, twisting, organic series of circular alleys that remind us of sort of a bazaar in a Middle Eastern city today, where only the locals knew how to get anywhere and, if invaders came in, they would be easily lost and rounded up again.

Nonetheless, Hippodamus believed in this—he believed in using the winds that prevailed in the area so that they would blow through the streets if the streets were oriented in the correct direction to the prevailing winds and bring fresh air; that the sunshine and its slanting rays in winter or summer would somehow be harnessed in order to keep the houses as cool as possible in summer and as warm as possible in winter. He was a great thinker, a very inspiring fellow, and he laid out a new city at Piraeus that developed in time to almost be a rival of Athens itself.

So Piraeus is now the headquarters of the Athenian fleet, thanks to Themistocles, and Themistocles went on with some other projects. He got Athens re-walled in spite of a Spartan opposition. He used his stratagems for that. He is, in general, trying to put himself forward again as the great leader, the great visionary of Athens. But he has too many enemies—he has rubbed too many people the wrong way. He doesn't have any political friends at all. He is outside the circle of Athenian old aristocratic families, and his reputation is tarnished.

He came into this whole Persian war period a man of very modest means, and he wanted to use the wars to get rich. He did so through some misappropriation of funds, some embezzlements, and some taking of bribes from foreigners. We have a long poem by one angry person who paid Themistocles a bribe so that he would be reinstated in his city after the Persian wars, and Themistocles didn't follow through, although he pocketed the money. So we get this very angry rant about how terrible Themistocles is.

Lots of people agreed with that, and he was eventually exiled from Athens, a price was put on his head, and he was declared a criminal for various crimes—probably some of them true and some of them trumped-up charges. Athens now had a very long arm. It could reach anywhere in the Greek world. He couldn't hide out with his friends in other cities. He eventually—irony of ironies—turned to the only safe place he could find: Persia.

He went to the coast of Asia Minor, evading Athenian and Delian League squadrons on the way, and surrendered himself to Xerxes. He spent a year on the coast learning Persian so that he could do his own diplomacy without interpreters. Then, by the time he went up to the court, it appears possible that Xerxes had died and his son Artaxerxes had taken over. At any rate, the Great King, whether Xerxes or his son, received Themistocles and probably regarded Themistocles as a great trophy to have on his side now, recognized him as a man of capabilities, and gave him three cities on the coast of Asia Minor—three Greek cities—that he would govern: Magnesia on the Meander, Myous, and Lampsacus up on the Hellespont. So he now has a little fiefdom of his own, and he's behaving like a Persian provincial governor for the rest of his life.

He was very popular in those cities, and they raised monuments to him in their marketplaces and put his image on their coins long after his death. But that was the sad end of the man who saved Greece through his cunning.

It's a striking thing to remember that when Themistocles was a boy, his father, Neocles, took him walking along the shore at Athens and pointed out the rotting hulks of some of the city's old triremes from the days before the big shipbuilding effort, abandoned there on the coast, and Neocles said to his son Themistocles: "Don't go into politics. You see how the Athenians treat their leaders when they have no further use for them."

But Themistocles paid no attention, and it was his father who turned out to have some insights into how democracies behave when their leaders, no matter what services they had performed, have lost the gloss of newness and current popularity—they are quickly cast aside. Who emerged as Themistocles's star was in the decline? The son of the hero of Marathon—that general Miltiades who had led the run of a mile across the plain of Marathon that defeated the Persian expeditionary force of 490 B.C.

His son's name was Cimon—sometimes spelled in the Latin way—C-I-M-O-N; in the Greek with a *kappa*—K-I-M-O-N. Cimon was everything Themistocles was not. He was born so rich that he was able to be the most generous and open-handed man in all of Athens. He had a fine crop of ruddy hair and a handsome, open-hearted manner; popular with everyone; friends everywhere—all the accomplishments of a perfect gentleman because he'd been brought up as a true aristocrat in his father's house. He'd been brought up not at Athens but up on the Hellespont in the family fiefdom on the Gallipoli Peninsula opposite Troy, back before the Persian wars.

Not only did he have that outside Athens experience, that Asiatic experience, growing up—looking across the Hellespont to Asia and talking to people from there—his mother was a Thracian princess. Miltiades, spending so many years from Athens, had met the king of Thrace and had fallen in love with the king's daughter and married her, and Cimon was the son of that union. So he's not a typical Athenian at all. He's a very charismatic, very glamorous sort of figure with a tremendous drive for naval affairs and military matters.

He emerges in the very first campaigning season of the Delian League as their new general. Under him, every year, the league goes out campaigning. The fleet marshals at Delos, or whatever place they have agreed to muster, and Cimon leads them into some new campaign: taking a city, making war in a Persian-held area, or just raiding and coming back home loaded with spoils.

I'd like to share with you the first year's campaign just to give you an idea of the kind of activities of the Delian League and how they kept their treasury filled with all of the loot. They went north from Delos in that first year to the river Strymon in what they called Thrace, the river that came down out of the gold-mining region around Mount Pangaion, and attacked a little town called Eion (E-I-O-N), still held by Persians, still loyal to the Great King, and under the rule of a Persian governor or military leader named Boges. Boges was there with his wife and his children, fanatically loyal to Xerxes, the Great King.

They only had mud-brick walls around the town, but this was a period that had not yet developed—as the Hellenistic world and the Roman world would—great siege machinery for breaking down walls. So the defensive armament of cities was much greater than the ability of armies to break through it. Behind those walls, the people of Eion sat feeling secure against Cimon.

Cimon was the son of Miltiades. Miltiades, you remember, had known Great King Darius and had spent time with the Persians, had seen their great engineering works. Cimon took a leaf from the Persian book, and he diverted the river Strymon, so instead of flowing in its bed past the town of Eion, it now flowed straight at those mud-brick walls and eventually washed them away so that there was a huge breech in the city where the river had eaten away at the mud brick.

As Boges, the Persian commander, saw what was happening, he went up, apparently by night—the Greeks didn't know he'd done it—and dumped all the treasure of the city into the river, which Cimon had brought over to flow against the walls, so it would be lost in the silt and lost to the Athenians. He then built a great funeral pyre. He, his wife, and children got up on the funeral pyre, had it set alight, and went up as a sort of a holocaust offering of their loyalty to Xerxes. Part of the city caught fire and burned along with them. Then, the people who were hoping to save themselves went up on the walls, signaled that they were surrendering, and Cimon took it over.

He shared the loot with the allies, but he made that mining district, to which Eion and the Strymon River were the keys, property of Athens. Athens then, thanks to Cimon's success there, sent out colonists and created new communities, Athenian colonies, so that they would control the mining district of Thrace. The man who will succeed Herodotus as the Greek world's next great historian, Thucydides, was tied into Cimon's family; he belongs to a younger generation, but he had Thracian ancestors and Athenian ancestors.

Where did Thucydides get his money? The gold mines of Thrace that came into the Athenian world at this moment as the Athenians used the leverage of the Delian League to expand their own territory. Where did Thucydides spend his own exile during the time of the Peloponnesian War, which he chronicled? Up there in Thrace, looking after the family gold mine. So Cimon is using the league to expand Athens's horizons.

Cimon felt that he certainly knew that the Athenians were standing a little bit below the Persians in a morale sense in that, for all the Persians, wars were holy wars. Ahura Mazda is the god of light. They are fighting as sons of light against the powers of darkness. He wanted that same kind of religious sanction and divine approval for the Athenian navy, for the Delian League. So he took steps to get a titular hero—divine hero—to preside over the Athenian navy, and that was the hero Theseus.

There was an island called Skyros, the dwelling place of pirates, south of the Strymon River, up in the northern Aegean. It was reputed that on the island of Skyros were the bones of Theseus—that he had died on that island in his final years after being exiled from Athens in his final years, in spite of all the good things he'd done for the Athenians, such as killing the Minotaur and freeing the Athenians from the overlordship of the Cretan King Minos. His bones were on that island, and Cimon managed to get an oracle that said he should recover the bones of Theseus—so he used that as a pretext to attack the island and rout out the pirates, take it over, and add it to the Delian League.

Then he went looking for the bones of this hero—long buried, no one knew where. Finally, he saw an eagle tearing at a mound of earth. It was probably trying to get a lizard or a snake out. Cimon had a vision. He said, "That is the place. Dig there." So they dug, and they found the bones of a giant man buried there. He said, "These are the bones of Theseus." So with great pomp and ceremony, he had them loaded onto a sort of a catafalque. He had it carried in a great parade down to the shore and loaded on his flagship—his own trireme—and conveyed back to Athens in honor.

When it was taken to the city, they built a new temple to the divine hero Theseus, the son of Poseidon. A painter named Mikon was hired to put paintings on the walls of this temple that would show the myths of Theseus's life. The one that had the most meaning, obviously, for Cimon, was the one in which the boy Theseus, on his way to Crete, has dived into the sea and has met the queen of the sea, the goddess Amphitrite. She is handing him a gold ring that used to belong to King Minos, the world's first thalassocrat—the world's first ruler of the sea. She is handing that ring to the boy Theseus to symbolize the passing of sea power from the ancient island of Crete to the new world of Athens.

In this way, Cimon is looking after the spiritual side of the Athenians and of their new naval enterprise, as well as the military side. Cimon loved the Spartans. He even named one of his sons Lacedaemonius—"the Spartan."

He thought the Spartans had the right idea: You should be active, vigorous, and public-minded, always at the service of your city. He spent the years after he took over the command of the Delian League forces "navalizing" the Athenians in the same way that the Spartans had been "militarized" on a permanent, never-to-be-demobilized basis by the Mycenaean wars.

This navalization went from top to bottom of Athenian society. At the top, every rich man in Athens was put on a list, and they rotated, taking it in turns year by year to be captains of the triremes. This was inescapable. There has never been a city like this. Venice itself, the Viking tradition, none of these included this kind of universal service on the part of the wealthy as commanders of warships—yet the Athenians, after Cimon, took it for granted.

Down at the other end, the lower classes are all now pulling the oars of the triremes. Instead of just doing it out of sort of public service to save their city, as they'd done at Marathon, and receiving just a sort of daily stipend to cover their costs, they're now enriching themselves through this service. It takes 170 rowers to pull the oars of each trireme. Athens now has a fleet of 200. That's a lot of rowers, and they didn't use slaves. This is a modern misconception about the ancient world. They are combatants also, and fighting men are supposed to be free men. So at the oars of those Athenian triremes are the poor citizens of Athens. Previously not quite disenfranchised but never allowed to hold public service or be of importance in their city's government, now they are what counts.

Twelve years after the Delian League began, Cimon learned that the Great King Xerxes, now in his very last years—he had kind of retired to his harem and tried to forget the disaster in Greece—had ordered his generals to mount another campaign against Greece. He also, I'm sure, had hoped for peace after the dreadful campaign of 484–479 B.C. Here were the Athenians and their Delian League allies continually harassing his territory; something had to be done.

He mustered, or told his generals to muster, a huge fleet—350 ships by one count, 600 by another—at the mouth of the Eurymedon River, which is on the southern coast of Turkey near the modern city of Antalya. So outside the normal Athenian sphere of activity, they were going to bring a great fleet together there and a huge army, and they were going to repeat the invasion of 480 B.C.—only this time, they were going to win.

Cimon heard about this. He put together a fleet of 200. He took them to a little Greek city called Cnidus at the southwestern corner of Asia Minor—

modern Turkey. Some of his ships were the veterans of Salamis, 14 years before. They were kind of creaky and not so fast anymore, so what he did with them was to deck them over and pile his troops—many more than normally would have been on a ship—on those decks. On normal troop transports, the troops had rowed themselves, but he wanted the ships to still have a full complement of rowers, so that they could be active in a sea battle, but at the same time carry a full complement of soldiers, so they would act like troop transports and carry his army into the heart of the king's territory in Asia Minor.

They made their way along the coast. They took the Persians a bit by surprise there at the Eurymedon River near Antalya, because the Persians had not yet even gathered all of their forces. There were still 80 more Phoenician triremes expected at any time. Without any hesitation, Cimon swept down with his fleet on the mouth of the Eurymedon River. The Persians scrambled to launch their much larger fleet to meet him, and came out, and the two fleets collided, and such was the force of the Athenian charge—along with their Delian League allies—that the Persians very quickly broke ranks, turned for the river, tried to row up the river, found that they couldn't all squeeze into that narrow stream, abandoned their ships at the water's edge, and fled for a fortified position on shore.

Cimon fought his way through the decks of the abandoned Persian ships, got on shore, and headed up and beat their army at the fortified place. He captured the navy and the army on the same day—a double victory the likes of which had never been seen. Then, hearing about the 80 Phoenician ships that had arrived on the coast but were still a bit of a distance away, Cimon took some of the Persian ships he'd just captured, dressed his own officers as Persians, and went off and took those Phoenicians by surprise (who thought it was just the Persian fleet coming to greet them). The Athenians were already on top of them and in their camp before they could resist.

This string of victories, like a string of firecrackers going off, lent a tremendous luster to Cimon's name. It was the climax of his career. He went back to Athens and made a gift. You remember Xerxes worshiping that beautiful plain tree—that sycamore on the Royal Road—Cimon brought back these plain trees from Asia, planted them in the marketplace—the Agora of Athens—so it would look like the park of a Persian king, and then took the loot from the great battle at the Eurymedon River (that climax of the Delian League's activities) and gave it to the assembly at Athens, the Athenian share.

The Athenians took it and rebuilt the fortifications of the Acropolis itself, creating on the south side of that great rock a new retaining wall (still visible today) and preparing on the summit a place for a new temple—a new temple to the goddess Athena, which would replace the ones burnt by Xerxes and would show that Athens truly, thanks to Cimon and the efforts of all the citizens, had risen from the ashes.

Lecture Thirteen
Launching a Golden Age

Scope: The democratic assembly of Athens launched an unprecedented series of wars and campaigns on many fronts; the most spectacular of these was an invasion of the Persian satrapy of Egypt. The Egyptian king shared rule with Athens for six years, until the relentless Persians took back the territory. In 449 B.C., King Artaxerxes I (the son of Xerxes) negotiated a peace with Cimon's brother-in-law, Callias, and established a new status quo: the traditional land empire of the Persians on one side and the new Athenian maritime empire on the other. Though still a democracy at home, Athens had, of necessity, become an oppressive imperialistic power abroad and demanded an annual tribute from its allies. These tributes enabled Athens to inaugurate its famous Golden Age under the leadership of Pericles, thereby resurrecting the spirit of Ionia in Athens.

Outline

I. The second half of this course on the Greek and Persian wars starts in a changed world.
  - **A.** With the defeat of the Persian land and naval forces at the Eurymedon River, for the first time, Persia was on the defensive.
  - **B.** In the future, Persia would attempt to weaken Greek internal combatants with payments of gold to one side or the other.
  - **C.** Persian forces no longer occupied Greek lands.
  - **D.** One unintended consequence of the "navalization" of Athens was the political and economic empowerment of the lower-class citizens (*thetes*).
    1. The *thetes* were usually the landless laborers of Athens.
    2. They wanted more control over their government, but the agenda for the democratic assembly in Athens was shaped by the aristocratic council of the Areopagus.

II. Four years after the events at the Eurymedon River, the naval heroes Ephialtes and Pericles staged a dramatic revolution in Athens.

- **A.** Ephialtes and Pericles stirred up the common people to demand full rights in the government.
    1. They eliminated the council of the Areopagus and broke its powers.
    2. They made public offices open to other citizens, not just the rich upper class.
- **B.** Cimon opposed these changes and opposed the hostility of the lower classes to the Spartans.
    1. The radical Athenian democracy stressed a pure Athenian heritage that Cimon lacked; his father, Miltiades, had married a princess from Thrace.
    2. Cimon, out of tune with this new democratic Athens, was ostracized.
- **C.** Though Ephialtes was assassinated during the revolutionary year of 462 B.C. to 461 B.C., Pericles survived and became one of the leaders of democratic Athens.

III. Athens's greatest campaign was in Egypt.
- **A.** Sometime around 460 B.C., Egyptian envoys asked the Delian League for help in overthrowing their Persian rulers.
- **B.** Led by Charitimedes, the Athenian fleet traveled south across the eastern Mediterranean and into Egypt, unexplored territory for most of the Greeks.
- **C.** The Athenians and other Greeks joined the battle between Persian garrisons and Egyptian rebels and won a tremendous victory.
- **D.** As payment, the new Egyptian king shared the rule of Egypt with Athens for six years.
    1. Athens established itself as a conquering force in Egypt.
    2. The Athenians used islands and coastal cities as stepping stones to connect the eastern Mediterranean under a new sphere of Athenian influence.
- **E.** Using the wealth of Egypt, Athens undertook two great projects.
    1. One was the creation of the pair of Long Walls from Athens down to the harbor city of the Piraeus to protect the city from sieges.
    2. The other was the construction of a monumental bronze statue of Athena on the Acropolis.

- **F.** Relentless, the Persians assembled a large naval and land force to reclaim Egypt.
  1. The Persian forces caught a reinforcement fleet of Athenian triremes as it approached Egypt.
  2. They defeated the Athenians at Memphis, forcing them to retreat to Prosopitis, an island in the Nile delta.
- **G.** At Prosopitis, the Athenians settled down to defend themselves but ultimately surrendered to the Persians and made their way back to Athens.

IV. By the 450s B.C., after almost 30 years of fighting between the Greeks and Persians, even the Athenians were starting to think about peace.
- **A.** Many members of the Delian League had long ago concluded that never-ending war was a bad idea. Fewer allies sent men and ships to the league's annual campaigns, opting instead to pay an equivalent monetary sum.
- **B.** At the invitation of the Persians, the Athenian Callias traveled to Susa to negotiate a peace with King Artaxerxes I, the son of Xerxes.
  1. The terms of the peace recognized the Athenian sphere of influence and recognized Athens as a power in the world with a right to its own territory.
  2. Persia agreed to stay away from the sea in Asia Minor.
  3. The Athenians agreed not to make war on Persian territories.
- **C.** The clause that ended hostilities against the Great King caused some problems for the Athenians.
  1. Now there was no justification for keeping the Delian League together or for compelling the allies to continue their annual payments.
  2. Pericles, however, stressed the idea of eternal vigilance to maintain the league and its funds.

V. The Athenians took advantage of the cessation of hostilities and the continued payments from their allies to launch their city into a Golden Age.
- **A.** Pericles gathered a group of sculptors and architects to create, in Athens, the most beautiful set of public buildings in Greece.
  1. The Parthenon was the centerpiece of the Periclean building program.

2. Some Athenians complained that Pericles was diverting money from the city's defense to fund the glorification of Athens and himself.
- **B.** During this time, Athens established philosophical schools and became a great center for drama and scientific inquiry.
- **C.** The centerpiece of Athenian civic pride each year was a parade in which the Athenians carried offerings to Athena on the Acropolis.
- **D.** The Golden Age of Athens, dedicated to the arts, unified the population and held up Athens as "the school of Greece."

Recommended Reading:

Camp and Fisher, *The World of the Ancient Greeks.*

Tuplin, *Persian Responses: Political and Cultural Interaction with(in) the Achaemenid Empire.*

Questions to Consider:
1. Geographically speaking, what made Egypt such an important territory for the Greeks and the Persians?
2. What are some other historical equivalents of the Golden Age of Athens?

Lecture Thirteen—Transcript
Launching a Golden Age

Welcome back. As we embark together on the second half of our course on the Greek and Persian wars, we find ourselves in a changed world. Up until the year 466 B.C., when Cimon beat, in a single day, the land forces and the naval forces of the Great King at the Eurymedon River in Asia Minor, the Persians had consistently been on the offensive.

That goes all the way back to Cyrus's taking over of the Ionian cities in western Asia Minor and the old kingdom of Lydia. Following his conquest of Lydia back in the 540s B.C., it went on with Darius's attempts to conquer Greece: the Mount Athos invasion, the Marathon campaign. It climaxed in Xerxes's first campaign in 480 B.C. and then met its end at the Eurymedon River in 466 B.C.

From now on, Persia will be on the defensive. To the extent that the Persians involve themselves in trying to weaken the Greeks, they will do so with payments of Persian gold to one side or the other in the hope of turning the Greeks into internal combatants. They, in fact, helped sponsor the final phases of the Peloponnesian War between the Spartans and the Athenians and, thus, wear down their enemies in a sort of remote-control kind of way. But we will no longer see Persian forces on Greek lands.

After the Eurymedon River, one might have thought that Cimon was in an unassailably high position, but of course, people like Themistocles had thought that before as Athenian leaders, and they'd been proved to be wrong. The Athenian populace was a very fickle one, and they would quickly turn on leaders if they no longer seemed to be in tune with the times.

Let's remember about Cimon that he was a great aristocrat; that he was pro-Spartan; and these two things together put him at odds with the growing tendency in Athens toward desire for a radical democracy. One unintended consequence of his "navalization" of Athens was the empowerment, the political and economic empowerment, of the lower class—that majority of about 20,000 lower-class citizens called *thetes* (T-H-E-T-E-S).

The *thetes* are the usually landless laborers of Athens. Athens's classes, by the way, were based on income, so that this is the majority sitting at the bottom. Now they want more control over their government. They've already had a democratic assembly, where it's one man, one vote. But the agenda for that assembly had been, in part, shaped by an aristocratic council called the council of the Areopagus, the sort of Athenian House of Lords.

Four years after the Eurymedon River, there was a dramatic democratic revolution staged by a couple of naval heroes, Ephialtes and young Pericles, who both won their spurs campaigning with the Athenian navy in eastern waters, attacking Persian sites. At this point in Athens, it's a credential required of all would-be politicians and leaders that they have been Persian fighters, that they have been out there in the campaigns with the navy.

Ephialtes is chief; Pericles is lieutenant. They stir up the common people to demand full rights in the government. They get rid of that council of the Areopagus; they break its powers. It's only left with the power of judging homicide cases and cases involving affronts to the sacred olive trees. This is not a very wide span of influence in political affairs for what used to be the sort of prime movers of Athenian policy.

So the Areopagus council has been broken, and the people also say that it's time that others than the nobles—others than the old, rich upper class—be able to hold public office. So the public offices become open to other citizens, as well.

Cimon opposed this, and he also opposed the hostility of the lower classes to the Spartans. The upper classes of Athens form part of an intercity—I was going to say international, but it's not quite international—but certainly a Panhellenic aristocracy that shares the same enjoyment of the Olympic Games (which was definitely a set of gentleman sports), of the same poets, worshiped at the same Panhellenic shrines, and had guest friends among other aristocratic families in other cities. At times, took their spouses from aristocratic families in other cities.

The radical Athenian democracy is opposed to all that. For them, it's Athens for the Athenians. They even passed citizenship laws that say you've got to have an Athenian father and an Athenian mother, which is a terrible blow to rich Athenians like Cimon. Yes, he had an Athenian father, but his mother was a Thracian. He would not even have been considered a citizen of Athens if they'd not grandfathered in the living citizens at the time of the change of law.

So Cimon, being so out of tune with this new democratic Athens, was exiled in that process called ostracism. It seemed that the floodgates had opened for aggressive, radical new policies at home and abroad, and Athens launched itself on a series of wars now, sometimes with the league—the

Delian League—sometimes without, fighting Spartans and fighting Spartan allies, as well as fighting the Great King and his dominions.

Shortly after this democratic revolution, which by the way, the architect Ephialtes did not survive—he was assassinated by parties unknown during that revolutionary year of 462–461 B.C. Obviously, feelings were running very high about what he had done. Pericles survives and becomes one of the new leaders of this new democratic Athens.

Their greatest campaign was a campaign to, of all places, Egypt. When the fleet of Athens and the Delian League was in Cyprus—either in 460 or 459 B.C., just a couple of years after the big democratic revolution—they were approached by envoys sent by a native Egyptian king, who said, "We Egyptians are going to rebel against the Persians, and we're going to throw out our Persian governors and reclaim the liberty of Egypt. Help us."

The Athenians liked to view themselves as the people who help those in need. Supplicants who came to Athens asking for help were traditionally given a very warm reception. Lots of their plays, their tragedies, show someone coming as a suppliant to the Athenians and receiving help. As one of my colleagues in the field of classics said (he's a bit of a wit), "What an Athenian would always ask himself in these ages was: 'What would Theseus do?'" What Theseus would always do is help the needy, help the oppressed, help people from overseas who came to you needing assistance.

So the Athenian generals, led by a fellow named Charitimedes, broke off their campaign in Cyprus and led the fleet south across the eastern Mediterranean until the sea turned brown from the sediment of the Nile River pouring out into the Mediterranean from the delta, and they finally saw that long, low, flat line of sand bars and waving palm trees and realized they had reached their goal.

Now they have embarked into an extraordinary new world. They enter the mouth of the Nile—the triremes row up the branches of the Nile River. They are surrounded by this world of villages, of endless wheat fields, of nodding palms. Everything is fresh, and fragrant, and moist. The Greeks, from their dry, rocky homeland—they'd never experienced anything like that.

Some of them, especially the Ionians, knew this area because there had been, as I said, an old Ionian trading city called Naucratis in the delta, where the Egyptians allowed Greeks to come and trade at this Greek-held emporium. I made the comparison to Hong Kong in China or the

Portuguese cities of Goa and Macao in India and China. The same sort of trading center for foreign merchants had brought many of the Ionians there. So there were pilots and there were members of the expeditionary force who knew Egypt already.

Nonetheless, for most of the Greeks, it was brand-new terrain and a place of marvels. It's extraordinary to think that at the time of annual flood on the Nile, the triremes could row right past the pyramids on the Giza plateau. They could see the gigantic monuments of the pharaohs, in places defaced with graffiti from earlier Ionian mercenaries who'd fought in Egypt in ages past.

There, they came to shore, and they unloaded their troops from the triremes; they formed an army. A battle was either happening when they arrived or about to between the Persian garrisons, who had been detailed to hold Egypt, and these rebel Egyptians, trying to get their country back into their own hands. The Athenians and the other Greeks joined in the battle and won a tremendous victory. The Persian survivors fled to the ancient city of Memphis and abandoned most of the city to the Greeks and the Egyptians but took refuge in a part of the city that the Greeks called the White Fortress, or the White Castle.

The rest of Egypt was theirs, and as a payment—as a gift for having shared the risks of the rebellion—the new Egyptian king shared the rule of Egypt with Athens for six years. Well, we have to realize this also should means they shared the revenues of what had been one of the richest provinces of the Persian Empire. There's no reason to think that the king stopped the payment down on the village level of all the annual tributes. They also had control, probably, of the tribute that came down the Nile River from the interior, from Ethiopia, where the Ethiopians, every year, were accustomed to sending to the Great King ebony logs, ivory tusks, and other treasures from central Africa. These would now be flowing into the hands of the new king of Egypt and his Athenian allies.

So they established themselves (and probably thought it was forever) as a presence in Egypt, a conquering force that was going to pay itself back for its risks and its services in this wealth. They took over a little port on the coast of Palestine, a place called Tel Dor that used to be a Phoenician stronghold. But the Athenians came down upon it and seized that little *tell*—that little artificial mound of ancient cities stacked one on top of the other that was there by a long lagoon—and from that base, they could reach Egypt in a long day's rowing. They could also get to Cyprus in a long day's rowing. In this way, they had stepping-stone sites—islands, coastal cities, Cyprus, Dor, and then, finally, Egypt—so that they could routinely get their triremes, with single-day hops, all the way around the eastern Mediterranean to this new sphere of Athenian influence.

What can we see at home that might show that they have started to have the wealth of Egypt pumped into Athens's economy? There are two great projects they undertake at this time. One is to run a pair of Long Walls from Athens down to this new city, the Piraeus, their harbor city. Within that corridor of walls is a protected road. No enemy can now cut Athens off from the sea. They are linked to the sea by the Long Walls and the defended road that runs between the Long Walls as if by an umbilical cord. Athens is now proof against sieges, and since they are controlling the sea, they are lords of the sea; nobody can blockade them.

They might as well now be on an island as far as being protected against the Spartans or any other enemies on land. That's one thing, and that was a gigantic fortification process because each one of the gigantic Long Walls is 4.5 miles long.

They also put up a sort of Statue of Liberty–type bronze image of Athena up on the Acropolis, and this is one of the early works of one of the first generation of Athenian artists of genius—a man named Phidias, who will go on in later life to create one of the official seven Wonders of the World: the ivory and gold statue of Zeus at Olympia, site of the Olympic Games. But here at Athens, at the time when Athens was controlling Egypt, he erected—on the open rock of the Acropolis—a towering statue of Athena in bronze. She was shown holding her spear up, and the spear point rose so high and had a polished tip so that when the Sun hit the tip of the spear, ships 4.5 miles away out at sea could see the glint of light up there and feel that they were being drawn by the light of the goddess into the harbor at Athens.

The Athenians ultimately came to grief in Egypt. The Persians, of course, couldn't afford to lose this province. At least that's what they thought. There are some tacticians who feel that it was always a fault of Persian strategy to think that they needed to hang onto Egypt. In the end, it probably wasn't worth the cost, and it created this permanent instability there on their southwestern frontier.

At any rate, the Persians are, of course, relentless. They ultimately assembled a large naval and land force. The land force marched through the desert, across the Sinai Peninsula, and into the northeast corner of Egypt, a place where King Darius's engineers had built a canal—predecessor of the modern Suez Canal—that joined one of the branches of the Nile delta to the Red Sea. They came back in that way on land. Meanwhile, the Phoenician fleet came along the coast to the Pelusian branch of the Nile River, as the Nile spreads out through the delta in many channels.

They caught, as it was approaching Egypt, a reinforcement fleet of 50 Athenian triremes that knew nothing of the Persian counteroffensive. They had been off guard now for six years, ever since the big battle that put Egypt into their hands, and as they entered that branch of the Nile, the Phoenician ships came swarming out from their hiding places, surrounded the Athenian ships, and destroyed them.

They then turned their attention to the Greeks in the interior. They were still besieging Memphis. For six years, the Persians inside that White Fortress had been able to hold out. So now they find themselves with Persians, both on the inside of Memphis and a Persian army on the outside. There are some skirmishes, and the Athenians are worsted, and they retreat to an island in the Nile delta with their ships. So they've taken the triremes of the league fleet, thousands of men, maybe still the original 200 ships—it's not clear from the accounts—which in this case were given to us by Thucydides, the historian of Athens and Athens's imperial power.

What happened was there was a place where the Nile branched in two as it headed toward the sea. The Egyptians had long before dug a canal to join those two branches, so there was a triangular wedge of land surrounded completely by water. They brought their triremes to this piece of land. It was called Prosopitis. They drew the triremes up on the shore, and they settled down to defend themselves. They defended themselves for a very long time. I said the sea battle happened in the sixth year; they, in fact, were not already in the sixth year of their occupation when the war with the Persians began.

For a long time, they were able to live off this island, which was a big space with farm land, and crops, and so on. Finally, the Persians put their mind to it: How can we get at them? Never forget the Persian genius for engineering, especially hydraulics; they diverted the river so that the canal would be drained of its water. Once the canal was drained of its water, they could send in the horsemen and the infantry straight across the dry bed and hit the Athenians very hard, without having to beat ships and carry out an amphibious maneuver.

After fighting for awhile, the Athenians surrendered. Some had been killed, and the rest were allowed to leave Egypt under a truce. They made their way westward into the Sahara Desert. They finally reached the Greek city of Cyrene up on the Mediterranean coast, and from there, the few that remained were transported back to Athens. That was the end of the attempt to make Egypt a part of the Greek world. But certainly I can't help but feel that those Athenians who got home, who had now seen the wonders of pharaonic Egypt—the temple at Luxor, all of those amazing pillared edifices of the pharaohs, and the pyramids, and the Sphinx—I just can't help thinking that their eyes were opened to what a great power should look like.

They had grown up in a small town (Athens), and they had seen that town leveled to be a sort of a ground zero after the Persians burned it and it was reduced to ashes. Now they came home with their heads full of this grandeur of Egypt, and it's going to play out, I think, very quickly in a new Athens that's going to rise on the remnants of the old.

Meanwhile, with the defeat of the Athenian expedition to Egypt—which probably happened about 454 B.C.—and some new campaigns by Cimon, who was back from exile—his 10 years' exile of ostracism—back in the saddle in Cyprus, both sides—Athens on the one side and Persia on the other side—both sides had now been battered. Both sides had now been beaten. Both sides had been involved in wars that had stretched for—the invasion of Xerxes was in 480 B.C. and we're now in the 450s B.C., so almost 30 years have gone by—a full generation of fighting. People were starting to think about peace.

The Ionians and the other Greeks who were part of the Delian League, they had long ago come to the conclusion that this never-ending war was a bad idea. More and more of them had stopped sending men and ships to the annual campaigns of the Delian League that had been led at first by Cimon, and they began to just pay money, pay an equivalent sum. As they sent that money to Athens, that tribute, the Athenians cared less and less about the opinions of those people as to the governance of the league and its policies. After all, these people were simply paying for protection, and as long as the Athenians gave it, they felt that they could make all the other decisions.

So it was that at the invitation of the Persians, conveyed to the Athenians who were campaigning in Cyprus, the Great King invited an Athenian to come to Susa to talk about the peace. Now in Athens, often you take over the status and the occupation of your family, your forefathers. There was a family called the Kerykes, the "herald's family," that were traditionally the heralds of Athens—the people who carried ambassadorial messages to other powers and represented Athens abroad. The current head of that family was a man named Callias, who was one of the richest men in Athens and was also the brother-in-law of Cimon, the great general.

Callias was sent up the Royal Road, all the way to Susa, that three month's journey, and there, he negotiated a peace with King Artaxerxes, the son of the Xerxes who had invaded. The terms of the peace recognized the Athenian sphere of influence, recognized Athens as a power in the world with its own right to its own territory.

The king agreed to stay away from the sea in Asia Minor. According to the somewhat contradictory accounts we have of the terms of the peace—no complete text of it has ever been found that was universally regarded as genuine—he agreed that his forces would not come closer to the sea than a three-day march on foot or a one-day ride on horseback. So there's now a Persian-free zone all along the coastal strip that guaranteed the Greek cities in Asia freedom from Persian interference.

The Greeks apparently, in turn, agreed not to make war on the king's territories—to give up that everlasting campaign that they had sworn to on Delos. Callias finished his negotiations. He came home with the peace that had been concluded with the Persians, and he also brought back a gift that the king had made to him personally: peacocks. The first ones ever known or seen in Europe were brought back as little trophies, little exotic items—presents from the Great King. Callias very proudly displayed these in his garden at Athens to anybody who would come and look at them.

The clause about giving up the hostility to the Great King (if it was in there—and it seems it has to have been or the Persians wouldn't have agreed to stay away from the coast) caused some problems for the Athenians. The justification for the Delian League had been: "We will wage war forever against Persia." Now, we're not sure that they swore that they would stop fighting, but we do know that now there were limits set to this Persian expansion, and we assume there were limits to the Athenians going in the other way. One is down south near the Eurymedon River at some islands called the Chelidonian Rocks, and the other is up at the Bosphorus, the Black Sea end of the Bosphorus near Byzantium. Those are sort of the limits beyond which the Great King cannot pass, but by extension, they must be the limits beyond which the Athenians will not invade.

What, then, is the justification for keeping the alliance together? What's the justification for compelling all those cities and islands to keep making their annual payments to the Delian League treasury, which has by now been, in fact, moved to Athens? Well, Pericles is the man who comes forward, apparently, and states the reason. He said:

> Eternal vigilance will be the price of our freedom. You must never stop paying to maintain this navy. Navies must be kept up through tremendous annual investment of money, and without our navy, the Persians will be back in an instant. [So the money can't stop; the allies cannot stop paying.] We may not be at war today, but unless we are always ready, as we transform [as we would say] our Department of War into a Department of Defense, nonetheless, it's going to cost us just as much, and the payments will not be reduced.

At this point, with almost all of the 150 allies paying money, with only three big islands up against the coast of Asia Minor—Samos in the south, Chios in the middle, and Lesbos in the north—still having navies of their own and contributing ships, it's very hard to tell the difference between the Athenian realm on the one side (with this imperial capital of Athens gathering the money from the allies) and the Persian Empire on the other side (with the king gathering annual tribute from his satrapies).

Athens shows us the anomaly—in some ways, a very terrible anomaly—of a very positive, very democratic city that has fought for freedom and democratic principles at home but somehow, through force of circumstances and through its own ambitions to keep the world free, has become a very oppressive imperialistic power abroad. Now there are revolts in the Delian League: people trying to rebel and get out from under the Athenian overlordship—just as in the Persian Empire there had been revolts by people like the Ionians, the Babylonians, and the Egyptians, who wanted to free themselves from the Persians.

This will be a dark side of the Athenian world for generations to come—this feeling that they are empire builders and that freedom was their banner at the beginning, but now domination is what they are really after. Nonetheless, the Athenians took advantage of this cessation of hostilities against Persia and this continued income from the allies to launch what we've come to call the Golden Age.

One of the visions that Pericles had was of transforming Athens into a great imperial capital. So with his friend Phidias, that great sculptor and artist, and with some architects of genius who had grown up in Athens, they decided to create for Athens the most beautiful set of public buildings in Greece. They would be temples—not just the ones set on the Acropolis in the heart of Athens but a rebuilding of the temple at Sounion, the cape where Poseidon was worshiped; or at a place called Rhamnus, to the goddess Nemesis; or at Eleusis, to the goddesses Demeter and Persephone, who were in charge of the Eleusinian Mysteries. All of these places in Attica would get brand-new temples.

They had taken an oath at the end of the Persian Wars that they wouldn't rebuild the temples destroyed by the Persians. They would remain as burnt testimony to the barbarism of that barbarian horde, the Persian horde, who came in and sacked Athens and burned Greece. But now, they didn't want to live with these shattered hulks anymore, and so they put up the most beautiful temples that the Greek world had ever known.

The Parthenon itself, sacred to Athena Parthenos ("Athena the maiden"), was the centerpiece of this whole Periclean building program. It was a temple of the greatest architectural refinement. It looks like a perfect sort of geometrical prism—a perfect set of rectangular forms with this triangular gabled roof—but, in fact, there's scarcely a straight line in it. It's all curves—entasis of the columns—tremendous sophistication in the architecture to give the illusion of a temple almost lighter than air, floating there on top of that rock.

It was a controversial temple. The people in Athens themselves, some of the aristocrats who were Pericles's opponents, said, "You're decking out our city like a pretentious woman. We are not happy to see you divert the money from our naval allies away from defense and put it into these buildings, only for the glorification of Athens and yourself." And Pericles is said to have responded, "The money does not belong to those who give but to those who receive. As long as we provide them with the defense against Persia that they have been guaranteed, we are free to do as we will with the rest of the money."

The Parthenon was itself, in part, a bank where the money was piled up from the tribute and guarded by the goddess herself. Her great statue inside the temple—which was of ivory for the face and the hands and of gold sheets over a wooden core for the rest of her body—was made so that the gold could be pulled off and melted down in case of a national emergency. That's no way to treat a goddess and her dress, but it became the centerpiece of a great cult of Athena that had its celebration each year at midsummer—the early days of the month of Hekatombaion, the Athenian New Year, and its first month began at midsummer. That was the great feast of Athena. *Hekatombaion* means "the month when you sacrifice 100." They sacrificed 100 oxen to Athena up on the summit of the Acropolis.

In this Golden Age that is going to see Athens getting its philosophical schools and being the great center in the world for drama and staging of new plays—tragedy and comedy—and sciences flourishing, and new inquiry in all sorts of fields, the centerpiece each year was a great parade—a procession where all the people of Athens (resident aliens, commoners, old aristocrats) got together and paraded through the streets of Athens, carrying offerings up to Athena on her rock.

The young girls of Athens, a few select ones, had been laboring for a year to weave and embroider a new robe—a *peplos*—for the statue of Athena. The goddess got a new dress every year, and the old one was put reverently away. How did they carry that new robe through the streets and the procession? Well, they had become now a city of the sea, so they had a little ship on wheels. The mast of that ship and its yardarm carried not an ordinary sail but the peplos itself—the robe of the goddess—to symbolize that in the sail of the ship, we are seeing Athena as the protectress of our great naval enterprise that has beaten the Persians and made us a city, a free city, that can look across the water at the Great King eye to eye.

So that ship on wheels was trundled through the streets. When it got to the bottom of the Acropolis slope, the sail was taken down, reverently folded, carried up to the Acropolis, and placed on the statue of Athena as her new garment for the next year.

In this great ceremony, the Athenians found the climax of their Golden Age—an age that had unified the population, an age dedicated to the arts, to creating the beautiful, and above all, to holding up Athens as, in Pericles's words, "the school of Greece," the place that taught people how to live.

We sometimes have the illusion in our history books that this was all a matter of pure intellect, of people in ivory towers thinking deep thoughts and creating wonderful artistic works, but it wasn't. It was the fruit of a war—it was the fruit of victories fought by a population of this city of Athens that had given up so much and deferred so much of their rewards to reach a point where they could rival any other city on Earth as the greatest market in the Mediterranean and as the most beautiful city in the entire Greek world.

Lecture Fourteen
Herodotus Invents History

Scope: The historian Herodotus of Halicarnassus is often referred to as the "father of history." His *Histories* sets out to record the Greek and Persian wars and is considered the first example of modern historical writing; it contains some fascinating accounts, including the strange world of the Scythians, the Phoenician circumnavigation of Africa, and the silent trading practices with Africans. Herodotus's greatness as a historian lies in his balanced view of both the Greeks and the Persians, his insight in identifying the overarching conflict between East and West (still an element of history in the modern world), and his willingness to record multiple accounts of events and to identify his sources. Endlessly fascinated by people and their stories and optimistic about the human condition, Herodotus was hopeful that an account of the Greek and Persian wars would renew feelings of unity among the feuding Greeks of his own time.

Outline

I. The middle of the 5th century B.C. spawned some of the most remarkable thinkers and creative artists in all of human history, including Sophocles, Euripides, Aristophanes, Thucydides, Socrates, Anaxagoras, Phidias, Hippocrates, and the focus of this lecture: Herodotus.

II. Herodotus, his name meaning "gift of Hera," was certainly a bequest of divine force to the human race.

   A. Herodotus was born in Halicarnassus just as the Greek and Persian wars were getting under way.

   B. Growing up Greek in the Asiatic world enabled him to see both sides of the wars.

   C. Herodotus clearly felt that the generation that fought in the wars was the greatest generation.

   D. Herodotus made it his life's work to travel to all the places that had been involved in the conflict and to create a work that would capture for all time what the wars had been like: *The Histories*.

      1. The Greek *historia* means "inquiry" or "research."

2. *Historia* became the process of finding and gathering together the truth about the past.
  E. Herodotus presents a modern view of history as an accumulation of the memories of many different people involved in the great events of the Greek and Persian wars.
   1. He often gives two or three contradictory versions of the same event.
   2. Amassing what people remembered, tying it together with overarching themes, and honestly displaying biases are some of his special achievements.
  F. The Greek and Persian wars seemed to Herodotus conflicts that achieved an epic status, worthy of treatment on the scale of Homer's *Iliad*.
III. Herodotus traveled throughout the Greek world and beyond, visiting such places as Athens or the site of the Olympic Games and telling stories about the wars in front of large crowds.
  A. He believed that history was the working out of divine purpose and destiny on Earth; thus, he spent a good deal of time talking about oracles.
  B. He often presented the Persians in a strikingly favorable light.
  C. Most of his listeners could only hope to share his knowledge of the strange peoples and distant places of the world.
  D. His recitals impressed the Athenians. In turn, Herodotus admired the Athenians and reminded other Greeks that Greece owed its freedom to Athens.
IV. Books created in the ancient world often encompass an oral element.
  A. Books of plays by Aeschylus, Sophocles, and Euripides are scripts based on what was originally spoken onstage; similarly, Homer's *Iliad* and *Odyssey* were originally oral recitations committed to memory and, ultimately, written down.
  B. The original text of *The Histories* was probably taken down by a scribe on papyrus scrolls as recited by Herodotus.
   1. The scrolls were edited by Herodotus with corrections and additions in the margins.
   2. To create copies of the book, a reader stood in the middle of a room filled with scribes and read the histories in a slow, clear voice.

        3. The copies made by the scribes were then sold in the marketplace.
    C. Certain aspects of the process make it difficult to know exactly what the original text of *The Histories* was.
        1. Sometimes, scribes would mishear what was spoken, leading to variant readings and interpretations.
        2. Sometimes, a scribe would miss a sentence, leaving a *lacuna*, a vacancy, in the manuscript.
        3. Herodotus's love of foreign names and terms must have puzzled the Greek scribes.
    D. *The Histories* was so vast that it took nine papyrus scrolls to complete.
        1. The work begins with a preamble about history.
        2. It ends with a return to Cyrus telling his fellow Persians that hard country breeds hard men—tough rulers rather than soft followers—and, thus, tying together Herodotus's themes of geography and history.
V. Herodotus was probably one of the most widely traveled people in the ancient world.
    A. After spending time on Samos, he embarked on travels that took him through Greece and into the region of the Black Sea.
    B. He met people who knew the Scythians (Indo-European horse lords) and recorded their traditions.
    C. He traveled along global market routes that conveyed commodities from the ends of the Earth to the great cities of the Mediterranean.
    D. Two of Herodotus's Phoenician stories offer examples of his legacy to the study of history.
        1. Herodotus's disbelief of a story about the Phoenicians' circumnavigation of Africa gave future scholars the information to prove that the Phoenicians actually *did* sail around the continent.
        2. Herodotus described the silent trading that took place between Phoenicians and Africans, a practice that seems to embody his philosophy of avoiding conflict and showing respect to one's fellow human beings.
    E. Herodotus also traveled through the Persian Empire.
    F. At some point, he wrote a 10th book about Mesopotamian history, which has been lost.

VI. Herodotus gave to the Greeks a picture of their place in the larger world, a history of their greatest and proudest moments, and a vision of harmony among peoples and nations.

Recommended Reading:
De Sélincourt, *The World of Herodotus.*
Myres, *Herodotus: Father of History.*

Questions to Consider:
1. Read through a few stories contained in *The Histories*. Which ones are your favorites and why?
2. What are some differences and similarities between Herodotus's method of recording history and the methods used by modern-day historians you have read?

Lecture Fourteen—Transcript

Herodotus Invents History

Welcome back. If it were possible for us to get in a time machine and go back to the Golden Age of Athens, of Pericles and the other great leaders, back in the middle of the 5th century B.C., we would have a chance to encounter some of the most remarkable thinkers and creative artists in all of human history.

There, at the Theatre of Dionysus, we would have been able to hear plays written by the likes of Sophocles and Euripides in tragedy and of Aristophanes in comedy. We would have been able to talk over military matters with Pericles himself or with Thucydides, who both led the Athenian fleet and then, later on, wrote a military history of the Peloponnesian War.

We would have been able to meet philosophers, like Socrates or Anaxagoras, the man who tried to replace a religious explanation of miracles with an understanding of the scientific principles of nature. We would have met great artists, like Phidias. But if I could have a chance to pick the person I would most like to meet in that Golden Age world, it wouldn't be an Athenian. We have to remember that Athens was a magnet for people from all over this new empire, and I should mention one more: Hippocrates—from the island of Kos, the man who is given the credit for inventing modern-style medicine—is a citizen of the Athenian Empire. He is a man whose home island is part of that Delian League and then, later, Athens and its tribute-giving allies.

But the man I would really like to meet is Herodotus—Herodotus of Halicarnassus—at the end of his life, having emigrated to a new Athenian colony in Italy, or Panhellenic colony founded by Athens, Herodotus of Thuriae, but just Herodotus. His name means the "gift of Hera," and he was certainly a gift of a divine force to the human race.

He had the good fortune to be born just as the Persian wars were getting underway. He was probably four or five years old when the queen of his city, Artemisia, queen of Halicarnassus, went off to fight at Salamis for Xerxes and came home entrusted with the task of bringing Xerxes's sons back to Asia from the debacle in Europe. This was his city. This was his queen as he grew up. He grew up hearing the stories of that great expedition, that great battle at Salamis, from eyewitnesses—people in his city who had actually participated in the battle.

He grew up a Greek within the Asiatic world. He was actually governed by Persian overlords when he was born. So he was a man who could see both sides of this great war and could interview people on both sides. He felt, to use a modern term, that the generation that fought in that war—both on the Persian side and the Greek side—was the greatest generation. And he made it his life's work to interview as many of them as he could, to travel to all of the places that had been involved in this conflict, and to create a work that would capture for all time, in the memories of the people who actually lived through that war, what it had been like.

I would like to give you his own preamble to that book that he wrote: "Herodotus of Halicarnassus here sets forth his *Historiae*"—we'll come back to that word in a moment—"so that mortal achievements may not become forgotten with the passage of time, so that great and marvelous deeds, some by Greeks, some by barbarians"—meaning the Persians—"may not be without their glory, and especially to show why the two peoples fought with one another, Greeks on the one side, Persians on the other."

Now that word *historia* has become our word "history." To a Greek, it meant "inquiry," "research." It comes from a Greek root that actually means "tracking things down." So it was all about the process of finding out the truth, finding out stories of what had happened in the past and assembling them together. It became our word *history*—meaning the past and the study of the past—because Herodotus used it.

He is the man who Cicero dubbed the "father of history," and that's the title he has kept ever since, except by those people who are so disturbed by Herodotus's credulity and the fact that he believed—or at least put into his great work—a lot of patently nonsensical stories from his informants; they call him the "father of lies." Nonetheless, he was a very honest man by his own lights. He said, at one point, after a particularly strange tale that he recorded, "This is what I was told. I don't believe it myself, but then it is my job to put down what those who saw these actions happen tell me. It's not my job to believe it."

He presents us with a very modern view of history as a gathering together of the memories of many different people who were involved in these great events and a recording of them for posterity—letting us know, in most cases, who told him what. What were his sources? Did he do the kind of documentary historical study and research we would have expected of a modern historian? Did he get into the old records and inscriptions, and try to figure out the Athenian financial outlay for the war, and things like that? No. In many cases, those documents were not present to him, and it's a funny thing that the Greeks were rather skeptical of inscribed pronouncements and so on—feeling that, apparently, those often have a lot of spin or government-based and biased attitude built into them.

They liked what Herodotus did, that he went around and talked to people. He often will give two and three different and contradictory versions of the same event, and this is why we credit him as the creator of this field of history. Before his time, there was chronicle. There was the idea of setting down—in chronological order—the facts of a period. But the idea of amassing what people remembered; the idea of tying it together with overarching themes, like the conflict between East and West; and above all, the honesty of displaying biases and weighing evidence—this is the special achievement of Herodotus.

He was inspired to create this first great work of history by the Greek and Persian wars. That conflict seemed to him so epic as to be worthy of a treatment on the scale of Homer's *Iliad* and *Odyssey*, and he certainly regarded the giant figures—like Xerxes, and Artemisia, and Themistocles—as worthy to stand beside Homer's heroes in the pantheon of human greats.

Well, Herodotus had an interesting life himself. He became politically undesirable in his home city of Halicarnassus due to infighting, and he became a sort of exile. It's interesting to me to consider how many of the great ancient historians were exiles from their native towns: Herodotus from Halicarnassus; Thucydides, historian of the Peloponnesian War, from Athens; Polybius, the chronicler of the Roman Punic Wars, from his home; and Josephus, who chronicled the Jewish war against Rome, an exile from Judea and now an adopted Roman himself.

There seems to be something about crossing over from your own birthplace into another world that helps people get the perspective and the motivation for creating what we now call "history." If you'd been in Athens—let's go back to our time machine—you've set the dial for sometime in the 440s B.C., and you've gotten out of the time machine, and you are in Athens. You are in the "agora," that "open space"—that's all that "agora" means—which was the market and the civic center for the city of Athens. It was also a place to go and hear philosophers, like Socrates, talking and interrogating young men of Athens about their beliefs and their ideas. It was a place to hear people from outside Athens come and give sort of public lectures. You could hear authorities on military tactics talking. You could hear scientists explaining marvels, and you could hear Herodotus.

Herodotus—having traveled the Greek world and beyond, and we'll talk about his travels in a moment—went to cities like Athens, or places like the Olympic Games at Olympia, wherever there would be a big crowd, and he'd stand up on some sort of pedestal, and he would just talk. Part of the charm of this incredible book that he created is it sounds as if he's there talking to you. It's a very conversational style and a very beautiful Ionic-influenced Greek.

As he rambles from story to story, as his mind is prompted by telling one tale to think of another and go straight onto it, regardless of chronology, one can feel one is lost in a labyrinth of the reminiscences of a brain—more than any other in human history—was stocked with an entire world of stories, memories, myths, geographical observations, and sites that he had seen and people that he had talked to. This is the world of Herodotus, and he would stand there in front of these crowds of people and tell his stories.

People remembered them, and people loved them; they were exciting. He had Thermopylae and Leonidas in the pass, and he had Xerxes sitting on his throne above Salamis, and he had Miltiades on the field at Marathon. He went all the way back into the origins of the whole conflict, with the kingdom of Lydia, the dynasty of King Croesus, and the invasion of Cyrus. All of this was in there.

He was a very pious man. He believed that history was the working out of divine purpose and destiny here on Earth, and so he spent a lot of time on oracles, and it's important he did that for us, because they certainly shaped the events of these peoples who believe very fervently what they received as messages from the gods through the oracles. So he's a typical man of his time, and his attitudes and the things he held important help us see that time as it was perceived by the people who lived it—but, in many ways, he is not a typical man of his time.

As he stood there addressing those Greeks who had come to listen to his stories, he would often be presenting the Persians in a strikingly favorable light. He did not demonize peoples. He seems to me to be the most tolerant, open-minded intellect that ever lived on this Earth, and certainly, his view of the world was one that most of his listeners could only hope to share—a man who had seen many strange peoples, visited many distant places, and had been interested in all of them. Certainly, there has never been anyone less judgmental than Herodotus was.

The Athenians were deeply impressed by his recitals. He came to love Athens as a second home. If it hadn't been for those citizenship laws, he probably would have liked to have been adopted as an Athenian citizen. He did the next-best thing. Athens had founded a Panhellenic colony in southern Italy, a city at Thuriae, sort of founded under Athenian auspices, and he joined the parade of remarkable people who went out there and joined that new colonial venture. At that point, he became Herodotus of Thuriae.

He admired the Athenians in return for the good impression they had of him, and he wanted to remind the other Greeks—who, by his day, were regarding Athens with suspicion, dislike, and resentment—that Greece owed its freedom to Athens: that if the Athenians had not made the financial sacrifice to create their fleet, if they had not stayed in Greek waters and fought for the rest of Greece after their own city had been taken, Greece would have fallen. He said at one point:

> I shall say something that I know will not be popular. It is the Athenians to whom we truly owe the Greek victory in the Persian wars. If they had gone away and left the rest of Greece to its own defense, what would have prevented the navy of the Great King from landing wherever it wished and taking the Peloponnese, as well as northern and central Greece?

This view of the Athenians was so pleasing to those people that they gave him a big financial gift in the course of his life, and we have to remember this is how itinerant people like Herodotus would live. No doubt he had private means, but it must have been a very pleasing thing that cities would offer him awards of gold and silver for coming and entertaining them with his wonderful stories.

Let's talk a little bit about how a book is created in the ancient world. There is often an oral element to the things. Our books of the plays of Aeschylus, Sophocles, Euripides, Aristophanes—those are scripts of what was originally spoken on a stage. Homer's *Iliad* and *Odyssey* were originally oral recitations—sagas committed to memory by bards, and recited at feasts, and ultimately, written down. We certainly get that feeling with Herodotus, especially the way he will put in little asides, or think forward to what he's going to say next, or hark back to an earlier story he has already told, or fit something in by saying, "Oh, I forgot to say," and then tuck it in there. We almost get a picture of him standing and reciting while a scribe quickly notes down all these stories.

That would have been the original text, probably not written by Herodotus himself but recited by him and written down by a scribe. It's being written down on scrolls of papyrus. Those scrolls will then be fixed up and edited by Herodotus, with little notes in the margin to correct them or add things that he thought of at the last minute. Then, to create the book, some reader will stand in the middle of a room filled with scribes, each one with their own papyrus scroll, and read the histories of Herodotus in a slow, clear voice. All of those people will be making a copy of their own, which can be distributed and sold.

There are certain things that make it difficult for us to know exactly what the original text was. Sometimes, they would mishear things, and so we will get, in different copies, variant readings or interpretations. Sometimes, they would not hear a sentence at all, and we'll have a *lacuna*, as it's called—a vacancy in one of the manuscripts. The Greek practice of not leaving spaces between words and not putting in all the accent marks of later Greek makes it sometimes ambiguous exactly what these people would have said. Certainly, Herodotus's love of foreign names and foreign terms must have been a great puzzlement to Greek scribes sitting there and trying to commit to paper something they were hearing recited in the room. Nonetheless, these copies would then be the source of future copies, and they would be taken in bundles of scrolls down to the marketplace and sold.

The size of the book determined the number of scrolls. Herodotus's *Histories* was so vast it took nine papyrus scrolls in order to make the whole thing. This is what they called the "books of Herodotus," and because there were nine, they thought of the nine Muses—those goddesses of inspiration—and the early copies of Herodotus had the name of a Muse—Cleo, for instance, was the Muse of history—as the title of each of the nine books of Herodotus's *Histories*.

He began with the statement you've just heard and then plunged right into things like the Trojan War and Jason and the Argonauts' expedition to the Black Sea as predecessors of the Greek and Persian conflict. He ended with the scene of the Athenians and the Ionians capturing the city of Sestos in the Hellespont, capturing the cables of Xerxes's bridges, and carrying them home to be trophies in the year 479 B.C. But he didn't want to end there. Where did he really want to end? He wanted to end with a moral lesson.

Herodotus had the view, unfashionable today in some circles, that history is meant to teach you things and that history is meant to teach you moral things—not just facts—but important things about choices you make and how you lead your life. This is one reason people turn—still today, 2,500 years later—to the pages of Herodotus, not just for entertainment of the great stories, not just for education about the facts of the Greek and Persian wars, but for that spiritual refreshment of a man who felt deeply on so many matters and wanted his book to be the carrier of these ideas to the future.

Herodotus ended by harking back to the hero from the first pages of his story, the Persian conqueror Cyrus, who rose from obscurity to lead his people to a world empire. In that story where Cyrus had challenged the Persians when they told him they wanted to move down on the plains and have a beautiful life enjoying the fruits of empire, you will remember he challenged them and said, "I'm not sure you really want this. Rough countries breed tough men; soft countries, the reverse. Do you want to be rough and rule, or do you want to live soft and be ruled by others?" As you will remember, they agreed with him, and that's why he built his capital up in the highlands of the Persian homeland.

That is where Herodotus chose to end this epic work, with Cyrus talking to the other Persians about what these choices mean. It's fascinating also that this ties together Herodotus's themes of geography and history. Time and time again, he attributes national characteristics of people to the kind of world, the kind of natural world, in which they live. How could he do this? It's because he was probably one of the most widely traveled people in all the ancient world.

From his original home in Halicarnassus, he moved to the offshore island of Samos. He lived there for a number of years, and then he embarked on travels. We know he traveled widely through Greece. We know that he went up into the Black Sea, and actually visited places like the Crimea and the area around the mouth of the Danube, and possibly even the far eastern end of the Black Sea, where Jason went to seek the legendary Golden Fleece.

He met people who knew the Scythians—those Indo-European horse lords who ruled the vast steppes of Eurasia. He saw the grain trade, the trade in salt fish, and the trade in slaves. He saw the makers of gold artifacts who lived up there in Scythia. He was fascinated by people the more different they were from him. So he recorded in great detail the Scythian traditions. He may have seen the funeral of a Scythian king. He saw the ceremonies of the horsemen for their king. He saw the erection of the great burial mound, with the king interred inside with his treasures. And archaeology in the 19th and 20th centuries has recovered some of those same mounds that Herodotus saw and brought to light again the treasures of the Scythian kings.

He was fascinated by anything that was out of the ordinary for the Greeks: the long midsummer days of northern latitudes, the snowfall in the north, which was such a rare thing in the Greek world. He brought all of these stories back out of the Black Sea.

Some people think he may have been a merchant because he's always interested in what is bought and sold. I don't know if that's really true that that means he was a merchant. There are people who think Shakespeare was a doctor, or a lawyer, or a merchant himself because he shows such expertise in the knowledge of the jargon of all those trades, and Herodotus is a bit like that.

At any rate, one of his interests in the Black Sea stems from the fact that after the Athenians captured the Hellespont and the approaches to the Black Sea in their counterattacks on Persia at the end of the Persian wars, they became masters of the waterway that brought the wealth of the Black Sea into the Mediterranean, and that was the route where most of the Mediterranean's wheat—or at least the eastern Mediterranean's wheat—was coming from.

It was grown on the vast plains of the Ukraine in southern Russia. The Scythians would then send it down the rivers to the Crimea and the ports there, many of which were now Greek colonies. It was loaded onto gigantic wooden ships—grain freighters—and carried across the Black Sea, down through the Hellespont, where most of it ended up going to the Piraeus, the new center of Mediterranean trade now that Athens is the center of sea power in the Mediterranean.

Herodotus knew all that. He was traveling on the routes that this global market was using to convey these commodities from the ends of the Earth to the great cities of the Mediterranean. He respected and admired another seafaring people—people on the Persian side of the divide—and those were the Phoenicians. We wouldn't know very much about the Phoenicians if it weren't for Herodotus because they didn't write a great deal themselves, or at least their writings have not survived.

I want to give you an example of something that we owe to Herodotus that, at the same time, shows us his mind at work. I'll take two things from his Phoenician stories. He tells us that about 200 years before his own time, the Phoenicians sailed around Africa—circumnavigated the entire continent. This is two millennia before Vasco da Gama, the Portuguese explorer who gets credit in modern books for circumnavigating Africa and for being the first. This is two millennia before his voyage in the 1490s. Here are these

Phoenicians making the same voyage all the way back in those early days before the Persian wars.

How did they do it? Herodotus gives us the story. He says there was a pharaoh of Egypt who wanted to know the limits of Africa and wanted to know if it was truly a landmass that could be circumnavigated. So he had a Phoenician fleet under his sponsorship start in the Red Sea, sail southward down the coast of Africa until they got to the tip, round that point, and come back in through the Pillars of Hercules (or Heracles) at the mouth of the Mediterranean, and then return to Egypt and the delta of the Nile River by that way.

He tells us that it took them three years to do it. He tells us that they ran out of food several times, went ashore, planted crops, waited for the crops to grow in the warm African sun, and then with the new harvest, set off again. He also tells us he doesn't believe the story. Here is why Herodotus is such an incredibly valuable historical source. Here is why we treasure so much his attitude toward his sources. He didn't believe this story.

If he'd been a Thucydides, he never would have put it in. Thucydides looked at the evidence and anything he didn't believe he excluded rigorously. His account was the one true account that he had determined to be factual. Herodotus puts it all in, but the fact is the element that he found cause for disbelief is the very point that proves to us the Phoenicians really did it.

Herodotus tells us that when they got to the southern tip of Africa—those seagoing Phoenicians—they were headed west to get around what we would call the Cape of Good Hope, and as they did so, they found, miraculously, that the Sun in the heavens at midday was on their right hand. Now if you're facing west and something is on your right hand, it's to the north. He's always interested in geography.

Well, in European terms, that's impossible—the Sun is always to the south. Herodotus had a circular idea of the world but not a spherical idea. He didn't understand that at the equator, everything changes: The constellations turn on their heads, and the Sun will be found to your north in the sky, not—as it was in Greece, throughout the Mediterranean, throughout the whole world that he knew—always to the south. He said, "Well, this is obviously an impossibility, so the whole story must be false."

His incredulity and his desire to explain why they're wrong have given us the information that proves they actually did it. The coast of Africa is, for the most part, north-south, all the way down that coast of the Indian Ocean. It's not until you get to the southern part by the Cape of Good Hope and swing around to the west, headed for the Atlantic, that you would have the Sun on your right hand—very clear evidence for us that the Phoenicians really made it.

There's one beautiful passage from Herodotus. Let's have another. He was interested in Phoenician trading. I told you he was interested in the world's merchandising and mercantile life. He knew that the Phoenicians and their friends, the Carthaginians—they're actually colonists of Phoenicians who settled down in what is today modern Tunis—they would go out of the Pillars of Heracles, into the Atlantic, and down the African coast, and they would be going after gold, and ivory, and ebony, and the other treasures of Africa.

He describes the most charming form of exchange that has ever been committed to paper. The Phoenicians would go to a place where there was a small offshore island, and they would gather their ships there, and then put together the things that they wanted to trade with the Africans at that point on the coast. These were probably cloths and manufactured goods from the Mediterranean, perhaps metalwork also. So they would cross over to the shore of the mainland, and they would lay out on the beach everything that they wanted to trade, and then they'd go back to their island, and they'd wait.

Onto the beach would then come the local people, who would walk around and look over the piles of Phoenician goods laid out for their inspection. They would then go back to their homes, and they would bring out a certain quantity of ivory, and gold, and other local products, and then they'd go away. The Phoenicians would now come back, look over the piles, and if they didn't think it was enough, they'd go back to the island. More would be brought out. The process was repeated until both sides were happy: the Africans that they had given as much as they felt they could for what was there; the Phoenicians that they were receiving as much as was right for the goods that they had brought. So with mutual respect and no possibility of hostilities, the two sides parted, each taking away the goods that the other had brought, each happy that they had come out well from the bargain.

This sort of silent trade is almost unique in the history of the world's markets, and I'm sure there would have been a lot less heartache over the economic expansions of Europe in the Renaissance if the same kind of respect for the people they were coming in contact with had been shown.

Herodotus obviously loved this story, and I think it symbolized for him the way people should treat each other: Try to avoid, if at all possible, anything that will lead to strife, to conflict, to violence; respect others; treat others as you would want to be respected.

He did the same kind of exploration in Egypt: He went up the Nile River, and he saw Elephantine, that cataract of the Nile near the Aswan Dam, where the ivory of Africa was brought. That's why it was called Elephantine. He went to southern Italy, of course, when he moved there, and he would describe for his Italian listeners things from around the globe that are given in sort of terms of what an Italian would be able to picture, because his audience is shifting from the Athenians early on to the Italians in the later book, now that he has become an Italian himself.

He traveled through the Persian Empire. The greatest loss is that somewhere along the line there was a scroll, a 10th book, apparently, that would have been what he called Assyrian stories, that is, Mesopotamian history. He did a whole book on the history of Egypt and its monuments. He did the same thing, apparently, for Nineveh, for Babylon, for Assyria and Mesopotamia. Those are lost, but he gives a wonderful description of the towering walls of Babylon, the amazing irrigation ditches, and the hanging gardens. It's all there in Herodotus to charm the mind, to awaken the spirit of inquiry and interest in all of his listeners and in all of his readers.

So in this way, Herodotus gave to the Greek world a picture of its great setting, where the Greeks fit into the world at large—a history of their greatest and proudest hours—those moments of victory over the Persian invaders, but he gave them something else. He gave them a vision to live up to—a vision of harmony between peoples who not only respect themselves but respect others, and at the same time, he reminded the Athenians and Spartans of his own day that there had been a time that they lived at peace. There had been a time when they accomplished great things because they worked together in unity and harmony, and it was Herodotus's dream that those times could come again.

Lecture Fifteen
Engineering the Fall of Athens

Scope: The fall of Athens began with the outbreak of the Peloponnesian War in 431 B.C. against Sparta. The first decade of fighting ended in a moral victory for Athens, but instead of resting content, Alcibiades goaded the Athenians to embark on a risky expedition against Syracuse that ended with a crippling defeat. In the wake of this blow, the Persian satraps Tissaphernes and Pharnabazus attempted to develop an alliance with Sparta. Disgusted by the double-dealings of Tissaphernes, the Spartans joined Pharnabazus in an effort to block the Athenian food supply, resulting in a series of battles during the summer of 410 B.C. and the spring of 409 B.C. that culminated with an Athenian victory at Cyzicus. An overwhelming victory for Sparta at Aegospotami in 405 B.C., however, ended the Peloponnesian War and cemented Sparta's dominance. Athens, it seemed, was finished—and Persia could take credit for engineering its downfall.

Outline

I. During the Peace of Callias (449 B.C.–413 B.C.), Athens and Persia nominally agreed to stop hostilities; nonetheless, elements of conflict continued that gave the period the flavor of a cold war.

   A. When the island of Samos revolted from the Athenians, the Great King clearly planned to aid the revolt, in defiance of the terms of the peace.

   B. When one of the Great King's officials in Asia Minor rebelled, the Athenians gave support.

   C. When the Peloponnesian War broke out in 431 B.C. between Athens and Sparta, the Athenians intercepted communiqués between Sparta and Persia.

II. After the first 10 years of the Peloponnesian War, a peace with Sparta was negotiated. The Athenians, however, allowed Alcibiades to goad them into invading Syracuse to destroy the city and eventually (they hoped) take over the island of Sicily.

- A. Certain Athenians dreamed of ruling the Mediterranean as the Great King ruled over Persia and the lands from the Himalayas to Thrace.
- B. The Athenians' desire to become even richer spurred them to vote in favor of the expedition to Syracuse.
- C. Exiled because of various crimes, Alcibiades fled to Sparta and gave the Spartans advice that enabled them to help the Syracusans defend themselves.
- D. In 413 B.C., after three campaigning seasons in Sicily, the Syracusans destroyed the Athenians in the harbor of Syracuse. No Athenians were left alive or remained free to report the news; thus, the Athenians at home believed they were winning in Sicily for some time.

III. Among those interested in helping to engineer the fall of Athens were a pair of satraps: Tissaphernes, who ruled west-central Asia Minor, and Pharnabazus, who ruled northwest Asia Minor.
- A. Both satraps sent ambassadors to Sparta offering Persian assistance in the destruction of Athens.
- B. Alcibiades advised the Spartans to join with Tissaphernes.
- C. The Spartans agreed to sign away the freedom of all the Greeks in Asia to the Great King on the condition that Persia provide Sparta with enough help to wage a successful war against Athens.
- D. The Athenians, to control the hemorrhaging of money from their treasury, appointed 10 counselors to limit the power of the assembly and govern through a series of referendums. In a few months, the new regime assembled an Athenian fleet and used the island of Samos as a base from which to attack the Spartans and Persians.
- E. When the Spartans were defeated at a battle outside Ephesus, Alcibiades ingratiated himself with Tissaphernes.
    1. He advised Tissaphernes to aid both the Spartans and the Athenians, strengthening each power just enough to weaken the other so that Persia would be the strongest of the three.
    2. The Spartans gradually became aware that Tissaphernes was undercutting the Spartan war effort.

- **F.** Some of the democratic Athenians in the fleet invited Alcibiades to return as commander; wanting nothing more than to get back to Athens, he agreed.
- **IV.** Giving up on the theater of war around Ionia, Ephesus, and Samos, the Spartans made a dash northward to the Hellespont.
  - **A.** The Hellespont was the lifeline of Athens.
    1. Athens depended on it for basic commodities imported from great distances, especially grain.
    2. The Spartans realized that if they grabbed the straits, they could starve Athens into submission.
  - **B.** With the help of Pharnabazus, the Spartans clashed with the Athenians twice in the Hellespont.
    1. Both battles resulted in unexpected victories for Athens.
    2. Though the Spartans lost the Battle of Abydos, Pharnabazus agreed to continue funding the war effort.
  - **C.** Learning that the Spartans had taken the former Athenian city of Cyzicus, the Athenians decided to reclaim it, ruin the Spartan naval effort, and discredit the Spartans with the Persians.
    1. Using a small force of Athenian triremes, Alcibiades lured the Spartans away from the harbor at Cyzicus.
    2. With the harbor undefended, the main body of the Athenian fleet moved into position and waited for Alcibiades to return before taking the city.
    3. With this failure, Pharnabazus lost interest in the Spartan effort.
- **V.** A few years later, the Great King sent his son, Prince Cyrus, to help the Spartans win the war against the Athenians as a means of securing tribute from the eastern Greeks.
  - **A.** Prince Cyrus befriended the Spartan commander Lysander.
  - **B.** Lysander secured funding and campaigned against the Athenians, finally defeating the fleet at Aegospotami and winning the Peloponnesian War.
  - **C.** Lysander then sailed to Athens, secured the surrender of the city, and tore down the Long Walls of Piraeus.
  - **D.** The Persians had gained from the Peloponnesian War exactly what they wanted: The Athenian Empire was broken, and the Spartans,

about whom the Persians were not particularly worried, had returned the Greek cities in Asia to the Great King.

Recommended Reading:

Kagan, *The Fall of the Athenian Empire.*

Plutarch, *The Rise and Fall of Athens: Nine Greek Lives.*

Questions to Consider:

1. Was Athens doomed to fall? How could it have withstood the machinations of such individuals as Alcibiades, Tissaphernes, and Pharnabazus?

2. What other reasons, if any, are there to ally oneself with a former enemy other than to achieve a strategic advantage?

Lecture Fifteen—Transcript
Engineering the Fall of Athens

Welcome back. That Peace of Callias—concluded in 449 B.C. between the Athenian maritime empire on the one hand and the great empire of Persia on the other—was to last 37 years. That may not seem very long, but since there had been 50 years of continuous fighting beforehand—from 499 B.C., when the Ionian revolt broke out, all the way down to that final conclusion of peace—that 37 years looked pretty good.

During that time, even though Athens and Persia were nominally agreeing to stop their hostilities and to agree to mutually exclusive spheres of influence, there were certainly elements of conflict that gave it the feeling of a cold war. When the island of Samos, which was a major player in the Athenian Empire—one of the Ionian states that they had brought in, first as an ally and then much more as a subject—revolted from Athens, it was clear that the Great King was planning to help with the revolt in defiance of the terms of the peace.

On the other hand, when one of the Great King's officials in Asia Minor rebelled against the Great King, the Athenians gave support. And finally the Peloponnesian War broke out in 431 B.C. between Athens and Sparta, that terrible Greek-against-Greek war that inspired Herodotus to write his history of the Persian wars and remind the Greeks of his own time—these warring Athenians and Spartans—that they were filling their world with calamities that didn't need to happen, that they should unite again with a common purpose as they had once done against the Persians.

Even during that Peloponnesian War, the Athenians managed to intercept a messenger, who was coming from the Great King Artaxerxes to the Spartans, and discover that the message that the fellow was carrying was a letter from the Great King saying to the Spartans: "I don't understand you. You keep sending me envoys and ambassadors. Every single one of them carries a different message. What do you want?"

It's not clear what the Spartans wanted. They certainly wanted the fall of Athens, and they wanted Persian help to do it, but they were aware that Persian help always came with strings attached, and they just couldn't seem to make up their minds. At any rate, this made it clear to the Athenians that although they were formally or informally at peace with Persia, the Persians were still to be feared as an element in their lives.

After the first 10 years of the Peloponnesian War, a peace with Sparta was concluded in 421 B.C. Athens seemed to have come very well out of that first 10 years of the Peloponnesian War. Then, like madmen, the Athenians allowed themselves to be goaded by one young hellion named Alcibiades into embarking upon a distant expedition that they didn't need to undertake. It was an attempt to destroy the great western city of Syracuse in Sicily and, ultimately, take over the whole island of Sicily—a great source of grain, rich Greek colonial cities, large populations. They would bring Sicily into their empire.

There were certain Athenians who dreamed of ruling the Mediterranean as the Great King ruled over Persia and the lands from the Himalayas all the way to Thrace. They thought that they could turn the Mediterranean into an Athenian lake once they had conquered Sicily; if they could just knock off the Carthaginians in North Africa and the Etruscans in Italy, it would all be theirs.

So they were very receptive in about the year 416 B.C.—five years after they had fought Sparta to a standstill—when this young Alcibiades came forward in the assembly and urged the Athenians to undertake this expedition to Syracuse.

They had a few trumped-up excuses and pretexts for attacking this fellow democracy among Greek cities, and the desire to become even richer than they were now spurred them to vote in favor of this big expedition going west to Sicily.

Our course is about the Greeks and the Persians, not about Greeks versus Greeks, so we will not follow them in detail. But suffice it to say that this expedition ended in tragedy for all concerned. Alcibiades, this brilliant, young Athenian commander and politician—brave as a lion, cunning as Odysseus, charismatic in a way that very few Athenian leaders had ever been—was the ward of Pericles, the architect of the Athenian Golden Age. He'd been brought up almost like a young prince in Athens, ready to take over the position as first citizen of the city. He was found guilty by his fellow citizens of various crimes and exiled.

He fled away to Sparta and took refuge there with Athens's enemies. He was so bitter about his treatment from his fellow citizens that he worked tirelessly through the years of the Sicilian expedition to ruin Athens—to give the Spartans advice that would allow them to help the Syracusans defend themselves against the Athenians and, ultimately, defeat the Athenians and also to tell the Spartans: "Get up there in Attica. Plant yourself a fort right outside Athens and lay siege to the city." The Spartans did that, and that was a terrific blow against Athenian independence and the prospects for the future.

So Alcibiades had now become an evil genius working against his home city from outside. It all came to a head in the year 413 B.C., when—after three campaigning seasons in Sicily—the whole thing ended in total disaster in the great harbor of Syracuse. The Athenians were trapped with their fleet and their men inside the great harbor, and the Syracusans destroyed them. More than 160 triremes were lost, thousands of men were killed or imprisoned, and that was the end of the Syracusan expedition.

How did the Athenians hear about the disaster? Well, the word was spreading through the Mediterranean, but there was no Athenian who survived alive or free to carry the message home to Athens. So a long time went by with the Athenians in the happy illusion that they were still winning in Sicily, when a stray mariner brought his ship into the Piraeus, walked into a barber shop for a shave and a haircut, and sitting there in the chair, said to the barber, "Terrible thing what happened to you Athenians in Sicily." The barber said, "What do you mean?" The man told him of the great defeat, and the barber ran all the way the 4.5 miles up to Athens to tell the archons of the city what had happened.

At that point, as the news spread that Athens had been defeated there, Athens's enemies and rivals everywhere joined together to destroy this great Golden Age city that had brought so many wonderful, creative things into the world but that had brought this very oppressive imperialism along with them.

One of the sets of people who were interested now in helping to engineer the fall of Athens were the Persians, and the two who took the lead were a couple of satraps—those provincial governors—whose territories abutted the eastern side of the Athenian Empire. These were the western satrapies of what is today Turkey, Asia Minor—one led by a wily rogue named Tissaphernes, whose capital was at Sardis and his satrapy was west-central Asia Minor, and the other was a noble Persian warrior named Pharnabazus. He ruled from a headquarters up near the Sea of Marmara, and he ruled over northwest Anatolia, northwest Asia Minor.

These two sent ambassadors (along with lots of cities and islands) to Sparta, saying, "Come to us first. There are Athenians right here who you can fight. We occupy a great territory for launching attacks on the Athenians. We will help you. We will fund your expeditions. Let us be the staging ground for the final destruction of Athens."

The Spartans weren't sure which way to turn. At this point, Alcibiades, still living at Sparta, advised the Spartans, "Pick Tissaphernes. Cross the sea to Persia. Cross the sea to Asia and join with Tissaphernes, this satrap at Sardis, and let's defeat the Athenians there." Alcibiades had his own reasons for wanting this to happen and for getting out of Greece. Irrepressible as ever, he had managed to have a love affair with the queen of Sparta—one of the wives of one of the two kings—and had managed to get her pregnant. She was bearing his child and was actually so besotted with Alcibiades that she was proud of it. He wanted to get out before his head was on a platter. So before the word got to this king that Alcibiades had cuckolded him, Alcibiades headed off in his ship, crossed over to Asia, and met with Tissaphernes.

He had finally met someone as wily, as unreliable, and as deceitful as himself, and the two got along like a house on fire Alcibiades negotiated a sort of meeting between Tissaphernes, this powerful Persian noble—this satrap—and the Spartans who followed Alcibiades over. In a disgraceful meeting, the Spartans agreed to sign away the freedom of all the Greeks in Asia—that freedom whose existence had actually triggered the whole Greek and Persian wars to begin with. The Spartans were willing to sign them over—lock, stock, and barrel—to the Great King if only the Persians would provide the Spartans with enough help—especially enough money—to successfully wage a war against Athens. So that was the final agreement that was concluded.

Alcibiades thought that that would be the end of it, but out of nowhere, the Athenians showed up. As Thucydides, who is the historian and chronicler of this period, says, "Democracies are always at their best in a crisis." Well, after the great defeat in the harbor at Syracuse in Sicily, the Athenians were at the supreme crisis of their history, and they rallied. They took extreme measures to control the hemorrhaging of money out of their treasury. They appointed 10 counselors to review all the proposals, to limit the democracy and the power of the assembly to vote anything. They basically governed through a series of referendums on every single issue, and now with these 10 counselors in place, there was a sort of a check on the power of the people—a balance to the impulses of the assembly to go one way or the other.

One of these counselors is a man that we should pause and look at for a moment. He's the famous tragic playwright Sophocles, whose most famous play today is *Oedipus Rex*. He was the most respected Athenian. He had actually served for a time as a naval commander during that rebellion of Samos. He had been a treasurer of the Athenian Empire, and now he was appointed counselor. He was a very old man by this time. His memory went all the way back to the Battle of Salamis, where he'd been a 17-year-old, the handsomest boy in Athens, and he had been chosen to lead the victory dance for the Battle of Salamis all those years ago.

Now he found Athens at the nadir of its fortunes, and he was among those old men working to pull the city up by its bootstraps. So successful was this new regime that within a few months, they had put together an Athenian fleet—they bought timber from the northern kingdom of Macedon, they built new ships, they conscripted everybody into the fleet again, just as they had done at Salamis, and sent them across to the island of Samos, using that as a base to attack the Spartans and Persians on Asia Minor, taking the offensive.

So there was a battle outside Ephesus. Alcibiades was with the Persian and Spartan side and had the mortification of seeing them—the Spartans—beaten on land by an Athenian expeditionary force. At this point, he said to himself, "These Spartans are losers. I'm fighting with the wrong side." So he went up to Sardis, and he ingratiated himself with the Persians there—with Tissaphernes, with all these nobles of the court. It was a very different life from what he'd been experiencing in Sparta—with the mess tents, and the black broth, and the hard bread, and the living tough, and talking short, and pretending to like Spartan ways. Now it was all cushions, gourmet food, perfumes, delicate music, and court intrigues.

Alcibiades, like a chameleon, managed to fit in there just as well as he fitted in at Sparta, and he soon became Tissaphernes's—the satrap's—best friend. He said something to Tissaphernes that became a thread of Persian policy toward the Greeks for the next 80 years: "Don't arrange for one side to beat the other; help them both. Keep them both just healthy enough that they can batter away, Athens against Sparta, and ultimately weaken each other so you, the Persians, will always be the stronger of the three."

This was very pleasing advice to Tissaphernes—he liked nothing better than double-dealing and double-crossing. So under the pretense of still helping the Spartans and holding up his end of that agreement—that if the Persians would give the Spartans help, the Spartans would turn over the Greek cities of Ionia and of Asia back to the king once the war was over and Athens was defeated—Tissaphernes was, in fact, continually undercutting the war effort for the Spartans, and the Spartans became gradually aware of this.

After a couple of years of this, in 411 B.C., an amazing thing happened. The Athenian fleet was still stationed on the island of Samos. You can swim across from Samos to Mount Mycale on the Asiatic mainland, so they were right there near the heartbeat of all of this intrigue and diplomacy. They were aware that Alcibiades was up at Sardis, and many of the common men, the democratic men in the Athenian fleet, longed for Alcibiades. They'd always liked him. They thought he was given a raw deal when he was exiled, and they sent a messenger to Sardis inviting Alcibiades to come and lead not the city of Athens but the fleet, which was becoming a breakaway power of its own.

He wanted nothing more than to get back to Athens. He was fed up with Spartans, and he was fed up with Persians, and he wanted to take his kinsman Pericles's place as the leader of his natal city, and so he agreed. He went down to Samos and became one of the generals of the fleet, now restored to Athens. How many reverses can one have in a four- or five-year period? Alcibiades went through all of them.

At this point, the Spartans, in disgust, remembered that that good, noble, reliable Persian up by the Hellespont, Pharnabazus, had also offered to collaborate with the Spartans in destroying Athens. So they gave up on Ionia, and they gave up on Ephesus and Samos and that whole theater of war, and—putting all of their troops into their triremes—they made a dash for the north and the Hellespont.

We've been to the Hellespont before. You remember, it's that channel of water that leads the waters from the Black Sea down into the Aegean; and it's the place where Xerxes spanned the straits with those pontoon bridges that allowed his Grand Army, in the spring of 480 B.C., to cross over into Greece; and it was the place where the Athenians had gone and recaptured the Hellespont and took those cables of the bridges and carried them back home.

The Hellespont was the lifeline of Athens. We talked a little bit before about how this is a time of global economy. Athens depended even for its basic commodities, like wheat and fish, on imports from great distances, and the Black Sea was one of the key areas of Athenian control. In fact, they had managed to add it to their empire in the 420s B.C., and Black Sea cities appear on the tribute list. They were inscribed in stone on the Athenian Acropolis.

It was a terrifying thing for the Athenians to learn that there were Spartans now in the Hellespont. Most of the grain that kept Athenians alive and gave them their daily bread came through that narrow pass—that channel of water—coming down in the great annual grain fleets of harvests of grain from the Black Sea area, from the Crimea, from the Ukraine. Athens depended for its existence on those ships, and finally, the Spartans had put two and two together and realized: "If we can grab those straits, we can starve Athens to submission without ever going anywhere near the city."

Pharnabazus—the noble, and reliable, and honorable Persian who led the king's forces up there along the Hellespont (the Sea of Marmara, the Bosphorus)—proved to be a completely different kettle of fish from Tissaphernes, his colleague to the south. He not only helped the Spartans, he actually joined them in the battles that succeeded this move, as the Athenians chased after the Spartans going up to the north, entrenched themselves in the Hellespont also, and clashed twice with the Spartan fleet in the stream of the Hellespont. Very difficult naval battles, where the water is sweeping you down all the time, like the current of a river, and you're trying to maintain place and keep battering away at the enemy in the straits.

At any rate, both of these battles resulted in victories for the Athenians, completely unexpected for all concerned. But in the second battle, called the Battle of Abydos—named after the town on the south side of the Hellespont where Xerxes had anchored his bridges—Pharnabazus was so fired up by the sight of these Athenian ships charging down on the Spartans and the Spartans fleeing to shore that he got on his horse, rallied his Persian cavalry, and they charged into the water to try to fight the Athenians—lances of the Persians sort of threatening these Athenian ships as they came in, hoping to save the Spartans, hoping to turn the tide of the battle.

A very impetuous man, Pharnabazus, and a very heroic one, but in spite of all of his efforts, they lost that battle. He agreed, however, to keep funding the Spartan effort over the winter—paying them for that one essential thing that Sparta couldn't afford, because Sparta had no treasury, Sparta had no empire, and Sparta didn't even really have money. They were a sort of honor society of militaristic folk who were called upon by all and sundry for help, but didn't build up great wealth themselves. How could they have a navy? Only if Persia would pay for the rowers—those hundreds, those thousands, of skilled oarsmen who were needed in these galleys.

Pharnabazus says, "I will keep paying you, and I will provide you a place to spend the winter."

He went back to his capital, a place called Dascylium, just south of the Sea of Marmara, and he entrenched himself there with his cavalry by a big lake, and then he built a fort for mercenaries that he paid for—Persian mercenaries—to be on the coast. Right by that mercenary fort, there was a city that the Spartans took over, a former city of the Athenian Empire, called Cyzicus. At this base, the Spartans kept their fleet over the winter and trained their oarsmen that were paid for by Pharnabazus the Persian, waiting for spring.

Alcibiades and his fellow Athenian generals learned that the Spartans had taken Cyzicus, and they decided they were going to get it back. They were also going to try to ruin the Spartan naval effort at sea and discredit the Spartans with the Persians, so the Persians would stop paying the Spartans—would lose their feeling of confidence in the Spartans to destroy Athens.

So under cover of darkness, the Athenians went from the mouth of the Hellespont, from Sestos, in their ships, slipping past all the Spartan guard posts in the night, so that there would be no word of their coming as they went up the channel and approached Cyzicus. They would row during the night, and they would sleep on shore, hidden during the day. Nobody knew they were coming. They spent the last night of their approach on an island in the middle of the Sea of Marmara, and Alcibiades called them in together, these Athenians.

He said: "We have no money left. We have nothing to support ourselves. If you want to feed yourselves, and if you want to go beyond that and be rich and free, you are going to have to fight on the sea. You're going to have to fight on land, and you're going to have to take walled cities—you're going to have to win your way back to prosperity and victory. Are you with me?" Well, of course, they were all with him; it was a very exciting moment, and he was always a great one for rousing the spirits of the men.

So that evening, they got into their ships, and they headed south toward Cyzicus, the place where the Spartans had holed up—right under that great fort of the Persian mercenaries and not too far from Pharnabazus's headquarters with his Persian cavalry.

At this point, the Spartans and Persians alike had begun to discount the Athenian effort. The Athenians had not been much in evidence during the winter, and it seemed very likely that they had just sort of split up and gone away. Instead, they were right there—headed down in the darkness—and their plan of approaching without being caught was very much favored by a heavy shower of rain that came down. So all the Spartan scouts on the coast went into their little huts and shelters, and the Athenian fleet approached with no one knowing they were there.

The Athenians first came into shore in the hours before dawn and put an army on shore—on the coast, north of Cyzicus—with orders to go up to the city wall and be ready to attack the city on the land side as the fleet attacked the city harbor at Cyzicus. Then they put into effect the last part of their plan. Alcibiades had spent a couple of years of his youth campaigning in northern Greece with a great Athenian general named Phormio, the greatest strategist and tactician the Athenians ever produced after Themistocles. Phormio had taught Alcibiades (and anybody else who was with him) how you draw an enemy away from a strong position. It's like the bird and the snake: You put a tempting little morsel in front of the enemy that they can't resist chasing after, and once they've left their secure position or broken up their fine formation, that's when you hit them.

Alcibiades volunteered to be the bird. He took a small force of Athenian triremes, and he rowed forward, burst out of the curtain of rain, and there was the sunshine, and there in the sunshine was the whole Spartan fleet out on the water, doing their morning exercises. They caught sight of Alcibiades and his little expeditionary force, assuming that this was a group of unwitting Athenians who foolishly had appeared, thinking Cyzicus was still a friendly city—not aware that the Spartans were there in force. They immediately stopped their exercising and set off after Alcibiades and his little squadron in dead earnest.

They chased them away across the Sea of Marmara, and as they left Cyzicus's harbor undefended, the main body of the Athenians moved into position and waited for Alcibiades to come back and join them in taking the city. But Alcibiades, unreliable as always, had gone sort of crazy out there on the water. As he turned and faced the Spartans who were chasing him, and they looked back and saw they were now between two fires—two Athenian fleets—the Spartans went for the mainland. Alcibiades, who should have, at this point, rejoined his fellows, chased after them—chased them to the shore—actually landed his few marines, formed up as if he had an army behind him (when, in fact, it was just a few hundred Athenian marines), and attacked the Spartan army that had come off the ships.

He was as brave as a lion, but he didn't always have a lot of sense. This time, his impetuosity paid off. His colleagues, his fellow Athenian generals, saw across the water what was happening. One of them decided to go help him immediately, and the other one went to fetch the army that was waiting on land for the appointed time to come over the walls. As Theramenes, the Athenian, went off to get the army, Thrasybulus, his colleague, landed the other Athenian force at the other end of the grounded Spartan fleet, came ashore, and started fighting the Spartans from that side.

Meanwhile, Pharnabazus's mercenaries had seen what was going on from the fort, and they came spilling in their hundreds down the mountainside to join in the battle. Things looked bad for the Athenians when, at the last possible minute, Theramenes, the third general, arrived—having picked up the troops from the city and landing them in time to turn the tide of battle. The Spartan general was killed—he was a man named Mindarus, in whom Pharnabazus had placed a lot of hope.

The Spartans were routed. The Athenians chased them back to their fort, and then when they heard the Persian cavalry and Pharnabazus coming at them, they retreated back to their ships. There was scarcely as happy a set of men in ancient history as those Athenians on the day that they beat the Spartans and the Persians together at Cyzicus.

They intercepted another message right after that, as the surviving Spartan leader sent word of this terrible defeat back to Sparta, asking the home folks—the *ephors* in Sparta—what to do. The Athenians were amused to find this very laconic message. (Our word *laconic* comes from *Laconia*, the Spartan homeland. It means to be short and terse in your speech.) This was the true telegraph kind of style of message, and it went like this: "Mindarus dead. Ships lost. Men starving. Don't know what to do."

They indeed did not know what to do because their failure had guaranteed that Pharnabazus lost interest in the Spartan effort. In fact, it was only the arrival a couple of years later of a new element in the scene, a Persian prince named Cyrus—after his great predecessor, the conqueror Cyrus who started the Persian Empire—sent out by his father, the Great King, with orders to help the Spartans win the war. The Great King finally realized that if we can just get all those Ionian cities back, we will once again have our tribute from the eastern Greeks. It was all about money.

Prince Cyrus became the friend of a new Spartan commander, Lysander, the greatest strategic genius Sparta ever produced. Between the help of Prince Cyrus paying for Lysander's crews—Lysander once looked gloomy at a feast with Prince Cyrus, and the Persian said, "What do you want? I'll give you anything." Lysander said to him, "I want one more *obol* a day for my crews." That was what he was thinking of—Persian gold to pay for Spartan military effort. He got the money, and he put together some wonderful campaigns against Athens, caught the Athenian fleet finally in the Hellespont at a place called Goat Rivers—Aegospotami—and trapped them on land due to his own clever strategies, and beat the Athenians. He won the Peloponnesian War, sailed to Athens, and tore down the city walls of Athens after Athens itself surrendered.

I shouldn't have said "the city walls." It was those Long Walls (that umbilical cord) that connected Athens to its port—the Piraeus—that were torn down. Showman that he was, Lysander had the pipers—the girls who played pipes at parties in Athens—come out and play tunes as the Spartan engineers dismantled the fortifications of Athens that had made it a great naval power.

It was all thanks to Persia. The Persians had gotten out of this war exactly what they wanted: The Athenian Empire was broken up. The Spartans, who they didn't worry about—although they should have—now did turn the Greek cities in Asia back over to the Persians, at least temporarily. As the Long Walls came crashing down, as a pro-Spartan government of Thirty Tyrants took over in Athens, and as that government of the Thirty Tyrants actually tore down the naval installations and the ship sheds in the Piraeus—the pride and glory of the Athenian fleet, the basis of Athenian power for half a century—everybody in the Greek world could have been forgiven for thinking: "This, at last, is the end of Athens."

But the Delphic Oracle had once proclaimed Athens unsinkable, saying that it would ride forever upon the waves of the ocean. Truly, although Persian gold had brought Athens down, now by a great twist of fate and to the astonishment of all, within 10 years, the Persians themselves would raise Athens up again.

Lecture Sixteen
Cyrus, Xenophon, and the Ten Thousand

Scope: In 404 B.C. (the same year that Athens fell), King Darius II died, and Prince Cyrus's older brother, Artaxerxes II, was named successor to the throne. Bitterly disappointed, Cyrus gathered an army of Asian troops and Greek mercenaries, known collectively as the Ten Thousand, and set out to take the throne from his brother in the spring of 401 B.C. Led by a rough Spartan named Clearchus, the army was accompanied by an enormous train that included personal slaves, cooks, craft workers, engineers, and a young Athenian volunteer, Xenophon, who later recorded the details of the army's march. Hiding his true intentions from the increasingly frustrated Greeks, Prince Cyrus marched through the Taurus Mountains, the Euphrates River, and barren desert regions before encountering Artaxerxes II and his forces (at Cunaxa). There, the two brothers met to fight a battle on a scale worthy of the prize: the Persian Empire itself.

Outline

I. In the spring of 404 B.C., Darius II died, leaving his elder son, Artaxerxes, as his successor.

   A. Darius's principal wife, Queen Parysatis, had two sons: the older Artaxerxes and the younger Prince Cyrus.

   B. Prince Cyrus was the favorite of the queen, who had fed him the notion of becoming king in spite of his age.

   C. Suspicious of his younger brother, Artaxerxes sent Cyrus to Asia Minor to serve as viceroy over the satraps there.

II. Prince Cyrus decided to raise his own army and march on the Persian heartland to seize the throne, which he believed was his by right of superior character.

   A. Cyrus used his gold to hire an army of about 13,000 Greeks (10,000 hoplites and 3,000 "peltasts," or light-arm troops) that came to be known as the Ten Thousand.

   B. One of the young men who joined the Ten Thousand was an Athenian named Xenophon.

1. The aristocratic Xenophon hated the democracy and felt alienated from Athens.
2. He had been a student of Socrates, who was against the idea of Xenophon joining the Persian army for fear that it would lead to the young man's banishment.
3. After visiting the Delphic Oracle, Xenophon traveled to Sardis to join Cyrus's army.

C. The leader of the 10,000 hoplites was a renegade Spartan named Clearchus, a former Spartan *harmost* (the head of a garrison) who had been stripped of his command.

III. The Ten Thousand set out from Sardis for the heart of the Persian Empire in the spring of 401 B.C.

A. Prince Cyrus had confided the true destination of the force only in Clearchus. The rest of the men were told that the goal of the campaign was to suppress troublesome hill tribes in the highland country of Pisidia.

B. In Cilicia, the men staged the first of many mutinies, refusing to go further until they had received full payment for their services thus far.
1. One way to keep troops loyal to a cause was to hold their pay until the campaign was over.
2. Prince Cyrus had enough money for the initial payments but not enough to give his soldiers the arrears of pay they were demanding.
3. The wagon train following the army, which Cyrus also had to support, included probably 1,500 wheeled carts carrying a variety of tradesmen, from weapon makers and bakers to weavers and carpenters.

C. To keep his soldiers happy, Prince Cyrus allowed them to plunder the troublesome area of Lycaonia.

D. Traders followed behind the army and resold plundered goods purchased from the soldiers; a large portion of this trade involved slavery.
1. In the ancient world, unlike in American history, slavery was regarded as a misfortune that could happen to anyone.
2. All slaves had the hope that they could earn their way out of slavery.
3. Slaves did not play important roles in ancient warfare.

IV. The journey the Ten Thousand made to the heart of the Persian Empire was called by the Greeks *anabasis* ("going up").
  A. The Greeks always spoke of traveling from Sardis to Susa, the capital of the Persian Empire, as "going up."
  B. The book that Xenophon wrote about the march was called *Anabasis* in reference to the army's progress along that route.
  C. Cyrus continued to lie to his army about its true destination, hoping to hold off sharing that information for as long as possible.
  D. At Issos, the army found 700 more hoplite soldiers (sent in thanks from Sparta for Persian support during the Peloponnesian War) and marched on through the Syrian Gates.
  E. Once the soldiers crossed the mountains, they vowed not to move until Cyrus promised to pay every man five *minae* of silver when the journey ended. Cyrus was forced to agree to keep the army moving toward the Euphrates River.
  F. On the other side of the Euphrates, the army reached the Wall of Media, which had been built between the Euphrates and Tigris to serve as a defense against forces like the Ten Thousand.
    1. The army passed the wall, expecting to find it held against them, but it was not.
    2. A Persian general who was in the region was so terrified of the size of Prince Cyrus's army that he had abandoned the wall and fled southward to join Artaxerxes II's forces.
  G. Two days after Prince Cyrus's army left the wagon train behind, it came across Artaxerxes II's massive army at Cunaxa.

Recommended Reading:

Trundle, *Greek Mercenaries: From the Late Archaic Period to Alexander.*

Xenophon, *The Persian Expedition.*

Questions to Consider:

1. Given the conflict between Prince Cyrus and his brother, Artaxerxes II, what role do family affairs play in the larger scheme of historical events?
2. How do you think the Ten Thousand would have reacted had they known of their destination (the heart of the Persian Empire) from the start?

Lecture Sixteen—Transcript
Cyrus, Xenophon, and the Ten Thousand

Welcome back. In the spring of 404 B.C., the same year in which Athens fell, the Great King—far away in Persia—died. There was a question as to who would succeed him. His principal wife, Queen Parysatis, had two sons: an older son named Artaxerxes and a younger son whom we have already met—that Prince Cyrus who was sent westward to Asia Minor to be the viceroy there and to bring about the fall of Athens and the return of the Ionian cities to the king's fold through helping Sparta.

Prince Cyrus was his mother's favorite. Parysatis had been feeding him with the notion that in spite of the fact that he was the younger son, he would be king. His sterling qualities as a commander and as a person would ensure that his father would name him. Well, his father did not, and so Prince Cyrus started the new regime with a great feeling of having been hard done by, which continued to be fed by his mother, the queen.

He was in the capital at Susa when his father died, and Artaxerxes, the new king, was suspicious—and quite justifiably so—of Prince Cyrus, his younger brother. So just to get him out of the way, he sent him back to Asia Minor—back to the west as some sort of viceroy over the satraps there. This was a new arrangement in Persian affairs at that time, but it was simply intended to get his brother out of the scenes of court intrigues and places where he might be able to stage a palace coup.

It's not clear what would have happened if Prince Cyrus had been kept at court and integrated into palace life. Perhaps he would have settled down, realized what his place was, and been a good brother to Artaxerxes. But knowing that you're under suspicion is a situation that often impels one to do the very thing that you are suspected of being about to do.

Prince Cyrus decided, as he was there in Asia Minor, that he was darn well going to raise his own army, and he was going to march on the heartland of Persia—his brother's kingdom—and seize the throne that he felt was his by right of superior character. Where was he going to get this army? Well, the Greek world was now at peace for the first time in 27 years of fighting this Peloponnesian War. Thousands of men who had been in the armies on the Athenian side or on the Peloponnesian and Spartan side and were now free—fully trained, no place to go.

The Greek economy was somewhat depressed by the fall of Athens as Athens had been the great economic engine of Greece, and so Cyrus decided to use his gold to hire an army—the army that came to be known as the Ten Thousand. It was an army of about 13,000 Greeks, the core of which was 10,000 hoplites—those heavily armed infantry shield men who fought side to side in the phalanx—and there was an additional 3,000 archers, slingshot specialists, javelin throwers, light-arm troops—the people that the Greeks called "peltasts" because they would pelt the enemy with missiles—not nearly so prestigious as the hoplite warriors.

The call went out through the Greek world. Through various channels, through agents of the Persians, the Greeks came to know, Greek young men came to hear, about this great opportunity. The tradition of being a soldier of fortune, and especially a soldier of fortune in the East, went back hundreds of years. In fact, it's my belief that the Greek hoplite tradition really began because these Greeks learned that they could find fame, glory, and wealth by learning how to fight in the hoplite phalanx and hiring themselves out to these potentates—everywhere from Iberia to the Nile.

So Cyrus was not really doing something new, but the scale of putting together an army of 10,000 to 13,000—that's the size of the army of Athens, not the fleet, but the actual land army of Athens was that same size, and now it's going to be a mercenary army under the leadership of one Persian prince, bound for the heartland of Asia.

One of the young men who heard about this opportunity heard about it from a friend of his in the Greek region of Boeotia—the area where the city of Thebes is, traditional enemies of Athens. This young Athenian who heard about it was named Xenophon. He was 27 years old at the time, still not a full age in the Athenian system. In Athens, you are able to go into the assembly, and start to sit, and listen to debates, and vote when you're 20, but you must spend the next 10 years listening, learning, and then at 30, you can both make your maiden speech in the assembly and you can also be elected to a magistrate's post, or elected general, or something like that. To be elected to some of the posts, like general, you also had to have married and had children so you had a real stake in the city's future.

Xenophon, at 27, was feeling very alienated from his city of Athens. He was, of course, disappointed to be living in a city that had just been defeated, but he hated the democracy. He was born an aristocrat, and he was a rider—a horseman. In later life, he wrote the ancient world's greatest book on horsemanship. He felt apart from the mass of Athenians. He had associated himself with possibly the greatest Athenian of all time, a teacher named Socrates—a great teacher who had no schoolhouse but, rather, could be found in the agora (the "open space") under the plain trees planted by Cimon—talking, inquiring, probing, driving people nuts with his endless questions about what did things really mean and what were they doing with their lives.

Xenophon was a student of Socrates at the same time that young Plato was a student. Socrates was like that other famous teacher of antiquity, Jesus, who never wrote anything down himself, but his followers couldn't stop writing about him, and what he said, and what it all meant. So Xenophon and Plato are, for us, the two lenses through which we can see back to Socrates and what it was like to be with him there in Athens. But they are very different lenses. They presumably each distort in a slightly different way what the true Socrates was like.

Plato was very interested in intellectualism: in ideas and ideals—the whole idea of the world really being about ideal forms that are hidden from us but which the material world is continually striving to assimilate itself to. That's in Plato, and that's his view of what mattered in Socrates's talk—this idea of the quest for beauty, for virtue, for ideal behavior patterns, and ideal understandings of the moral world.

Xenophon remembered Socrates as the most practical person he'd ever met—practical in the sense of wanting to talk to people about being the best possible soldier you can be, the best general you can be. He talked about tactics—about approaches to everyday life—using very humble similes all the time from everyday life. So we get two very different visions of Socrates from Xenophon and from his contemporary and rival—the two obviously didn't get along very well—Plato.

Xenophon went to Socrates, his teacher, and told him what he was planning to do. Now Socrates had been a soldier. In fact, early on, Socrates was a friend of Alcibiades, that notorious Athenian whom we met last time. When Alcibiades, as an 18-year-old, enlisted under the famous Athenian tactician and military leader Phormio—whom we also talked about last time—he and Socrates had gone together under Phormio's command to the north of Greece, had fought in a winter campaign there, and had had many adventures.

Alcibiades had fought his way through to the enemy position and had fallen from a wound. Socrates had placed himself over Alcibiades's fallen, wounded body and kept the enemy at bay until help could arrive. Socrates was given the prize—well, Alcibiades was initially given the prize for valor in that fight—a suit of hoplite armor by the great general Phormio, and Alcibiades promptly gave it to his beloved Socrates as a token of his love and his friendship.

It was a wild time, and everybody in Athens was involved in the military. That was part of the mark of a citizen. So Socrates was no stranger to warfare. On the other hand, because we're going to drift away from Socrates in a moment, I just would like to say that Xenophon puts us in touch with what was perhaps the younger Socrates. Socrates himself said he started off his philosophical life inquiring after things, like how far is the Sun from the Earth, and what do you suppose the Sun weighs, and natural historical questions of what we would consider a scientific nature. Then he decided partway through his adult life: "What am I doing? What does all this matter? It's what's inside people that counts. It's the moral decisions that you make; it's the way you lead your life. It's your thoughts. This is what I should be talking about—men, not nature."

So he shifted over to the kind of philosopher that we know of from the writings of Plato and a little bit from Xenophon, as well. He had, therefore, become a magnet for young men in Athens who wanted to think deeply about the choices they were making in life. Socrates called that his "second voyaging." He said, "It's as if you're out on a ship. You've got the sail up to begin with; that's what I was on my first phase of philosophy: I was sailing along with the wind, and then the wind dropped. Well, I ran out the oars, and I went ahead by rowing. That was my 'second voyaging,' and that's what I'm doing now. It's manpower at the oars I'm studying—people, men, human beings—what can I do to help you see yourself, know yourself—in the Delphic Oracle's terms—and make the right choice?"

He was very against this idea of Xenophon's—of going off with the Persians. The reason was this: Prince Cyrus was known in Athens to have funded the Spartan drive that finally succeeded in destroying Athens and taking away the Athenian Empire. Prince Cyrus of Persia was the man that Xenophon was planning to go and swear his allegiance to and fight for. Socrates was very concerned that this would result in Xenophon's banishment—exile from Athens—by an angry fellow citizenry, who would regard Xenophon then as a traitor. He didn't want that to happen to this beloved young man.

So Xenophon said, "I'll go to the Delphic Oracle, and I'll ask for advice." He went across the mountains to Mount Parnassus in Delphi, and he went into the temple and down that long ramp that the Athenian envoys and the Lydian envoys had all gone down before him, into the crypt, into the darkness. He asked his question of the woman, but he didn't really remain true to Socrates's hope that he would say, "Should I go on this expedition?" He said, instead, "If I go on this expedition, which gods should I sacrifice to for success?" He got an answer from Delphi. He went back and told Socrates what he'd done. Socrates was annoyed with him but gave him his blessing, and off went Xenophon to that city we've been to so often: Sardis, near the western coast of Asia Minor—the capital of the old kingdom of Lydia, where our story began with Croesus 150 years before Xenophon sets off.

Xenophon arrived and found that the leader of this group of mercenaries that Prince Cyrus was putting together was a Spartan, a renegade Spartan—a notorious man named Clearchus who had been among the Spartan leaders who were put in charge of various cities around what had been the Athenian Empire and what was, at the speed of light, turning into a Spartan Empire.

The Persians had not imagined this happening. They still thought of the Spartans as rather stodgy people who would never spend much time away from home. They had reckoned this without Lysander—that imperialist, that genius, that strategic mastermind who'd figured out how to catapult Sparta into the same position Athens had held as leaders of the Greeks at large. As for Lysander—who is denied the possibility of ever being king in Sparta because he's not of the royal line—this is the way that he hopes, as Themistocles once hoped, to be the first man among the first people in Greece—through this idea of a great maritime empire.

The people that the Spartans placed as Spartan heads of garrisons in these various cities that they are now ruling, some of which were cities they had promised to give back to the Persians—to the Great King—were called *harmosts*; H-A-R-M-O-S-T is the way we put it in English. These *harmosts* got a terrible reputation for brutality, for tyrannical behavior, for harsh treatment of the local populations. Pretty soon, the locals were longing for the Athenians to come back—tributes, tax payments, and all—rather than put up with these Spartans.

Clearchus in the great city of Byzantium—that's modern Istanbul; it's on the Bosphorus. It's another one of those cities along the grain route that can control the flow of commodities from the Black Sea into the Aegean, and it was an old colony of the little Greek city of Megara long before. There at Byzantium, Clearchus behaved so outrageously that he was stripped of his command by the Spartans and sent off in disgrace. He was then hired very quickly by Cyrus, who needed a tough, hard-as-nails commander to weld together this 10,000-hoplite force from all over the Greek world—many different cities represented there—and lead them, following Prince Cyrus, into the heart of the Persian Empire.

They set out in the spring of the year 401 B.C. We are now three years after the Great King's death, three years after the accession of Artaxerxes, and three years after the fall of Athens. On a spring day, they set out from Sardis. The only person in the whole army of the Ten Thousand, as far as we can tell, who really knew where they were going was Clearchus himself. Prince Cyrus had taken this general into his confidence. The rest of the men were told: "We're going a little way eastward to the highland country of Pisidia, and there are some troublesome hill tribes there, and we're going to suppress them and bring them to order."

A simple campaign, the pay was good, the distance was not great, and they all trooped off. Although any of them who'd sat down to think: "Why does it take 10,000 Greeks and another"—well, the ancient sources say 100,000, it was probably more like 20,000—"tens of thousands more Asian troops to put down a few bandit tribes?" But nobody seems to have asked the question until they got into the middle part of Asia Minor, working on the system of royal roads, and went right through Pisidia and out the other side. They got to Cilicia, which lies beyond, and the men staged their first mutiny—their first of many—and said, "We're not going any further until we get full pay for what we've done so far."

One of the ways of keeping troops loyal to a cause, or at least keeping them in line and present for duty, was holding up their pay until the campaign was over, so that once they've invested a certain number of days in the effort, they're going to be very unwilling to break ranks and leave. Cyrus was in sore straits here. He'd had enough money for the initial payments that brought everybody in, but he didn't have the money to give them the arrears of pay that they were demanding. We have to remember, it's not just the soldiers that are Cyrus's headache; they are surrounded by an equally large number of auxiliaries—camp followers.

Let's go down the list of who is marching with them but invisible most of the time in the ancient historical accounts: There is a wagon train following the army of probably something like 1,500 wheeled carts; there are the drivers for the carts and the grooms for the animals—the pack animals, like the mules, and the draft animals, like the oxen and mules that are pulling the carts. Remember, the army can't move any faster than the slowest cart. It's like that saying about the caravan moving no faster than the slowest camel. There are all those people. There are armorers, and leather workers, and weapon makers who are going to make or repair the weaponry of the soldiers. There are doctors who will bind up their wounds. There are women who will accompany these men and attend to their needs. There are bakers to make the daily bread, because the army travels with un-ground grain. It has been parched—it will last a long time. As soon as you grind it into flour, it's subject to spoilage very quickly, so they can't take along flour ready for mixing and kneading into dough and baking bread every day. There are portable ovens for baking the bread that these bakers are in charge of. There are weavers for making cloth. On, and on, and on: carpenters for putting up the temporary forts, engineers for building the bridges that will span the rivers, and interpreters who will deal with the various people they meet along the way.

Finally, in sort of an outer cloud around this city on the move are the traders. Soldiers are getting loot. One of the things that Cyrus immediately does to kind of keep his Ten Thousand happy is—there's a little area called Lycaonia; it's famous for causing trouble for the Persian kings. He said, "Plunder it." Well, then, they can go house to house, farmstead to farmstead, looting, raping, pillaging, behaving as they all want to behave in their wildest dreams as soldiers of fortune. What are they going to do with a bedstead? Well, there's a trader who is following the horde that is on the move, and he will pay money for that bedstead, take it away, and sell it for a much higher price on the market somewhere else.

Of course, the big trade was in slaves. You capture people, haul folks out of their beds and carry them away. They are then sold to the slave traders, who were like vultures around the sides of all these conflicts, and they are then pushed into the international market of slavery. Since we're with these slaves, let's just spend one moment talking about slavery in the ancient world. It was different from slavery in American history.

Slavery in American history was also tied to a caste system. Once you belonged to the group of people who are identified as the slave caste, it was very hard to get out of it. It wasn't true in the ancient world. Slavery was regarded as a misfortune; it could happen to anybody. It could happen because you fell into debt, or it could happen because you were a prisoner of war, or it could happen just because your parents were slaves. But all slaves had the hope that they could earn their way out of that position.

I mentioned when we talked about the Greek galleys that we have the image—partly from *Ben Hur*, with Charlton Heston chained to his oar—that those galleys were powered by prisoners or slaves, unwilling to be there. That's not true in this classical period that we're talking about. Most of the people pulling the oars in those hundreds and hundreds of triremes and other warships are free citizens or free agents who have come as resident aliens to a place like Athens, and hired their services out, and must be paid. It was a very good way to earn a living as a young man.

So slaves were not as important in ancient warfare. It was part of the identity of a citizen to fight for the city. You don't want slaves co-opting that role, and so slaves were kept to the rear, as the helots of Sparta were typically kept to the rear, although they were taken along on the campaigns to serve their masters and carry the army's shields, and spears, and so on from one battlefield to the next—do the cooking and tend to the needs of the actual warriors.

Slavery is different from what we're used to, and freed slaves could often go on and become millionaires. We're going to stop now because it's too interesting a topic and too important a one to pretend that we can do any more justice to now.

At any rate, Cyrus is now in the center of this vast mass of people. He has to deal with supplying them with food. If his total numbers were something like 30,000, with 10,000 to 13,000 Greeks and the rest Asiatics, you've got to double that—that was the standard rule of thumb that ancient historians used for estimating how many people were on the move—double the size of the fighting force, and you've got the actual numbers of people that are in the horde. So just picture possibly 60,000 people all squeezing along these narrow roads through these mountain passes.

I come from a town in Indiana—New Albany, Indiana—we've only got 40,000 people in the whole town, and I can't picture us hiking from New Albany to the tip of Florida, which would be the kind of thing that they were bound on. Even with all of our modern skills, and logistical support, and easy availability of food, it would be a huge undertaking, and this is what Cyrus is attempting to do.

I think one of the lessons we get from the close, detailed story that Xenophon gives us of the march of the Ten Thousand is that we're very wrong to think of there being anything small-time or primitive about these ancient peoples. They had worked up a very sophisticated way of dealing with the world on a very complex, intricate, and successful level, and that's proved by the successful march of the Ten Thousand into Asia.

By the way, what they were doing was what the Greeks called "going up." The Greeks always said if you start at Sardis and go to Susa, the capital of the Persian Empire, on the great road, you are "going up" to Susa. The Greek word for "going up" is *anabasis*. So the book that Xenophon is going to write about this journey has as its name *Anabasis* (*Going Up*). But they will also—as we're going to see in the next lecture—have to get home, and that will be "going down."

Cyrus, at this point, is luring them from place to place. He's continuing to lie to them about their true destination. He wants to hold off as long as possible before letting them know where they're going. They come down to the sea. By the way, I never explained that he got money from Cilicia, from the queen of the country, whom he had obviously been secretly dealing with, and whom he must have told, "Once I am king, I will remember those who have aided me, and you will be enriched beyond your wildest dreams." So she, as an investment for the future, came down with the wealth of Cilicia and paid him the money he needed to provide his troops with their pay so they would keep going.

They came down to the sea at the absolute northeast corner of the eastern Mediterranean, where Syria becomes the country that's on the coast—you're out of Asia Minor now—at a place called Issos. We're going to be coming back to Issos. That's the place where Alexander will face King Darius in a great battle in the last stage of our history of the Greeks and the Persians. But for now, Issos was just the last port that they would encounter before they turned away from the sea altogether, and there they found 700 more hoplite soldiers from Sparta sent out to Cyrus by the Spartan government, although he was paying them like mercenaries. This was an official move on the part of the Spartans at home to say thank you for the support that Cyrus had given them that allowed them to destroy Athens and win that Peloponnesian War.

He joined the 700 to his main body of troops, and they marched on through the Syrian Gates. This word *gates*—*pylae*—is what the Greeks called "passes," like Thermopylae in Greece—"hot gates," "hot pass." Finally, at a place called Myriandrus, they saw the Mediterranean for the last time and turned inland. He still hadn't fully leveled with them. He was still claiming they were just going to pass a little further into Syria and find there a Persian army that they were going to help him destroy.

So they kept marching, lured onward by these tales that it's just the next stage, it's just over the next mountain range, that's the limit of our intention, and always goaded onward by the promise of more money. But they finally settled down and said, once they got over the mountains, "We want a promise here. You're going to have to promise to pay every man five *minae* of silver when this is all over, or we are not going any further. We want a pledge from you, Cyrus."

Five *minae* of silver—that was a year's worth of pay, and he had to agree. They had him where they wanted him. At all costs, he had to keep that army moving. Twelve days from the Mediterranean coast, they came to that fabled river, the Euphrates, and now they were approaching Mesopotamia, which is the land between the rivers—the two rivers being the Euphrates on the west and the Tigris on the east—and those great cities of antiquity, Nineveh and Babylon, were located on or between these two rivers.

So now they had to go south, but first they wanted to cross the Euphrates. They were at a place called Thapsacus, or Zeugma—*Zeugma* is the Greek word for "pontoon"—where there used to be a pontoon bridge. Cyrus had taken them there, hoping to get them across the bridge. The Persian who was ahead of him—this Persian general who was retreating in front of him, the man loyal to Artaxerxes—had burned the bridge and burned the boats, which were the pontoons for carrying the bridge.

How were they going to get across? The whole thing might have been derailed there because they had to cross the Euphrates, and there weren't many places to get an army across. But by what they considered a miracle, that river—which should have been full and brimming with water coming down out of the mountains of Armenia—was lower than anyone had ever seen it at that time of the summer. They were able to walk across the Euphrates and even get the draft animals and the carts across and get to the other side. It seemed truly that the gods were with this expedition.

Once on the other side, they turned south. It had taken them 12 days to get to the Euphrates from the sea, and now they had 13 days through increasingly arid territory. Xenophon describes this as the "desert of Arabia," and although that's very far north of where we draw the limit of Arabia today, clearly, the Greeks realized that the sandy wastes that they were looking at to their right stretched all the way down through the Arabian Peninsula to the place in Yemen where they got their frankincense. They were looking at an ocean of sand, an ocean of aridity, filled with strange animals that they could see as they marched along: ostriches and bustards among the birds, antelopes, gazelles, and wild asses roaming in herds among the shrubs that grew on that plain, because there wasn't enough water for trees.

If Cyrus had not, through his careful planning, had with them enough supplies to get through these 13 days of what amounted to a desert trek, they never would have made it. They owed it all to his foresight that they had their supplies with them, with this huge baggage train, and could go on.

At last, they saw looming up ahead of them a gigantic wall. It was called the Wall of Media, and it had been built between the Euphrates and the Tigris to serve as a defense against people coming out of the north, exactly as they were doing now. It was 100 feet high and 20 feet thick. It was made of mud brick that had been cemented together with bitumen, which they took from the petroleum seeps that came up in various places in the Near East at that time, and which they had no further use for than as a building material to cement mud brick together or as pitch to make the ships proof against ship worm.

They passed by the wall. They had expected to find it held against them; it was not. That Persian general was so terrified of the size of Prince Cyrus's army that he was simply fleeing southward to try to join Artaxerxes. They kept on moving down. They came to a great canal that connected the Tigris and Euphrates. They got across it and then to a trench that Xenophon was under the impression had just been dug to try to stop them. We're not sure that that is true, but at any rate, one more barrier to cross.

At this point, they left the baggage train behind. Cyrus began to feel that the moment of crisis was at hand, and sure enough, two days after leaving the baggage train, as they were walking along at their ease, confident since the landscape was so eerily empty—that Artaxerxes, terrified by their numbers had decided not to confront them. One of the scouts who had been sent on ahead, a Persian noble, was suddenly seen coming up over the horizon at a gallop, and as he approached, he shouted to Cyrus, "Artaxerxes is coming. He has an army with him." When the scout was questioned, it turned out Artaxerxes's army was even larger than their own.

So we have brought Xenophon and his Ten Thousand into the heart of the Persian Empire, and there we must leave them until next time.

Lecture Seventeen
The March to the Sea

Scope: When the dust settled over the plain at Cunaxa, Prince Cyrus was dead and the Ten Thousand found themselves leaderless and without supplies in the heart of the Persian Empire. After the deaths or arrests of their commanders, the soldiers convened to choose new generals for the various divisions of the army; one of those chosen was Xenophon. The reorganized army fought its way north through rough terrain, attacks from local tribes, and crippling hunger and cold, eventually reaching the southeast corner of the Black Sea and voyaging back to Greek territory. When Xenophon returned to Greece, he settled in the Peloponnese and wrote books on horsemanship, hunting, and personal heroes, including Socrates. His most well-known book, however, was *Anabasis* (*Going Up*): the incredible tale of the bravery of the Ten Thousand and the extraordinary turns of fortune they encountered and finally overcame.

Outline

I. Artaxerxes II of Persia, with his 40,000 to 50,000 troops, and Prince Cyrus, with his Ten Thousand, met in battle on a vast plain near a village called Cunaxa.
  - **A.** To meet Artaxerxes's forces with a united front, Prince Cyrus prepared a particular battle order.
    1. He would be in the center with his prime Persian cavalry.
    2. To his left was his faithful noble, Ariaeus, with the light-armed Asiatic troops.
    3. To his right were the Greek hoplite phalanxes, marching four men deep instead of the usual eight men.
    4. Prince Cyrus wanted his front line long so that the Greeks reached from the edge of the Persian cavalry formation to the Euphrates River, which could be used as a barrier against Artaxerxes's forces.
  - **B.** Artaxerxes arrayed his troops in a similar formation.
    1. He was in the center, with his cavalry.
    2. On the right was a mass of Asiatic troops.

- **3.** On the left was Tissaphernes, commanding Artaxerxes's best forces.
- **C.** The demoralizing effect of the size of Artaxerxes's army was probably greater than its strategic effect.
- **D.** Prince Cyrus ordered the Greek general Clearchus to move from the right to the center, but Clearchus kept his position—a decision that probably lost the battle for Cyrus.
- **E.** As the Greeks moved forward, the left wing of Artaxerxes's army seemed to draw back. The Greeks, convinced that they were winning the battle, pursued the Persians southward.
- **F.** Cyrus fought his way through and broke up Artaxerxes's cavalry but, like the Greeks, made the mistake of pursuing an early advantage impetuously. After wounding his brother, Cyrus was surrounded and killed in battle.

II. With the death of Cyrus, the surviving troops found themselves in a hostile city of armed men, in the middle of a great empire, without a leader.
- **A.** Tissaphernes visited Clearchus and offered Persian provisions if the remaining Greeks agreed to leave the realm. The Greeks accepted his offer.
- **B.** Tissaphernes intended to lead them into mountainous territory, where he hoped they would become lost, starve to death, or surrender in small groups and never again pose a threat to Persia.
- **C.** Morale among the Greek troops was incredibly low. The Greeks, appalled at their situation, wanted only to return home as quickly as possible.
- **D.** The army crossed the Tigris River and headed north into the modern-day Middle East, following Tissaphernes stage by stage into hill country.
- **E.** A fight, probably instigated by Tissaphernes, broke out between some of the Persians and Greeks.
    - **1.** Clearchus demanded an explanation and brought his four generals and 20 subordinate officers to meet with Tissaphernes.
    - **2.** The Greek leaders were ambushed and killed by the Persians; one soldier escaped and managed to relay the news to the Greek camp.

3. The Greeks sought to engage the Persians in a pitched battle, but Tissaphernes had no intention of fighting them head-on. Rather, he intended to subject them to endless harassment on their march.

III. The remaining Greek army elected five new generals, one of whom was Xenophon, chosen to command the rear forces.
  A. The soldiers decided to continue northward, as Tissaphernes initially had recommended, and fight their way through the mountains.
     1. Tissaphernes launched lightning-like attacks on the army's rear.
     2. The hill tribes, also refusing to engage in a pitched battle, attacked the army from above the trails.
  B. In midwinter, the Greeks found themselves caught between the army of Tiríbazus (who did not want the Ten Thousand in his province) and the hill tribes.
     1. The local tribes were averse to confrontation, and a small squadron of Greek soldiers forced them to retreat.
     2. Tiríbazus's army was so overwhelmed by the spectacle of a Greek phalanx on the move that it fell back and let the Greeks pass.
  C. Five days after leaving the village of Gymnias, the Ten Thousand came to the Black Sea.
     1. The soldiers piled up a gigantic cairn as a monument to their arrival.
     2. A few years ago, an archaeological team discovered the remnants of the cairn.
  D. At Trebizond, the army managed to find ships and began the final stages of the journey back to Greece.
  E. Xenophon arrived in Greece to discover that his mentor, Socrates, had been tried and executed.
  F. In exile from Athens, Xenophon settled down in the Peloponnese as a guest of the Spartans and wrote books, including *Anabasis*, which became a textbook for Greeks interested in Persia and later inspired Alexander the Great.

Recommended Reading:
Smith, *Greece and the Persians*.

Waterford, *Xenophon's Retreat: Greece, Persia, and the End of the Golden Age.*

Questions to Consider:
1. If you were Prince Cyrus, how would you have approached the Battle of Cunaxa? How would your military strategy differ from the one that led to Prince Cyrus's defeat?
2. Make a case for the march of the Ten Thousand as an example of both shameful retreat and heroic survival in the face of impossible odds.

Lecture Seventeen—Transcript

The March to the Sea

Welcome back. King Artaxerxes of Persia had not been willing to believe that his younger brother, Cyrus, would ever make it as far as Babylonia with an army, and so he'd been very slow to collect an army of his own.

When that messenger came over the horizon telling Prince Cyrus that his brother Artaxerxes was approaching, it was with an army that Artaxerxes still did not feel was ready to meet his brother. The reason Artaxerxes was so worried was because of those Greeks—those 10,000 hoplites. He had nothing to put up against his brother's force that was equally fearsome, equally respected as an armed force.

We have to remember that for all these people out on this field, their last memory of an actual pitched battle between Greeks and Persians was all the way back 65 years earlier at the Eurymedon River, when Cimon the Athenian stormed ashore from his victorious fleet, brought his troops to land, and attacked the Persian position there. There had not been a pitched battle even at Marathon early on, where the Persians had managed to prevail over Greek hoplites.

So it was with terror that Artaxerxes had learned that his brother had managed to put together this 10,000-strong force of hoplites and bring them down into the heart of the kingdom. Nevertheless, they had arrived in Babylonia long before they were expected. Artaxerxes took the troops he had. It has been estimated he probably had 40,000 to 45,000, and he brought them north to meet his brother.

They met on a vast plain near the city of Babylon and near a village called Cunaxa. Cunaxa has given its name to the battle that took place on that plain. The horsemen arrived at a very awkward moment of the day for Prince Cyrus and his men. It was so early in the day that it was clear that the battle would probably happen before nightfall. It was late enough in the day that the men had not had their dinner, their all-important midday meal, and there was no time to prepare it. In fact, the 30,000 or so troops of Cyrus were spread out in a long, casual marching order. It was all that they could do to get the troops together, form their lines, and be prepared to meet Artaxerxes with the united front when he finally appeared over the edge of the plain ahead of them.

This was the battle order that Cyrus decided upon: He would be in the center with his prime Persian cavalry; to his left would be a faithful Persian noble, loyal to his cause, named Ariaeus, and with all of the Asiatic troops, who were mainly light-armed mobile troops with lances, small spears, and javelins; to the right are the Greeks—10,000 strong, four deep. Normal hoplite phalanxes marched eight deep if you can imagine that—eight ranks—so that the front rank is jammed up against the enemy, and the rear rank is ready to come forward, walking over the dead bodies of their comrades, if necessary, to take their place in trying to mow down the enemy.

Why did they do only half the normal depth? Why was it four deep? Because Cyrus wanted his front line long. He knew he was outnumbered by his brother. It's a terrible thing for an ancient army or any army to be outflanked, and he wanted to get the Greeks all the way from the edge of the Persian cavalry formation all the way to the Euphrates River. That way, the river could be the barrier on his right wing that would prevent Artaxerxes's forces from getting around.

Over the edge of the horizon came Artaxerxes. The Greeks were very dismayed, as Xenophon remembers. They had told themselves that they would be facing an undisciplined horde—nothing could be further from the truth. They had expected barbaric war cries and yelling of savages trying to keep their spirits up. Artaxerxes's army came forward in dead silence.

He had arrayed his troops in a very similar way to Cyrus. His center was also his cavalry, and he himself was facing his brother across the plain, center to center. On the Persian right, which was facing Ariaeus and the left wing of Prince Cyrus, there was a mass of Asiatic troops. On the Persian left—King Artaxerxes's left—there was the satrap Tissaphernes, brought all the way back from Lydia—from Sardis—to command the best forces that Artaxerxes could find (except for his own household cavalry) in an attempt to deal with the Greeks.

There were Egyptian foot soldiers; there were men from all over the empire, and in front of them, something that the Greeks had never seen: chariots to which scythes—that were normally used out in the field to harvest the wheat—had been attached to the axels of the chariots. As the wheels spun, these long scythe blades spun also, extending out on either side of the chariot. There were more blades below the chariot body, so that any Greek unlucky enough to fall down and have a chariot pass over would be sliced up by these wicked blades.

The demoralizing effect was probably greater even than the strategic effect would have been, but the Greeks were certainly shocked to see this much preparation, this much serious thought going into how you deal with a hoplite phalanx. Of course, with the hoplite phalanx, cohesion is all. If a scythed chariot can charge its way through and break open a gap in the phalanx, all is lost.

Prince Cyrus left his station in the middle and paraded down the front of his army, talking to the men, cheering them on, encouraging them. Young Xenophon remembers stepping out of the ranks and having a word with Prince Cyrus as he went by. Cyrus reached Clearchus, the general, and called him forward. He said:

> I've now seen my brother's disposition of troops, and we need to change our plan. I want you to shift so that you move into the center, and you tackle the cavalry. I don't want you facing these scythed chariots, and I don't want you facing an inessential part of my brother's army. I want you hitting my brother himself.

Clearchus said to Cyrus, "And I want you out of the battle. We're fighting for you. What's the profit to us if we win a battle, and you, our leader, have died in the course of it?" Cyrus said, "I cannot back down. This is a duel between myself and my brother. I would lose all honor if I stayed behind and sent my men forward to do the dirty work for me. But," said Cyrus, "you will move to the center." Clearchus gave him an ambiguous answer, saying, "I will deal with it."

Clearchus had no intention of obeying Cyrus's order. His right wing was up against the Euphrates River, and that meant it was protected. Hoplite phalanxes have a curiosity, an eccentricity—they are terrified for what will happen on their right wing. Remember, every man has a shield on his left arm. That means every man is protected by the shield of the man to his right, except the soldier on the far right of the position. Here, they were in a dream position: The banks of the Euphrates River—which could not be traversed by Tissaphernes's troops—were next to that right-hand man in each of the four ranks. If they move away, as Cyrus had commanded, into the middle of the battlefield, those right men are exposed, and they have no armor on their right hands. That simple strategic concern caused Clearchus to tell his men, "Keep your position," and that decision probably lost the battle for Cyrus.

As they joined battle, as the trumpets sounded, as at last the war cries were let loose and they surged forward, a remarkable thing happened: The

Greeks, moving forward at a quick march, saw the enemy melt away in front of them. It seemed like a dream come true: "We won't have to fight a battle after all." They were drawn further and further back, beyond the main army of Artaxerxes, as they pursued this unresisting left wing of the enemy formation. With Tissaphernes leading his troops—he is mounted himself on a little detachment of cavalry—they are falling back, and the Greeks are following them, rejoicing in the fact that their enemies seem to be giving up.

Meanwhile, Cyrus has charged straight at the center, having realized that the Greeks were not going to do anything. By the way, I forgot to mention, those scythed chariots—they proved to be no use at all. Remember, they hadn't been used before. The horses became very unruly. The charioteers turned the horses back around toward the rear and tried to retreat with them. A few of the horses were so hard to handle that they threw the charioteers from the chariots, and then those were the ones that turned around and charged at the Greeks. The phalanx found all it had to do was open its ranks, let the scythed chariot run through, and then close up again after it.

Only one man was foolish enough to get in the path, and he was run over. So that wasn't a very serious outcome from the scythed chariots, and the Greeks, full of conviction that they were winning this battle—and certainly they were on the right wing—pushed onward, southward.

Cyrus fought his way through and hit his brother's cavalry with such force that he broke it up, and he was able to penetrate. But, like the Greeks, he made the mistake of pursuing an early advantage too impetuously. He forged his way right into the heart of this melee of horsemen, trying to get at his brother, whom he hated with a passion. There was this dream that he would be the one to cut his brother down.

He managed to get close. He actually managed to throw a javelin—or thrust in with a javelin—and wound his brother in the chest. Artaxerxes was then taken by his doctor, a Greek medic named Ctesias of the city of Cnidus (who was sort of a descendant of that Greek doctor Democedes of Sicily, who was King Darius's trusted doctor before the Ionian revolt and he was sent by Darius to do a scouting mission of the Greek world). Here, we have another Greek in place, and he goes with Artaxerxes and his companions to a hilltop. He dresses Artaxerxes's wounds. He ultimately wrote another account of the battle, which provides an alternative view to Xenophon's, although since it's mainly lost, we only have fragments and references to go on.

At any rate, Artaxerxes has now been pulled out of the fight, and Prince Cyrus finds that he has forged ahead too far, and he has left the main body of his own cavalry behind, and he is surrounded by his brother's supporters. They get him off his horse, and they kill him on the ground. That's the end of Cyrus.

That should have been the end of the battle—except how do you let people know the battle is over? It's very difficult in the ancient world, and in fact, the Greek right wing never learned that Cyrus had been killed. There were counterattacks from Tissaphernes—they finally did have a battle on their hands, and they were surrounded at one point by people who outflanked them. They finally saw a hill in the distance covered with Persian cavalry, and they marched up to that hill, and the enemy melted away in front of them.

So they sent some of their forces up on the hill—they ultimately all went up on the hill—looked out on this vast plain filled with clouds of dust, a melee of shifting forces of cavalry, chariots, and foot soldiers. They just couldn't see what was going on, and they were puzzled that they had received no messenger from Cyrus, their prince and leader, about how he had fared at the battle.

The Sun was going down. The battle was over. Cunaxa had ended. The Greeks felt it had surely ended in a great victory, and they had nowhere to go, so they spent the night hungry (without their dinners, without their suppers) and tired but scarcely having lost a man. The Ten Thousand settled down on that hill and waited for morning.

With morning came the terrible news. They might have won their half of the battle, but Cyrus had been killed. Without a leader, what were they? They were the strangest thing that anyone in the ancient world had ever experienced: a hostile city of armed men plunked down in the middle of a great empire that didn't know what to do with them.

Artaxerxes found them a tremendous embarrassment. He couldn't pay them, and he couldn't take them into Persian service; he wasn't sure he could defeat them if he actually confronted them. What was he going to do? Some negotiations were opened. He asked them to surrender, thinking, "Well, at least that's a start," and they refused.

Finally, Tissaphernes, that wily satrap who had dealt with the Greeks all along, offered to be the go-between. He went to Clearchus and the other leaders of the Greeks, and he said, "The king will provide you with provisions if you will agree to leave his realm." All they wanted to do was get home. They could have, in fact, probably gotten to the edge of Persian territory somewhere and established a Greek city there, but that held no attraction to them. These were men who had left their homes, seeking their fortunes—they'd hoped to make themselves rich in this war—and they wanted to get back, each to his own city.

They accepted this offer, and Tissaphernes rounded up the baggage train and said, "You can't get home by the way you came here." He had several reasons for saying this—one of which was that that way led back through his satrapy, and the last thing he wanted to do was have the Ten Thousand at loose on the plains of Lydia and causing trouble for him. He had a larger plan in mind. He is intending to lead them into mountainous territory where they will become lost, and he hopes they will either starve to death or have to surrender in small groups, but at any rate, they will never again pose a threat to him or to any other Persian.

They don't know what to do. They have no geographers or mapmakers among them. Their baggage train has been looted—that was the great loss. They are now without most of their own supplies, and equipment, and camp followers, so with the remnant of the baggage train, they agree they will go north, following Tissaphernes.

They pass northward through the plains of Babylonia. This time, they cross not the Euphrates to get home but the Tigris. They get to the other side and now the mountains are starting to rise up ahead of them. Tissaphernes tells them that is their destination. They will go into the hills, and he will take them up through Armenia and to the Black Sea. That, he says, is the nearest body of water for them, which actually was true.

We must never forget that their morale was incredibly low. Because they had allowed Cyrus to trick them—stage by stage, luring them deeper and deeper into Persia—by the time of Cunaxa, they found themselves exactly where no Greek ever wanted to be—1,500 miles from the seacoast of Asia Minor. Remember back to the beginnings of our story, the year 499 B.C., when Aristagoras of Miletus brought his map to Sparta and showed the Spartans the way into Persia from Sardis and Lydia and explained that it's a three-month journey in, and that was enough to make the king of Sparta, back in 499 B.C., say, "Get out. I will not talk to anyone who wants to take the Spartans that far from the sea."

Most of the Ten Thousand felt the same way. They were appalled at what had happened to them, and they just wanted to get home as quickly as possible, and like most men in that kind of situation, they weren't always thinking as clearly as they should have.

They now are in the heart of what we might call the Middle East. To the south of them is Babylonia and to the southeast is Persia itself—the great Iranian plateau and the city of Susa; off to the east, the way of the rising Sun, is the central Asiatic plateau—completely unknown and impassable to them. On to the north are the mountains. Off to the southwest, they would come down into Syria and, ultimately, the eastern Mediterranean, the coast of the Levant and the Phoenician cities. And, finally, to their west is that land that they traversed initially, the great block of land that we call Anatolia, or Asia Minor—modern Turkey—the one way that they've decided they won't go back.

So northward seems the only possibility, and they followed Tissaphernes stage by stage into these hills. They crossed a branch of the Tigris again, and they are now surrounded by the Carduchian Mountains—real wild territory. They are, in fact, out of Persian territory. There was a wedge of wild, mountainous country that the Great King had never managed to conquer—even he—and the wild tribes there were very much a law unto themselves. Tissaphernes was hoping that this would be the killing ground where the Ten Thousand would finally be eaten up by the rigors of an Asiatic winter, by the mountains, by their getting lost on the trails, and by the hill tribes—doing the work for him.

A little fight broke out, probably instigated by Tissaphernes, between some Persians and some Greeks. Clearchus, the Greek general, went to Tissaphernes and demanded an explanation. Tissaphernes said, "I want to work this out with you. Please come to my tent." He had a great field pavilion, like the one Xerxes had had during the Salamis campaign. He said, "Come to my tent and bring your colleagues with you." So Clearchus, truly not thinking clearly, got together all four of the other generals of the Ten Thousand, including that *proxenos* of Boeotia who had been the friend of Xenophon, who recruited that young man to the cause, and they brought with them about 20 of their subordinate officers and a whole lot of attendants.

What was Clearchus thinking? "I shall make a grand show. I shall show this Persian satrap, Tissaphernes, who is really the powerful one here." But this show was his undoing. They got into the tent. Only the five were admitted. They are by a river whose name would live in infamy in Greek memory, the river Zab—the Greater Zab—and as they got in the tent, they were seized, these five generals, and bound as prisoners. They, in fact, lived for a considerable length of time. Tissaphernes took them back into Babylonia, and they were executed there for the pleasure of King Artaxerxes.

The 20 outside, the subsidiary officers—equally important for the cohesion and command of the 10,000 troops—were cut down to a man. They were all killed where they stood. Then, the Persians mounted their horses and rode out among the attendants who were milling here and there on the flat area in front of the pavilion, and with no warning and working silently, they killed them one after the other with their lances.

One man got away. He'd been cut across the belly—one of these Greeks—and he managed to get on his horse and get back to the Greek camp, where Xenophon and the other Greeks had no idea of what was happening until they saw this man coming, holding his guts into his body and shouting, "Treachery! Treachery! The generals have been killed!"

Immediately, the Greeks grabbed their shields and formed their lines, but Tissaphernes had no intention of fighting them. They were to be left to their own fate. He would dog their steps as they moved through the mountains, but he would never offer them what they truly wanted: a pitched battle that they knew they could win. This endless harassment, which is what they were now treated to, was something that they weren't sure they could survive.

What did they do, these Greeks—10,000 or so strong—in the heart of Asia? They behaved like Greeks. They sat down, and they had a town meeting. Everybody had to have their chance to speak. Every idea was put forward. Let's remember old Herodotus and his statement: "It's important that many views be expressed. How else can the best be selected?"

So as each one made proposals and talked, the army finally decided they would elect five new generals. Xenophon, this young Athenian in his 20s, this somewhat bookish scholar of Athens who had been a student of Socrates—he was chosen to be the general at the head of the rear of the army. There were four others, some more prominent than he—all more prominent than he—ahead of him, right up to the vanguard.

They got on the march, and they decided—because they didn't know what else to do—to continue northward, as Tissaphernes had initially recommended, and just fight their way through the mountains. It's hard to express how much courage went into this. It was the time that winter was coming on. Down on the plains of Babylonia, in what would have been the month of August or September, they had fried in the heat. Now, these cold winter winds were starting to blast them. They didn't have adequate clothing. They barely had adequate supplies. The one reason that Tissaphernes had made it easy for himself to lure them there was that there was plenty of fresh water. That was the one thing that they didn't have a problem with—lots of springs, lots of mountain streams. Otherwise, they were in desperate, desperate shape.

They forged northward, just going by the North Star and their sense of where the trails were leading them; Tissaphernes was behind, launching little lightning-like attacks on their rear, where Xenophon was. Then the hill tribes appeared, also refusing to engage them in a pitched battle; they would get on the cliffs above their trails that they were following and roll rocks and avalanches down on them. Many of the men were being killed in this most difficult of all situations for a Greek hoplite—no level field on which to deploy, no space in which to form the phalanx, strung out on these mountain trails. It's a miracle that any of them got through, and they were very demoralized. They continually had meetings. There were many different ideas—some to go back, and some to try to bring Tissaphernes to battle—but onward and onward, northward and northward, they went.

At last, sometime probably in absolute midwinter, they came to a river and were told by the locals that on the other side was civilization at last—a satrapy of the Persian Empire called Armenia. But there on that other shore—they had so longed to get back to civilization—there was a Persian army. It was the army of the satrap Tiríbazus, satrap of Armenia, and he didn't want the Ten Thousand in his province. He was there to try to stop them. He was convinced that simply a show of force along the edge of the mountain torrent would be enough to prevent the Greeks from crossing.

Meanwhile, behind them came the hill tribes now having caught the Greeks, the Ten Thousand between themselves and the river, they had decided to wipe them out and take all of their armor and enrich themselves with all the things that the Greeks had been carrying. Not even on the battlefield of Cunaxa itself had the Ten Thousand been in such peril and they owed their preservation to alertness, a stroke of luck, and their readiness to seize the advantage when they saw it.

Two young Greek soldiers, out gathering kindling for their fire, went half a mile along the river and saw locals on the far side near a rocky place behaving in a way that suggested there might be a crossing. The two young Greeks stripped off their clothes, waded in naked except for their daggers, and discovered to their joy that at this point there was a hidden, a concealed ford across the river, and the water did not even come up to their crotches. So they ran back to the camp; they told Xenophon himself who shared this information with his colleagues, and they decided upon a plan.

Half the army moved along the shore with the baggage train behind them in full battle array. Xenophon, with the other half, brought up the rear. They went down to that newly discovered crossing place saying the great battle hymn. Even the camp followers, the women that had shared their ordeals and followed them through thick and thin, sang along with the soldiers, and then they faced into the river several columns abreast and forged down into the stream. The horsemen on the far side came down, but they couldn't get to the opposite side at the crossing place because of the rocks.

Meanwhile, Xenophon turned and ran back toward the original crossing place with that rear half of the army, and the horsemen on the other side fearing that they might be caught in a pincher movement between these two groups of Greeks, fled into the hinterlands. Then Xenophon came back, covered the crossing of the baggage train, and led a charge straight up the slope into the mass of the hill men who were coming down trying to pick off the Greek rear guard. The leaders of the Greeks sent back the archers and the javelin throwers. They covered Xenophon and his men as the crossed and in this way the entire army got to the other side.

On the far side of the river, now in Armenia, they encountered deep snows and the Persian's satrap of Armenia, Tíríbazus. He wanted them out of his province as rapidly as possible. He promised them safe passage if they would, in turn, promise not to plunder his domain. So they agreed and they forged on through the snow but it became clear that he was dogging their footsteps with his own troops and as soon as they came to a vulnerable place, he intended to strike.

By good luck, scouts discovered where Tíríbazus's camp was, now very lightly defended since its master was out on the road following the Greeks, and the lightly-armed Greek auxiliaries in a daring dash crossed over to Tíríbazus's camp, captured his supplies, captured his own tent, his bakers, and his silver-footed couch, and now very well-supplied, and with great satisfaction, the Ten Thousand were able to continue their way north, north, and north passing mountain ranges, vast plains, villages, finally to their joy in the springtime, they came to a city, the first one they had seen in months, a place called Gymnias, and the people there said: You're very close, it's just a matter of days from here up to the Black Sea. So with hope in their hearts, they forged on northward.

On the fifth day after leaving Gymnias, Xenophon (in the back) found himself and his rear guard following the rest of the army up this immense slope toward a high pass. They were a mile and a half up. The air was thin; they were at the top of some sort of great mountain massif, and suddenly, Xenophon heard, tumbling back down the line of men, the sound of shouting—a sound he had not heard for months. It sounded like battle cries. As each line got to the crest, they started shouting, too, and his great dread was that they were at last facing, in this more open terrain, an army of Persians that had been sent to block their way and that, in fact, they were in a trap, and that this pass would be the place where they all met their end.

In an effort to try to find out what was going on, he spurred his own horse up the slope, and as he got into the center part of the army, he could finally hear what the men were shouting: "*Thalassa*! *Thalassa*!"—or, in the other dialect of Greek—"*Thalatta*! *Thalatta*!"—"The sea! The sea!"

He came up to the brink of the pass, and an extraordinary vision met his sight. There was the Black Sea spread out before them—its beautiful waters blue in the sunshine. He was surrounded by crusty veterans who were weeping and hugging each other. They had seen that thing that is more dear to Greeks than any other: the sea—that universal mother of all the Greeks. None of their cities were very far from the life-giving sea. They were much more accustomed to go from place to place in their ships than on land. At last, they felt—although they were still 1,000 miles from Greece itself—the vision of that water made them feel they were home.

Each man took a stone from the surrounding slopes, and they piled up a gigantic cairn as a monument to that great moment when the army of the Ten Thousand finally, once again, beheld the sea. It's an exciting thing that that mound was searched for, for years, by archaeologists, by historians, but no one could find it. No one was sure where the pass lay until, at last, just a few years ago, a team discovered not only the remnants of the cairn but a most unusual thing—a vast plain up there on that upland mountainous slope with no loose rocks at all. Every single one had been picked up 2,400 years ago and carried into the cairn. So we know exactly where it was now that Xenophon and his comrades beheld the sea.

They made their way down the other side. Their adventures were by no means over. They had arrived at the absolute southeast corner of the Black Sea in an area where there are beautiful rhododendron bushes on the slopes.

They were all in bloom, and the bees were producing honey. So here it seemed like a gift of the gods—combs dripping with new honey. The men ate it uncontrollably, not knowing that rhododendron honey is toxic. The last horror for this army of Ten Thousand was the writhing, dying men on the ground who were in delirium from this honey that they'd eaten—but that was the last of the terrible trials of their march.

They reached Trebizond, as the Byzantines called it—the modern city of Trabzon and the ancient Greek city of Trapezus—and after waiting there for a long time, they managed to find ships and begin the final stages of their journey back to Greece.

Xenophon arrived in Greece and discovered that he was just too late for what he considered the most tragic event of his time. The Athenians had arrested Socrates, and they had tried him and executed him in the year 399 B.C., and it was a grief to Xenophon for the rest of his life that he had not been there to help his master in his hour of need.

Xenophon remained in exile from Athens. He settled down in the Peloponnese, a guest of the Spartans. He wrote books on, as I said, horsemanship, but also on hunting and on one of his heroes, King Agesilaus, and on the greatest of his heroes, Socrates—a whole book called *Memorabilia*, which is the conversations of Socrates that Xenophon could remember. But the work that he was best known by was that *Anabasis*—that *Going Up*—that incredible tale of the bravery of the Ten Thousand, all of the extraordinary turns of fortune that they encountered and that they finally overcame.

That book became a textbook for the Greeks—who wanted to learn about Persia, who wanted to learn about warfare, learn about courage—and above all, it fell into the hands of a young man (several generations after Xenophon) named Alexander the Great. It was reading Xenophon's book that inspired the young Alexander with the idea: "Yes, truly, that march can be made."

Lecture Eighteen
Strange Bedfellows

Scope: When Xenophon and the Ten Thousand finally reached the Greek mainland, they found that Agesilaus had assumed the Spartan kingship and was pursuing a war against Persian power in Asia Minor. In 394 B.C., Artaxerxes II assigned Pharnabazus and Conon, an Athenian naval commander, to lead an expedition to keep Spartan expansion in check; the combined forces confronted and overwhelmed the Spartans at Cnidus in the same year. Afterward, Conon proceeded to liberate the Asiatic and Aegean Greeks from their Spartan *harmosts*. One of these Spartans was Dercyllidas, who still controlled the city of Abydos even though, according to the recent Spartan-Persian alliance, the city should have been part of Pharnabazus's satrapy. Enraged, Pharnabazus took steps to help Conon restore Athens, reverse the outcome of the Peloponnesian War, and resurrect in Athens a Golden Age that the Athenians had believed they would never experience again.

Outline

I. When Xenophon and the Ten Thousand finally reached the Greek mainland in the early 390s B.C., they discovered that the world had changed while they were away in Persia.

A. When they left Greece back in 401 B.C., Persia and Sparta had teamed up to destroy the Athenian Empire. The Persians would soon change their allegiance and support Athens against Sparta.

B. The Greeks began to hate the oppressive Spartans (under Lysander) in a way they had never hated the Athenians. The Greeks began to long for freedom from their former liberators.

II. The Persians also began to resent the Spartans for attacking Persian holdings.

A. Lysander meant to be a great invader of Persia who would ultimately make himself king of Sparta.

1. He paid to have oracles make pronouncements in favor of his kingship.

2. Denied the throne, Lysander opted to rule through King Agesilaus, whom he believed would be ineffective.

3. When Agesilaus began his rule, however, he co-opted Lysander's plans and removed him from the picture.
B. Agesilaus waged an incredibly vigorous war against the Persians in Asia Minor for control of the old Greek cities and additional territories.
C. While Agesilaus was raiding, Pharnabazus requested that the Persians confront the Spartans at sea to remove them from Asia Minor.
D. Artaxerxes II enlisted Conon the Athenian as a commander.
   1. Conon was the only Athenian commander who had escaped capture at Aegospotami.
   2. Conon set himself up in Cyprus with his son Timotheus and became a leader in exile.
   3. He traveled along the trail of the Ten Thousand to consult with Artaxerxes at Babylon about strengthening the navy; Artaxerxes II agreed to all of his demands.
E. Pharnabazus joined Conon, and together, they assembled a fleet to head to the Aegean to confront the Spartans.

III. The Spartans learned of the invasion and made preparations for battle.
   A. Agesilaus appointed his brother-in-law, the dimwitted Peisander, as admiral of the fleet.
   B. Peisander took the fleet to Cnidus, on the southwest corner of Asia Minor.
   C. Conon sent spies and scouts to learn more about the Spartan forces. Not realizing the extent of Peisander's inexperience at sea, he assumed that luring the Spartans into battle would require cunning.
      1. Conon used his Athenian squadron as a vanguard to tempt the Spartan ships.
      2. He then brought up the main fleet to face the charge from Peisander and the Spartans.
      3. When the Spartan ships saw the rest of the Persian naval formation, in addition to Conon's squadron, they abandoned Peisander.
   D. When Agesilaus, campaigning on land in Greece, received word of the Spartan defeat, he feared it meant the end of the Spartan Empire. He lied to his troops about the outcome of the sea battle to keep up morale and avoid informing Sparta's enemies.

- **E.** At Coronea, Agesilaus won a battle but could not follow up on his victory; thus, Sparta's enemies—Thebes, Corinth, and Athens—scored a tactical victory.
  1. The battle at Coronea signified the end of the Spartan Empire.
  2. After Cnidus, Conon and Timotheus liberated the Greek cities in Asia Minor from their Spartan governors.
- **F.** One such governor, Dercyllidas, tried to deny Pharnabazus and Conon access to the Hellespont. The two commanders gathered the navy for a second campaign.
  1. Pharnabazus funded the war against Sparta and allowed Conon's fleet to remain in Athens to carry on the war at Sparta's doorstep.
  2. Conon reinstituted the Athenian navy and rebuilt the Long Walls that linked Athens to the Piraeus to protect the city from attack.
  3. The Athenians built a monument to Themistocles, and Conon built a temple to Aphrodite—the goddess who looked over his victory at Cnidus.

IV. The restoration of Athens launched a new Golden Age in the city, a resurrection of glory and beauty that the Athenians had believed they would never experience again.

Recommended Reading:

Briant, *From Cyrus to Alexander: A History of the Persian Empire.*

Xenophon, *A History of My Times.*

Questions to Consider:

1. What does Lysander's payment of the oracles to support his bid for the kingship of Sparta suggest to you about the supposed divine nature of their other pronouncements?
2. The Spartan ships' abandonment of Peisander at the Battle of Cnidus is another instance of retreat delivering the fatal blow to a battle. Do you think the Battle of Cnidus could have been won for the Spartans had their ships remained to fight? Why or why not?

Lecture Eighteen—Transcript
Strange Bedfellows

Welcome back. When Xenophon and his army of 10,000 Greek mercenaries finally succeeded in fighting their way out of the Persian Empire and returning home to mainland Greece, they discovered, then, in the early 390s B.C., that the world had changed during the years when they were in Persia.

When they left Greece back in 401 B.C., Athens was in the depths of defeat and despair. Persia had teamed up with Sparta and the Spartan allies to destroy the Athenian Empire, to force Athens to surrender, to tear down the Long Walls that tied Athens to its port city of Piraeus and guaranteed Athenian freedom and sea power. All this was gone, and it seemed gone irrevocably.

A famous Athenian named Thucydides, who wrote a history called the *History of the Peloponnesian War*, had assumed also that his home city of Athens was finished, and that year, 404 B.C.—the year of Athens's surrender—was the year that he marked as the end of the war, the end of Athenian sea power and independence; a war that had lasted 27 years was finally over.

The only reason Thucydides thought this was that he didn't live long enough to see the resurgence of Athens. Just as Persian gold and Persian support for Sparta had been able to defeat Athens, in the years to come, the Persians changed their allegiance. They now supported Athens against Sparta, and we will see this time how they got Athens back on its feet in a way that Thucydides never could have dreamed and brought his city back to prominence.

There was at this time, of course, in Sparta, a man named Lysander. He was the great charismatic visionary who had seen the right way to defeat Athens: "Win the friendship of Persia, secure the gold of Persia so we can pay rowers—oarsmen—to power our galleys, and then we will catch the Athenians unsuspecting, and we will beat them." That's exactly what happened.

Lysander was so puffed up with pride about this that he started a sort of Spartan Empire. Instead of letting all the Greeks be free, as had been the slogan 27 years earlier when Sparta started the Peloponnesian War—saying, "We are fighting for the liberty of the Greeks against these oppressive

Athenians"—the Spartans, led by Lysander, simply took over the Athenian Empire and now forced all those Greek cities to pay tribute to them.

Where the Athenians had been quite just and quite rigidly adhering to a rule of law, the Spartans didn't obey any laws at all. Any Spartan was viewed as a tyrant whose word was law. The Greeks began to hate the Spartans in a way they had never hated the Athenians, and they began to long for freedom from their liberators. So this was the ironical situation that Xenophon found when he got back from Persia.

The Persians, too, are beginning to resent the Spartans because the Spartans are beginning, in their hubris—that word which we think just means "arrogance" but to a Greek meant "arrogant violence"—to attack Persian holdings. Lysander meant to be the sort of great invader of Persia who would have ultimately made himself king of Sparta. He was born, not a commoner but a noble Spartan who was not in the direct line to inherit one of the two royal positions as king, and he didn't like that. He felt he should be king. He tried to pull the oracles in to help him.

He actually paid to have oracles pronounce that would declare that the Spartans should take steps that would result in Lysander becoming king. One of the oracles he went to was in Africa. Out in the Libyan desert there was an oracle of Zeus Ammon that was very famous. It was at an oasis called the oasis of Siwa, and Lysander went there to manipulate the oracles and get favorable pronouncements about his own claims to rule Sparta.

He came back to Sparta; the Spartans managed to get around him, and so he thought, "Well, if I can't be king myself, I will make a king of my choice and rule through him." There was at this time a debate about who would succeed the old king who had just died—a king named Aegis. This was the man whose wife had had a passionate affair with the Athenian Alcibiades, whom we visited a few lectures ago. Everyone believed, and it's probably true, that her son was Alcibiades's child and not the child of the king of Sparta, her own husband.

Lysander fomented doubts about this boy and said, "No, no, we must not have a half-Athenian on the throne of Sparta. Let's take this man," and he pointed to a kinsman of the dead king—a little fellow called Agesilaus. The Spartans really prized physical stature and strong, heroic bearing. Agesilaus was one of the shortest Spartans of his generation. He was sort of one of these stocky, little, bandy-legged guys that you could overlook in a crowd, and he had spent his early life avoiding notice. He'd adhered to all the rules of Spartan upbringing: He was quiet; he was obedient to his elders. No one really knew him.

Lysander the king-maker thought, "Here's a perfect person with no character of his own, whom I can make king, and then I'll rule through him." Well, he couldn't have been more mistaken. As soon as Agesilaus became king of Sparta, he took over all of Lysander's plans. He said, "If there is to be a war in Asia, I shall command it." He took Lysander along just as one of 30 advisors, and when Lysander tried to strike out a policy of his own, he completely sidelined him and put Lysander—the great hero of Sparta a few years earlier—completely out of the picture.

Agesilaus then waged war, incredibly vigorous war, against the Persians in Asia Minor—modern Turkey—fighting for control of those old Greek cities and even beyond. He was so successful that Sparta's former ally, the Persian satrap, or provincial governor, Pharnabazus—who really was the mastermind and the friend of Sparta who enabled them to beat Athens—called for a meeting with Agesilaus, and the two of them met on a grassy plain. Pharnabazus was having his attendants—in normal Persian style—spread out the carpets on the grass, and the cushions, and the refreshments, and he saw Agesilaus the Spartan arrive and go over and sit on the cold, hard ground—cross-legged, no ceremony at all.

Pharnabazus walked over and just sat down right in front of him, ignoring all of the beautiful preparations, and he said, "Why are you doing this to me? I was Sparta's friend, and now you are burning my farms—you are raiding my territory. I can't get dinner because you are forever destroying my crops. Is this any way to treat a friend? Is this justice?" Agesilaus was so ashamed—because he'd never really had anybody rebuke him for Sparta's faithlessness to Persia—that he was silent for a long time. Then, finally, he said, "You have made me feel remorse for what we have done. I beseech you, leave your master, the Great King of Persia, and fight with us Spartans, and together, we will win you a kingdom of your own."

This is the first time anybody put into a satrap's head the idea of rebelling from their Persian overlord and setting up a province to be a new kingdom. Pharnabazus was too loyal to do that. He said, "As long as the Great King has appointed me his servant, I am loyal to him and to nobody else." He got up, and he walked off to his horse. Agesilaus was very impressed with this and ran after him and said, "I cannot help admiring you. I promise that in future I will leave your territory alone and only raid those of other Persian satraps."

Pharnabazus's son, who was with his father at this meeting, ran back to Agesilaus, gave him a gift, and said, "I want to make you my guest friend." So in this way, a friendship, a formal friendship, was formed between this king of Sparta and Pharnabazus.

Unfortunately, damage had already been done. While Agesilaus was raiding, Pharnabazus, who held a lot of clout in the Persian system, had sent a messenger up the Royal Road from Asia Minor all the way to the king—he was at Babylon at this time—saying, "The Spartans are attacking us. The only way to get them out of Asia is: Attack them at sea; draw them away from our territory. We should be looking around for a naval commander."

This had always been the problem for Persia: How do we fight these Greeks, who are the greatest seafarers around? They even surpass our Phoenicians who fight for us at sea. How do we do this? So the king, Artaxerxes II, began looking around for a commander, and amazingly, he found one who was in his own realms, who had tremendous experience and a fair amount of success. But this man was an Athenian. His name was Conon—Conon the Athenian.

After the last battle of the Peloponnesian War at a place called Goat Rivers (Aegospotami), up in the Hellespont, Conon was the only Athenian commander who escaped the universal capture of the Athenian fleet on shore by Lysander and the Spartans. Conon had kept his men together while the others were, in an undisciplined way, scattering away from the Athenian camp, resting, and looking for a meal around in the countryside. Conon kept his crews tight by their ships, and as Lysander swept down without warning and captured the Athenians on shore, Conon got away with just eight ships out of what had been a fleet of almost 200.

Those eight got away, and Conon, looking for a safe haven now that the whole world was going to be a Spartan domain, fled away to the island of Cyprus. We think today of Cyprus as a divided island, today divided between Greeks and Turks. In antiquity, it was divided between Greeks and Phoenicians, but one of the Greek kings was very friendly to the mainland Greeks. His name was Evagoras. His kingdom was centered at a little city called Salamis in Cyprus, and it was to that little city of Salamis—named for Salamis back by Athens and founded by those Greeks who, after the collapse of Greek civilization in around 1200 B.C., had gone to Cyprus as refugees (so they were cousins, sort of, of the Athenians)—that Evagoras welcomed Conon and his eight ships.

Any commander with eight good, trained crews and eight good, ram-tipped triremes is going to be welcome anywhere. So Conon set himself up there. He had his son Timotheus with him, and he became this leader in exile. To him came all of the Athenians who wanted to resist Sparta but couldn't do it at home. So here was this admiral who had participated in a number of Athenian naval campaigns back in the glory days of Athens, and the king sent a message to him in 397 B.C., appointing him admiral of the Persian fleet.

The Persian naval efforts for the last 100 years had always suffered from what I think of as erectile dysfunction—a lot of determination to follow through and a lot of fine talk up front, but it never came to anything. They just couldn't seem to deliver, and that's what happened now. The Great King had told Conon he was admiral, but when Conon asked for ships from the cities of the Persian Empire that could have supplied them—the Phoenician cities, the Cilician cities—they sent back messages saying, "Well, it will take a few years to get new ships built and to assemble the crews." Everything began to peter out, and he had a vision of the impotent result of all of this effort, and he wasn't going to put up with that.

He followed the trail of the Ten Thousand that we followed a couple of lectures ago. He wanted to see Artaxerxes himself, and he decided to go to Babylon to do it. So he crossed over to that port at Issos, and he went inland to the Euphrates River, and he took a boat down the river to Babylon—which was the king's residence and was rapidly becoming a sort of unofficial additional capital of the great Persian Empire.

Now he's in Babylon, and he's ready to talk to Artaxerxes, but there's a problem. Persian kings had become very different from what they were in the days of Cyrus the Conqueror, back 150 years earlier, back in the mid-6th century when the Persians were young, vigorous conquerors spreading out across the globe and the king was everywhere—at the front of his forces, talking to enemies and friends alike. Now the king was an unapproachable figure. He was surrounded by the court; you had to petition for a chance to speak to him. There was no meaningful dialogue, and the ceremonies were things that the Greeks just found abhorrent.

The most abhorrent of all was what was called *proskynesis*—"getting down on your knees," "kowtowing." You had to kiss your hand to the king; you had to bow. It seems, apparently, some of the Greeks even called it "prostration." You had to just almost lie on the floor before the king would recognize you and allow you to speak.

Part of the idea of Greek *eleutheria*—"freedom"—is not just the freedom of your city; it's the freedom of yourself. You are an independent, free man. You don't bow to anyone. To do that would be what the Greeks called "slavish," and when Socrates, as recorded in Plato's *Dialogues*, wants to tell a young Athenian to act in the right way—stand up for yourself; be a virtuous man—he says, "Don't be slavish. Don't be someone who obeys the orders of others. Think for yourself. Act for yourself." So it was inconceivable that Conon should ever go into the presence of Artaxerxes because he would have had to bow.

There's a funny story that one Greek ambassador from the city of Thebes was so upset when told he had to bow to the Great King in order to have an audience with him that he dropped his ring on the floor in front of him and then reached over to scoop it up, so that the rest of his Greek embassy could be told by him later, "I was just picking up my ring," but Artaxerxes (or whichever Great King it was) would have seen this bow.

At any rate, Conon and Artaxerxes stayed in separate rooms, and they sent go-betweens back and forth. Conon listed his complaints about this failure of the Persians to follow through on the naval effort, and Artaxerxes, respecting him tremendously, agreed to all of his demands. So he confirmed Conon as admiral, and he gave him more funds—all the funds he wanted—to pay his crews. Let's not forget that these aren't slaves who are rowing these ships—170 rowers in each trireme—and they've all got to be paid every day. He gave Conon a tremendous war chest.

He sent orders to the satraps and the local rulers that they must obey this man's request for ships and for men. Finally, he said to Conon, through the go-betweens, "I would like you to have a Persian to command with you." Part of the reason people have been slow was Conon, of course, is an Athenian. They have been the demons in Persian eyes for so long that he is not a congenial figure for these Persian types to collaborate with.

Conon, knowing very well the reputation of Pharnabazus for fairness and for valor, asked for Pharnabazus, the satrap of Asia Minor, and so that was agreed to by Artaxerxes. As soon as Pharnabazus—whom you may remember riding his stallion into the sea almost to try to attack the Athenian ships on horseback up in the Hellespont, and we just saw him being very plain and straightforward with Agesilaus at that meeting on the grass—he comes down to the sea. He joins Conon, and together, they put together a big fleet very quickly and head west toward the Aegean to meet the Spartans.

The Spartans learn that they are coming, because during all the months of delay that were driving Conon crazy, a merchantman—a freighter from the city of Syracuse in Sicily, a traditional enemy of Athens ever since the Syracusan expedition of 415 to 413 B.C.—this sea captain was in the harbor at Cyprian Salamis, saw the preparations for this invasion, realized what was going on, and hurried off to tell the Spartans back home: "You're about to be attacked at sea."

Agesilaus probably should have commanded the defense at sea himself, this new king of Sparta. Instead, he appointed—in an act of true and despicable nepotism—his own brother-in-law to be admiral, a man named Peisander who had no naval experience and whose only recommendation was he was the king's kinsman. Peisander was not a sensible person, and he was not a person who understood tactics. He just thought the way to win battles was the Spartan way—go straight at them. Don't hesitate. Be the bravest, and you will win.

We all know by this time—having seen Themistocles at Salamis and some of these other great naval tacticians—that it's not like a hoplite battle on land. It's not two lines of men confronting each other and having a shoving match along the front line and seeing who can shove the hardest. Naval battles are won by tactics, by stratagems, by knowing the terrain, knowing your enemy.

Peisander didn't understand that. He took his fleet to a city at the absolute southwest corner of Asia Minor, a beautiful city called Cnidus, sacred to the goddess Aphrodite. We may not immediately associate Aphrodite with the sea—we think of her as the goddess of erotic love, beauty—but the Greeks thought of her as a great deity of the sea. She was supposed to have been born from the foam of the sea near the island of Cyprus. Cnidus was on a promontory sticking far out into the sea, and her temple was up on a height, looking out to the horizon over the blue waters where the Aegean met the eastern Mediterranean.

So under the goddess's gaze, the Spartans marshaled their forces, and Conon sent spies and scouts ahead to find out how big they were. He'd discovered that they had a smaller fleet than his, once he'd combined with Pharnabazus and all of these Athenian ships. So many Athenians had flocked to his standard now because they were desperate to get their city back on its feet, and he seemed their only hope. So he had a bigger fleet than the Spartans did, and not knowing what an idiot Peisander was, he assumed it would take some stratagem to lure him into battle.

Half of winning a battle is often persuading your enemy to fight a battle that they shouldn't—a battle that, in fact, they would be destined to lose and would know it if they understood the whole situation. So he pulled that same stunt that we saw Alcibiades pulling at Cyzicus. He took his own little Athenian squadron as a vanguard and paraded across the bay in front of Cnidus, with Pharnabazus behind with the main body of the Phoenicians, and the Cilicians, and the other Persian ships hidden.

Well, Peisander saw this tempting target, these few Athenian ships—the hated Athenians—like a red rag to a bull. He loaded all of his men onto the ships and launched his full force immediately and set off in pursuit of these Athenians. Conon then swung his fleet around to face this charge from Peisander and the Spartans. I say "the Spartans," but the Spartans have no seafaring tradition—they're like the Persians in that. These are not Spartan ships, or Spartan men, or Spartan rowers or pilots; they're all mercenaries. They're all hirelings from Asia Minor, or from the islands, or from the Greek cities that the Spartans have basically conquered, and many of them don't like the Spartans at all. They're just their paymasters. So this is not a good situation for Peisander.

At any rate, he plunged into the midst of the Athenian fleet. They were battling hard, when suddenly, the left wing—or the left "horn," as the Spartans would have called it—of their naval formation was able to see, rounding the point, Pharnabazus and the main body of the enemy fleet. They thought they were attacking the whole thing with this Athenian vanguard, and here was a fleet that outnumbered them—fresh, ready for combat, and showing up across the sea. They all abandoned Peisander the Spartan, turned for shore, and fled.

Peisander saw this happen, but he kept on fighting, and he was ultimately killed. As soon as he was seen to die, all of those Spartan ships turned back and ran for shore. We've seen it again and again, starting with Marathon. In a rout, you've got your undefended back to the enemy, and the casualties can be huge. Conon and Pharnabazus managed to snap up 50 enemy triremes in the short run from the field of battle out in the bay before they got to the shore. Thousands of the enemy oarsmen leapt overboard and swam to shore, trying to escape from the Athenians and the Persians—and even with that, they managed to capture 5,000 others as prisoners.

This is a great deal in ancient warfare, because you can ransom your prisoners, and that helps pay for the campaign. So it's a tremendous victory for the Athenians and for the Persians. I just want you to reflect on the irony here—piled on irony—that now Athens and Persia, which were, in the year 480 B.C.—almost a century earlier—confronted vicious enemies to each other, fighting it out at the Battle of Salamis, and finally, the Athenians beating the Persians and launching their Golden Age under the banner of resistance to Persia. Now, they're the best of friends, fighting against Athens's former ally, Sparta.

The word got around immediately of this disaster. It came to Agesilaus, the king of Sparta, when he was campaigning. He was already back in Greece at this point, and we know all about it because Xenophon, our hero of the march of the Ten Thousand, looking for a congenial leader to whom to hitch his own star, had joined Agesilaus, and he was there on the day when word came of the defeat of the Spartan fleet at Cnidus. He was there when the messenger came to Agesilaus's tent—the Spartan army's tent—and said, "We have lost a great battle at Cnidus. The Spartan navy is destroyed."

On that day, there was an eclipse of the Sun. We've had one earlier when Xerxes set out on his great march to invade Greece—there was an eclipse of the Sun there. The Greeks always viewed eclipses as portents of disaster. So Agesilaus, fearing that this might be the end of the Spartan Empire, went out and lied to the troops, because word was percolating everywhere: "There has been a great battle. My brother-in-law Peisander fell valiantly fighting for Sparta, but the navy won. We are still masters of the sea." He wanted to keep his own men's courage and heart up, and he didn't want the enemies of Sparta, who were surrounding them at this point—he knew a battle was in the offing—he didn't want them to know, or they would have fought with renewed vigor against him.

Well, the battle happened very shortly after that at a place called Coronea, and although Agesilaus survived, he fell in the front line. He was leading, as Spartan kings do, in the front, but he was so small, so short that he got pushed over in the crush of the phalanx, trampled on, and almost killed. His officers finally pulled him out and got him back on his feet. He survived the battle, and the Spartans were not beaten, but it was a tactical victory for their enemies, the Thebans and the other states—the old allies of Sparta, like Corinth and Athens, that are now fighting against Sparta. He made his way home, and that was the end of the Spartan Empire—this Battle of Coronea on land, this great defeat of the naval forces at sea.

That might have been the end of it. Conon was allowed, with his son Timotheus, to go around to the Greek cities in Asia and in the Aegean and liberate them from their Spartan governors. If they had managed to just end it there, probably there, then, would have been this equipoise: Athens and Sparta sort of in balance. But there was one Spartan governor, Dercyllidas, up at Abydos on the Hellespont—that city where the south end of Xerxes's bridges had been anchored back in 480 B.C.—who would not give up. He was so popular with the local people that when he said, "We can defy the world," he sort of infused them with this desire.

It would have been a lot better for Sparta if he had been defeated and thrown out with the rest, because Abydos was in the satrapy of Pharnabazus, and Pharnabazus—getting home after this big naval effort and beating the Spartans at sea—is enraged to discover at his doorstep another Spartan still hanging on, still denying him access to the Hellespont. He went back to Conon and said, "We are going to Greece."

So in the following spring, 393 B.C., they gathered the navy again, and they crossed over to Greece. They took the island of Cythera—that beautiful island sacred to Aphrodite off the southern tip of Sparta—and they put in an Athenian governor. They went up to the Isthmus of Corinth. Pharnabazus, Persian satrap and prince, went ashore on Greek soil and was an honored guest of the Athenians, the Corinthians, and the Thebans—all of the anti-Spartan Greeks. He said, "Keep fighting this war against Sparta," all because of that annoying Spartan up in Abydos. "Keep fighting the war. I will fund you; I will give you treasure; I will give you gold."

When Conon asked him for the fleet to remain in Athens to carry on the war at Sparta's doorstep, he said to Pharnabazus the magic words: "If you do this, you will hurt the Spartans more than you could do in any other way. If you take away from them the rule of the sea, if you restore Athens and Athens's naval power, as you are the only man in the world that could do, you will have injured them more deeply than you imagine."

This was music to Pharnabazus's ears. He left that fleet of ships with Conon. He left Conon a tremendous war chest. Conon went back to Athens, and Pharnabazus went back to Asia Minor, and Conon—received like a hero at the Piraeus—was able to bring back Athens seemingly from the dead. With those ships, he reinstituted the Athenian navy. With all that money, he rebuilt the Long Walls that linked Athens to the port of Piraeus, so once again, the city was impregnable by attack on land, and he rebuilt the Piraeus, which in the years after the fall of Athens had been wrecked. No one wanted to see this emblem of Athenian sea power ever to be a strong naval base again. He rebuilt it.

The Athenians—wanting a sort of presiding genius to hover over the Piraeus—remembered Themistocles, that sea hero of long ago who had won the Battle of Salamis for them with his stratagems and his tricks. They built for him a monument on the point of land—you can still see it today at the entrance to the great harbor at the Piraeus—the one that faces west into the straits of Salamis. Archaeologists found this little place where a monument to Themistocles was set up, and there was an inscription: "Here you lie on a high point of land. You look on the merchantmen coming from all the world. You see the galleys racing in and out from this place."

In addition to a cult of Themistocles, which the Athenians in general took over to do justice to him, Conon built a temple to Aphrodite—Aphrodite of the fair voyage—because she's the goddess who looked out over his great victory in Cnidus. In the new Athenian Golden Age that was launched by this victory and this restoration of Athens—the Golden Age of the philosopher Plato, the orator Demosthenes—there was a great sculptor, Praxiteles, who glorified the female form as no one ever had done before.

The Greeks had been kind of hung up on male nudes up to this time. The first person to show a female nude was Praxiteles, and he created—what else?—a famous statue of Aphrodite to go in that temple at Cnidus, where the sea battle that turned the world's history around had been fought. She was shown with her robe slipping off her, getting ready to step into her bath—that goddess who was part of an element of water—and she was so beautiful, front and back, that they put doors at the rear of the temple so people who wanted to see her 360 degrees could get in there and admire her from the rear as they did from the front.

So all this feeling of happiness, of joy, that Athens had never thought to experience again came back with Conon, with Pharnabazus, with the turn of their fortunes—and we have truly seen, in almost the space of just a decade, the world turned upside down.

Lecture Nineteen
The Panhellenic Dream

Scope: In 386 B.C., the Spartan Antalcidas and the satrap Tíríbazus worked out the terms of the King's Peace (also known as the Peace of Antalcidas). This Spartan-Persian initiative protected the Spartans and limited resurgent Athenian expansion but at a horrible cost: The Great King of Persia had, at a stroke, been recognized as overlord of the Greeks almost without having had the trouble of fighting a war. The reactionary Panhellenic crusade, spurred by the orations of Lysias and Isocrates, sought to unite all of Greece against Persia. A key source of the Panhellenic dream was Isocrates's epic speech "Panegyricus," which turned Lysias's themes into a cosmic vision by claiming that Persia suffered from *malakia* ("softness") and calling for a united Athenian-Spartan leadership in a war on the Great King. Some 30 years later, with no unity in sight, the aged Isocrates appealed to a new power: the energetic King Philip of Macedon.

Outline

I. The Greeks were dismayed by the inability of the city-states, including Athens, Sparta, Corinth, and Thebes, to create a Panhellenic (Greek-wide) sense of unity.

II. With the revival of the Athenian navy, Athens once again resumed its imperial mission to liberate the Greek cities of Asia Minor.

    A. Athens felt no obligation to Artaxerxes for his help against the Spartans and set about supporting a rebellion against the Persians on Cyprus and making war to reclaim the Hellespont.

    B. The death of the Athenian general Thrasybulus as he tried to extend Athenian influence was symptomatic of the chaotic years when Athens and Sparta both vied for leadership of Greece—with Persia perpetually considering itself injured by whichever state was ascendant.

    C. To put a check on Athenian expansion, the diplomat Antalcidas and the satrap Tíríbazus developed the King's Peace (also known as the Peace of Antalcidas), which made Persia the arbiter among

the Greeks and allowed the Spartans to continue operating without fear of Athenian naval reprisal.
  1. The Greek cities in Asia would belong to the Persian king.
  2. Empire building among the Greeks would cease.
  3. The Great King would enforce the peace by making war—"with ships and with money"—on any power that violated it.
 D. The Greeks were not enthusiastic about the King's Peace, but they signed it nonetheless. Many Greeks were appalled to think that, a century after overcoming Xerxes, they had now turned over to the Great King the ability to dictate their affairs.

III. With the King's Peace, the Greeks saw what their disunity had brought them to—an issue that seems endemic to city-state systems.
 A. A city-state (what the Greeks called a *polis*) consists of a city and its surrounding territory; the territory feeds the city, and the city defends the territory.
 B. Throughout history, city-states have come into conflict until welded into a single kingdom by a greater power with a dictatorial central government.
 C. The city-state system, however, engenders remarkable innovations, competition, free enterprise, and entrepreneurship.
 D. The perpetual warfare in the Greek city-state system has been called the "wound of Greece."
 E. Certain aspects of their cultural lives drew the Greeks together, including the oracle shrines and such competitions as the Olympics and the Panathenaic Games, but politically, the Greeks were disunited.
 F. The Athenian orator Lysias made an appeal for Panhellenism at the Olympic Games, calling for the Greeks to unite in a war against Persia.

IV. In 384 B.C., the Athenian Isocrates presented the "Panegyricus" ("the thing in praise of all kinds of things"), which became a manifesto for Panhellenism.
 A. Isocrates gave numerous orations on this theme, promoting a common purpose to engender Panhellenic unity: war on Persia.
 B. Isocrates was born in 436 B.C. and was a pupil of Socrates.
 C. The practice of oratory involved putting philosophy to work through deciding the right course of action and making speeches to

guide one's fellow citizens in making the right choices. In Athens, the place of oratory was a speaker's platform on a hill called the Pnyx.
- **D.** Isocrates combined his philosophical interests with his genius for crafting speeches and opened a school where he taught others.
- **E.** The theme of the "Panegyricus" is that the Greeks were disgraced because of the King's Peace, which allowed the Persians to rule over them.
    1. The common purpose for the Greeks would be a war on the barbarians (the Persians).
    2. Two reasons for promoting this war were unification and the prospect of more wealth.
    3. Athens must lead the unified Greeks, but the Spartans needed to join in.
- **F.** Isocrates in particular accused the Persians of *malakia* ("softness"). He held up the march of the Ten Thousand as a shining example of the weakness of the Persian Empire, which could not prevent the Greeks from going wherever they wished.
- **G.** Thirty years after the delivery of the "Panegyricus," Isocrates still looked for some way to unify Greece. At the end of his life, he found the man he believed could be such a leader: King Philip II of Macedon.
    1. Isocrates begged Philip II to take on the burden of unifying the Greeks and leading them on a war of conquest into Persian territory.
    2. Philip II took advantage of this friendly overture and began to lay plans to unify Greece under himself and make the attack on Persia a reality.

Recommended Reading:

Isocrates, *Orations.*

Olmstead, *History of the Persian Empire: Achaemenid Period.*

Questions to Consider:

1. Thinking back to earlier events in this course, make a case for the Panhellenic dream as both an achievable mission and wishful thinking.
2. Read Isocrates's "Panegyricus." Would you have been convinced enough to support its message for Panhellenism? Why or why not?

Lecture Nineteen—Transcript
The Panhellenic Dream

Welcome back. With our last lecture, we saw the resurgence of Athens as a great naval power—thanks to, ironically, Persian support. If your head is beginning to ache from all these reversals in the Greek world, you are not alone. The Greeks themselves were dismayed by the inability of the city-states of Greece—Athens, Sparta, Corinth, Thebes, and the others—to create a stable world. That's going to be the theme of our lecture this time: this quest for a "Panhellenic"—a Greek-wide—mission, a sense of unity that so far has been lacking in Greek affairs.

However, we're going to start, pick up the story, with the coming back to the light of the Athenian navy, Conon's rebuilding of the Long Walls, and the situation there in the late 390s B.C. as Athens, once again, resumes its sort of imperial mission at sea.

Of course, no sooner do the Athenians get their navy back, than what do they do? That old mission to liberate the Greek cities of Asia comes back into their minds. Most of those cities are still now in the hands of the Great King. One of the results of the fall of Athens in 404 B.C. and the payment of the Spartan war debt, as it were, to Persia was the handing over of Greek cities in Asia to the king. Many of them have not yet been liberated, and so the Athenians start fighting the Persians.

This may seem like a great betrayal after all the help that King Artaxerxes gave to the Athenian Conon, but remember, that was using Conon for his own purposes. Athens as a city-state felt no obligation or debt to Artaxerxes for what he'd done. They set about, first, supporting a rebellion against the Persians on Cyprus itself and, then, making war to get the Hellespont on both shores—Asiatic and European—back into Athenian hands. They even go around to that site where Cimon, back in the 460s B.C., won the great Battle of the Eurymedon River against the Persians on land and sea.

An Athenian general named Thrasybulus, a radical democrat, takes the Athenian fleet there and is actually killed in action by local tribes as he's trying to extend Athenian influence further and further into Persian territory. This was symptomatic of the years—approximately six years—that followed the great victory at Cnidus and the reversal of Spartan hegemony at sea. It is a chaotic time, where Athens and Sparta are both vying for the leadership of Greece, and Persia is still feeling injured by whoever is the leading Greek state.

Eventually, the Spartans begin to fear: "If we don't somehow put a check on Athenian expansion, we will be right back where we were before we seemingly beat them at the end of the Peloponnesian War." So a Spartan diplomat named Antalcidas, who seems to have had a way with getting along with Persians, went over to Asia Minor. He presented himself to one of the satraps, a man named Tíribazus, whom we last encountered on the banks of a river with his army, trying to prevent Xenophon and the Ten Thousand from wading across and entering the satrapy of Armenia.

Tíribazus and Antalcidas get together, and they come up with a document, which King Artaxerxes endorses, that will take for Persia the role of arbiter among the Greeks. Remember, this is all a Spartan scheme. It's a way of having the Persian king show up with the big stick to enforce peace and harmony among the Greeks—but, in fact, it's so that the Spartans can go on operating without fear of Athenian naval reprisals.

At any rate, in the winter of 387 to 386 B.C., all the Greek city-states receive invitations from the Great King, from Artaxerxes, to attend a conference in that city we have visited so often, the city of Sardis, in the old kingdom of Lydia. They meet there, and they find that Antalcidas and Tíribazus have drafted this document. What does the document say? "It seems good to the king that the Greek cities in Asia shall belong to the king as of old." That is, "as of old" before 480 and 479 B.C., when the Athenian navy, along with the other Greeks, liberated them from Xerxes.

"Second, all the other Greeks shall be autonomous and free." In other words, there shall be no more building up of empires among the Greeks. There shall be no Spartan Empire, no Athenian Empire. The only exceptions being that a couple of islands the Athenians had come to view as their own, Lemnos and Skyros—these are stepping stones up to the Hellespont, the grain route that brings Athens its wheat from the Black Sea—these are thrown in for Athens—Athens's property—as a little sop to Athenian pride, as a way to induce the Athenians to quit fighting and sign the peace.

"If anyone breaks this peace, the Great King shall be the enforcer, and he will make war on those who violate the peace with ships and with money"—a very funny way of describing making a war.

The Greeks were not enthusiastic about this, but they signed. So in 386 B.C., a new world order came into being for the Greeks, mandated by their hereditary enemy, the Great King of Persia, who has now set himself up, through this document, as overlord of the Greek world. It's as if Athens and

Sparta are bickering children who cannot stop fighting on the playground, and finally, the teacher comes out, knocks their heads together, and says, "Behave." Artaxerxes was the schoolmaster for Greece.

When the delegates returned from that meeting back to their cities, lots and lots of ordinary Greeks were appalled to think that a century after beating Xerxes—defeating the Persians, showing that the Greeks were a greater fighting force than all of the massed armies and navies of Asia combined—it had come to this. That without the Great King ever having to fight a great war or defeat them in any kind of decisive way, just because they couldn't unite, they had turned over to him the ability to rule them—to dictate to them.

This may not seem so gigantic to us, but the fact is that that's what empires were in the ancient world. I've made this point before, but let me make it again. The Roman Empire gives us a false impression of normalcy among empires. Usually it was a conquering people, a conquering dynasty, who took over, changed regions filled with city-states and brought them together, and basically dictated their foreign policy to them and demanded tribute from them. That was all. There wasn't a tremendous amount of interference. There was no attempt to build Roman-style temples, Roman-style marketplaces, and all the rest of it everywhere. Persians didn't behave that way.

So for the king to dictate the foreign policies of Greek states was tantamount to saying, "You are now part of my empire, and I will keep the peace that you seem unable to keep yourselves." This created a reaction among the Greeks. They were now up against it. They really saw what their disunity and their disharmony had brought them to. We might point out here that this seems endemic to city-state systems.

City-states, what a Greek called a *polis*—and from that word we get "politics," "politician," "political," "cosmopolitan," and "Indianapolis" ("city of Indiana")—all of these *polis* words. To the Greeks, that didn't just mean an urban area. That *polis* is a city-state, and that's why we have to use that cumbersome hyphenated term to duplicate it in English.

It's a city and its surrounding territory. The territory feeds the people in the city with its farms and its produce, and the city defends those who are out in the countryside by giving them safe walls to hide behind in case of an invasion. There have been city-state systems in Sumeria in southern Mesopotamia—what is today Iraq—those ancient cities like Ur, and Uruk, and Erek that show up in the Bible and in the ancient accounts of

Gilgamesh. They couldn't get along. They were at war with one another all the time until Sargon of Akkad, the world's first great emperor—unifier of city-states—welded them into one kingdom with a dictatorial central government.

There were city-states in Maya country in Mexico and in surrounding modern nations, like Guatemala, where these individual little ceremonial centers each supported a king, a court, an army, astronomers, and grand public buildings. There was perpetual warfare, as we now know since the code of the Maya has been cracked by archaeologists. We can read their records of continuing strife.

The Renaissance in Italy was marked by competition between city-states: Venice, Padua, Pisa, Florence—fighting it out, irrepressibly unable to unite until finally outside conquerors come in and do the unification for them.

So the Greeks are part of a system in which warfare simply seems endemic, systemic, part of the inevitable way of life that's engendered by city-states. What's the plus side? There has never been a system in human affairs that engendered more remarkable innovations, competition, free enterprise, and entrepreneurship than city-states. So we're left with this unfortunate paradox that the system that seems to get humans the furthest the fastest seems to have warfare bred into its very bones.

Where do you find stability? Where could ancient peoples look out and see stability? Egypt—never a place of city-states, always a unified kingdom around the Nile River. Look over at Mesopotamia, the empires of Asia. Once the city-states of Sumeria had been unified, then you get this world of the two rivers, the Tigris and the Euphrates, with single emperors—kings of kings—ruling over it, and stability, because the individual city-states have been suppressed. Of course, when we get to Rome, we will have the same sort of thing.

This situation was the identifying character of Greek civilization—that character of being a city-state civilization. How did the Greeks expand? They'd start from one city-state—Athens, Megara, Corinth—and they'd send out colonies. Those colonies would land on a coast somewhere— Spain, France, Sicily, Italy, North Africa, the Black Sea, Asia Minor—and what would they create? A new city-state independent of the mother city and sometimes fighting wars with the mother city. So this isn't a colonial expansion where you build empires typically from one city—it's just creating new cities on the model of the old ones in central Greece.

This is what was sometimes called the "wound of Greece"—that this perpetual warfare seemed to be something they couldn't break out of.

There were certain things that drew the Greeks together. We've already talked about one of them: the oracle shrines—places like Delphi, places like Dodona, the oracle of Zeus up in the mountains of northern Greece. At these oracular shrines, the Greeks, who all worship the same gods, would come together, and pray, and give offerings, and show their commonness—their "Greekness"—as they worshiped Apollo. There were also the big games. We're most familiar with the Olympic Games, which were held at Olympia in southern Greece. They were in honor of Zeus, but there were also Pythian Games to Apollo, Isthmian Games under the pine trees at the isthmus. Those were in honor of Poseidon. More games to Zeus set in Nemea in the Peloponnese. Those are the four crown games, where instead of getting a cash prize, you're given a crown of wild leaves. That was all. You competed for the honor of that crown.

But Athens also sponsored something called the Panathenaic Games, to which all comers could come. So with these games; with these shrines and common sanctuaries; with their common language and their common sense of independence, freedom, and personal worth, the Greeks were united culturally but disunited politically.

After the King's Peace was handed down by Artaxerxes in the 380s B.C., an Olympic festival took place in 384 B.C. To that festival came an Athenian orator. He was actually a resident alien in Athens. The status of those who came to Athens as resident aliens is a little like modern America: It was a place of opportunity for people in other cities whose economies were not so robust. They would come to Athens, and they would have chances to shine. This man's name was Lysias. He'd made a mark as the greatest orator in Athens. Ultimately, he was so impressive that the city turned over to him, after one of their wars against Sparta in the 390s B.C., the right to give the public funeral oration for the heroes who had fallen in that war.

In 384 B.C., Lysias traveled from Athens to the Olympics. Our modern Olympics are modeled on the ancient Greek Olympics, so they happened every four years, and they were always at Olympia. He went there because that was a Panhellenic place. You could count on meeting Greeks from all over the Greek world. Lysias read out an oration, because at the Olympic Games—it was not only the track and the field, and the chariot races, and so on, but it was a chance to hear people talk.

You may remember Herodotus. In addition to reciting his history of the Persian Wars in Athens, he'd also done it at Olympia, and people had heard him talk there. So they were used to hearing orators. Here was this man from Athens, Lysias, who gave an appeal for Panhellenism—that the Greeks should unite in a war against Persia.

This speech was not the first on that theme. The very next Olympics that followed that amazing Battle of Cyzicus—where Alcibiades led the Athenian fleet against the Spartan fleet sponsored by Pharnabazus back in 409 B.C.—a speaker named Gorgias from Sicily had come to the Olympics to make the same plea.

Sicily at that time was being attacked on the far side by Carthage—colonists of the Phoenicians, Asiatics, who were also trying to take over the western Greek world, just as the Persians from the east seemed to be trying to take over the central Greek world.

So Gorgias had presented this idea and, a generation later, Lysias, and then, in 380 B.C., the big publication was made of the thing that became the manifesto for Panhellenism, an oration called the "Panegyricus"—"the thing in praise of all kinds of things"—by an Athenian named Isocrates. I'd like to take a moment to tell you about this remarkable man because this Panhellenic dream is going to become linked especially to his name.

He wrote oration after oration, letter after letter on this theme. It became his cause. He was a bit of a dreamer. He stayed outside of politics himself, and maybe in some ways, this idea of the Greeks uniting was just a pipe dream, but he was so eloquent about it that he kept the dream alive for decades. He was 99 when he died, and he was still writing about this theme of Panhellenic unity and what was going to make the Panhellenic unity a common purpose—war on Persia.

Isocrates is our hero for this lecture. He's the great prophet of Panhellenism. Let's get to know him a little bit. He was born in 436 B.C. He was born into one of those rich manufacturing families of Athens, where their money came not from ancient ownership of land and noble rank but just from hard work. His father owned a factory, where they manufactured those pipes, those musical instruments that were played by the pipers at parties. They are often mistranslated in modern texts as flute girls, but they aren't flutes—they're much more like oboes. They're actually like the medieval instrument a shawm.

If you picture the chanter of a bagpipe, the thing that the pipers hold in their hands and play on, that has a double reed in it, and the pressure of the air forced through from the bag produces an incredibly strong reedy sound that you can hear for miles. It's an outdoor instrument. They played it at the theater, and they played it in the warships. The Spartans had their pipers accompany the men into battle to keep them in step.

This was a factory owned by Isocrates's father, manned by slaves, who produced these pipes and the reeds that went in them. They lost all their money in the Peloponnesian War. Like many Athenian families, they were ruined by the conflict with Sparta, and so Isocrates, in his 30s, was suddenly thrown out in the world with no obvious means of making a living or supporting himself.

He had been a pupil—like so many other important Athenians of that latter part of the 5th century B.C.—of Socrates, the philosopher. In one of Plato's *Dialogues*, he shows Socrates, his master, referring to this young Isocrates and saying, "I know he will make a great mark on the world, either in oratory or in philosophy."

Philosophy didn't mean quite the same thing to an ancient Greek that it does to us, even though we derive our philosophy from the ancient Greeks. To the Greeks, it meant simply "love of wisdom," which is what the compound word means: *philosophia—philos* ("love"), *sophia* ("wisdom"). So it could embrace all kinds of things: natural sciences, the path that Aristotle is going to follow; abstract thoughts and reasoning about the virtues and the right way to live one's life—that's Plato's theme. All kinds of things are included in *philosophia*.

It was about thought; it was about the intellect. Oratory was putting philosophy to work by deciding the right course of action and making speeches to guide your fellow citizens in making right choices. In Athens, the place of oratory was a speaker's platform on a hill called the Pnyx (P-N-Y-X)—the crowded place—where the 30,000 or 40,000 citizens would gather (or at least a quorum of them) about three times a month and debate the issues confronting Athens in a sort of gigantic town meeting.

Isocrates, with his oratorical gifts—his ability to craft a good speech—seemed marked out by nature to be one of those citizens who would have a tremendous impact on Athens. He would stand on that platform in the open air, looking across on the one side to the Parthenon on the Acropolis, looking on the other side over to the sea, to the straits at Salamis, to the great naval installation at the Piraeus, and out in front of him all of his fellow citizens were waiting for him to talk, ready to cheer, or jeer, or express their own opinions immediately afterwards. But he couldn't do that.

He had a very weak voice, and he was very shy, and if people interrupted him, he was put off his stride. He couldn't engage in the back and forth that was expected of an effective orator in the political scene. So he put his philosophical interests together with his undoubted genius for crafting speeches, and he opened a school. It was a school in which he taught others to make speeches. They came to him from all over the Greek world. Timotheus, the son of Conon, enrolled in Isocrates's school, and he loved his master and revered him.

He brought Isocrates to the attention of people in Cyprus—Greeks in Cyprus—who had helped Conon and Timotheus when they were exiles. So Isocrates built up around him an academy, a school for oratory and philosophy the way that out at the grove of Academe—the Academy—Plato, among the olive trees, was creating a school for those who wanted to enquire into abstract philosophy. Then out at the Lyceum, Aristotle was going to come along a generation later and create a school of those interested in politics, ethics, and natural science.

This was the kind of transformation that made Athens into a university town that endured long after the imperial Athens went under. Isocrates was part of that transformation.

At 56, he went to that Olympic festival of 380 B.C., and he took with him the text of this gigantic work, the "Panegyricus." He probably distributed it as a pamphlet. It's possible that he had someone else stand on a stone at Olympia and read it to the crowd. It's awfully long. It would have taken many, many hours to recite.

What's his theme? His theme is: "We are now disgraced, we Greeks, because of the King's Peace. We are allowing the Persians to dictate to us. It's time for someone to come up with some good ideas." He starts off by using the fact that he's at the Olympic festival to make a comment that is still relevant today in our sports-crazy world. "You know," he said, "if you were to double the strength or the athletic ability of every athlete on earth—double it—you would do nothing to better mankind in general. It would have no impact whatever. But if you were to do the same for just one human being in terms of their intellect—their ability to perceive new ideas—you would benefit all of humanity who could share that insight."

I have to say that to stand up and say this at the Olympic Games—the holy shrine of athletic mania—took some guts, whether he had somebody else do it or just published his little pamphlet. He then goes on to make his concrete proposal: "We must unify. What unifies people? A common purpose. What's the natural common purpose for Greeks? War on the barbarian—the Persian. That's the way it should be. That's what our tradition is. That was the only time that we united in the past was against the Persians, and we must do it again."

He has two reasons—first is the one I just said: unification. The other one is: "Let's get rich." The Greeks were very open about their desire to gain material advantages, gain wealth from warfare. We in the modern world are much more prissy about saying that that's a motive, but they were very upfront about it. "We should be enriching ourselves through wars. Not wars on each other, not Athenians taking from Spartans and Spartans taking from Thebans, but let's all get together and hit the biggest pile of wealth on earth."

Remember, he's just repeating here that argument of Aristagoras of Miletus way back in 499 B.C. when he showed up in Greece and tried to persuade, first, the Spartans and, then, the Athenians to participate in a grand war against Persia that would end in the capital city of Susa—way off beyond the Tigris River, 1,600 miles from the sea—and dump into the victorious Greeks' laps all the wealth of the treasury of the Persian Empire.

Money, gold, and wealth—this is something to make a Greek sit up and take notice. How is this going to be done? Athens must lead, but the Spartans need to join in. They need to forget their differences. He spends a lot of the "Panegyricus" going over recent Greek history, showing the track records of the different states.

Remember, in an age before you could go to libraries, and pull down books off the shelves, and read these histories and authoritative accounts, it was this kind of speech—whether it was a funeral speech praising the noble dead or a political speech like this one, trying to promote a certain new course of action—that was where people got their history. It's kind of amusing to us today to see that Isocrates, like other orators, will twist facts to make a point. So gradually, the reality of what went on in the past, we can see getting a special spin on it from all these successions of orations—especially by Athenian speech-makers.

There was one argument he made in particular. He accused the Persians of *malakia*—"softness." We spent a couple of sessions with Xenophon and his

Ten Thousand going into and then fighting their way out of the Persian Empire. Isocrates mentioned this. He may have met Xenophon. He certainly could have at the Olympic Games because Xenophon, though an exile from Athens, lived very near Olympia. He held this up as a shining example—the Persian Empire was so weak that even with its millions, it still could not prevent 10,000 armed Greeks from going wherever they wished in the king's domain.

There was a powerful argument. We will see in the future that Isocrates and the other orators exaggerated the *malakia*—the "softness"—of the Persian Empire. But at this point, it still rang very true to his Greek listeners. Nonetheless, however much intellectual agreement the "Panegyricus" and Isocrates's other speeches on this theme may have won for him and for his idea, the Greeks just are not capable of this. They may rationally say, "This makes sense, and this is the right course of action," but the on-the-ground political situation is that every one of those cities is continually going to be vying with its nearest neighbor.

So 30 years after that famous event, the Olympic Games where he presented this to the world, the octogenarian Isocrates—and he helps us get over the idea that it's only in modern times that people have long, fruitful life spans—is still looking for some way to unify Greece. It's at the end of his life, in the 350s B.C. that he finds the person he thinks is a champion. I mentioned the fact that city-states continually fight each other. Kingdoms can be at peace and stable.

On the north end of the Greek world, there was a kingdom called Macedon. You may remember back in the winter between the Salamis campaign and those final battles of 479 B.C., when Xerxes's forces were finally destroyed by the Greeks, a king named Alexander of Macedon came down to Athens and tried to bring the Athenians over to the Persian side because the Macedonians themselves had already bowed to the inevitable and surrendered to Xerxes.

There was a successor of that King Alexander of long ago. That King Alexander, by the way, had been recognized as a Greek, although his kingdom was so far off to the north. How was he recognized as a Greek? He was allowed to participate in the Olympic Games. That was the assurance that you are truly of Hellenic blood and descent, because only Greeks were allowed at the Olympics, and that old King Alexander was welcomed at Olympia.

His successor was the new strongman on the Greek scene. Old Isocrates from Athens sent him a letter begging him to take on, himself, the burden of unifying the Greeks and leading the Greeks on a great war of conquest into Persian territory—a war that would finally bring Aristagoras of Miletus's dream to reality: that the Greeks should conquer the Persians on their own land.

The name of this king up in Macedon was Philip. It's certainly one of the coincidences of history that the man to whom this Panhellenist Isocrates looked to unify Greece and to lead the Greeks on a war into Persian territory was a man whose thoughts were going on exactly those same lines, though in ways that the Athenians and the Spartans—if they'd been able to look into the mind of Philip—would have frightened them into uniting against him.

As it was, Philip took advantage of this friendly overture from this very influential Athenian Isocrates and began to lay his stratagems, his plans, and his maneuvers to put the unification of Greece under himself as war leader—as hegemon—into action and make the attack on Persia a reality.

Lecture Twenty
The Rise of Macedon

Scope: In the mid-4th century B.C., the remarkable Philip II ascended to the throne of Macedon, becoming to his kingdom what Cyrus II had been to Persia. He set about uniting the Greek world using a combination of old and new strategies—conquest combined with diplomacy and dynastic marriages. Philip saw that involvement in foreign conflicts had scattered Greek mercenary armies throughout the Mediterranean. In contrast, he created a professional fighting force that owed allegiance to the king of Macedon alone. He then set out on campaigns to win an empire, tackling the fragmented city-states of Greece one by one until finally defeating the armies of Athens and Thebes at Chaeronea. The Athenian orator Demosthenes had warned his fellow citizens that Philip was a threat to Greek freedom; Isocrates, however, continued to see Philip as the only hope for a unified Greece.

Outline

I. The Macedonians were those people who inhabited the kingdom of Macedon in the Balkans, the immense mountain range to the north of Greece.

    A. Unlike the seafaring Athenians, the Macedonians were a terrestrial people.

    B. Nevertheless, Macedon had the best supplies of timber for shipbuilding, and the Macedonians grew wealthy from trade with the Athenians and eventually became ambitious.

II. The man who fulfilled the Macedonian dream of uniting this mountainous territory into a larger kingdom was King Philip II.

    A. Philip II knew the Greeks very well.
        1. He and his mother were rescued from dynastic struggles by the Athenian general Iphicrates.
        2. He hired the philosopher Aristotle, who had trained in Athens, to tutor his son Alexander.
        3. He was sent as a hostage in his teens to Thebes during the time when the Theban general Epaminondas was living there.

- **B.** When he came to the throne, Philip II used new strategies for taking over territories, combining conquest with diplomacy and weddings. Perhaps the most famous marriage he arranged was his own, to Olympias from Epirus.
- **C.** Philip II, like Cyrus II, took a remote hill people who seemed far from the centers of civilization and world control and, through training, inspiration, and a new vision of warfare, raised them to become a formidable fighting force.
- **D.** Philip II paid particular attention to the Greek and Persian world after the King's Peace.
    1. Greek involvement in the war in Egypt between native Egyptians and the Persian Empire had drawn the fighting forces of Greece to distant parts of the Mediterranean, rather than keeping them focused at home.
    2. Agesilaus's humiliation of Persian captives to illustrate the vulnerability of the Persians diminished the Persian Empire's prestige and fearsome reputation in the eyes of the Greeks and Macedonians.

III. Philip II set out to conquer the small, fragmented kingdoms and city-states surrounding Macedon.
- **A.** The fighting force he created seemed to resemble the traditional Greek phalanx.
    1. The chief difference was the Macedonians' weapons: spears called "sarissas" that were twice as long as those of the Greek hoplites.
    2. The army was a permanent one that owed its allegiance to the king and trained year-round.
    3. The cavalry, traditionally neglected in Greek city-states, became an integral part of the Macedonian army.
- **B.** Philip II assaulted the towns along the Hellespont that brought the wealth of the Black Sea down into the Mediterranean.
- **C.** Because the Greeks could not reach consensus about unification or national priorities, Philip II was able to circumvent their defenses and ingratiate himself with a number of city-states and peoples.
    1. He appeared at and competed in the Olympic Games.
    2. He used money to buy the support of the Greeks.
- **D.** The most prominent opponent of Philip II was the Athenian orator Demosthenes.

1. He warned the Greeks that Philip II only appeared to be a friend and was, in fact, bent on robbing the Greeks of their freedom.
2. Demosthenes was countered by Aeschines (an Athenian actor in Philip II's pay), who claimed that Demosthenes was motivated only by self-interest.
3. With conflicting opinions in play, Philip II was protected against Demosthenes and other detractors.
   E. At last, Philip II brought his armies into Greece and met the united forces of Athens and Thebes at Chaeronea. The result was a Macedonian victory.
IV. The victory at Chaeronea made Philip II the hegemon of all the Greek city-states except Sparta. Accordingly, he called a council at the Isthmus of Corinth.
   A. He wanted the people of the city-states to believe they were autonomous, even though he now governed their foreign policies.
   B. He announced to the Greeks the start of a campaign to conquer the Persian Empire.
   C. It was at this time that he received a letter from Isocrates promoting the Panhellenic dream.

Recommended Reading:

Adcock, *The Greek and Macedonian Art of War.*

Plutarch, *The Age of Alexander: Nine Greek Lives.*

Questions to Consider:

1. How do you imagine the Panhellenic vision playing out without the crucial role of Philip II?
2. Do you think Philip II had the best intentions of the Greek world at heart with his campaign to conquer the Persian Empire, or was he merely power hungry? Why or why not?

Lecture Twenty—Transcript
The Rise of Macedon

Welcome back. To the north of Greece stretched the immense mountain range called the Balkans, and 2,500 years ago, just as today, it was divided among many peoples. It was a dangerous place. The Greeks felt it was only partially civilized because it was only on its margins that the Greeks had colonized and set up those familiar city-states. In the interior were little kingdoms and chiefdoms, mountain valleys connected by precipitous trails over passes, divided by rushing torrents of rivers—each little place ruled by its own people.

The people who inhabited the Balkans—where the mountains came down to the northwest corner of the Aegean Sea—were called Macedonians. It's their story and the story of the king who elevated them to greatness on the world stage that we are going to tackle in this lecture.

Macedon was a kingdom of mountains, forests, rivers, and lakes. They were a terrestrial people rather than seafarers, like the Greeks, in spite of the fact that they had the best supplies of shipbuilding timber in that entire part of the world. Ironically, the Athenians, who are ultimately going to be subdued by the Macedonians, helped to enrich and empower the Macedonians by sending Athenian gold and silver north to buy shipbuilding timber from these people, who still commanded immense forests of pine and oak at a time when Athens and the other Greek states had deforested their own home territories.

In fact, the first environmental comment we know of in all the world's literature came at the time when the Athenians were sending all that money north, and it was written by Plato, that great Athenian philosopher. What he said was that: "When we look at Attica today, the territory of Athens, we are seeing the wasted skeleton of a once-healthy body. In the time of our grandfathers, these hills in Attica were covered with tall trees, trees whose trunks provided beams for temples and for the keels of ships. They've all been cut down. The soil has eroded down into the sea, and all that those hills are good for today is the raising of bees on the heather."

Where did the Athenians go for their timber? They went to Macedon, and they had continuing treaties with the kings of Macedon so they could get that wood to build their ships: oak for the keels, pine for the planking, and fir for the oars. Those were the three kinds of trees that they were after, and that was Macedon's main source of wealth: exporting those trees.

So the kings of Macedon began to become rich. As they became rich, they became ambitious. It was their dream that they could unite a lot of that mountainous territory into a much larger kingdom. The man who fulfilled this dream, Philip, knew the Greeks very well. When he was a little boy, he and his mother were caught up in the dynastic struggles that in these kingdoms inevitably accompany the death of a king and the choice of a new king.

They were rescued at a time when they were about to be exiled, or imprisoned, or even killed by an Athenian general who happened to be in the area—a man named Iphicrates. By saving the mother and her sons, he managed to ingratiate himself with the new dynasty in Macedon and actually was adopted in as sort of an honorary son of the family, too. So Philip got to know Athens through this link with Iphicrates, the general who had saved him as a boy.

Ultimately, when he grows up and has a son of his own—Alexander the Great, we call him—he hired a tutor for Alexander who was a philosopher who had trained at Athens. He was the son of the former king of Macedon's court physician, and that philosopher is very familiar to us. His name is Aristotle. He served as the tutor at the court of Philip for Philip's son Alexander. That was the link to Athens.

He was linked to other Greek states. When he was in his teens, Philip was sent as a hostage to the great city of Thebes, down in the central part of Greece. This was a very common thing in the Greek world. If you had ties with another state or kingdom and wanted to ensure peace and good relations, each side would have some important people held hostage at their main city, so that there would always be a great threat against the safety of these people should war break out, and both sides would think twice about misbehaving, breaking oaths, and so on.

Philip was lucky enough to be at Thebes during the time when the greatest military genius—one of the greatest that Greece ever produced—was living at Thebes. He was a Theban general named Epaminondas. His story doesn't come much into our Greek and Persian war story, but he was the one who brought the Thebans to a high level of perfection and professionalism in the hoplite phalanx. At the battlefield of Leuctra in 371 B.C., he performed the seemingly impossible feat of defeating the Spartan army—that once invincible military machine—brought low by Epaminondas and the Thebans.

Philip had a front-row seat for all this. As a hostage, nobody paid too much attention to him; just as when he was a little boy with Iphicrates, he was just a pawn in the dynastic struggles. So he grew up not much regarded, not much noticed, and people didn't have great expectations of him when he assumed the throne after the death of the old king and another dynastic struggle. But as soon as he had control of Macedon in his own hands, he embarked on a career of conquest.

He had different ways—different strings to his bow—when it came to taking over territory. Of course, there was always war and invasion, but Philip liked subtler means: diplomacy and weddings—marriages. He had a number of wives, and most of them were politically motivated weddings because he would find a daughter of an important chief or king, marry her, and then bind that man and his territory to himself, Philip, through that link of wedlock.

The most famous of these marriages was to a princess, the daughter of a king of a Balkan realm off to the west of Philip's Macedon. Her name was Olympias. He met her on an island in the northern Aegean, an island called Samothrace. It's within sight of Troy. It's a place we have heard of once before. If you remember in the Battle of Salamis, those brave javelin throwers from Samothrace who were serving in Xerxes's—the king of Persia's—fleet. They were seen by Xerxes from his hilltop to do a heroic act when they were rammed by a Greek trireme. They seized their javelins, and boarded the ship that had rammed them, and took it over, cleared the decks, made it their own, and went off and continued to fight in this captured vessel. So they were tough folk, these islanders.

They were also great craftsmen. They were near the metal-producing regions of the north. They brought the metal to Samothrace, and they had a cult of craftsmen there—and of spirits who supervised the success of metal workers and craftsmen. On this island, there were mystery cults. There were strange festivals that were held in honor of these spirits. Philip went to one of these on Samothrace, and he found there this woman: Olympias was her name. She was a devotee of strange cults—snake cults, various cults worshiping different demons and spirits.

He saw her, and he fell passionately in love with her, and the two of them were married. The result of that union was this boy, Alexander, one day to be called "the Great." They didn't live in harmony for very long. Olympias had a fiery temper of her own. Once she had a son to promote, she was all for Alexander's interests and very upset with Philip for continuing to marry other women—each of whom she was afraid would supplant her as principal wife. It was a stormy relationship, but he got what he wanted. He got that alliance with her family, her father, and therefore, added that area in the central Balkans to his own sphere of influence.

As far as military matters were concerned, he was someone who did for Macedon exactly what Cyrus the Great had done for Persia two centuries earlier. He took a remote hill people who seemed far from the centers of civilization and world control, and through training, through inspiration, and through a new kind of vision of what warfare could be, he raised them to the most formidable fighting force on the planet in a single lifetime.

We know all about Alexander the Great today—books are written about him, and films are made of his life—but most people who have studied that time feel that Philip is the one who should get the credit for transforming Macedon from a remote hill region into a place that could really consider taking over this great empire of Persia.

How did he do it? Well, he looked out at the world around him, and he saw the Greeks and their kind of warfare, and he saw the Persians. Let me fill that in for you—what he was seeing at the time. The King's Peace of 386 B.C. has already been in effect for about 30 years when Philip comes to the throne. That has guaranteed that the mercenary armies of Greece are free to go off and do service for pay overseas. In fact, the Great King actually said at the time when he mandated the King's Peace in 386 B.C.: "This is partly so I can hire the mercenary armies I need. If Athens, and Sparta, and the other city-states are continually fighting each other, the mercenaries I want are tied up in domestic wars. I would like them on the market, available for hire for my wars."

He certainly succeeded in that. Not only did the king of Persia manage to hire entire armies, commanded sometimes by Spartan kings or Athenian generals who were also in the pay of Persia, but rebel states: Egypt trying to break away from the Persian Empire; the island of Cyprus; and at times, the satraps of Asia Minor, who would go to war against their lord and master, the Great King, and try to become independent. All these also would hire Greek mercenary armies to fight for them.

A climax was reached in the 340s B.C., when there was a war in Egypt between the native Egyptian king—who wanted to liberate Egypt from Persia—and the armies of the Great King coming in on the eastern front, trying to subdue those Egyptians and bring them back to the fold of the

Persian Empire. Each side mainly rested their hopes on big Greek mercenary armies.

We were impressed enough by Xenophon and his Ten Thousand back in 401 B.C. There were 35,000 Greek mercenaries fighting on the two sides in Egypt: Athenians and others on one side and Spartans and others on the other side—35,000 Greek troops clashing along the banks of the Nile. Ultimately, the king won, and Egypt went back into the Persian fold. But it remained a fact that the great minds and the great fighting forces of Greece were scattered through the Mediterranean rather than focused at home, carrying out the policies of any one city. So Phillip sees Greece united, and he sees their best strategists and their best fighting forces abroad, disunited, scattered over the face of the map.

Now look at Persia. Persia has gotten used to other people fighting their wars. The Persians themselves do not train. He had grown up at the time that Agesilaus, that king of Sparta, was out fighting on Persian soil. Agesilaus himself eventually became a mercenary captain in Persian pay, just as Iphicrates, the savior of Philip when he was a boy—Iphicrates, the general of Athens—became a mercenary captain for Persian pay.

When Agesilaus wanted to make the point to his Greek troops about how soft and how vulnerable the Persians were—that quality of *malakia*, "softness"—he did something that was an outrage to Persian sensibilities. He brought all of his troops together, his Greek troops, and then Agesilaus ordered some Persian captives to be brought in and stripped naked. Maybe to the Greeks this didn't seem like the horror that it was to the Asiatics, but all Asiatic peoples had a horror of exposing their naked bodies. We are very familiar with this through the Old Testament in our mainstream American tradition—the horror that the Jews had of nakedness. The first thing that Adam and Eve do when they discover a consciousness and are able to look at themselves is make some aprons out of fig leaves so they will hide their shame, hide their nakedness.

Greek men didn't feel this. They didn't feel this shame about the body—they were proud of stripping down for their athletic contests, and their wrestling, and their running, displaying the male nude in sculpture and art. But to these Persians, they were being shamed and degraded to have their robes pulled off and their white, untanned bodies put on public display.

What was Agesilaus's point? Persians didn't have an athletic tradition. Individual Persians were not in great physical shape the way most Greeks were because of all of their training in the gymnasium. So he was saying,

"Look at these people. These are the rulers of the world. These are the rulers of the powerful empire that you fear and that dictates to you. Look at them. They're pale. They're weedy. They're un-muscular. Why are we fearing these people?"

That display, which so angered the Persians, left a very indelible mark on the minds of people on the other side of the Aegean—the Greeks and the Macedonians. A lot of Persian prestige, a lot of the aura of fear that they had been carrying around about the Persians, was diminished by considerations like that.

So to Philip, it all looks doable. He has a problem that Cyrus the Great did not have two centuries earlier when it came to turning a small kingdom into a great empire. Cyrus the Great's Persia was an upland plateau on the edge of a great empire. The cousins of the Persians, the Medes, as you will remember, had already conquered the world from central Asia to the middle of Asia Minor—modern Turkey. All Cyrus had to do was conquer the Medes—one people—and he had an empire that had now fallen into his lap fully formed. Using that as a base, he then went on to conquer Lydia, the Greek cities of the Asiatic coast, Babylonia in Mesopotamia, and ultimately, died trying to add even further parts of central Asia to his new Persian kingdom back in the 6th century B.C.

Philip did not have that luxury. Philip was surrounded by small, fragmented kingdoms: realms, city-states. He had to tackle them one by one, but he was a man of tremendous patience, intelligence, foresight, and energy. With these qualities, he set about—from that time in the 350s B.C. when he got the throne of Macedon—the process of conquering the world.

The fighting force that he created to be the match of Greeks, or Persians, or the Balkan hill tribes all around him looked at first a lot like the traditional Greek phalanx. The men trained with round shields, and they trained in closely knit lines—shield to shield—and they came forward mast, several lines deep. The big difference was their weapon. He invented a spear called the "sarissa," twice as long as the spear of the Greek hoplite, so it was almost 20 feet long, certainly over 18 feet. It's much more of a pike than a spear. The front row of the phalanx would have their spears coming out over their shields, and then the row behind would also have their spears protruding forward, and another row. So there was this wall of steel points facing the enemy, and the ordinary hoplite couldn't get anywhere near the front row of the Macedonian phalanx, yet the Macedonians were already delivering deathblows with these formidable weapons.

It took a lot of training. Philip militarized Macedonia. He created this army that was a permanent army, owing their allegiance to the king, training all year round, making themselves tough and hardy. If you remember back to Cyrus the Great's comment about: "Hardy lands breed hardy men," well, Persia certainly fit that bill until the Persians decided to move their centers down onto the plain. First, they were at Susa. Now, they have started camping out at Babylon, the ultimate whore of cities of easy living and high luxury.

Macedon is still rough. [Philip is] able to command the loyalty of these men who are fierce fighters almost from boyhood but keep them tied to the throne—no mercenary service for them. They are going to be at home serving the interests and the policies of their King Philip.

Remember his name, *Philhippos*, "lover of horses." He was very interested in the cavalry also. In Greek warfare, typically, cavalry—the Greeks didn't know what to do with it. If you remember back to the *Iliad*, the charioteers are basically taxi drivers who deliver the heroes to the front: They hop out of their chariots and then fight a duel with somebody, get back in the chariot, and go home. This is no way to use horses in a battle.

Philip saw as he looked at the Greek city-states that although there are aristocrats, like Xenophon, trained as cavalry men, they didn't use the cavalry in a sensible way. They hung around on the fringes of the action, and they might make an initial charge on a hoplite phalanx, trying to disorganize it, and certainly during a rout, the cavalry would come into their own, chasing down fleeing soldiers and spearing them in the back, but they were not organic to the system.

He treated the cavalry seriously. He had horses and his phalanx of sarissa-wielding soldiers work together to be this formidable duple, or doubled, force that could be very mobile and quick, with the cavalry, and then this immovable bloc of armed men, with the infantry.

He studied the art of war, and he also studied sieges because he was after cities—all those Greek cities along the coast, the Greek cities that guarded the famous gold mines of Thrace. He captured them, and therefore, all of the wealth of those mines came into his treasury. He went up to the Hellespont and began to tackle the towns that guarded that lifeline of trade that brought the wealth of the Black Sea—with its grain, its salt fish, its slaves—down into the Mediterranean. He began to assault those cities from land and sea. He would mount catapults and siege engines on his ships and tackle these port cities from the waterside.

He was a thinker, and he was an innovator (he was willing to try everything), and he didn't mind failures. There's something inevitable if you read the short version of Philip's life. He just seems to have rolled to success. It wasn't like that at all.

If the Greeks had really gotten together to oppose him—had called all their mercenary armies home, gotten their good generals out of Asiatic service, where they were getting rich and staying far away from the troublesome democratic mob in Athens, a little like American politics today—any high-ranking person is going to have their private life pried into, is going to suffer all kinds of slurs, is going to be limited in their actions, and may be hauled into court—it was much better to live as a mercenary warlord in Persia and fight for the king, reaping the rewards of your ability. The Greeks, if they had done that, could have stopped Philip, but they didn't.

Of course, that's why they got in the fix they were in. They couldn't act in a serious, concerted way about unification or about national priorities. So, one by one, he began to tackle the defenses of Greece. He managed to ingratiate himself with a large number of Greeks—first through a religious series of steps. He appeared at the Olympic Games, and he also competed, as his predecessor Alexander of long ago had done.

He became a protector of the Delphic Oracle. He joined religious movements in Greece as an important supporter of Greek religious life and the various sanctuaries. That was one of his methods. He also used money, just as the Great King did. Macedon is rich now. It had all that money from selling the timber. Now it has the gold mines of Thrace. Philip is a sensible man. Anything that gets people to open their gates, he's willing to try. There's no great sense of honor about him. He has already been involved in one siege that cost him one of his eyes. He was inspecting his siege equipment, and somebody up on the wall shot an arrow down and took out one of his eyes and left him with a bad wound.

He's quite willing to buy his way in, and so he buys the support of people all over Greece. In Athens, he found an actor named Aeschines who was interested in getting into politics. Yes, if you've got a good actor's training, and you've got a good voice, and you can play different parts, you're the perfect politician. Aeschines was in Philip's pay, as it turned out later on, and all the speeches he made in the Athenian assembly were paid for by Philip to promote the idea of not resisting Macedon: "Our policies lie along the same path. We should welcome this partnership with Macedon, and we should let Philip do what he wants to do."

Then there were quite disinterested Greek politicians—like Isocrates, not strictly a politician but certainly a political thinker—who just admire Philip. They've given up on the democracy of Athens, they've given up on the independent Greek city-states, and they're looking for a strong unifier, and they think Philip is that man. So they admire him without being paid. They're quite genuine in thinking he's the answer. They tended to be upper-class people who just felt that we need, at this point, a strong hand.

Now there were resisters, and the most prominent of these was the Athenian orator Demosthenes. It came to a point, finally, where it seemed that there was one little, scrawny Athenian, Demosthenes. A boy who was born with a stutter that he overcame by standing on the seashore and putting pebbles in his mouth. He would shout at the waves in order to master his tongue, and learn to enunciate properly, and build up the chest and the lungs that would allow him to dominate the assembly, as he wanted to do when he grew up.

Demosthenes gets up in front of the people of Athens again and again—from the 350s B.C. onward—and warns them against Philip: "He is the great threat. He appears to be a friend of the Greeks. He appears to be a protector of Greek sanctuaries. He appears to be someone who is only bent on carrying Macedon to its natural limits and creating order and stability in the north of Greece. But beware, my fellow citizens. He plans to take over all of us. He is the evil genius who will rob us of our freedom."

He would, then, be immediately countered by Aeschines, the tool of Philip, getting up and denying everything that Demosthenes said, and saying that Demosthenes was only motivated by self-interest. The Athenians should send yet another embassy to Philip to ask about his plans. While that was going on, Philip would take two or three more cities or rob the Athenians of yet another port somewhere in the northern Aegean.

With this playing off of one group against the other, Philip was pretty proof against Demosthenes and the other detractors. Demosthenes made a beautiful point, or at least a beautifully put point, at one stage of this conflict that I think bears keeping in mind today. He stood up in front of the Athenian assembly and said, "Do you realize how difficult it is for me to combat someone like Philip? Here I am, a private citizen of Athens, and all I can do is try to persuade you—the voters, the citizens—to vote one way or another. I have no real authority—I can't command anything or anybody. I am subject to having everything I say contradicted and put in the wrong light by the next speaker on this platform. Everything I say about strategy, and policy, and new initiatives is said in the open air to thousands of people and immediately carried to Philip by spies from this assembly, and I know you are out there."

What does Philip do? He concludes in his own mind, as absolute master of his kingdom, what will be his next step, and without asking permission of anyone or telling anyone what he is doing to give advance warning, he orders it, "I am one man. He is a kingdom. How can I hope to succeed?"

Here, we see the difficulty that real democracies have in waging war. The deliberative process slows things down. Elements can be brought in that, in fact, impede a straightforward, energetic pursuance of an objective. So the dictator always has it easy when it comes to facing a democracy when they come to battles and military campaigns.

Through all this, Philip was succeeding more and more, and at last, he brought his armies down into Greece and met the united armies of Athens and Thebes at a place called Chaeronea, not too far from Thebes on the Boeotian plain. There was the army he'd known when he was a kid as a hostage in Thebes—the famous sacred band of 300 Thebans. There were the Athenians, the descendants of the people who had beaten the Persians at Marathon, and here was his army, Philip's army—his tremendous Macedonian phalanx with those long pikes and his son Alexander commanding the cavalry.

The two armies met, and it was a tremendous victory for the Macedonians. These Athenians, these Thebans, some of them died heroically on the field, and many ran away. Demosthenes, who was there, was one who threw away his shield and ran away, so that he could live and fight another day, but very ingloriously, very shamed, giving his opponents a handle against him for all time to come.

Right after this great success, which dropped Greece into Philip's lap as a place he could control, as a place where he would be hegemon (war leader) for all the Greek city-states—as I say, he has not added them to his kingdom. They are still independent, and he wants them to be happy, to think they are autonomous and independent, but he now governs their foreign policies. He summons them to the Isthmus of Corinth, that traditional place for bringing the Hellenic League together, and he recreates the league that fought Persia. He announces to the Greeks: "We are going on campaign. I will be your leader, and at last, we, united, we Greeks, shall conquer the Persian Empire."

It was at this time that he received a letter from Isocrates, incredibly, in 338 B.C., still alive at the age of 99, and still writing and still promoting the Panhellenic dream. Isocrates wrote in this letter to Philip: "It is now in your hands. You have shown yourself able of fulfilling all of our hopes and wishes for you as the strong leader that Greece has been yearning for. Unite the Greeks and conquer Persia. Take for yourself the wealth of that continent, and there will be nothing beyond that for you to do but become a god."

These are prophetic words spoken by the voice of the oldest living Greek to the newest figure on the political scene. As we shall see next time, the prophecy was to be fulfilled, but in ways that neither Isocrates nor Philip could ever have imagined.

Lecture Twenty-One
Father and Son

Scope: Philip II's son Alexander III (better known as Alexander the Great) would prove to be instrumental in ending the Greek and Persian wars. With a volcanic temper and an unquenchable yearning for what lay beyond his reach (*pothos*), Alexander was such a precocious warrior and commander that Philip II assigned him the command of troops in the Macedonian battle line. At age 20, Alexander was appointed regent of the kingdom during Philip II's absence in Asia. After his father's assassination, it took Alexander almost two years to secure his rule at home. Once home rule had been achieved, Alexander ferried his army across the Hellespont into Asia in the spring of 334 B.C. As the young warrior leapt ashore, he threw a spear into Asian soil—inaugurating the final great campaign against the Persians. After more than two centuries of confrontations between Persians and Greeks, the final contest between the East and West was at hand.

Outline

I. In 356 B.C., Philip II's son Alexander III (who would later become known as Alexander the Great) was born.

   A. The burning of the temple of Artemis in Ephesus by a madman on the same day seemed to cast a prophetic glow over Alexander's birth.

   B. Alexander, influenced by his mother, Olympias, grew up accustomed to the mystical idea that spirits, demons, and gods were everywhere.

   C. Philip wanted to raise Alexander as a prince who would succeed him and create a Macedonian dynasty to rule the Greeks and, possibly, Persia.

   D. Leonidas of Epirus, a kinsman of Olympias, gave Alexander a tough physical education.

   E. A group of companions was assembled to accompany Alexander in his studies. One of these companions was the Macedonian youth Hephaestion, with whom Alexander developed a deep friendship.

- **F.** Aristotle tutored Alexander in his formal studies.
    1. Aristotle was interested in applied knowledge and believed that the universe was held in balance by opposing forces. A healthy life took all these forces into account.
    2. Aristotle's calm, intellectual nature contrasted with Alexander's desire to go to the ends of the Earth and achieve great things.

II. Three elements of Alexander's character set him apart from others.
- **A.** The first element was *enthousiasmos*, an inspiration by the breath of divine force to take up things with joy, excitement, and a feeling of spiritual linkage between oneself and the object of one's love.
- **B.** The second element, in contrast, was *mênin* ("wrath"). This aspect of Alexander's nature sometimes resulted in titanic rages.
- **C.** The final element, *pothos* ("yearning"), referred to Alexander's desire to see what lay beyond the next horizon, his drive to seek what others had not attained.
- **D.** Of all the stories of Alexander's childhood, Plutarch relates one, the taming of the wild horse Boukephalos, that illustrates his relationship with both his father and the natural world.

III. At 18 years of age, Alexander was entrusted with command of the left wing of the Macedonian army at the Battle of Chaeronea, in a new, effective formation designed by Philip.
- **A.** On the wings was the cavalry, which attacked the enemy on its flanks and crushed it between the cavalry and the immovable front line of sarissas.
- **B.** Alexander was able to force the Greek hoplites to retreat and create chaos in the Greek ranks, resulting in an overwhelming victory for Philip.
- **C.** After an argument with his father at Philip's wedding to a Macedonian woman, Alexander left Macedon and campaigned in the Balkans. He ultimately was called back when Philip completed preparations for a campaign in Asia.

IV. After Philip's assassination, Alexander seized the reins of Macedon, eliminated possible contenders for the throne, and inherited his father's mission to conquer Asia.

- **A.** He summoned the Greeks to the Isthmus of Corinth and was elected their commander-in-chief.
- **B.** After a visit to the Delphic Oracle, he assembled his troops and moved toward the Hellespont.
- **C.** Alexander took a single trireme in an effort to create a moment that would encapsulate his arrival into Asia as a conqueror.
    1. As his trireme's prow approached Asian soil, Alexander threw his spear into the sands of the beach so that he could then claim all of Asia as his "spear-won land."
    2. With Hephaestion, he went to Troy and performed ceremonies at the tomb of Achilles.
    3. He wore a suit of armor said to be from the Trojan War as a talisman.
    4. Alexander's vow to avenge the burning of the Greek temples by Xerxes linked him to the earlier Greek and Persian wars and the longstanding conflict between East and West.

Recommended Reading:

Green, *Alexander of Macedon.*

Renault, *The Nature of Alexander.*

Questions to Consider:

1. What made Alexander different from his father, Philip II? How did these differences help him to succeed where his father failed?
2. What character flaws can you find in Alexander that weakened his ability to conquer and maintain control over Asia?

Lecture Twenty-One—Transcript
Father and Son

Welcome back. At the end of our last lecture, we were with Philip, the king of Macedon, following his victory over the Greeks at Chaeronea in 338 B.C. and his assumption of the role of hegemon (war leader), commander-in-chief of all the Greeks for a united campaign against Persia.

Now we're going to go back in time, back all the way to the year 356 B.C., when the son of Philip is born on a summer day, the son whom he names Alexander—an ancestral name in his family—and the son whom we know as Alexander the Great. Alexander the Great was born, according to tradition, on a very remarkable day. A madman far away in the Greek city of Ephesus on the coast of Asia Minor had burned down one of the Wonders of the World: the temple of Artemis in Ephesus.

He burned this down so that his name would be remembered forever, and just to frustrate his wish, I will not say it now. At any rate, that concept, that image of a fire in Asia associated with the birth of this young prince in Macedon, seemed to cast a glow of prophecy and portent over this young man's birth.

He grew up in a household with possibly the two strongest-minded parents anybody has ever had. First of all, Philip—this Herculean, burly figure, a giant of a man, both in achievement and in intellect, cool as a cucumber under fire, but nonetheless able to inspire great passion in these Macedonian troops that he had spent his life training and a man who had accomplished the seemingly impossible—the unification of the Greeks behind him.

He was a man of strong physical appetites: hard-drinking, hard-living, a man with a huge appetite for food and for sex. He had lots of lovers (female and male), lots of wives, and lots of children, a man who lived life to the full—both the earthy, physical side of life and the intellectual side.

What he lacked on the spiritual and mystical side was made up for in his wife, Olympias, who was his third wife and whom, you will remember, he met at a religious festival on the island of Samothrace. She brought into the palace at Pella, his capital in Macedon, a tradition of snake handling, arcane cults, and Earth goddesses. She brought this over from her people, who were northern Greeks of the area called Epirus. In this alien world, Alexander found things that weren't part of the traditional Macedonian way of life but became part of his own nature.

He grew up accustomed to the idea that spirits, demons, and gods were all around you. When we find in later life that he begins to think perhaps he's one of them, we can trace that idea back to his mother, Olympias, a woman of whom he stood in awe all of his life long.

Alexander was subject to a lot of careful thought on the part of his father as to training. He wanted to raise up a prince who would succeed him and create a Macedonian dynasty to rule, certainly the Greeks but possibly Persia, as well, because Philip fully intended to carry out that vision, that dream of the Panhellenists, like Isocrates, and forge his way into the Persian Empire and make it a Greek domain.

So he got the best teachers possible for young Alexander. His physical training was turned over to a kinsman of Olympias, a man with the appropriate historical name of Leonidas—bearing the same name as that famous king of Sparta who died in the pass of Thermopylae with his 300 Spartans, trying to block the way of the Persians into Greece. Leonidas of Epirus, the kinsman of Olympias, gave Alexander a very tough physical training.

So this slight, short, almost delicate-looking youth—very different from his father—with his short-cut blond hair and that beardless face—never grew a beard all of his life long. He always looked like the eternal youth, which was a very strange thing in a Macedonian or a Greek. He was subjected to the rigors of learning how to hunt; learning how to wrestle; learning how to hold his weapons; and learning how to endure privations, hunger and thirst—all under the guidance of Leonidas.

To accompany him in his studies, a little group of companions was assembled. They were boys who weren't as young as he was—because Alexander was so precocious, boys his own age couldn't have kept up with him—but they were of his generation. They became a circle of friends with whom he maintained close ties all his life long. The chief of these friends among the companions was a boy, a Macedonian, named Hephaestion, with whom Alexander established a deep, lifelong friendship that had sexual overtones and even, later on, sort of administrative overtones of turning over to Hephaestion lots of responsibility in Alexander's new realm. He was a loyal friend, and he ensured that these people rose along with him, since they had shared these childhood experiences with him.

For his formal studies, that son of a former Macedonian court doctor, Aristotle, was chosen. He was, at the time, examining marine life in a lagoon on the island of Lesbos when he got the call to give up his studies there and come to Macedonia.

Aristotle had made a name for himself. He'd been a pupil of Plato in the Academy at Athens, but he had parted company with Plato. Plato's ideas were all on higher things, and the intellect, and abstracts. Aristotle was very interested in applied knowledge. There were two slogans on the temple at Delphi, where we started our whole story long ago. One of them was "Know thyself," and I think that would be Plato's vision of what's important about philosophy. The other one said, "Nothing to excess"—nothing too much. That's the middle range of Aristotle's thinking: that the universe is a great cosmos held in balance among opposing forces, and that a healthy life includes them all.

He had come up, finally, with the idea that there were four elements, water, earth, air, and fire, and that all of creation was a compound in various mixtures of these four elements. Well, that certainly didn't apply to his pupil, Alexander, who seems to have been pure fire. It's hard to think of a master and pupil who got along less well or were less likely to be in harmony than Aristotle—the calm, intellectual inquirer into nature, the man who sought these patterns of balance—and this boy who simply wanted to go to the ends of the Earth and achieve things nobody had ever achieved before.

But Alexander did remain loyal to Aristotle to the extent of taking with him scientists (when he eventually invaded Asia) and sending specimens back to Aristotle, who—once Alexander was out and in the world—went back to Athens and founded a new philosophical school at the Lyceum. He would get these bundles of things from his former pupil: exotic specimens and descriptions of plants. Aristotle's pupil Theophrastes—who wrote the first book on botany—was able to describe mangrove swamps on the Indian Ocean because Alexander sent word back of these wonders that he was seeing on his journeys.

Alexander had three elements in his character that I think set him apart from any other person who has ever lived. He is truly someone we could say is a unique individual. I'll give them their three Greek words. The first one for me is always *enthousiasmos*. He had "enthusiasms." *Enthousiasmos* means you have a god inside you—you are inspired by the breath of divine force, and you take up things with joy, with excitement, with a feeling of spiritual linking to some object of your loves.

Alexander had enthusiasms for people. He had enthusiasms for books. He had enthusiasms for this great book by Homer, the *Iliad*. He slept with a copy of it under his pillow, hoping that some of Homer's heroic ethos, and especially the ethos of the great hero of the *Iliad*, Achilles—with whom the young Alexander identified himself—would seep up through the pillow and into his own mind and soul. He had enthusiasms for Greek culture: He loved the city of Athens. Athens certainly did not repay the love, but he idolized Athens. He had a romantic streak in him with these enthusiasms that made him at times a very joyful person to be with.

Contrasted to that was an Achillean quality, *mênin*—that's the first word of Homer's *Iliad*. It means "wrath" or "anger." Achilles was a hero famous for his rages, famous for his heroic sulks, where he would go off and sit in his tent while the Greeks came around and begged him to lead them again. He refused because his honor had been slighted.

Consciously or unconsciously, Alexander followed this part of Achilles's nature also and was famous for his titanic rages, in which he would, at times, and sometimes under the influence of strong drink—which was an important social element in Macedon—he would kill friends at banquets in these rages. His father didn't have that. Philip was always thinking, always rather cool in balancing one thing against another, and looking into people, and I think being a little amused by the passions that he raised in other people.

Alexander always took life personally, and that really set him apart from his father. So we've had the *enthousiasmos*, and we've had the *mênin*—the wrath. The final thing was something his own contemporaries talked about—that they marveled at in him. It's a Greek word, *pothos*, and it means "yearning," "longing," always wanting to see what's beyond the next horizon, always wishing you had what you don't have, always trying to get beyond—driven to seek things that other people have not attained. That *pothos*, that *mênin*, that *enthousiasmos*, I think define the character of this remarkable prince.

He was lucky in his biographers. Many people wrote about him, although most of those works are lost—lost in great fires at places like the Library of Alexandria, the city that Alexander founded in the delta of the Nile River that was to become the greatest city in the Greek world. The loss of those books deprives us of the contemporary accounts of Alexander's childhood and later life, but they were read by biographers, such as Plutarch in the late 1st century A.D. Plutarch took it upon himself in his *Life of Alexander* (he was doing parallel lives between the Greeks and the Romans) to compare Alexander to Caesar.

He collected stories of Alexander's childhood, much as Parson Weems in early-19th-century America collected stories about George Washington because he thought you've got to know a man through what he was like when he was a boy. So he collected, among those stories, one that I think is very illustrative of Alexander and his relationships with his father and the natural world.

These Macedonians were horse lovers, and every year, there was a great horse fair held at Pella in Macedon. Horse dealers from all over the Balkans, northern Greece, even some coming out of Asia with Mycean horses—a famous breed—would come to Macedon to sell horses to the king and the Macedonian nobles.

In a year when Alexander was still in his early teens, a stallion was brought to the horse fair. It was called Boukephalos—or Bucephalus is the more Latinate way to say it—and that means "ox-head." It's speculated that there was either a blaze of white on the horse's face (looking like the horned head of an ox) or that that was the brand that was on the hindquarters of the horse.

At any rate, this stallion was brought in, and the horse dealer tried to sell it to Philip. The horse reared up as Philip approached and lashed out at him with his forefeet. Philip said, "This would be a terrible horse in a battle, exposing itself to the spears of the enemy." Philip and his groom tried again and again to calm the horse and mount him, to no avail. They were walking off when Alexander said out loud for everybody: "Well, what a shame; that's the best horse in the show."

This almost-criticism of Philip as a man who couldn't manage a good horse was something that really stung him. He was already at odds with his son. He recognized that his son had a different nature than his own, that his son took more after his mother. They were continually butting heads, but nothing had been as bad as this. Plutarch works up into a wonderful scene what happens next.

Philip then called his son forward, planning to teach young Alexander a lesson, and said, "So you think you could do better?" The boy said, "Yes, with this horse, I could." His companions were there watching him. Everyone at the horse fair had gathered around by now to see what was going on. The price on the horse was immense—several talents. A talent is

60 pounds of metal—60 pounds of silver or 60 pounds of gold, and it was worth many of these talents.

Philip said, "Well, what are you going to do?" Alexander said, "I will ride this horse. If I will ride it, you pay for the horse. If I can't ride it, I will pay." Philip said, "Well, I hope you are serious about this."

Alexander had noticed something that everyone else had overlooked: Boukephalos was afraid of his own shadow. They had consistently had him facing away from the Sun so that his shadow was cast before him. Every time the horse saw the shadow move, he was spooked, and he would rear up or shy away. Alexander ordered the grooms that had come with the horse dealer away. He felt that they'd become loathed presences to this noble creature. He immediately came up, seized the reins with great conviction, and turned the horse's head into the Sun—and the shadow disappeared.

He then got the horse in motion. Plutarch describes very beautifully the movement from a standstill, the first hesitant steps, then getting the horse running, and just before the horse is moving too quickly, Alexander, who is so short compared to this massive stallion, throws himself up and over onto the horse and is now astride.

Everyone is terrified that he's going to be thrown or run away with, and they are then amazed to see he's in control. This boy has mastered this animal exactly as he said he would. He kicks the horse's sides, and they go racing off together, and finally, they return in parade style—the horse almost marching along to Alexander's will. Alexander slides to the ground in front of his father, who is weeping and grabs him and says, "My son, my son." They feel in that moment unified in a way that perhaps they never were before or after in their lives together.

That scene of Alexander winning Boukephalos—finding an animal nature that matched his own—is one of Plutarch's emblematic scenes for the events in the boyhood that really made the man. Alexander remained loyal to Boukephalos—Boukephalos became one of his enthusiasms—and he was taken along on all of Alexander's campaigns. Even when he was too old as a war horse to go into battle, Alexander would mount him for the parade to the front and then slip onto a younger horse for the actual fighting.

Alexander was 18 years old when the Battle of Chaeronea took place. Philip entrusted to him the all-important command of the left wing of the Macedonian army, facing the best Greek hoplites on the right enemy wing, therefore giving Alexander command of the cavalry.

You'll remember last time we talked about how Philip created a new kind of fighting force. He took the idea of the phalanx but gave his Macedonian warriors—who are now professionals working all year round—these immensely long pikes with very small iron points, very good for stabbing through armor. They had the force of perhaps an 18-foot-long handle or spear shaft behind the blow of that little iron tip. To have his pikemen ranks leveling those spears forward—sometimes the ranks are 10 deep, and there's this bristling wall of spear points facing any hoplite or other enemy that comes at them—that was the centerpiece of his battle formation. That was the great bloc that pinned the enemy down.

He would have cavalry on the wings, and he had another group who were called shield bearers who were also involved, but the critical thing was that the cavalry would split off on the wing, attack the enemy on the flank, drive them against this great prickly wall of spear points, and like a hammer driving down on an anvil, would crush the enemy between the cavalry—whom, you'll remember, had not been used much in Greek warfare for centuries (certainly not used in a sensible way)—and that immovable front line of the sarissas—those super-long pikes.

Alexander's job, then, was to part from the center, swing around, and attack the Greeks on their right side. You will also remember from our talking about the hoplite phalanx and hoplite tactics that with their shields on their left arms, everybody in the hoplite phalanx was protecting the man to his left. But the man at the far right of the formation had nothing and nobody protecting him.

You will remember back to the Battle of Cunaxa with Xenophon and the Ten Thousand on the plains near the Euphrates River, under Cyrus, the prince of Persia, that the Greeks refused to move away from the river because it would have left those right-handed men (those men at the far right-hand end of the phalanx) without protection.

Alexander swung his cavalry around at Chaeronea, and suddenly, he was facing the rows of Greek hoplites on their exposed side and was able, in his charge then, to push them and make them retreat and create chaos in the Greek ranks. The result was an overwhelming victory for Philip.

At the victory party that night, Philip—hard-drinking as usual—got drunk, and he led a sort of chain dance through the camp in front of the pens where the Greek prisoners were kept. He was reveling and singing. He'd wreathed ivy around his head, and he was playing the part of Bacchus, or Silenos, or a satyr. One of the Greeks shouted out to him: "King! Nature cut you out for Agamemnon. Why do you play the part of Thersites?"

Thersites is a figure of very low caste and low aspirations in the *Iliad*—a man who opposed Agamemnon and was very anti-heroic. Immediately, at this insult, Philip sobered up and had that man who had called out to him brought out and dressed, and fed, and treated well. That got him out of his mood of semi-barbaric revelry.

Philip and Alexander went then to the isthmus, and that is where (as you will remember) Philip had himself proclaimed hegemon—commander-in-chief—of the Greeks for a campaign against Asia. The only Greeks who held out were the Spartans, and that holding-out is going to cast a bit of a shadow into the future for Alexander: the fact that the Spartans would never join in this surrender of their foreign policies to Philip—the recognition of Macedon as their leader. That had been Sparta's traditional role. Think back to the great year 480 B.C. of Xerxes's invasion. Sparta fought very hard—both to keep the Persians out and to hold onto their own position as the leaders of the Greeks. They weren't about to turn that over to the Macedonians, and given the mountain fastnesses in which the Spartans live, it just didn't seem worth it to Philip to go down and wage a campaign against them.

He returned to Macedon with Alexander, and in the ebullience of his nature, he took another wife, a young girl named Cleopatra. She was of good Macedonian stock. Remember, Alexander himself is a bit of a half-breed. His mother is an Epirut Greek, and his father is a Macedonian. At the wedding feast, when everybody is getting drunk, the bride's father drinks a toast to the upcoming nuptials and hopes that the union of Philip and young Cleopatra will result in a true-born Macedonian heir to the throne.

Alexander is sitting right there listening to this deathly insult. He has inherited from his mother paranoia about whether or not he will actually succeed his father. Macedonian royal families—in fact, as with many Indo-European tribes—have a royal line, but the warriors elect out of the royal line who shall succeed the dead king. Alexander is not guaranteed, even as first-born son, that the succession will be his.

He stands up and throws his drinking cup at this father of the bride and hits him. Philip then—in a rage—gets up, pulls out his sword, and is ready to fight with his own son and perhaps kill him, but fortunately, there's a low table in the way, and Philip stumbles over it and falls on his face. Alexander looks at him in complete contempt and leaves not only the hall of feasting but Macedon itself, and he goes west into the Balkans to campaign there—to get as far away as he can from his father.

Ultimately, he's called back because Philip is now ready to campaign in Asia to launch that war. He has already sent two generals—Parmenio and Attelas—with a Macedonian army across the Hellespont into Asia Minor—modern Turkey—to soften up the resistance and prepare the way for the main invasion force. But there's a ceremony to go through before he goes, and he wants Alexander by his side. He wants to show everyone he has mended his fences with his son. Alexander, at the age of 20, will be left behind (the year is 336 B.C.) as regent in Philip's place while Philip is gone conquering Persia.

So they enter the great theater at Aegae together. This may have been the place where the great Athenian playwright Euripides first presented his masterpiece, *The Bacchae*, in which a king is torn apart by *maenads*—by women made into a frenzied state by exposure to the god Dionysus—kind of an ill-omened play for kings. At any rate, Philip enters the theater—it's part of another royal wedding, not his own this time. Alexander is by his side. Philip is not wearing armor, just a white robe. He wants to show everyone, all these foreign guests who have come for this grand celebration, that he rules by love, not by fear.

Ironically, one of his own bodyguards—a man named Pausanias, with whom Philip had once had a torrid romantic relationship and then cast aside—has nursed a grievance for years and takes advantage of the king's exposure to run forward, stab him, and kill him.

Philip is dead instantly and falls in the dust of the theater. Pausanias is surrounded. There was a horse nearby waiting to carry him to safety. He trips on a root and falls down. The Macedonians are on him and kill him at once. So nobody ever found out who was behind this. Lots of people took credit, and lots of people were suspected. The Athenians were believed to maybe have had a hand in it. Alexander and his mother, Olympias, were thought perhaps to be the instigators of Philip's death. The Great King of Persia, way off in Susa, took credit and said, "I'm the one who guided the hand that killed Philip for having the temerity to say that he would invade my kingdom."

At any rate, Alexander immediately stepped forward, seized the reins of Macedon, eliminated possible contenders for the throne, and made himself the new Great King, inheriting not only the realm but his father's mission: to conquer Asia. It took him two years to solidify his position at home and to go back down into Greece and get those rebellious Greeks behind him—because as soon as Philip was dead, they all thought, "Well, the strong man is gone. We are free now to follow our own devices."

Alexander soon disabused them of that notion. He summoned them back to the isthmus, and he got them behind him as commander-in-chief, the way they had been behind his father. Alexander also took advantage of being in Greece to go visit the shrine of the Delphic Oracle. We started our story in Delphi, on the slopes of Mount Parnassus, way back in the 540s B.C., more than 200 years ago, as far as Alexander is concerned, when Croesus of Lydia—the king who feared the approach of the Persians—sent envoys to Delphi to ask the oracle's advice.

Alexander was now going the other way. He was going into Asia from Greece, and he wanted the oracle's advice and the gods' blessing. So he went to the temple. He arrived in early winter, of the month we would call November, and the oracle was closed. She shut down for the winter. She didn't like to prophesize on wrong days. Apollo himself went away in the winter, and his rather dark and impulsive half-brother Dionysus took over—so it wasn't a time you could normally consult the oracle.

Alexander had one of his rages, and grabbed the woman, and was actually pushing her down the ramp into the crypt where she would prophesize when she turned to him and said, "Boy, there is no resisting you." He took his hands off her at once and said, "That's oracle enough for me." It was exactly the words that he'd wanted to hear, and so he left her there, went home, assembled his troops, and moved toward the Hellespont.

You will remember there's still a Macedonian army on the other side, so the Persians are not able to get up to the Asiatic coast and block his passage. He calls for the fleets of the Greeks who are allied to him—the Athenians send 20 ships, and others send more. He has a fleet of over 100 triremes. He has many merchant vessels. Along that strip of water between Sestos on the European side and Abydos on the Asiatic side—the same place where Xerxes had suspended his two pontoon bridges in 480 B.C.—the great ferrying of the army begins.

Meanwhile, Alexander has a special role in mind for himself. He takes one trireme. He goes down to the coast opposite Troy, and he steers that trireme across himself—a little like MacArthur in the South Pacific—wanting to have that moment that will encapsulate the arrival of the conqueror. As his trireme's ram was approaching the soil of Asia, he ran forward to the prow, grabbed his spear, and threw it over into the sands of the beach so that he could then claim that all of Asia was spear-won land by him, the irresistible conqueror.

He then joined his friend Hephaestion. They went to Troy, performed ceremonies at the tomb of Achilles, and made offerings at the site of Troy. There in the temple, they were shown by the local inhabitants a suit of armor that was said to go back to the Trojan War. Alexander stripped off his own armor, took that instead, and carried it on his campaigns as a talisman—a good-luck token—as something that linked him not just to that avowed claim—that PR claim—that he and his father were going to avenge the burning of the Greek temples by Xerxes but tied into something that Herodotus had put into people's minds: The world is divided between East and West. The Trojan War was just one episode in that great conflict, and any Greek who involves himself in the war with Persia is partaking of this great struggle—the greatest of struggles in history.

Next time, we will follow Alexander down the coast as he sets about carrying out his promise to liberate the Greeks of Asia.

Lecture Twenty-Two
Liberating the Greeks of Asia

Scope: With the defeat of the Persians at the Granicus River, the way into Asia now lay open for Alexander and his forces. As Alexander moved south, most cities, including Sardis and Ephesus, opened their gates to him. At Miletus, quickly overrun by Alexander's army, the priest at the oracular shrine of Apollo at Didyma sent word to Alexander that the sacred spring there, which had ceased to flow when the Persians destroyed the temple 150 years earlier, had bubbled up again at Alexander's coming, predicting success for his mission. Continuing through Caria and Halicarnassus, Alexander eventually barred the Persians from every harbor on the western coast of Asia Minor. He then turned east and proceeded to Gordion, where he untied the legendary Gordian knot by slicing through it with his sword. Having fulfilled yet another local prophecy, it seemed apparent that Alexander would soon rule Asia.

Outline

I. Many modern histories claim that Alexander and Philip initially were motivated by a simple desire to reclaim the liberty of the Asiatic Greek cities, but the idea of the Greeks conquering the Persians had been a preoccupation since 499 B.C.

II. When Alexander crossed the Hellespont for the first time, he came into contact with the armies of the Great King Darius III.

  A. These later Persian kings took on the names of the earlier Achaemenid monarchs so that they would be seen as linked to the kings before them.

  B. Darius III inherited Xerxes's mentality—the belief that victory was to be achieved through the use of the largest force possible.

  C. Darius gave orders for the western satraps in Asia Minor to amass a great force of Persian cavalry and find a plain on which to deploy it in an effort to stop Alexander.

  D. Darius's best commander was a Greek nobleman named Memnon, who suggested a scorched-earth policy to make it difficult for Alexander's forces to stay in Persian territory.

- E. This plan was overruled, and Darius's army, allegedly 20,000 troops, found itself on the eastern side of the Granicus River, where Alexander was sure to pass on his way south.
III. Alexander was numerically outnumbered in all of the three great battles he fought to win the Persian Empire. The first of these battles took place at the Granicus River.
    - A. Alexander had his normal military arrangement: sarissa-wielding infantry in the middle, his general Parmenio and some cavalry on the left wing, and Alexander himself and his cavalry on the right wing.
    - B. Alexander waited until late in the day to attack to limit the possibilities for disaster for his army.
        1. The infantry and cavalry on the left wing attempted to cross the river first, drawing the attention of the Persians.
        2. Alexander took advantage of the Persian focus on the front line to break off, bring his horses onto the enemy side of the river, and attack from the flank.
        3. Between the cavalry on the right wing and the infantry, the Persians were crushed and forced to flee.
    - C. Alexander was outraged to find the Greek hoplite mercenaries fighting against him.
        1. He took the fact that these Greeks had not joined his Panhellenic crusade as a personal insult.
        2. After the battle, he sent the Athenian prisoners to work as slaves in the gold mines of Thrace.
IV. After the victory at Granicus River, Alexander headed south.
    - A. Most of the cities, such as Ephesus and Sardis (with its great windfall of Persian treasure), opened their gates to him.
    - B. Alexander left Macedonians behind to garrison the cities, allowing them to choose their own governments. Typically, oligarchies were replaced by pro-Alexander democracies.
    - C. Alexander met his first resistance among the Greek cities when he reached Miletus, a city that sought to remain neutral.
        1. Darius planned to stop Alexander at Miletus by stirring up trouble at sea.
        2. Alexander, in opposition, occupied every possible port on the mainland.

3. The Persian fleet landed at Mycale and watched helplessly as Alexander besieged and captured Miletus.
4. At the oracular shrine of Didyma, the sacred spring, dry for the last 150 years, bubbled up when Alexander approached, signifying that Alexander would meet success in his Asian mission.

D. Alexander wrapped his progress through the Greek cities in the cloak of religiosity, divinity, oracles, portents, and contacts with the gods.

E. Beyond Miletus was the district of Caria, where Alexander met the female ruler Ada; the pair joined forces to tackle the city of Halicarnassus.
1. No longer needing his Greek fleet, Alexander sent it home, keeping only 20 Athenian triremes to carry siege engines.
2. In late summer, Alexander began attacking the city but was kept at bay for some time by effective defensive measures.
3. A small night guard of Macedonians, with the aid of some Greeks, staged an improvised charge that captured the walls of the city.
4. With the fall of Halicarnassus, Alexander completed the liberation of the Greek cities along the western coast of Asia Minor.

V. Alexander then turned east along the shores of Asia Minor and, near Antalya, led his troops inland.

A. The troops met with the army of Parmenio, and together, the two forces traveled to the ancient city of Gordion, where they encountered the Gordian knot.
1. The knot was the twisted bark from a tree; it was said that whoever could untie the knot would be the ruler of Asia.
2. Alexander cut through the knot with his sword, exposing it as a trick.

B. Having received the blessing of Apollo at Didyma and having "untied" the Gordian knot, Alexander felt more than ever that he was indeed the man chosen to wrest Asia away from the Persians.

Recommended Reading:

Andronikos, *The Search for Alexander: An Exhibition.*

Wood, *In the Footsteps of Alexander the Great: A Journey from Greece to Asia.*

Questions to Consider:

1. What would have been the effect of Memnon's scorched-earth policy toward Alexander's army had the plan not been overruled?
2. How do such events as the bubbling of the spring at Didyma affect your view of Alexander's right to rule Asia? Do you consider them portents of his success or mere natural occurrences?

Lecture Twenty-Two—Transcript
Liberating the Greeks of Asia

Welcome back. You will read in many modern histories about Alexander the Great, that he and his father, Philip, were really initially motivated simply by a desire to reclaim the liberty of those Asiatic Greek cities. This was their motive, and that was all they were trying to do. When Alexander crossed the Hellespont, at the head of his great army, he really wasn't looking any further than Ionia—than western Asia Minor—but one thing led to another. Success bred success, and he finally found himself willy-nilly in the heart of the Persian Empire.

I think nothing could be more naïve than this view. I think it would really please Philip and Alexander to know that their PR machines were still working in the 21st century. After all, it was they who promulgated the idea that this was, in the words of Isocrates the Greek, "More a sacred mission than a military expedition." In other words, Isocrates viewed it as a liberation campaign, and that is the label that, first, Philip and, then, Alexander put on the expedition to make it palatable to the Greeks.

We are fighting to avenge the wrongs that Xerxes did to you when he came into Greece and burned the temples at Athens and at other places, and we are fighting to liberate the Greeks in Asia—those people that had been in and out of Persian domination ever since the time of Cyrus the Great in the mid-6th century B.C.

I think if we look at what French historians call the *longue durée* (the "long run") of history—look beyond individual events, battles, and personalities—and think what are the preoccupations of populations, of peoples, of rulers over the long span of history, we can see that right back to 499 B.C.—with Aristagoras and his map of the Persian Empire and his trying to lure the Spartans all the way to Susa to capture the treasure of the Persians and make themselves as rich as Zeus—the idea of Greeks conquering Persia has been a preoccupation.

Alexander would have had to have been dead to all kinds of longstanding beliefs, and ideas, and senses of purpose in Greek politics if this wasn't on his mind. At any rate, when he crossed the Hellespont for the first time, he came in contact with the armies of the Great King trying to stop him. Persia had a new Great King, and his name was Darius III.

I should explain that these names of these 4th-century Persian kings are throne names. These are young men who were not born named Artaxerxes or Darius; they were born with other names, not knowing that they were going to grow up to be king. But once the struggles for succession had passed with the death of their predecessors, they would take on a name of one of those earlier Achaemenid conquering monarchs, so that they would be seen to be in the line of these Great Kings who had gone before them.

Darius III is the man on the throne. He was only distantly related to the previous king. He came to power at the same time as Alexander. He was a bit older than Alexander, but he was a warrior, too. He had performed feats of strength in his youth. He was ruling from Babylon and from Susa, and he was very, very slow to act. He, unfortunately, inherited not Cyrus's—the first Cyrus's—beliefs about acting quickly and with speed, and seizing the initiative, and using your mind against the enemy; he still had Xerxes's mentality about god is on the side of the big battalions: "I just need to throw the largest number of people I can, and inevitably, we will win."

How anyone could go on believing that after a century and a half of rough handling at the hands of these Greeks who use their *metis*—their "cunning intelligence"—to turn even great forces' strength, and power, and massiveness against them in the same way that a judo wrestler will use the weight of his antagonist against the antagonist himself. It's hard to understand, but that's what Darius did. He gave orders for the western satraps in Asia Minor to amass a great force of Persian cavalry and to find a plain on which to deploy it.

He sent some of the flower of Persian nobility up there to join in this effort to stop Alexander. What should they have done? They should have tackled that little preliminary army of Philip's that was sent across under Parmenio and Attelas. They had the power to wipe them out if they'd taken that seriously, and then they would have been able to line the shores of the Hellespont and stop Alexander's ships from landing. We all know from D-day and a thousand other examples that landing an armed force in an amphibious maneuver is one of the toughest things in all of military science, and that was the place to block Alexander.

Darius's best commander was a mercenary—a Greek nobleman from the island of Rhodes. His name was Memnon, and he was one of the great military geniuses of the age. He was serving Darius, and unfortunately, that meant he was a Greek among Persians. The other Persian nobles and commanders paid him little heed or respect. Memnon pointed out to them that now that Alexander had crossed, their best course was to practice a scorched-earth policy—to cut down the fruit trees, burn the crops, strip the countryside of provisions for Alexander and his army—and make it very difficult for them to stay in Persia the longer they remained in the Great King's territory.

The satrap who was in charge of that northwest corner of Asia Minor didn't want to see his revenues take a tumble, and so for this very short-run motive of "What will my tribute look like next year?" this excellent plan was overruled. They simply found, on the eastern side of the Granicus River, a little stream that ran from Mount Ida (south of Troy) northward into the Sea of Marmara, emptying into the Sea of Marmara not far from Cyzicus. This is where we saw our great battle between Greeks and Persians—Greeks, and Greeks and Persians—back in 409 B.C. They found a field, a vast plain, where their 20,000 cavalry (allegedly) could deploy, and they planted themselves there, sure that Alexander would come through on his way east.

I am not giving you regularly the numbers that are assigned in the ancient sources to both sides. Some people think that Alexander's numbers are being quoted correctly because they seem reasonable, and the Persian numbers are incorrect because it's very unlikely that Darius could really field 600,000 here and a million there. I think they're all suspect. You're certainly welcome to look at the sources and draw your own conclusions, but we need to face the facts: We don't really know, and they may not have known, how many people were on the field at any given time.

At any rate, bear in mind that Alexander is numerically outnumbered in all of the three great battles that he is going to have to fight if he wants to win the Persian Empire. The first one is at this Granicus River. Alexander makes his way along with his army already sort of half-deployed in battle formation, because he does not initially know where he will find the enemy. He just knows that a big force of cavalry and a very small force of mercenary Greek infantry lie somewhere out there ahead to oppose his passing.

He comes to the Granicus River, and he sees a deep-cut stream—one of those typical Asiatic or eastern Mediterranean streams—which is filled with turbulent, rushing water in the winter from the winter rains and the snowmelt in spring but then dies down in the summer. He's there in late spring/early summer, and he finds there's water in the river. Also, there's a slippery, muddy slope on the far side. This is going to be very tough for his horses.

He has his normal arrangement. He has his infantry with their sarissas in the middle; and he has, off on the left, Parmenio with some of the cavalry; and he has his own cavalry on the right wing. On the other shore, the top of that bank, he sees the thousands upon thousands of Persian horses—the cavalry of Persia—waiting for him: very mobile, able to flow up and down the streamside and tackle anybody who attempts to come across. He sees off in the distance, on a little rise, the Greek mercenaries—the formidable hoplite phalanx that has been recruited by the Persians with their gold from all over the Greek world—these soldiers of fortune.

Alexander waits until late in the day. I believe he's doing the same thing that Themistocles and Eurybiades did long ago in the battle at Artemision— that naval battle where the Greeks first tried to stop Xerxes's fleet from getting into Greece. They wait until late in the day—why? There are only a few hours of daylight left, no matter how badly the battle may go, and just as Artemision was the first time that the Greeks had tackled the Persian armada, Granicus River is the first time that Alexander has actually come head to head with the Persian army. He doesn't really know what will happen. But if you limit the number of daylight hours in which the engagement can occur, you limit the possibilities for a huge disaster for your own army.

He sent his infantry down into the ravine. This may have been something that the Persians did not expect. He takes some of his cavalry and puts them in a line in front of the infantry. The men are up on their horses, and they have small shields—and since the Persians will be shooting down from their high place on the riverbank, these lines of cavalry can help screen, to some extent, the troops wading through the Granicus River behind them.

The horses splash through the river first. They get to the far side. The Macedonian cavalry are holding up their shields and trying to defend themselves against the barrage of missiles that's coming down, and behind them come the sarissa-wielders—the infantry of Alexander—moving across. Among those first horsemen to cross—that initial crossing of the horsemen—the casualties are pretty high. The Persians, seeing easy pickings and not being as disciplined as Alexander's troops, draw together and focus on what looks to them like the main attempt to get across.

Meanwhile, Alexander takes advantage of their focus on his front line and the center to break off—as he so often does with the right cavalry wing— and goes upstream. He's in the river, too, and it may have been that the current was stronger than he thought, because it took a long time for him to get beyond the last of the Persians, who were all distracted by the action going on in the center. But he finally gets upstream far enough so that he can get ashore, get his horses up onto the enemy side of the Granicus River, and now attack them from the flank.

Once this happens, the battle is effectively won. The Persians have failed to prevent him from crossing. They could have done it if they had stuck to their original plan of lining the shore, but they fell into his trap. They focused on the first ones to try to get across—it is like little kids playing a soccer game: It's just all a cloud of dust following the ball—and Alexander gets across.

He fights against the cavalry. He is one of those people like Cyrus the Great of the Persians at the very beginning; he fights at the forefront. He risks his own life every step of the way. We saw this go wrong with Prince Cyrus during the battle of the Ten Thousand at Cunaxa, where the prince effectively won the battle but lost the war because he got himself killed. But there's a tradeoff here, and commanders have to decide: "What is my goal? Is it to inspire my troops so that they will go on fighting and carrying out this impossible campaign, or is it just to survive?"

Unfortunately, this is a cleft stick of a decision. You've got to be lucky. You've got to be lucky and get through those battles, and Alexander was willing to take the risk. In fact, it was in his nature to abhor the idea of standing back, being on his horse on a high place, looking out over the plain, and directing his forces from there. He was on the frontline. He was almost killed a couple of times in this Battle of the Granicus River.

It's said that his spear broke at one point, and he was able to fight on with that spear-butt spike that we've met before—that bronze point that was on the butt-end of the spear shaft. He turned it around and kept on fighting with that. At one point, a Persian was about to aim a killing thrust at Alexander, and next to him was a friend—one of his companions from his youth, a man named Clytus—who cut off the Persian's arm just before the blow fell that would have killed Alexander. Clytus remembered for the rest of his life that he saved Alexander at the Granicus River.

After the melee, the fighting, the confusion there at the top of the bank, the infantry—now with the Persian cavalry distracted—is able to get up the slope themselves and onto the plain. Between the hammer of the cavalry and the anvil of those infantry with their big sarissas the Persians are first crushed and then flee.

This brings Alexander up to the place where the Greek infantry—the hoplites—are waiting on their knoll—Darius's mercenary force. He wades right into them and kills many of them. They try to surrender under terms—which means that: "Oh, if you'll grant us certain conditions, we'll lay down our arms." He says, "No terms." He is outraged to find Greeks fighting against him. He can't understand why they haven't joined this Panhellenic crusade, and he takes it personally.

Of course, these Greeks have never heard of any Panhellenic crusade—they've just been earning a living as soldiers of fortune—and now they're up against this insane person, this psychotic commander. When the battle is over, and he has won, and he has erected his victory trophy, he comes and looks over these prisoners. He picks out the Athenians among them, because they make him madder than anything else, that Athens—which once fought Persia and was the bulwark against Persia—should now have sons fighting against him, opposing the war to conquer Persia.

He sends those guys off—it's something you shouldn't normally do to a prisoner of war—to the gold mines in Thrace to work like slaves deep in the tunnels under the mountain and bring up more wealth for him, and they probably die within a very short time.

He also remembers that this war is for revenge on Xerxes—so he takes 300 suits of armor from the Persians that were dead on the field, and he sends them back to Athens. Athens had been filled with mixed feelings about following Alexander. Athens prized its freedom—it never liked following Sparta, and it didn't like following Macedon, but the Athenians had been loyal to Alexander. They sent ships when he asked for them, and in the troubles that lie ahead—he will, in fact, find behind him uprisings in Greece—Spartans who try to derail the whole effort by reclaiming their hegemony over Greece. The regent he left behind, a man named Antipater, will have to bring a Macedonian army down and fight in Greece. If it had gotten much worse, Alexander would have had to go home and give up the whole campaign. The thing that saved him was: The Athenians did remain loyal to him. They did not mobilize their immense fleet of 400 triremes to fight against Alexander. So he sends back to the Athenians a gift—a gift of 300 suits of Persian armor with instructions that they are to be dedicated on the Acropolis to the gods, with an inscription saying that Alexander, the son of Philip and all of the Greeks, except for the Spartans, dedicates these to the god from the spoils of Asia.

If you go to the Parthenon today and look up at the east façade, the actual front door—and that's the one that's away from the gate that gets you up onto the Acropolis—you can see the holes where the Persian shields were hung in a long row above the entrance to the Parthenon by the Athenians. You can see the tiny holes where bronze letters were originally placed with that dedication: "Alexander, the son of Philip and the Greeks ..." and so on.

So there's a desire on Alexander's part to memorialize, with these gifts and with these inscriptions, this epic undertaking that he has now embarked on.

From Granicus River, he heads south. The word of what he achieved there has gone ahead of him. Most of the cities open their gates—cities like Ephesus. When he gets to Sardis, that great former capital of the kingdom of Lydia, that place that has played such a role in our story of Persians and Greeks fighting each other, the Persian governor comes out and meets him on the road with the keys to the citadel. Since Sardis was the provincial capital, that means that a great windfall of treasure has fallen into his lap.

This is very welcome. He has to pay his troops, and he has to buy provisions all the way along—so he's partly fighting as Alcibiades did once in the Sea of Marmara. He is fighting for the very money—the very wealth—that will allow him to continue the campaign.

He leaves Macedonians behind him to garrison these cities and to serve as governors of the cities, but he does pose as a liberator. He tells these cities that they can now choose their own governments—typically, those are democracies that are pro-Alexander, where the "oligarchies" (the "rule of the few") had been pro-Persian. But it's clear they've got to make contributions. What the exact distinction was that a Greek would have seen between the tribute they used to pay to the Great King and the contribution that they now have to give to Alexander is not entirely clear, but it was certainly clear to him: "I have liberated you."

He met his first real resistance among the Greek cities when he got to Miletus. That was the greatest city of Ionia, and it wants to be neutral now. In this new world order that seems to be emerging, they would like not to be Persian and not to be one of Alexander's little cities that he has a garrison and a governor in—so they have a huge Greek mercenary army inside.

Finally, Darius has gotten himself together and taken Memnon's advice to try to stir up trouble at sea and draw Alexander away. So a fleet—I said I wasn't going to give you the numbers, but the claims are it's 400 ships. I don't believe that for a minute, but lots and lots of triremes come up from

Phoenicia, and Cyprus, and Cilicia, and they are planning to stop Alexander at Miletus. What's Alexander's method of opposing fleets that come against him? He occupies every possible port or beach on the mainland where those fleets could land, and they are neutralized.

These galleys cannot stay at sea for long periods—they have to go off and find an island somewhere to make their base. They initially go to Mycale, that mountain place with a beach below, where, back in 479 B.C., Xanthippus the Athenian and the other Greeks caught and burned Xerxes's fleet while it was ashore. So it was well known to the Persians. They land there, and then from the sea, they have to watch helplessly as Alexander brings up his siege engines, storms the walls of Miletus, and captures it.

It was an extraordinary scene. The mercenaries inside—fearing what Alexander would do to them—took their shields, put them like little skiffs in Miletus's harbor, and tried to paddle away and get out to sea, using their hands as oars to propel themselves across the water, so desperate were they to try to escape. But it did not succeed. He rounded them all up and took this greatest city of Ionia.

Miletus had attached to it a shrine—an oracular shrine—called Didyma, founded by priests from Delphi long, long before and rivaling Delphi at one time as a great place for prophecies. People from all over the eastern Greek world would come to Didyma near Miletus and ask for prophesies from the priestess who spoke for Apollo there.

In the time of the first Persian wars, Darius and Xerxes—the Persians—had burned the temple, and the sacred spring that brought the gases to the surface dried up. It had been dry for 150 years, but when Alexander approached, the water started bubbling up again from the rock. The priest sent a message to Alexander, thanking him for restoring the force of nature, letting the god speak again ,and assuring Alexander that the god had, indeed, foretold Alexander would meet success in his mission in Asia.

Alexander was very happy with this. He gave him some money to rebuild the temple. He also tried to rebuild that temple in Ephesus, and they said to him—these Greeks in Ephesus whose temple of Artemis had fallen and been burnt—"It's not right for one god to build a temple for another god." It was not clear why they wouldn't take the money, but they did not want to, and so he had to pass on, having failed to carry his point there.

Nonetheless, he was trying to wrap his progress in this cloak of religiosity, of divinity, of oracles, portents, contacts with the gods, and services to the gods—all the way south through Ionia and the rest of the Greek cities.

Beyond Miletus, he got into hill country. He's now in the district called Caria. Caria was a place, traditionally, where there were strong female rulers—a real anomaly in the Mediterranean world. If you think back to Artemisia, that queen of Halicarnassus who was the admiral of her little contingent in Xerxes's grand armada at Salamis, back in 480 B.C., she was one of these Carian queens. There's one living now up in the hills, and her name is Ada. She and Alexander meet.

She's an older woman. He seems to have had a mother fixation and was always pleased to be in the company of older women, and they liked him. He hit it off with Ada, and they joined forces to tackle the next big city in Alexander's path, Halicarnassus—Herodotus's hometown, a Dorian city sitting at the southwest corner of Asia Minor. It was very heavily fortified by double walls to protect the city on the landward side and by a great circular, fortified harbor—one of the best harbors in all the Mediterranean—facing the sea. There, Memnon of Rhodes had brought the Persian fleet, intending to hold out there.

There was an Athenian mercenary in charge of the defense of the city who was a descendant of that same Ephialtes—and actually bore the name Ephialtes—who, back in the time of Pericles, had started the great dramatic democratic revolution in Athens. Ephialtes, that first one, had been a naval commander attacking the Persian Empire. Now his descendant, certainly his namesake, is in charge of the garrison at Halicarnassus.

Alexander needs those siege engines again. He's tired of the Greek fleet that has been with him so far. They haven't done much. He doesn't like ships—after all, there aren't any sea battles in the *Iliad*, so it doesn't seem part of his nature to collaborate with ships. He had turned down the proposals of his own generals to use his fleet as a real naval arm of the expedition. So he sends them all home. He keeps the 20 Athenian triremes for one last purpose: He loads onto their decks the gigantic siege equipment—these battering rams. There may have been catapults also. They take them to a beach on the north side of the peninsula, where Halicarnassus is on the south side, and there's a fairly level road for him to tow the siege equipment from the beach over to Halicarnassus.

Once he has rendezvoused with those ships, he tells them to hang around and wait until the siege is over. Then, in late summer, he hauls the siege equipment over the hills to Halicarnassus and starts to attack. He can look down into the beautiful circular harbor, and he can see the hundreds of Persian ships there holed up within that fortified port, but he is kept at bay for a long time by that double ring of walls, by very effective defensive measures on the part of Ephialtes and Memnon.

He's getting very frustrated. We have to remember that he lives at a period when the defense of cities had reached a higher art than the offensive machinery to bring down the walls or sap them. Alexander tries everything. Having finally broken through the outer defenses, he simply finds that the defenders go within the next ring of walls, and he has to do the whole thing all over again.

Finally, they break through in a very funny way. There's a small night guard in the Macedonian army who get bored with night duty and dare each other to go tackle a certain tower in the offensive lineup. They rush in, alarms are sounded, fires are lit, and all the Greeks wake up and realize what has happened—the Greeks and the Macedonians—and they rush forward to help their friends. In rushing forward, they actually stage a charge that captures the walls, and Halicarnassus falls.

Memnon sees what is happening and slips out with his ships before Alexander can get down to the port. So Persian sea power is still intact, but the city of Halicarnassus, the old hometown of Herodotus the historian, is now in Alexander's hands. He has now completed that run down the coast of Asia Minor that has "liberated" all of those Greek cities from Persian rule. The dream that had been born back in the 6th century B.C., when Cyrus took them over, has now finally been brought to pass.

Alexander then turns east and goes along the shore of Asia Minor. He sends some of his troops inland. The Athenian triremes carry the siege engines to a place on the Meander River, and then those ships go home. Alexander is right along the coast. You're not supposed to go on the coast. There are royal roads inland for carrying traffic, but he likes to attempt the impossible. He gets to a place where the cliff comes right out into the sea—there's no road at all. He and his soldiers strip down, carry their armor on their heads, and wade in the sea to get around this obstacle and keep going.

At last, they come back to the road near Antalya that carries them up into the heartland of Asia Minor. They meet Parmenio, who has followed the Royal Road from Sardis, and together, they all go to this ancient city of Gordion. Gordion is the place where King Midas (he of the golden touch) was once the ruler—that mythical figure, but who was actually a very wealthy ruler, and whose tomb has recently been discovered. There was at Gordion an object that was very famous. It was called the Gordian knot.

It was bark from a tree that had been twisted together into this sort of bowling-ball–sized object, where you could see lots of straps and pieces of the bark—no clear ends. It held a span for a team of oxen to the yoke, and it was said that whoever could figure out how to untie that knot would be the ruler of all Asia. This was not a challenge that Alexander could pass up, and so after the local priest had explained it to him—this object was kept in one of the temples—he went there, and he looked over the Gordian knot.

After he had studied it for a while, he just pulled out of the scabbard his sword and sliced right through it. Once he did that, it was seen that the whole thing had been a trick. It was not a single strand of that bark in a rope that really had a way to unknot it; there were many different pieces—all their ends met together—hidden in the middle of the ball. The only way to get through it was violence—a single blow or slice to cut that knot.

At any rate, having received the blessing of the god Apollo at Didyma, having performed this wonderful feat at Gordion, Alexander felt more than ever that he was fulfilling prophesies—that he was, indeed, the man chosen by destiny to wrest Asia away from the Persians. He had still not met Darius himself, his chief antagonist, but in a short time, these two kings would come face to face on a battlefield at Issos, and it will be the task of our next lecture to follow them there.

Lecture Twenty-Three
Who Is the Great King?

Scope: As Alexander and his army marched through the highlands of central Asia Minor, Darius III began to realize that the Macedonian king represented what the Persians had always dreaded: an invader who could strike all the way into the heart of the Persian Empire. Passing through the Cilician Gates, Alexander tarried at Tarsus, then moved on to Issos, where he finally confronted the Persian king and emerged victorious. Instead of pursing the retreating Darius, Alexander consolidated his rule in the Levant and began a campaign in Egypt. Inspired by the biblical story of Daniel, he proceeded toward the Tigris and Euphrates rivers and clashed with Darius at Gaugamela. It was on this plain that the Greek and Persian wars truly ended; Alexander's victory won for him not just the territory around these two rivers but lands of the traditional Persian homeland to the south and east.

Outline

I. Darius III soon realized that Alexander was not a flash in the pan but what the Persian Empire had always dreaded: an invader who could strike all the way into its heart.

   A. Darius marshaled one of the largest armies ever assembled, calling upon all of the Persian heartland to contribute troops.

   B. Darius sent forward a force to hold a narrow pass called the Cilician Gates. Alexander, moving quickly, got through the pass and into Tarsus before Darius reached it.

   C. After a swim in a local river, Alexander caught a terrible fever. Darius took great hope that Alexander's progress had been checked; however, the Macedonian soon recovered and was back on his feet.

II. Alexander led his troops into Syria and the seaport of Issos.

   A. He believed that Darius would not venture to this port because it did not offer a large enough expanse for him to deploy his massive army.

- **B.** Darius, however, decided to go around the mountain range, follow behind Alexander as he traveled through the expected passage that led into the heart of the Persian Empire, and attack him from the rear.
  1. Darius captured Alexander's field hospital at Issos and mutilated the sick and wounded in an effort to diminish Alexander's confidence.
  2. Alexander turned around immediately and came back to Issos.
- **C.** The Battle of Issos was launched in the morning and ran for most of the day. Ultimately, Alexander used the same tactics at Issos that he had at the Granicus River—with the same victorious result.
  1. Alexander took off to the right with his cavalry and defeated the Persians on their left wing.
  2. He then came down on the flank of the main Persian force and distracted the enemy while the infantry moved in from the other side of the river.
- **D.** Alexander attempted to fight Darius, but the Great King fled, leaving behind his army, his mother, his wife, and his children.
  1. Alexander treated Darius's family with the utmost chivalry and assured them that they would be under his protection.
  2. A messenger arrived from Darius asking for the return of his family; Alexander replied that Darius should petition for them in person and advised the Great King to look out for his own safety.

III. Scholars have been puzzled by what happened after the Battle of Issos.
- **A.** Many believe that Alexander should have followed up his success immediately by pursuing Darius into the heart of the Persian Empire and capturing him before he could rally another army.
- **B.** Instead, Alexander decided to consolidate his rule over the Levant (the area of Phoenicia and Palestine) and take Egypt to ensure that no regions in the rear would be left unconquered to cause trouble in the future.
- **C.** He received word that the Spartans still opposed him in the Aegean, but he left such issues to the regent in Macedonia.
- **D.** Alexander's first targets were the Phoenician cities of Tyre, Sidon, and Byblos, which had become some of the richest cities in the world through global trade.

        1. Sidon and Byblos surrendered immediately, but the people of Tyre refused.
        2. Alexander settled down to a six-month siege that ended in success.
    E. Alexander then proceeded down the coast to Egypt, where he was welcomed as a liberator by the rebels against Persian rule and recognized as a new pharaoh.
    F. He capped this experience by visiting the oracle of Zeus Ammon, where he was told that Zeus, not Philip II, was his true father.
    G. Alexander left Egypt and went back into Palestine, where he claimed to be the future conqueror of Asia foretold in the Book of Daniel.

IV. A year after the Battle of Issos, Alexander received word that a reassembled Persian army was ready to face him on a vast plain called Gaugamela on the Tigris River.
    A. A Persian corps of engineers leveled out the rough spots on the plain so that the army's scythed chariots and cavalry could be deployed without obstacles.
    B. Fearing a sneak attack, Darius placed his camp miles away and brought his troops to the battlefield the night before the confrontation. This miscalculation resulted in a lack of rest for his men.
    C. Alexander deployed his army as always: infantry in the middle, cavalry on the ends. Darius spread the scythed chariots across the front of his array and placed some of his best forces on the wings.
    D. Different sources give different views of this battle, but it is possible to form a consensus of what happened that day.
        1. Darius's elephants and scythed chariots proved to be of no use.
        2. As usual, Alexander parted from the center, but he was followed by Darius's left wing.
        3. An enormous gulf opened up between the center and the wings, in which the two armies collided.
        4. Alexander, attacking the Persian left wing, closed in on Darius.
        5. Alexander charged to the other end of the line to help Parmenio and his cavalry; unified at last, the Macedonian army swept forward and crushed all resistance.

V. The Greek and Persian wars ended at Gaugamela. Alexander was now master of the territory around the Tigris and Euphrates rivers and the Persian homeland; subsequent campaigns would carry him all the way to the Indus River valley (the eastern frontier of the empire).

Recommended Reading:

Harper, *The Royal City of Susa: Ancient Near Eastern Treasures in the Louvre.*

Heckel and Jones, *Macedonian Warrior: Alexander's Elite Infantryman.*

Questions to Consider:

1. Was Alexander's decision to consolidate his rule over the Levant instead of immediately pursuing Darius III into the heart of the Persian Empire a puzzling one? Why or why not?
2. What do you think made Gaugamela the capstone battle in the Greek and Persian wars?

Lecture Twenty-Three—Transcript
Who Is the Great King?

Welcome back. We left Alexander and his army in the highlands of central Asia Minor following the dramatic episode in which Alexander sliced through the famous Gordian knot and, therefore, could be recognized as the future ruler of all Asia.

King Darius, by this time, was thoroughly alarmed. He realized that this was not a flash in the pan—a sort of come-and-go attempt on the part of the Greeks (like so many before) to move into Persian territory. This was the real thing. This was what the Persians had always dreaded: the possibility of an invader who would strike all the way into the heart of the Persian Empire.

So Darius began to marshal one of the largest armies ever put together. He still had all of the Persian heartland to recruit from—as far away as Afghanistan and Pakistan, into the Arabian Peninsula, Mesopotamia, Iran itself, the Near East—all were called upon to contribute troops for this immense army that Darius was putting together.

Meanwhile, the slowness with which Darius moved was sort of counterpoised by the rapidity of Alexander's advance. Darius sent forward a commander with a force to hold a narrow pass called the Cilician Gates, which led from the center part of Asia Minor down to the coastal plain near the great city of Tarsus—later to become famous as the hometown of that Saul (later, Paul) who wrote all of those important works of early Christianity.

Tarsus was a great mining town. It was a target in itself, and Darius thought that if he simply sent someone up there, they could hold the pass. Well, he needed to get on the stick. He didn't send the people in time, and Alexander was through that pass and down into Tarsus before Darius was even aware that he had started moving forward.

But Alexander had moved so fast—he had gotten so overheated in this last dash to get to Tarsus that he—in his usual impulsive, boyish way—decided, "I'll go for a swim," plunged into the local river and caught a terrible fever. So he is now laid up for weeks, and some of his companions—desert people—think he is going to die, that this is the end. But of course, it was only natural that such a great expedition would eventually peter out.

Darius took great hope from the fact that Alexander's progress seemed to have been checked. His physician prescribed a certain draft of medicine for Alexander to take for his fever. Alexander is surrounded by rivals—people who are competing with one another for his attention, for his favor. One of these is his father's old general, Parmenio. As Alexander was about to take the medicine, a message arrives from Parmenio (who has been left behind on the trail), saying, "I've received word that your doctor is trying to poison you."

Alexander (in a typical show of bravado) handed the letter from Parmenio to the doctor and said, "Read this," looked him in the eye, and drank the medicine just to show his faith in this person who was treating him and his courage to dare anything rather than appear timid or hesitant. Of course, the draft had a violent initial effect, but it did cure him, and he was then back on his feet.

He led his troops, then, now following the trail blazed originally by Xenophon and the Ten Thousand and that great army of Prince Cyrus half a century earlier. He led his troops east to the place in the coast of the eastern Mediterranean where there is a deep embayment. The Greeks call it a *koilae*, a "hollow." The sea comes into the land, and we then find Syria on one side and Anatolia—modern Turkey—on the other side, where Alexander is now.

He passes at that place into Syria, getting much closer to the heart of the Great King's realm. He is now at a place called Issos. This is a seaport. It is where Prince Cyrus picked up 700 Spartan troops when he was making his bid for kingship of the Persian Empire. At Issos, on a narrow plain, Alexander feels that this is a spot Darius will not come because there is not a large enough expanse for Darius to deploy his great army. He is assuming the king will block his progress further on at a place called Myriandrus, where the road bends away from the sea, passes through the Syrian Gates, and leads to a huge plain. He thinks that is where the battle will be.

He leaves in Issos all of his wounded and his sick. He sets up a field hospital there, and at the port of Issos, he leaves them behind. Darius, however, in the only tricky move of his entire career, decides he won't face Alexander on the great plain. He will go around the mountain range the other way while Alexander is coming through the expected passage that leads into the heart of the empire and the road to the Euphrates. Darius will have led his troops around to Issos, follow behind Alexander, and take him from the rear. What a great idea it seemed—but it wasn't.

That problem with the narrow, constricted plain at Issos was something Darius just didn't take into account. He came down on the city of Issos like an avalanche. He captured that field hospital, and in an act of the kind of thing that gave the word "barbarism" its modern meaning, he cut off the right hands of all of the Greek wounded and sick that he found in the hospital and cauterized the stumps with hot pitch. He didn't do this personally, but he had it done on his orders. Then, he sent some of them after Alexander.

Taking a leaf out of Xerxes's book—when Xerxes was at Sardis in the fall of 481 B.C. and insisted on saving Greek spies who had come to spy out the land and sending them home with a full report for the Greeks who were facing him, of exactly how gigantic his army was—Darius sent to Alexander these now-handless Greeks and Macedonians to tell Alexander exactly how big a force he would face, hoping with this war of nerves to diminish Alexander's confidence.

Alexander turned around immediately and came back along the coast, between the mountains and the sea, to that narrow place at Issos—and this is where the great battle was fought. He was thanking his stars that Darius had done anything so insane as to give up the possibility of deploying his immense cavalry on the open plain and come down to the sea. So Alexander is now marching along, and he is with the right wing up against the slopes.

The plain is so narrow that the Macedonian army is initially in column, and it's only as it widens out a little bit near Issos that he is able to form that center with his sarissas, and the right wing, and so on. Darius is facing him in a chariot. He has put himself in the center of the Persian line, where Persian kings always fight. Alexander is off to the right, and there's our great infantry with their sarissas in the middle.

As at Granicus, there is a riverbed in between Greeks and Persians. The engineers, who have always played such a big role in Persian affairs, have taken advantage of the delay of Alexander in getting back to the battlefield to put pointed stakes facing downward into the riverbed, so that any Macedonians and Greeks who try to get across will face this array of stakes and be unable to reach the other side.

Of course, Darius also has his Greek troops fighting for him—his thousands of Greek mercenaries—he has his Persian horse, and he has a large number of troops this time, including infantry from all over the Persian Empire, who have answered the king's call. The battle is launched in the morning, and it runs for most of the day. Initially, the infantry has a terrible time with these stakes—with these sorts of palisades in front of them as they try to reach the Persian center—but, ultimately, exactly the same thing happened that happened at Granicus.

Alexander got off to the right with his cavalry. He went up the slopes. He defeated the Persians on their left wing, and then he was able to come down on the flank of the main Persian force, where the king was, and as he distracted those Persians from defending the line of the palisade, up came the infantry out of the gully where the river ran onto the other side. So in a way, it was a repeat of what had happened, or seems to us to have happened, at Granicus River.

Alexander felt very differently about Issos. I'm sure he still felt a tremendous amount of rage over what had been done to his men—having their hands cut off. He also—remember, this is a man who always takes it personally—sees out there Darius in his chariot, the head, the chief of all the power of Asia, and he personally undertakes to cut his way through to Darius and fight with him hand to hand.

Darius saw him coming. It must have been like seeing a forest fire making its way toward you in a strong wind—Alexander hacking his way through the Persians, who are rallying around their king. And in a scene that has been made famous for us by a great artwork discovered at Pompeii of all places, on the Bay of Naples in Italy. One of the great houses buried by Mount Vesuvius was decorated with a huge mosaic that showed the battlefield at Issos with Alexander on Bucephalus, his wonderful stallion, fighting his way through the swarm of Greeks, and Persians, and Macedonians all around, and Darius looking at Alexander, reaching out toward him ambiguously, as Darius's charioteer lashes the horses, turns them away from Alexander, and breaks out of the field to save the king.

Both Darius and the charioteer remember what happened at Cunaxa. They remember that the battle was won, but because the pretender to the throne was killed, the victory went for nothing. At all cost, the Great King's life must be saved. What a demoralizing thing for those Persians to suddenly realize that their king is in flight and they are being left to face the Macedonians alone—something that Alexander would never have done.

As quickly as he could, Darius got out of the chariot, onto a horse, and sped away into the dry land beyond the battlefield. Alexander pursued him. They pursued him until darkness, but they could not catch up with the fleeing Darius. So it was clear that he would live to fight another day.

Alexander came back to the battlefield, to the heaps of the dead and the wounded, and to the place where the king's tent—his immense pavilion—was still standing. Water was ready for the king's bath after the battle, and wine, and the sweetmeats, and the fine feast were all prepared—and, extraordinarily, the pavilion of the women—Darius's mother, wife, son (a baby), and two daughters—had all been traveling in entourage with the king, and he had left them behind.

So Alexander went into the tent—one of his generals was with him—stripped off his clothes, settled down in the hot tub that had been prepared for Darius, and quoted a line from Herodotus. Herodotus remembered that earlier scene on the field at Plataea in 479 B.C., where the Spartans, and the Athenians, and the other Greeks had beaten the Persian army that Xerxes left behind and had killed that great general Mardonius of the Persians, had taken Mardonius's field tent, and as the Greeks walked into the tent, their leader said, "So this is what it is to be a king." As Alexander settled into the tub, he quoted that line: "So this is what it is to be a king."

Once he had bathed, he went with his friend Hephaestion into the women's quarters. Alexander was so short and Hephaestion was so tall and handsome that the queen mother bowed to Hephaestion and not to Alexander on seeing the two of them together. Alexander said one of those things that show us how dear to his heart this Hephaestion was—he said, "It's all right, mother; he's Alexander, too." At this point in his career, there is still something about Alexander that harks back to the old Macedonian days when they fought as a band of brothers, when the king was merely a first among equals, and in which the nobles and the royal house together felt a sense of equality that is soon to disappear from Alexander's worldview.

He treated the women of Darius's family and his baby son with—as many authors have very appropriately used the term, the "utmost chivalry." He treated them with respect; he did away with all of their fears, and he respected their privacy—none of this nightmarish treatment of Asiatics that we saw Agesilaus, the king of Sparta, deal out when he stripped Persian captives naked in public to show off their soft, white bodies.

Instead, he respected them, and then said that they would be under his protection. Very soon, a messenger arrived from Darius with a letter asking for his mother, and his wife, and his family back and also making an offer. He made a number of offers to Alexander in the time ahead, and his offers consisted of half the kingdom—all of the kingdom from the Euphrates westward would be Alexander's—and the hand of Darius's daughter in marriage.

Alexander was beginning to feel a great contempt for this man who would run away and leave not only his army but his family behind. He wrote a letter to Darius and said:

> In your letter, you do not address me as you should. I am the lord of Asia, and you should not be addressing me as an equal. If you want your women back, come and ask for them. I can be persuaded, but you must petition me. As for your kingdom, it is all mine. I am the lord of your lands. As for the hand of your daughter, I can marry her if I will—whether you give your permission or not. Now look to your own safety. Do not run away because I will follow you wherever you go.

With this terrifying message, the herald was sent back to Darius.

People have been puzzled by what happened next. It would seem that Alexander, who so far has been blazing a path at high speed through the king's territory, should have immediately followed up his success at Issos by pursuing Darius into the heartland of the Persian Empire and catching him before he could rally another great empire. But for whatever reason, Alexander did not do that. He turned aside and decided that he would consolidate his rule over the seacoast there in the Near East, the Levant— the area of Phoenicia and Palestine (modern Lebanon and the coast of Israel)—and that he would take Egypt so that he would be tidying up behind him and leave no messes in his rear that could cause trouble later on.

He was still getting word from the Greek world that the Spartans were causing trouble. They had advanced out into the Aegean and had actually taken the island of Crete to oppose Alexander. There were remnants of Persian naval forces on the Aegean Islands, but he realized he had gone too far now to deal with those troubles at home. The regent in Macedonia, Antipater, would have to handle that. He must continually look forward.

His first target was the Phoenician city of Tyre. These grand, old Phoenician cities, of course, are the heirs of that terrific seafaring tradition that had gotten around Africa back in the 7th century B.C. and planted great colonies, like Carthage and Utica, on the North African coast. They had traded all the way to Britain to bring the Mediterranean world its tin to alloy with copper and make the bronze that everybody needed. Off this global trade, the Phoenician cities of Tyre, Sidon, and Byblos had become some of the richest cities in the world. They also made that famous purple cloth from the dye of the murex shells that stains wool, or linen, or silk a lovely, rich crimson or purple color, and it was worth its weight in gold on the international market.

Sidon and Byblos surrendered immediately. Tyre received a message from Alexander saying he wanted to come in and worship his ancestor Heracles at the temple in Tyre. Tyre had a god named Melchar, whom they identified with the Greek Heracles, and Alexander was just asking to come in and worship. But the people of Tyre—the Tyrians—realized this was just a way of getting their gates open, and once he was inside, he would stay as a conqueror, so they refused.

Alexander settled down to a siege of the city, which was located on an offshore island that held him up for six months. He used every sort of approach: battering rams, siege equipment mounted on ships, and moles built out from the shore of rock and sand to try to make a highway to the city gates. The Tyrians fought back desperately, and Alexander, at one point—according to a romantic later story that technically is possible—went down in a glass diving bell to look at the underwater fortifications of the city of Tyre. The medieval artists loved to depict him under the water in his glass bell.

This is the kind of ancient technology that an earlier generation of modern scholars dismissed as fantasizing. But ever since that Antikythera device has been identified as the world's first computer and dating to just a couple of centuries after the time of Alexander, I think people have realized we have to keep a more open mind about what the ancients could and could not achieve.

At any rate, Tyre finally fell, and Alexander proceeded on down the coast to Egypt. He was welcomed in Egypt as a liberator. Here at last was the warm welcome he had really been hoping for. Remember, the Egyptians have been fighting for their freedom from the Persians almost from the beginning. They staged rebellion after rebellion, often helped by Greek armies, and here at last is this man, this Greek, this Macedonian, who will make their freedom permanent. They are happy to recognize him as their new pharaoh, to invest him as the head of a new dynasty of pharaohs, and to recognize him as a god. Every pharaoh was, in fact, the incarnation of the god Horus on Earth.

Alexander was already feeling that he was walking in a cloud of divine power and presence. This Egyptian tribute was tremendously gratifying to him. He decided to put the cap on his Egyptian experience by going westward into the desert from the Nile, into the sands of Libya, where there was an oasis, Sebah, and where the oracle of Zeus Ammon—*Zeus* to the Greeks, *Ammon* to the Egyptians—pronounced the destinies of humans.

He made the long and difficult crossing of the desert, and he arrived at the oasis. He was taken into the oracular temple, and in private with the god (or with the priests speaking for the god), Alexander was told that the god recognized him as his own son—that Zeus himself had come down in the form of a snake and had coupled with Alexander's mother, Olympias. Philip was not his real father. He was the son of a god.

To a boy who had never gotten along with his father very well, this was very pleasing news. It also made it clear that his achievements were his own—his own divine force in this world—and not something he owed to that earthly father, Philip.

He came back from Sebah, from the oasis and the oracle there, with the same kind of glow that one imagines Moses having come down from Mount Sinai and his encounter with God. He left Egypt behind, and he went back up into the area of Palestine, and according to Jewish stories, he came to Jerusalem, which was certainly in his path and was a big city. He was shown there the Book of Daniel. Daniel was the prophet, you may remember, at the time when Cyrus took Babylon.

The Jewish prophet Daniel was in Babylon with that last ruler, Belshazzar, as Cyrus brought his troops in on the dry riverbed of the Euphrates that Cyrus's engineers had diverted so that the riverbed would be available as a highway for the Persian troops and their sneak attack. Daniel had predicted the fall of the Babylonian Empire. The Book of Daniel also summoned up the idea of a future conqueror who would rule Asia and would be a Greek. Alexander, being shown this book, thought, "I am the man. Yet again, the prophets have foretold my coming."

With all of these wonderful experiences behind him, about two years after the Battle of Issos, he returned to that location and headed inland, again following the path of the Ten Thousand and Xenophon until he reached the Euphrates River. He had received word that Darius had, indeed, taken advantage of the year to put together one more gigantic army—this time, an army that included elephants and 200 chariots with scythe blades attached to the axles, just as Artaxerxes II had had at Cunaxa—and that he was ready for Alexander.

Alexander considered going south along the Euphrates through that same desert that Xenophon and the Ten Thousand had once traversed, but he decided not to. He went east until he reached the Tigris and crossed the Tigris River. Now he learned that in anticipation of his movements, Darius had come north to meet him with this massive army.

Darius this time was going to pick the battlefield. He knew Alexander had to come wherever he was. Alexander could only win this war through a battle. It was now Darius's initiative to choose where the battle should take place. There was a vast plain on the Tigris River, not too far from a city called Arbella. The plain was called Gaugamela—that *gamel* at the end is "camel"—and the name meant something like "house of the camel" or "stall of the camel."

The last service that the Persian core of engineers ever did for a Persian Great King was to go to the plain of Gaugamela and level out all the rough spots so that those scythed chariots and the cavalry of the Persians could deploy without any obstacles or dangerous places out there on the plain. Alexander learned where they were, he led his army toward Gaugamela in turn, and he camped on a rise overlooking the field—a proper camp with the tents and the baggage train nearby and everyone getting a good dinner.

Darius had made one miscalculation. The place for his camp was miles off. He brought his army up the night before the intended battle, and they had no place to camp. They did not have their tents, and they did not have their support and auxiliaries. He didn't want them. He was afraid Alexander was going to stage a sneaky night attack, and so he told his soldiers, "No one shall sleep tonight. Everyone will stay at their post, ready for an attack."

History was repeating itself. If you remember back to the Battle of Salamis in the autumn of 480 B.C., the sneaky message of Themistocles to Xerxes that induced Xerxes to send his amazing armada into the straits of Salamis to face the Greeks caused the Persian fleet—with all of its rowers and all of its men at arms—to pass a night working and preparing in readiness for a Greek engagement that never happened.

So they started the next day without sleep, without rest, and with the frustration of having missed their night's rest for nothing, because Alexander did not make any attempt that night. All he did was go down on the battlefield in the moonlight and tour it on horseback with some of his generals. He slept soundly. In fact, he overslept the next morning, and his generals were afraid to wake him up. So this last battle of all in this great epic series of wars between Greeks and Persians started with the general on the Greek and Macedonian side—Alexander—so confident that he didn't even wake up in the morning.

They finally got him out of bed about midmorning, and he went out and looked at the field and deployed his army as always: infantry in the middle and the cavalry on the ends. Darius had spread the scythed chariots across the front of his array—he himself was in a chariot in the middle—and he had some of his best forces out on the wings to face the Macedonian cavalry.

It was summer. The plain was dusty. Since our different sources give very different views of this battle, we have to assume that there were such clouds of dust and the forces were so gigantic that nobody could see from one end of the line to the other, that nobody really knew how this battle went. Let me try to give some sort of consensus opinions of what might have happened.

First of all, let me say right away, the elephants proved to be of no use. They had made that long trip from India through the Khyber Pass and all the way across Iran to this point, and all they did was, perhaps, shed a little color and glamour on the event on the part of these Macedonians, who weren't used to seeing elephants across from them on the other side of the battlefield.

The scythed chariots were also of no use. That lesson probably should have been learned at Cunaxa, where the phalanx simply parted as the chariots would approach. You can't get horses to steer straight into a mass of men with spears pointed at them. They just won't do it. They would see the parting of the phalanx and go for the opening, and the result was: The men could then throw their javelins at the charioteers as the scythed chariots passed through and pick them off or even grab the reins and just stop the things. So these things that Darius had counted on—elephants, scythed chariots—were nullified in the event.

What happened was Alexander started one of his normal partings from the center, with his cavalry going off to the right. In strict normal Greek battle tradition, this isn't a good thing to do. You're supposed to keep the wings tight to the infantry, but this is the risk that Alexander took time and time again. If you go off to one side or the other with your flank, with your wing, with what they call the "horn" of your army—you will either draw the enemy with you, in which case, you break their formation, or you will outflank them.

In this case, Darius told his left wing to follow Alexander and parallel him, so that he couldn't outflank the Persian position. Alexander kept going further, and further, and further until this enormous gulf opened up between the center and the wings on each side. Into that gulf the two armies began to pour and to collide.

Meanwhile, on the far wing, where Parmenio is, as always, leading the Macedonian left, things are going very badly for the Macedonians. They're facing the right wing. If you always put your best people on the right, they will face the enemy's least good people on the enemy's left. So there is sort of this uneven give and take on the two ends of a battle line, and that is what happened at Gaugamela—very bad consequences for the overwhelmed Macedonians on the left wing. But Alexander, finally wheeling and attacking the Persian left wing—who he has managed to completely detach from the main force—now is making short work of them—hacking his way through them, destroying this right wing, and closing in on the king, who is in the center.

He then receives a message from Parmenio, his general—his father's old general, who is now maybe 70—on the left wing, saying, "We are hard-pressed. We desperately need help." Alexander charges to the other end of the line, seeming to be in two places at once, and saves the day there, and together—unified at last—the whole Macedonian army sweeps forward and crushes all resistance. Once again, Darius fled away, but once again, Alexander was master of the field.

Truly, the Greek and Persian wars ended here at the "camel's stall"—at this Gaugamela field—the last great battle between Greeks and Persians, led by this young Macedonian conqueror, Alexander, who here had won his greatest victory—the victory that dropped into his lap not just the territory around the Tigris and the Euphrates rivers but all the lands between where he stood now and the Indus River.

In our final time together, we will follow him to the ends of the Earth as he pursues his way through the distant Persian territories, and as he then—as conqueror of it all—tries to do the thing that the Greeks and Macedonians who followed him least expected: create a unity and a harmony between two worlds.

Lecture Twenty-Four
When East Met West

Scope: After the submission of Babylon and Susa, Alexander rode into the Persian heartland, then campaigned in the territories of modern Afghanistan, Pakistan, India, and Iran. On returning to Babylon, he conducted two ceremonies that symbolized, after decades of conflict, the union of Greece and Persia: a massive intercultural wedding and a harmonious intercultural feast. Alexander, in the Persian manner, was now a Great King. He continued to depart from his role as conqueror on behalf of Greece—for example, he trained 30,000 Persian youths in the Macedonian way and called them his "Successors"—and his army mutinied. Shortly afterward, Alexander died, either from natural causes or from poisoning, and with him perished the short-lived political union of Persia and Greece. Cultural interactions between East and West, however, would endure for centuries and become a major force in shaping our modern, multicultural world.

Outline

I. The Battle of Gaugamela in 331 B.C. marks the last stage of the epic journey of this course.

A. After the battle, Alexander and his army moved south to Babylon, which opened its gates to him; Susa, which yielded up its great treasury; and the royal cities in the southernmost part of modern-day Iran.

B. Alexander was filled with reverence for his Persian predecessors and greatly disappointed his army by refusing to let it loot, pillage, and rape its way through the empire.

C. At Persepolis, Alexander went into winter quarters until May, when he prepared to set out again to pursue Darius III.

    1. Alexander was concerned that the dethroned Great King might suddenly become the focus of resistance against Macedonian rule.

    2. At a feast, a young Athenian woman named Thais rebuked Alexander for failing to pay the Persians back for the

destruction of the Acropolis; goaded by her, Alexander started a fire that eventually destroyed the great hall at Persepolis.
- **D.** Though Alexander's relentless need to conquer ended the Greek and Persian wars, it also launched new conflicts.
- **E.** From Persepolis, Alexander headed into Bactria (modern-day Afghanistan), where he caught up with Darius III near the Caspian Sea.
    1. Darius had been tied to a cart, speared through, and abandoned by his exasperated companions.
    2. According to one ancient source, Darius was already dead (the most likely case) when Alexander discovered him. Other sources suggest a final conversation between Darius and Alexander, in which the former passed on the kingship to the latter.
- **F.** From Afghanistan, Alexander passed southward into the plains of the Indus River and announced that he would lead his troops past the Ganges River to the end of the world.
- **G.** His troops mutinied, refusing to go further.
    1. The troops faced enormous difficulties on the return to Persia, largely because Alexander did not understand the geography of the area.
    2. Many men died of hunger, thirst, and exposure along the march through the Gedrosian Desert.
    3. Dispirited by the failure of his men to share in his vision, Alexander finally rejoined his fleet and returned to Mesopotamia.
- **H.** Alexander's next destination was Babylon, which he intended to make a world capital.

II. Alexander now wanted to unify the Persians and the Greeks in the same that way his spiritual ancestor, Cyrus, had unified the Persians and the Medes.
- **A.** To achieve this goal, he behaved in ways that horrified his Macedonian followers.
    1. He adopted Persian dress.
    2. He appointed 92 Macedonians to take 92 noble Persian women as brides in a mass marriage.
    3. He bred a generation of young Persians to be culturally Macedonian and called them his "Successors."

       4. He held an enormous feast, to which he invited Macedonians and Persian nobility and suggested that they rule the world in harmony as partners.
   B. The Greeks were still autonomous at this point, having submitted to the idea of Alexander as hegemon as long as they retained self-government.
   C. In 324 B.C., an envoy of Alexander was sent to Olympia with the Exiles Decree.
       1. The decree ordered all the Greeks to allow the return of their exiles, many of whom were part of Alexander's army.
       2. This decree, along with a message claiming that Alexander could be worshiped as a son of Zeus, turned the Greek world against Alexander—even as he won wider popularity in the Persian Empire.

III. The death of Hephaestion during this time brought Alexander to despair and triggered thoughts of his own mortality. While in Babylon, he fell sick and died.
   A. Some bad portents seemed to foreshadow Alexander's death.
       1. A Macedonian sailor rescued Alexander's hat when it blew into the water and placed it on his own head, an act that symbolized the passing of royal power.
       2. A madman was found seated on Alexander's throne.
       3. These portents may have worked on Alexander's own psychology.
   B. Modern writers are divided on whether Alexander's fever was a natural illness or the result of poison.

IV. Alexander's passing, and the subsequent struggle for possession of his empire, launched what modern historians call the Hellenistic period, known at the time as the "Period of the Successors."
   A. Alexander's empire was immediately cut up among his Macedonian commanders, divided into warring kingdoms.
   B. Throughout the Near East and the eastern Mediterranean, powerful Macedonians set themselves up as rulers over chunks of Alexander's empire.
   C. The Persian Empire passed away with Alexander along with his vision of harmony between Persians and Greeks.
       1. Alexander had spread Hellenic ideas to Asia.

>   **2.** A new kind of civilization emerged in the cities that grew in the wake of his conquests.
>
> **V.** The true legacy of the centuries-long conflict between the Greeks and the Persians was the foundation for our modern, cosmopolitan, multicultural world. We can trace many of its elements back to the line of giants—from Cyrus to Alexander—who made these transformations possible.

Recommended Reading:

Bengtson, *The Greeks and the Persians: From the Sixth to the Fourth Centuries.*

Farrokh, *Shadows in the Desert: Ancient Persia at War.*

Questions to Consider:

1. Was Alexander's *pothos* (his drive to expand his empire beyond the known world) his undoing? Why or why not?

2. What are some similarities and differences between the East-West conflicts of the Greek and Persian wars and the East-West conflicts of our modern world?

Lecture Twenty-Four—Transcript
When East Met West

Welcome back. My friends, we have come to the last stage of our journey together on this great epic that has carried us through more than two centuries of history—and over a vast span of Europe, Asia, and Africa. Like Henry Fielding at the beginning of the final part of *Tom Jones*, I would like to address you as fellow travelers on this journey and tell you what a pleasure it has been for me to be in your company and how much I hope that you have enjoyed the journey also.

We left Alexander and his army triumphant on the field at Gaugamela in the autumn of 331 B.C. We can date it pretty precisely because about 10 days before the battle, there was an eclipse of the Moon. The soothsayers of Egypt, who were now in Alexander's train, obligingly interpreted this as a great sign of good fortune for Alexander and for his army.

Alexander moved south from Gaugamela. Babylon opened its gates—it was now one of the great capital cities of the Persian Empire—and he entered the city with flowers being showered down upon him, with the priests of Marduk singing hymns in his praise. He entered it like a conqueror, like a king, like a god.

From Babylon, he proceeded onward to the great official capital of the empire at Susa, that city on the plain in old Elam, which the descendants of Cyrus the Great had chosen as the capital once they abandoned Persis, their old homeland. They came down into Mesopotamia to rule the world from there as so many earlier conquerors had done.

After he took Susa, with its great treasury, he set his sights on the final royal cities—those that Cyrus the Great and Darius had created up on the high plateau of ancient Persia itself, in the southernmost part of Iran. He was filled with a reverence for these Persian predecessors, and he greatly disappointed the Macedonians and Greeks in his army by refusing to let them loot, pillage, and rape their way through Persia. After all, this was no longer a land to be plundered. This was his kingdom, and they must treat it with respect.

He went to Pasargadae, that place where Cyrus had hoped the Persians would always make the seat of their rule. You will remember—I've quoted it so many times—the anecdote with which Herodotus closed his great history of the early Persian wars when he reminded us that Cyrus told his followers: "Don't move down on the plains. Don't go down and join the Babylonians and the others. Hardy countries breed hardy men. Stay here in Persia."

Alexander came to that park-like place. He went to the simple little tomb of Cyrus the Great and marveled that such a fantastic conqueror should have ended his earthly time by having his remains placed in this simple little hut of stone at the top of a few steps.

Then he went on to the greatest prize of all: Persepolis, the city of the Persians, the grand ceremonial center begun by Darius and finished by Xerxes long, long before Alexander's time. Persepolis was, of course, one of the most famous places in the world and one of those few off limits to ordinary travelers. You had to be a Persian or a Persian subject to go to Persepolis for one of the great New Year's ceremonies, which happened every spring, in our month of April. Not only did the people bring their tribute from all corners of the empire to the Great King there, but they were received in audience by the king, seated upon his throne. In their national dress, they would be led forward by these courtiers who were descendants of the original Medes who joined with the Persians to conquer the world. They would have their moment face to face with that normally unapproachable figure, the Great King.

Alexander brought his army there. It was autumn, and he went into winter quarters and stayed the whole of the winter there—making Persepolis his base, glorying in that gigantic hall of columns, those immense pillars. Each pillar was crowned by an image of a bull or a lion holding up the roof beams; those original cedar logs sent to Darius way back in the 6th century B.C. from Lebanon by the Phoenicians were still in place overhead.

There came the month of May and the time to be going out again. Alexander at this point still had not caught Darius, and there was still sort of a political reason for pursuing him. He might always suddenly become the focus of some resistance and rebellion against Macedonian rule. But it was really Alexander's *pothos*—his "yearning," his desire to see what was beyond the horizon—that was driving him on.

So he was taking leave of Persepolis, and he had a great feast there in the spring of 330 B.C. to which all of his Macedonian officers and all of their women, their camp followers who, through thick and thin, had been following them through Asia Minor, the Levant, Egypt, and now Mesopotamia and Persia. These women came, too. They had flowers to wear as garlands—men and women alike—and they poured into the great hall at Persepolis, and the drinking began.

There was a famous harper there to sing songs to the lyre, to praise Alexander. As the evening progressed, the drinking got heavier and heavier, as it always did. The inhibitions were cast aside, until finally, a young woman of Athens—one of Alexander's favorites—a young woman named Thais stood up and rebuked the king for failing to really complete his mission. Her city had suffered from Xerxes long ago. The Persians had come and burned the temples on the Acropolis at Athens. What had Alexander done to pay the Persians back for that outrage?

Goaded by Thais, he seized a torch, and he went over to the side of the hall where the rich hangings came right down to the floor, and he threw the torch into the tapestries and the curtains. The fire ran up through the dry cloth, and his fellows joined in the fun. Some of the pillars were wood instead of stone, and as they threw their torches against them, the fire took over this vast hall.

Alexander apparently sobered up pretty quickly and realized he was burning his own most magnificent building, but it was too late. They couldn't put the fire out, and it burned to the ground. When one visits Persepolis today, one sees what those early explorers saw in the 19th century: columns still standing on this desert plateau on that high platform whose walls are engraved with the images of the Persians and their subjects, the camels, the trees, the flowers, the gifts of tribute from all over the known world—and rising above all, a few gaunt columns still cracked, blistered, and blackened by the flames of that May night so long ago. Nearby, you can see some of the fallen capitals, the bulls, the lions—that once held up the cedars of Lebanon—now on the ground.

A great English poet of the 17th century, John Dryden, made that scene the subject of a poem called "Alexander's Feast." He described Alexander and all of his men crowned with those wreaths. He described the beautiful women, and he described the songs that roused them to remember their great victories—that reminded them of the unburied, un-honored fallen among the Greeks and the Macedonians who lay behind them, whose souls still cried out for revenge against the Persians, and finally, of Thais herself. Thais led the way, and like another Helen, she fired another Troy.

Before Dryden gets to that conclusion, he puts in some lines in which he tries to address Alexander himself and all conquerors—people who spend their time blazing their way through the world, leaving wars, and hurt, and trouble in their wake—and asks these conquerors: "What was it all for?" These are the lines:

> "War," he sung, "is toil and trouble;
> Honour, but an empty bubble;
>   Never ending, still beginning,
> Fighting still, and still destroying:
>   If the world be worth thy winning,
> Think, O think, it worth enjoying;
>   Lovely Thais sits beside thee,
>   Take the good the gods provide thee—"

Alexander was not one to heed that call. For him, the battle was unceasing, the quest was eternal, and the calm sitting back and enjoying the fruits of one's labors was something that he never dreamed of doing. His restlessness helped to turn the world upside down, and although it brought much new and good to the world and its history, it was also the cause of the destruction of peace for many peoples for many years to come.

From Persepolis, Alexander headed north. He caught up, finally, with Darius near the Caspian Sea. Darius had been abandoned, finally, by his own exasperated companions, who had despaired of this king who seemed unable to turn, to fight, to rally. When Darius refused to go any further with them, they tied him to the throne that sat on a sort of a cart. They put golden chains on him, and they speared him through and left him to be dragged wherever the horses would take him.

The horses went to water, and it was there at the water hole that Alexander found—deserted and alone—the body of the man that he had come so far to defeat. One ancient source says that Darius was already dead, which is certainly the most likely. That source is the writer Arrian. But all the others like to stage a final conversation between this past lord of the world and this new conqueror, this new Great King, in which Darius wishes Alexander well and passes on the kingship to him as legitimate heir.

Alexander had already been sort of adopted as a son by the queen mother—Darius's mother, who never saw or spoke to her own son again but really liked Alexander—but that wasn't a very official thing. It really would have helped him if Darius had been known to have named him successor. Without that, all that Alexander appeared to be in the eyes of the world was the man who had taken this empire by conquest—that was his only right. With Bessus—a Persian noble who was a kinsman of Darius—still alive, there was still a rightful claimant to the throne.

It may be that the accounts of a deathbed encounter between these two great men were partly invented to give Alexander this claim upon the throne—some semblance of real legitimacy. As we will see, this is becoming very important to him. He doesn't want to be just conqueror; he wants to be the rightful king of a new world empire.

He went into the country we today call Afghanistan, which to him was Bactria. From Afghanistan, he continued through the Khyber Pass and down onto the plains of the Indus River and Pakistan. At one point, he actually crosses over into what is today modern India. He fights battles against Great King Porus there, who has many elephants and knows how to use them. But still, Alexander and his hardened Macedonian troops are ready for anything and succeed in winning their battles and taking, by siege, the cities that they make their targets in the Indus Valley.

At this point, someone has told Alexander that if he will just go east a little further, he will be at the headwaters of another river, a river that flows eastward—the Ganges, a sacred river. Alexander announces that this is where he is going, that they will get to the end of the world. His troops, who have followed him now for so many years—all the way from Macedon—mutiny and tell him they are not going any further.

So Alexander—not defeated by nature and not defeated by enemies—was finally defeated by his own men. They could not share his *pothos*, his yearning to see what lay beyond. They just wanted to go home. After one of his heroic sulks in his tent—Achilles-like, waiting for them to come around—he finally realized, this time, they're not going to. He was on his own, and he had to cave in.

They went down the Indus River. Alexander had fallen sick. He was carried on a galley, and the other galleys had to follow at a distance, lest the crashing of their oars into the water disturb the sleeping king.

They had a terrible time of it, getting back to the centers of the civilized world. He didn't understand geography; he was given bad advice about the terrain between India, and Pakistan, and Mesopotamia. He didn't understand it was one of the driest and most difficult deserts on Earth, and so while some of his ships went back by sea under the command of a companion from his boyhood days, Nearchus, he himself led his troops through the Gedrosian Desert.

He managed to get a lot of them through, but many died of hunger and thirst along the march and of exposure, so it was a very beaten army, certainly beaten in terms of their sufferings in the desert. Alexander, somewhat beaten down in spirit by this failure of his men to share his vision, finally rejoined with the fleet and came back to Mesopotamia.

He had to follow the road past the Behistun Rock that we visited long ago, as King Darius had carved there—Mount Rushmore-like—an image of himself triumphing over the rival claimants to the throne back in the 6th century B.C., and a trilingual inscription detailing the events of his seizing of the throne, and the greatness of Darius, King of Kings. Alexander, now the new Great King, was able to look up and see his illustrious predecessor above him.

His target was Babylon, which he now intended to make a world capital. He had plans in which his head was full of ships—he was going to create a great armada of thousands of ships and conquer the whole of the Mediterranean. He was going to run a highway from Egypt to the straits of Gibraltar or the straits of Heracles. He was going to use that highway as a military road for conquering the Carthaginians and beyond. Europe was going to be his next target, but not the only one. Another fleet would circumnavigate Arabia, and another one would cross the Caspian Sea and take control of whatever lands lay beyond.

There was no end to his ambition. We are often told that Alexander the Great died weeping because there were no more worlds to conquer; that was not the case. He died weeping because with a universe full of worlds, he had not even managed to fully conquer one.

To Babylon he came, and the priests came out and met him on the way before he could enter the city gates and said, "Do not come to Babylon. The portents are unfavorable; the gods have prophesied you are putting your life at risk if you come into this city." Alexander didn't like threats. He didn't like the idea that he would ever back down. Remember the moment where he drank the draft that had been prepared for him by the doctor whom he had just been told intended to poison him—yet he would not back down.

So the effect of this warning from the priests of Babylon was not what they expected. He did ask, "What is the proper direction from which to approach the city?" He led his whole army around to the other side and came in by the other gate, but he would not back down, even in the face of the gods.

At Babylon, he carried out a number of moves—initiatives—that showed what a changed man he was from that 20-year-old about 10 years earlier who had crossed over the straits at the Hellespont and led this fresh, young army into Asia. His vision has changed. He now wants to be king of Persians, and Macedonians and Greeks. He wants to unify those two peoples together in the same way that this man he now thinks of as his spiritual ancestor—Cyrus the Persian, the founder of the great Persian Empire—had unified the Persians with the Medes—whom they had just beaten—a partnership of victors and vanquished into a new harmony.

So he did several things that horrified his Macedonian followers. First of all, he started appearing in trousers, wearing Persian dress. Second, he decided that the only way to really get these people together was to really have some forced marriages, so he appointed 92 Macedonians, himself included, to take 92 noble Persian women as brides. There at Babylon, there was a public mass marriage as all of these unions were sanctified and all of these couples were formed—half-Persian, half-Macedonian or Greek.

He also bred up a generation of young Persians to be culturally Macedonian. He called them the "Successors," and he had them put through standard Macedonian training, and they joined him at Babylon and were the target of a great deal of attention and affection from Alexander.

He then had an enormous feast, and to this feast, he invited all of his Macedonians, and all the Persian nobility and commanders, as well. He said to them at the feast as they sat down together around him: "Let us rule the world in harmony as partners." Different Persian nobles were being given appointments by Alexander as governors or as commanders in the army. He began to act more and more this part of the god, until finally, there was another mutiny of his veterans. They said, "Go on with your wars alone. Your father, Ammon, will no doubt fight with you." Alexander, this time really furious, waded into the ranks, laid about left and right, and ordered some quick executions of the ringleaders of this mutiny.

He had already killed in one way or another a lot of his companions who had followed him along the way and whom he suspected of treachery. In this way, he became more and more like that oriental monarch of Greek nightmares—the absolute autocrat whose will is law, who is not bound by any human sense of justice.

As for the Greeks, Alexander remembered them—those distant, troublesome people. He decided that as he disbanded his armies and sent his Greek soldiers home, he would ensure that they got a warm welcome in their cities.

Remember, the Greeks at this point still feel that they are autonomous. They have submitted to Alexander as hegemon (commander-in-chief), but they haven't turned over their cities and governments to him. So it was a tremendous shock for them in the Olympic year of 324 B.C. when an envoy of Alexander's showed up at Olympia—that place where Herodotus had once recited the histories of the Persian wars, that place where Isocrates had pronounced to the world his new philosophy of the Panhellenic dream of Greek unity and a war against Persia. To the Olympic Games came this envoy of Alexander's with what the Greeks called the Exiles Decree.

Many of the men serving in Alexander's army came from Greek cities from which they had been exiled as troublemakers. Alexander now ordered all the Greeks to take back their exiles. This may not seem like a gigantic thing to us, but we have to remember that all these men were landowners whose lands had now been taken away and given to somebody else, or they were political undesirables who posed a threat to the state. The Greeks bubbled over with resentment and rage against Alexander for this interference in their affairs.

The Exiles Decree turned the Greek world against him. What was his legitimate claim to be able to do this? "I'm a god." Along with the Exiles Decree came a message from the envoy saying, "And Alexander may be worshiped now, fittingly, as a god, as a son of Zeus," to which the cynical Athenians replied, "Well, let him be a son of Zeus if he wants and a son of Poseidon, too, if he likes." They were not impressed with his claims to immortality and to godhood.

More and more people who had been part of Alexander's youth began to turn against him even as he won wider and wider popularity in the Persian Empire. They had dreaded his coming as an unstoppable, ferocious conqueror and found him, instead, to be a man who wanted to respect the local traditions, who wanted to fuse Greek and Persian into a new world culture.

During this time, after Alexander's return from India, his best friend, Hephaestion, died very unexpectedly. He was quite a healthy young man, but he just died, apparently after an enormous drinking party and a fever. After disobeying his doctor's orders not to take any heavy food or strong drink, he ate a whole chicken and downed it with a lot of wine, and he died.

Alexander behaved as if the great love of his life was gone. He mourned for days. He apparently was trying to will himself into death so he could go with Hephaestion to the next world. Hephaestion had always been the legendary Patroclus to his Achilles, and now he felt that half of himself had disappeared. So he ordered, for Hephaestion's funeral, a mountain of ships to be created as a funeral pyre. There were going to be *quinquiremes* in long rows. These were ships even bigger than triremes that would form a square and then another square smaller on top of that—platform upon platform of these ships with their glittering rams facing outward. On the top: Images of the Sirens, who had once lured mariners to destruction. In each statue of a Siren was going to be a human being, singing like the voice of the unseen spirit of the Siren within.

It's not clear to me whether these people were going to be burned up, too, in the funeral pyre, but Alexander wasn't thinking in very rational or logical terms. Hephaestion was going to be placed, then, on this pyre and sent to the gods in a fitting way. That pyre, by the way, was never finished. It was just too much to think of a whole fleet of ships being burned up in this profligate manner.

Alexander's own despair and feeling of mortality were really triggered by this death of Hephaestion. There in Babylon, he, too, fell sick. There were some bad portents that happened. Alexander was out on the river, and his hat blew off. Whatever hat you wear is, if you're a king, a crown. It blew off in a gust of wind into the water, and one of the men onboard the ship—a Macedonian—jumped overboard, fetched the hat, and now, having to swim back to the ship and needing two hands, put it on his own head in order to keep it dry, and made his way back to the ship.

He was rewarded for saving the hat. He was flogged for having done anything so ill-omened as to put the king's crown on the head of another—himself—something that symbolized the passing of royal power from Alexander.

There was a tradition in Babylon that once a year, whoever was the rightful monarch would step off his throne, and a substitute king would sit down—a sort of foolish king for a day who was mocked and ridiculed—and everybody got to say to this jester figure all the things they bottled up all year long and really wanted to say to the king but couldn't. So there was a tradition of the surrogate in Babylon. There was one wonderful occasion back in the days of Babylon's glory—back in the Bronze Age—when the surrogate was sitting on the throne, and word came that the real king had died that day, and the surrogate refused to get up. He became the new king.

This tradition was eerily echoed when a madman was suddenly found seated on Alexander's throne in Babylon, and nobody knew where he came from or how he got there. There just seemed to be piling up these ill-omened portents of something terrible about to happen to the king. They may have worked on Alexander's own psychology.

At any rate, not long after the death of Hephaestion, he fell sick, as well—fell into a terrible fever. Modern scholars are divided, as ancient people were, on whether this was a natural illness or he was being poisoned. Some people think it might have been Roxane, a native girl whom he had married and by whom he was about to have a child. But there were hundreds of people who would have wished him dead, and any one of them might have been administering the poison to him.

He went into sort of not quite a coma but a state in which he could barely speak and barely move. His troops, learning that his last days were at hand, filed by him there in Babylon to take their leave—weeping now that this man who had turned them into gods and supermen also was now passing out of this world. So in Babylon, Alexander died. His body was embalmed—it was prepared for return to Macedonia, the land of his fathers—and a great struggle for possession of the empire that he had created began.

We call the period that was launched the Hellenistic period because he had carried Hellenic traditions and culture into the heart of Asia, where it fused with local traditions to create a hybrid world—partly Greek and partly local. They themselves, at the time, called the period after Alexander the "Period of the Successors." But with that world, we and our course have nothing to do, because the Persian Empire and the world of the free Greek city-states both ended in that year of Alexander's death, 323 B.C.

His empire, his political earthly empire, was immediately cut up among his successors—divided into warring kingdoms. Ptolemy, his general, became pharaoh of Egypt and started the last dynasty of Egyptian kings—the one that ended several centuries later with the famous Cleopatra, a descendant of the Macedonian Ptolemy. All over, powerful Macedonians set themselves up as rulers over chunks of Alexander's empire.

That empire was the Persian Empire, and it was no more. It had passed away with him. But that other vision that he had had in his last days—that vision of a harmony between Greek and Persian—that endured. He had brought Greece to Asia; he had spread Hellenic ideas of city planning, architecture, government, philosophy, art, and religion everywhere he went. Little Alexandria's and Alexandropolis's popped up in his wake, and in those cities, a new kind of world civilization emerged.

That was his true legacy. That was the true legacy of this centuries-long conflict between these peoples—Greeks and Persians. It was the foundation for our modern world, our cosmopolitan world, our multicultural world, which still can trace so many of its elements back to that line of giants—from Cyrus to Alexander—who made these transformations possible.

Maps

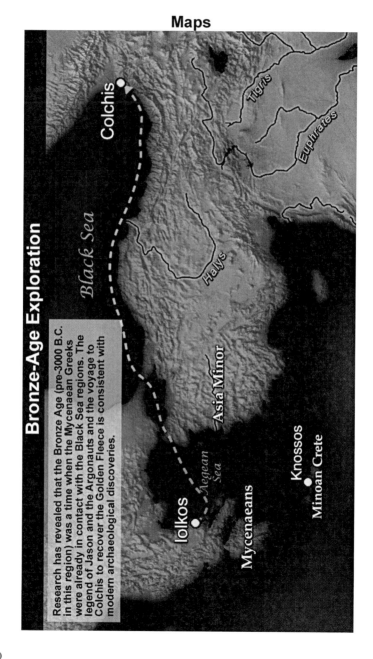

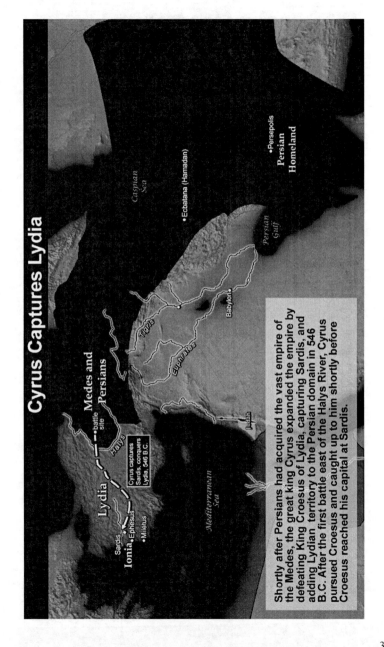

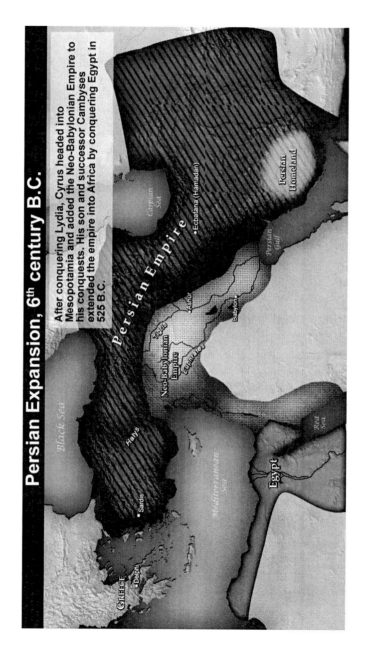

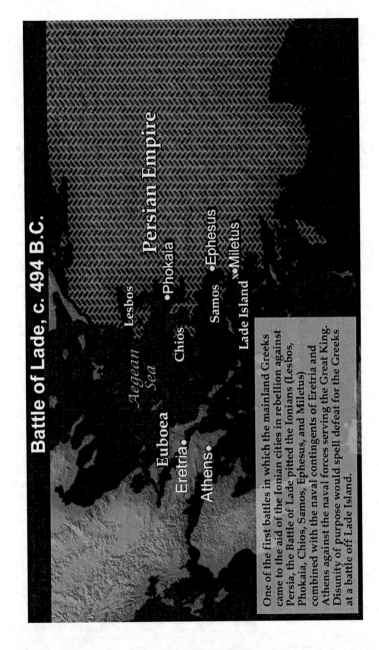

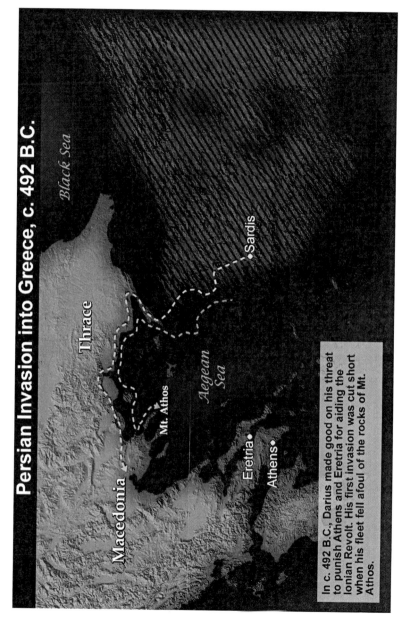

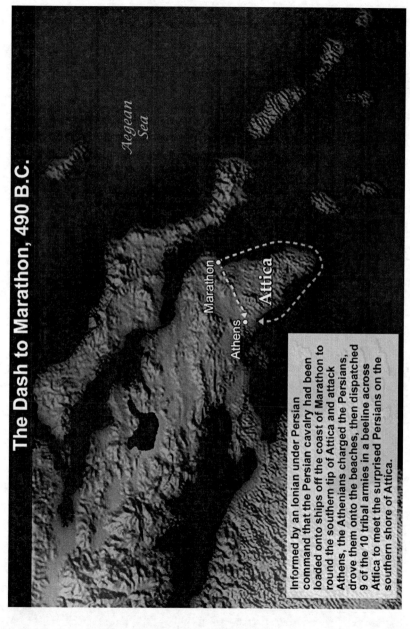

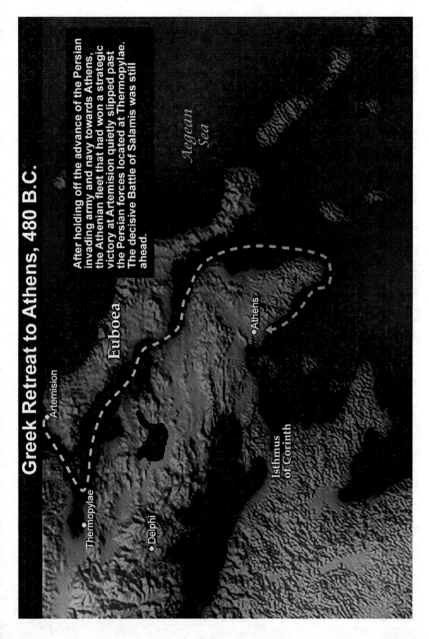

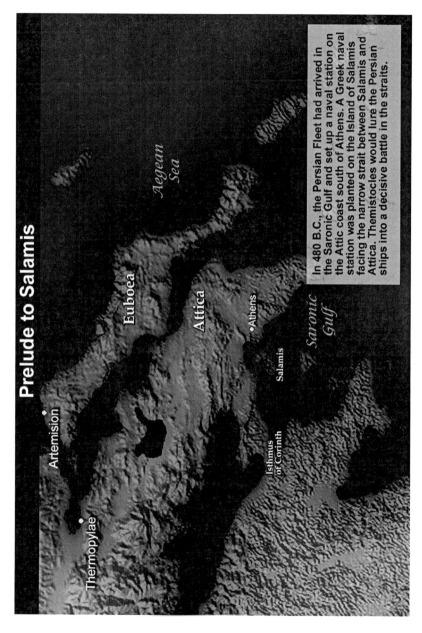

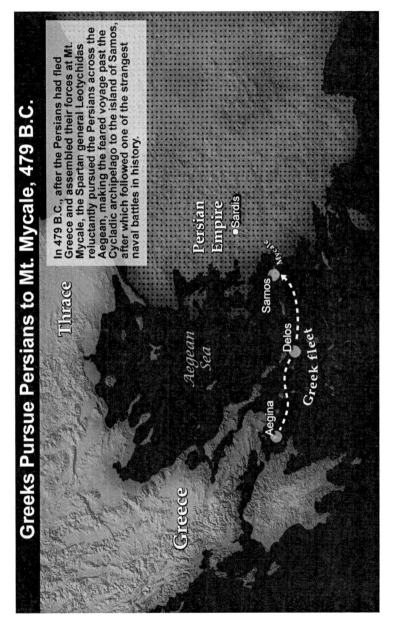

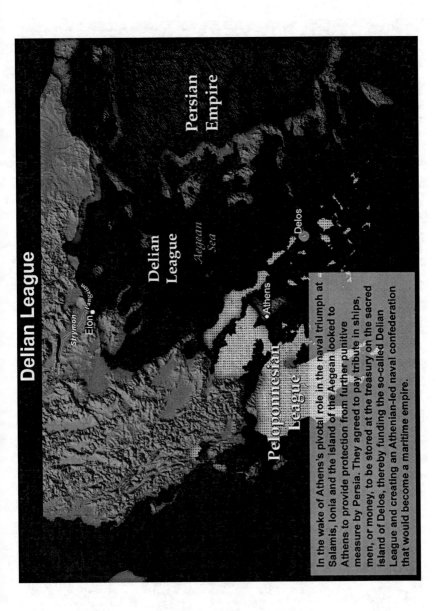

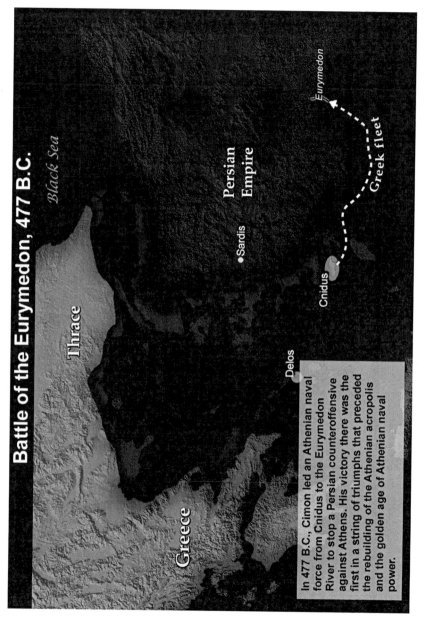

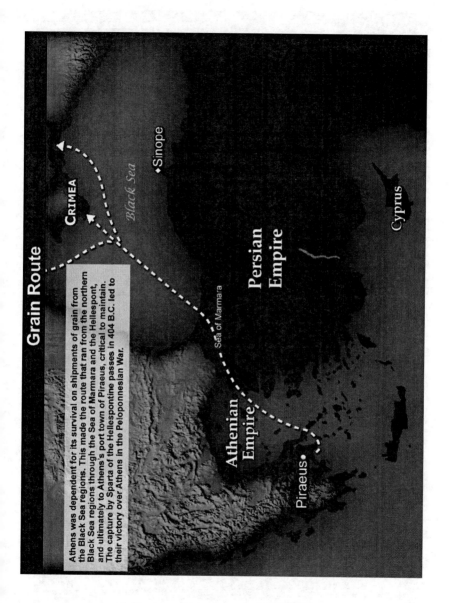

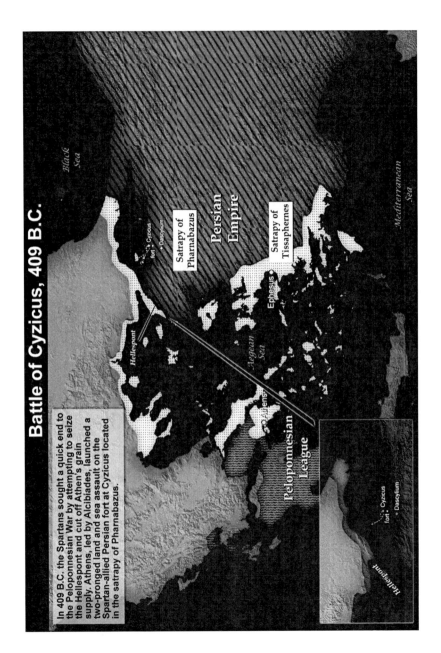

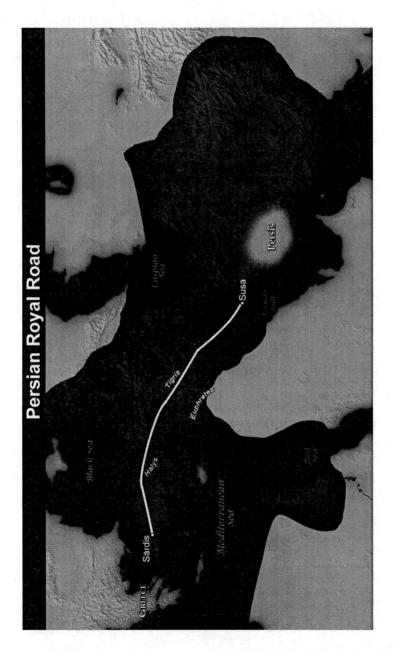

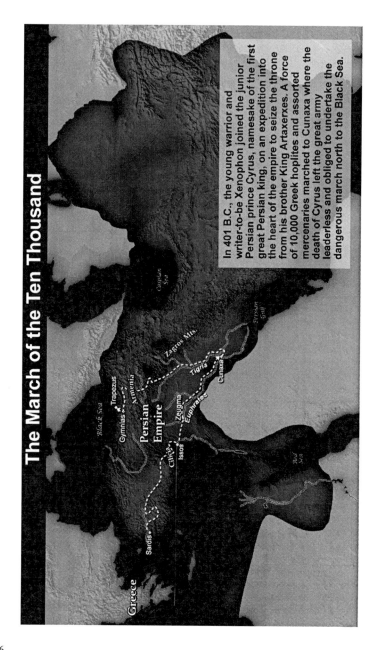

Alexander's Conquest of Ionia, 334–323 B.C.

Following in the footsteps of his father Philip's consolidation of hegemony in mainland Greece and the regions of Thrace, Alexander made good on the centuries-old promise to settle affairs with Persia once and for all in the name of Greek freedom, launching his conquest in the East by crossing the Hellespont and plunging his spear into the beachhead of Abydos.

Macedon

Thrace

Hellespont
Abydos

Aegean Sea

Persian Empire

Sardis
Ephesus
Miletus
Caria
Halicarnassus

Greek city-states

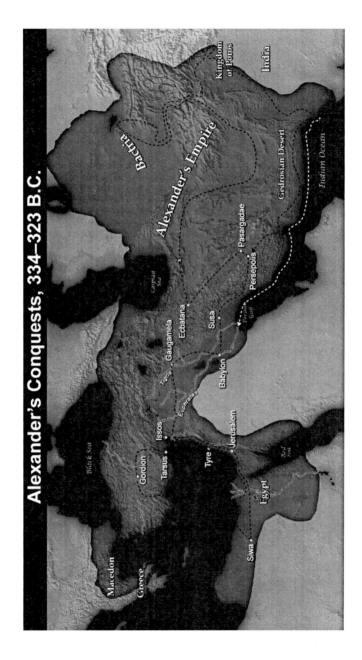

Overview of Major Phases

Note: A handy companion to the study of historical dates is E. J. Bickerman's *Chronology of the Ancient World* (London: Thames and Hudson Ltd., 1980).

546 B.C.–482 B.C.
Initial Contact between Greeks and Persians

The Persian kings Cyrus II, Cambyses, and Darius I add to their empire the ancient Greek cities of Asia Minor, the islands of the Aegean Sea, and the European mainland as far west as Macedonia. Persian attempts to conquer Greek city-states are checked by a naval disaster in a storm off Mount Athos in 493 B.C. or 492 B.C. and by the Athenian victory over a Persian expeditionary force that landed at Marathon in 490 B.C.

481 B.C.–479 B.C.
Xerxes's Invasion of Greece

In a massive three-year operation chronicled by Herodotus, the Persian king Xerxes leads the largest armed force ever seen westward into Greece, which he invades by land and sea. The major clashes of the invasion are the battles of Thermopylae and Salamis in 480 B.C. and the battles of Plataea and Mycale in 479 B.C.

478 B.C.–450 B.C.
Athenian Maritime Alliance Campaigns

The Athenians take over the role of hegemon (war leader) from the Spartans and lead annual campaigns of retribution against the western maritime territories of the Persian Empire. Allied with them are the Greek islands and cities that were liberated from the Persians during or after Xerxes's invasion. Modern historians often call this group of allies the Delian League.

449 B.C.–413 B.C.
The Age of Peace

After the Athenians negotiate the Peace of Callias with the Persian king Artaxerxes I, major hostilities between Greece and Persia cease.

412 B.C.–386 B.C.
The Weakening of Athens and Sparta

The Persian kings and the satraps of Asia Minor use their gold to fund the wars between Athens and Sparta, thus playing the two leading states of Greece against each other and fatally weakening both. The Persians pay for a Spartan fleet, which gains victory for Sparta at the end of the famous Peloponnesian War in 404 B.C.; 10 years later, Persia restores the naval power of Athens. In 386 B.C., Persia imposes a peace on all the Greeks, attempting to stabilize its western frontier.

385 B.C.–335 B.C.
Mercenary Armies and Campaigns

The half-century that follows the King's Peace sees the prominence of mercenary armies whose campaigns influence relations between the Greeks and the Persians. Some of these armies fight to support rebels (such as the Egyptians); others fight on behalf of the satraps; and others still are hired by Persia to fight the king's wars.

334 B.C.–323 B.C.
Conquests of Alexander the Great

The Greek and Persian wars come to a close with the rise of young Alexander III (Alexander the Great) as king of Macedon. Championing the Greek cause, Alexander leads an army into the heart of the Persian Empire; defeats the Persians at the Granicus River, at Issos, and at Gaugamela; and reigns briefly as Great King himself. More lasting than Alexander's military success is his dissemination of Greek culture throughout the old realm of the Persian kings, which launches the Hellenistic Age.

Timeline

Note: A handy companion to the study of historical dates is E. J. Bickerman's *Chronology of the Ancient World* (London: Thames and Hudson Ltd., 1980).

B.C.

546 .... Cyrus II (known as Cyrus the Great) conquers Lydia, brings a number of Greek cities under Persian control, and initiates direct contact between Persians and Greeks; Cyrus ignores the warnings of a Spartan emissary who tells him to leave the Greek cities in peace.

530 .... Cyrus dies and leaves his empire to his son Cambyses.

525 .... Cambyses conquers Egypt with the participation of Ionian and Asiatic Greek forces and extends the Persian Empire into northern Africa.

522 .... Cambyses dies, and a noble Persian named Darius I takes the throne, recording his triumphant accession in inscriptions and reliefs on the cliff face at Behistun and marrying Cyrus's daughter Atossa to strengthen his claim to the throne.

520 .... Darius I embarks on the construction of Persepolis: the grand ceremonial center in the heart of the Persian homeland.

c. 515 .... Darius I sends Democedes and a contingent of Persians on a reconnaissance mission into Greek waters, with a view toward a future Persian campaign of conquest.

c. 512 .... Darius I leads a major expedition (again, with the assistance of the Ionian

Greeks) across the Bosphorus into Europe to conquer the Scythians and the rich, grain-producing lands that border the Black Sea.

c. 499.. Aristagoras, the Greek who governs Miletus in Asia Minor on behalf of the Persian king, plots a rebellion against the Persians in the hope of liberating the Ionians; Aristagoras crosses the Aegean to mainland Greece to seek assistance for his rebellion from the Spartans (who refuse) and the Athenians (who send a force of hoplite soldiers); the Greek forces take the Persians by surprise at the Battle of Sardis but suffer a severe defeat after their victory.

c. 494.. The Persians suppress the Ionian revolt, defeat the Greek fleets at the Battle of Lade, and take the city of Miletus after a siege; the Ionians and the Greeks of Asia either flee or submit to Persian rule.

493 .... Themistocles is elected archon (chief magistrate) of Athens and persuades his fellow citizens to build massive fortifications at the promontory of the Piraeus to create a secure base where Athenians can either wait out a Persian siege or safely embark for a new home in southern Italy.

c. 492.. Darius I sends forces into Europe under the command of his kinsman Mardonius and conquers the coastal regions of Thrace and the kingdom of Macedon; the Persian fleet is destroyed by a great north wind as the ships try to round the promontory of Mount Athos.

490	Darius I sends an expeditionary fleet with horse transports directly across the Aegean Sea; under the leadership of Datis the Mede, the Persians capture Eretria and carry off the population to a new home in the heart of the Persian Empire; the Greeks, led by Miltiades, manage to inflict an astonishing defeat on the Persians at the Battle of Marathon.
c. 489	The Athenians, believing that they have no need of elaborate naval installations, abandon their work at the Piraeus with the walls having reached only half their proposed height.
486	Darius I dies while preparing a third invasion of Greece, and Xerxes inherits both the throne and his father's ambition to conquer the Greeks; the Persian satrapies of Egypt and Babylonia revolt.
c. 484	Xerxes starts to assemble the Persian armada and the Grand Army.
483	Xerxes sends engineers to Mount Athos to cut a canal through the neck of the peninsula; Themistocles persuades the citizens to devote the wealth from a recent silver strike in their mines to the purpose of creating a fleet of triremes.
481	Xerxes sets out from Susa with his Grand Army; a council of Greeks led by the Spartans meets at the Isthmus of Corinth to plan the defense of their homeland.
480	A Greek force under the command of the Spartan king Leonidas holds back the Persian army for three days at the

	Battle of Thermopylae; the Persian fleet suffers a decisive defeat at the Battle of Salamis.
479	Mardonius, left behind in Greece by Xerxes to finish the job of conquest, burns Athens but is defeated by a grand alliance of Greeks at the Battle of Plataea; the remnant of the Persian fleet is caught on shore at the Battle of Mycale and destroyed by the Greeks.
478	The Ionians decisively reject the Spartan hegemony and ally themselves with Athens instead, creating the maritime alliance known today as the Delian League.
477	Under the command of Cimon, the fleet of the new Athenian maritime alliance embarks on the first of many seasons of attacks on Persian holdings and territories; Themistocles convinces the Athenians to complete the transformation of the Piraeus into the best-fortified naval base and commercial port in the Greek world.
472	Aeschylus's tragedy *The Persians* is produced by Pericles at a dramatic festival.
471	The Athenians turn against Themistocles and vote to ostracize him from the city.
c. 466	Cimon leads the naval and military forces of the Athenian alliance to their greatest victory at the Eurymedon River; using the spoils from the battles, the Athenians fortify the southern side of the Acropolis (thus preparing a

	terrace where the Parthenon will one day stand).
465	Xerxes is assassinated; his son Artaxerxes I succeeds him.
462	The empowered lower-class majority of Athenian citizens participates in a radical democratic revolution and reorganization of their government; Cimon opposes the reforms and is ostracized.
c. 460	The Athenians conduct a fresh series of campaigns against the Persians at the Hellespont, at Cyprus, and at Phoenicia; the Athenian fleet aids the Egyptians in a rebellion, thus inaugurating a six-year period in which Athenians share in the rule of Egypt with a native monarch.
454	The Persians defeat the Athenian forces in Egypt and reclaim the country.
450	Cimon, back in authority as a general after his 10-year ostracism, leads an attack on Persian holdings in Cyprus but dies during the campaign.
449	Callias travels along the Royal Road to Susa and negotiates a peace with Persia, leading to the cessation of hostilities.
448	Pericles begins to use the wealth from Athens's new maritime empire to usher in a Golden Age, with remarkable achievements in the fields of art, architecture, science, drama, history, political thought, and philosophy.
c. 440	Herodotus collects information about the Persian Empire and the invasion of Xerxes, writes *The Histories* (a massive work that forms the cornerstone of the

new discipline of history and historical research), and presents it orally at such sites as Athens and Olympia.

431 .... Fearful of growing Athenian power, the Spartans and their Peloponnesian League attack the territory of Attica, beginning the Peloponnesian War.

423 .... Artaxerxes I dies and is succeeded by Darius II.

413 .... The Athenians lose a huge fleet and army in an ill-advised expedition against the city of Syracuse in Sicily; Tissaphernes and Pharnabazus send envoys to Sparta promising large-scale financial support for a campaign against Athens's overseas allies and areas of imperial control.

412 .... On the advice of Alcibiades, the Spartans set out to destroy Athenian power in alliance with Tissaphernes; Alcibiades himself urges Tissaphernes to use Persian gold and diplomacy to wear down both the Athenians and the Spartans; the Spartans swear an oath to return the Greek cities on the Asiatic mainland to the Great King if the Persians will help them destroy Athens.

410 .... When the resurgent Athenians maintain their power on the Ionian seacoast, the Spartans seek the support of Pharnabazus; the Athenians win two naval battles against the Spartans in the Hellespont.

409 .... Alcibiades helps engineer a stunning victory over both Spartans and Persians at Cyzicus.

404	The Spartans defeat the Athenians at the Battle of Aegospotami—the last battle of the Peloponnesian War; thanks to the Persian gold provided by Prince Cyrus, the Spartans overcome the Athenians and Athens falls; Darius II dies and is succeeded by Artaxerxes II.
401	Prince Cyrus marches into the heart of the Persian Empire with the Ten Thousand to claim the throne and dies at the Battle of Cunaxa; Xenophon helps lead the Greeks on their famous march to the sea.
c. 400	Native rulers in Egypt revolt against Persia and (aided by Greek mercenaries) maintain their independence from Persian for more than half a century.
394	Pharnabazus persuades the Great King to place Conon in charge of a combined Persian and Athenian fleet that breaks Spartan naval power in a battle off Cnidus; Pharnabazus provides Persian gold to help rebuild the naval fortifications of Athens and restore a balance of power between Athens and Sparta.
389	The Athenians antagonize the Persians by supporting a revolt of Cypriote Greeks against the Great King.
386	To stabilize his western frontier, Artaxerxes II imposes the King's Peace on the Greek city-states.
384	Isocrates makes a speech at Olympia urging the Greeks to unite in a Panhellenic crusade against the Persians.

c. 366	Aided in part by Greek mercenaries, the satraps of the western Persian Empire unite in a rebellion against the Great King (which is ultimately suppressed six years later).
361	Artaxerxes II (with the aid of Greek mercenaries) suppresses a revolt in Egypt.
359	Artaxerxes II dies and is succeed by Artaxerxes III Ochos; Philip II becomes king of Macedon.
356	A madman burns down the temple of Artemis at Ephesus; Philip II's wife, Olympias, gives birth to Alexander III.
346	Isocrates recognizes in Philip II the leader who will unite the Greeks in a war against Persia.
c. 343	Artaxerxes III Ochos successfully reconquers Egypt.
340	Athens declares war on Philip II; Artaxerxes III Ochos opposes Philip II's attempt to conquer the city of Perinthus, providing the Macedonians with a justification for attacking Persia.
337	Philip II convenes a council of Greeks at the Isthmus of Corinth and proclaims a Panhellenic war against the Persian Empire.
336	Philip II is assassinated; he is succeeded by his son Alexander III (known as Alexander the Great); Artaxerxes III Ochos dies and is succeeded by Darius III; Alexander summons the Greeks again to the Isthmus of Corinth and reaffirms his father's mission to conquer Persia.

334	Alexander moves his army through western Asia Minor, defeats a Persian army at the Granicus River, wins over or conquers cities, and deprives the Persian fleet of any harbors in the region.
333	Alexander treks through southern Asia Minor, cuts the Gordian knot, and routs the army of Darius III at Issos.
332	Alexander besieges and captures Tyre and conquers Egypt; the oracle of Zeus Ammon at the oasis of Siwa tells Alexander that he is the son of the gods.
331	Alexander founds Alexandria and leads his army to Gaugamela, where he inflicts a decisive defeat on Darius III and captures the heartland of the Persian Empire; Alexander chooses the Persian capital of Persepolis for his winter quarters and burns the great hall of the Persian kings.
330	Darius III is assassinated by men who form the remnant of his force; Alexander becomes Great King (as well as king of Macedon and general of the Greeks) and embarks on a series of initiatives aimed at unifying his own people with the Persians.
324	Alexander creates the Exiles Decree, which orders all Greeks to take back their exiles (many of whom were part of Alexander's army).
323	Alexander dies in Babylon; his Macedonian "Successors" cut up the realm, igniting a power struggle amongst the Hellenistic kings that succeed Alexander.

Glossary

Achaemenid: The dynasty of Persian kings (of which Cyrus was the first major representative), so-called because of their supposed descent from a legendary ancestor known as Achaemenes. The line of descent was broken on a number of occasions, but the designation is still applied by modern historians to the line of Persian kings down to the last one, Darius III.

agora: The open public space at the heart of every Greek city. It served as a civic center, a religious sanctuary, and a marketplace.

Ahura Mazda: The god of the Persians. A deity of the sky, light, and fire.

archaeology: The scientific and humanistic discipline of recovering, analyzing, and interpreting the physical remains of past cultures. From the Greek for "study of ancient things."

archon: In Greek, a general term for any ruler or overseer; in Athens, the title of the chief magistrate who gave his name to the civil year from one midsummer to the next (the *eponymous archon*). Athenian archons were originally chosen by vote; shortly before the Greek and Persian wars, however, the method shifted to choice by lot.

barbarian: In Greek, *ho barbaros*. A term usually applied specifically to the Persians. The word had a more general application for anyone who spoke a non-Greek language and whose speech sounded to a Greek like "bar-bar-bar" (or, as we say in modern English, "blah-blah-blah"). It did not necessarily carry the modern connotation of "uncivilized savage," but it was not a compliment either.

"Black Athena" debate: A scholarly controversy launched by philologist Martin Bernal concerning the debt that classical Greek civilization owed to innovations and discoveries borrowed from Egypt and the Near East.

cuneiform: A script developed in ancient Sumeria in Mesopotamia and widely used for millennia to record different languages throughout the Near East. Not a simple alphabet like that used by Phoenicians, Hebrews, and Greeks, cuneiform employed hundreds of characters that represented phonetic elements, complete words, and determinative qualities. Though often inscribed on stone, the script was originally used to incise signs on wet clay with the wedge-shaped end of a scribe's stylus (*cuneus* being Latin for "wedge").

daric: Gold coin first minted under Darius I and used throughout the Persian Empire. Sometimes called an *archer* because it bore the image of the Great King brandishing a bow or other weapon.

drachma: A common silver coin in the Greek world (also a unit of measure). During the 5th century, a drachma represented a day's pay for a skilled rower or artisan. One hundred drachmas made a mina (roughly equivalent to a modern pound); 6,000 drachmas made a talent.

ephor: One of five annually elected magistrates who ran the Spartan state. The only real check on their executive and judicial powers were the votes of the open assembly of all Spartan citizens and the fact that they presided for only one year and could not hold the office more than once.

eunuch: A castrated male, normally abhorrent to the Greeks but important in Asiatic societies in roles ranging from the palace bureaucracies of Near Eastern kingdoms to the priests who served the mother goddess Cybele.

Great King: The traditional Persian title for the Achaemenid monarchs from Cyrus to Darius III, meaning a "king of kings" or ruler of an empire. The Greeks knew the term but generally used the generic term *ho basileus* or "the King."

hegemon: A war leader, particularly of a powerful state (such as Sparta, Athens, or Macedon) that leads an alliance of other states.

Hellenistic Age: The period launched by Alexander the Great during which Greek (Hellenic) civilization spread throughout the Near East and northern Africa.

helot: One of a class of slaves in Spartan territory who worked the land for the Spartans during peacetime, accompanied their masters to battle during war, and in general (according to Xenophon) would have been happy to "eat the Spartans raw."

hemerodromos: A professional courier in the Greek world capable of running all day to carry messages at high speed.

henotheism: The religious practice of the Persians, who were monotheistic themselves but tolerant of polytheism in other societies.

hoplite: A heavily armed Greek soldier who fought in the tightly arrayed phalanx. Full hoplite panoply consisted of a helmet, a breastplate, shin guards (greaves), a round shield, a spear, a sword, and possibly, a dagger.

The name probably comes from the term for the round shield (*hoplon*), less likely from the general Greek word for gear (*hoopla*).

hubris: To an ancient Greek, not merely arrogance but unjust or impious violence arising from arrogance. The Greeks held Xerxes to be guilty of hubris for his acts of violence against nature in bridging the Hellespont and cutting a canal through the promontory of Mount Athos.

magus (pl. magi): A magus was a Persian wise man, star-watcher, magician (hence the English term *magic*), and priest of Ahura Mazda. Magi carried the sacred fire altars when Persian kings went forth to war.

Medizer: To a Greek, a Medizer was a turncoat who had chosen to collaborate or submit to "the Mede" (the Persians).

metis: In Greek, cunning intelligence. Homer had King Nestor praise the power of *metis* and devoted the *Odyssey* to showing how Odysseus used *metis* rather than brute force to overcome his opponents. Themistocles and Alcibiades in their different ways employed *metis* in battle. The Persians in general despised such cunning schemers—and suffered accordingly.

oracle: A site where public divination was practiced and where it was believed that one could receive guidance directly from the gods; also the religious person who spoke the prophecies (*mantis*) and the prophecy itself.

paian: The war cry and victory hymn of the Greeks, sung before battle by both sides and after the battle by the victors. Familiar in English by the Latin form *paean*, the word derives from an epithet of Apollo as the healing god.

Panhellenism: An ideal championed by such 4th-century-B.C. writers and orators as Isocrates, who envisioned a Greek world united in a crusade to conquer Persia, the common enemy, rather than continually caught up in internal wars.

paradeisos: Greek version of the Near Eastern term for a royal pleasure park planted with trees. In the Septuagint (the Greek version of the Hebrew Scriptures), Eden is termed a *paradeisos*, hence the modern word *paradise*.

peltasts: Lightly armed troops who used missiles at close quarters rather than swords or spears (as hoplites did).

phalanx: From the same Greek word that serves for "finger," the military phalanx was an array of hoplites in tightly packed lines, often eight deep.

They advanced with spears held before them and, provided the terrain was level, were almost invincible unless outflanked.

***polis* (pl. *poleis*)**: In Greek, not merely a city but a city-state, comprising the walled urban community and the surrounding lands. Some *poleis*, such as Athens and Sparta, grew to incorporate many other communities in their territory, but each was still thought of as a *polis*.

Royal Road: To a Greek, the Royal Road was the limited-access highway that ran for 1,600 miles from Sardis in western Asia Minor to the Persian capital at Susa beyond the Tigris River. There was, however, a network of royal roads throughout the Persian Empire, and the Great King depended on them for the rapid movements of his couriers, envoys, and armed forces.

sarissa: The pike or long, heavy spear with which Philip II of Macedon equipped his soldiers. At roughly 17 feet in length, the sarissa outclassed the older Greek spear used by hoplites, but its use required a much more intensive level of training.

satrap: English rendering of the Greek term for a Persian governor who governed territory (a satrapy) on behalf of the Great King. Most satraps were Persian nobles; all were required to muster troops at the Great King's command and serve as war leaders for the contingents from their own satrapies.

satrapy: English rendering of the Greek term for the territory or province that a Persian governor (satrap) ruled. Each satrapy seems to have had a fixed quota of tribute that the satrap collected each year and sent to Susa or Persepolis.

trireme: The big-oared galley that served as the ship of line in naval battles throughout the time of the Greek and Persian wars. According to ancient sources, the Phoenicians first built triremes long before their city-states were incorporated into the Persian Empire; they used these 120-foot-long galleys for trade, exploration, and colonization. The concept of a galley with a large crew of rowers arrayed in a triple-tiered arrangement was then taken up by the Greeks. During the Greek and Persian wars, the principal naval power on the Greek side was Athens, with its fleet of 200 to 400 triremes; on the Persian side, the principal naval power was the Phoenicians, in particular, the mariners of Tyre and Sidon.

Biographical Notes

Aeschylus (c. 525 B.C.–455 B.C.): Athenian poet, tragic playwright, and veteran of the battles of Marathon and Salamis who wrote the oldest dramatic work surviving today: *The Persians*, which commemorated the victory at Salamis.

Alcibiades (450 B.C.–404 B.C.): Athenian general in the later stages of the Peloponnesian War, notorious for his sexual escapades, his chameleon-like changes of allegiance, his disastrous advocacy of the Athenian expedition to Sicily in 413 B.C., and his contribution to the Athenian victory over a combined Spartan and Persian force at Cyzicus in 409 B.C.

Alexander III, or Alexander the Great (356 B.C.–323 B.C.): Son of Philip II of Macedon and Olympias and tamer of the stallion Boukephalos, Alexander inherited his father's kingdom, army, and mission to conquer Persia when he was only 20 years old. He proved equal to every challenge, defeating Darius III of Persia and waging successful campaigns from Egypt to the Indus River Valley during his reign (336 B.C.–323 B.C.). His death in Babylon has been suspected by some to be the result of poisoning.

Antalcidas (c. 430 B.C.–370 B.C.): Spartan commander and diplomat who achieved prominence in the decades after the end of the Peloponnesian War. He engineered the King's Peace (or the Peace of Antalcidas) in 386 B.C., which imposed peace on the warring city-states of Greece, acknowledged the Great King as an arbiter in Greek affairs, and handed the Greek cities of Asia Minor over to Persian control.

Aristides the Just (c. 520 B.C.–465 B.C.): Athenian general and statesman who is said to have served as general of his tribal regiment in the Athenian victory over the Persians at Marathon in 490 B.C. and was the commander-in-chief of the Athenian forces during the Battle of Plataea in 479 B.C. He earned his nickname as an arbiter, but his reputation for fairness did not save him from ostracism after he opposed Themistocles's navy bill in 483 B.C. In 478 B.C., at Byzantium, the Ionian Greeks appealed to Aristides and the other Athenians to lead them in a new maritime alliance against Persia, thus creating the organization known to modern scholars as the Delian League. Aristides was entrusted with the task of assessing the annual monetary contributions expected of each ally.

Aristotle (384 B.C.–322 B.C.): Greek philosopher, student of Plato in his younger days, tutor to Alexander, and head of a new school at the Lyceum in Athens (where he wrote many of his immortal treatises on science, politics, and other subjects). He believed that cultural groups such as the Persians were inherently inferior to Greeks and, therefore, that Alexander should subjugate them—advice Alexander refused to take. Aristotle is said to have received botanical and zoological specimens from the remote regions of Asia, sent back by Alexander.

Artaxerxes I (r. 465 B.C.–423 B.C.): This son of Xerxes is best known in the context of the Greek and Persian wars for having concluded a peace with the Athenians in 449 B.C., for recognizing the Athenian sphere of influence in the Aegean and eastern Mediterranean, and for agreeing to end hostilities. The peace is called the Peace of Callias, but its terms—and even its very existence—are still fiercely debated by some scholars.

Artaxerxes II (r. 404 B.C.–359 B.C.): As Great King, Artaxerxes worked through the Spartan diplomat Antalcidas to impose the King's Peace of 386 B.C. on Athens, Sparta, and the other warring city-states of Greece. In doing so, he regained the Greek cities of Asia Minor but lost Egypt, which was not recovered until the days of his son and successor, Artaxerxes III Ochos. In the early years of his reign, Artaxerxes II successfully withstood a challenge from his brother Cyrus and Cyrus's army of 10,000 Greek mercenaries. He was wounded at the decisive Battle of Cunaxa in 401 B.C. and was tended by the Greek physician Ctesias.

Artaxerxes III Ochos (r. 359 B.C.–340 B.C.): The Great King who restored order to much of the Persian Empire and succeeded in reconquering Egypt. His attempt to prevent Philip II of Macedon from capturing the city of Perinthus near Byzantium sparked an undying hostility on the part of the Macedonian kings toward Persia. Artaxerxes III was assassinated through the intrigues of a eunuch named Bagoas.

Artemisia (r. early 5th century B.C.): As ruler of the Dorian Greek city of Halicarnassus in southwest Asia Minor and of the nearby island of Cos, Artemisia was also a vassal of the Great King. In 480 B.C., she commanded the contingent of five triremes that Xerxes levied from her territory for his invasion of Greece. The only female combatant among the hundreds of thousands of men who followed the king, Artemisia won Xerxes's respect through her plain-speaking and sound advice, according to Herodotus (who was born at Halicarnassus under her rule). She was a special target of the Athenians at the Battle of Salamis but survived and was given the honor of transporting some of Xerxes's sons back to Asia aboard her ships.

Atossa (c. 550 B.C.–475 B.C.): Persian queen, daughter of Cyrus, wife of Darius I, and mother of Xerxes. Aeschylus brought her onstage with a major role in *The Persians*, in which she anxiously awaits the return of Xerxes from his expedition against Athens and summons up the ghost of her late husband, Darius I, to seek his wisdom.

Cimon (c. 507 B.C.–450 B.C.): Athenian general and son of Miltiades (the victor of Marathon). Cimon's mother was a Thracian princess, and he grew up outside Athens. He was too young to take a leading role in the defense of Greece against Xerxes, but his natural gifts for leadership, his wealth, his aristocratic heritage, and his affability made him the people's choice as general for some 15 years during the wars between the Delian League and the Persians. A great admirer of Sparta, Cimon "navalized" Athens in much the same way that military leaders had long before militarized Sparta. His greatest victory was won at the Eurymedon River in Asia Minor in about 466 B.C. Shortly thereafter, he became unpopular with the Athenians for his Spartan sympathies and his opposition to radical democratic reforms. After 10 years in ostracism, Cimon returned to the generalship but died while campaigning in Cyprus.

Conon (c. 445 B.C.–390 B.C.): Athenian naval commander who escaped from the disaster at Aegospotami in 405 B.C., maintained an exiled Athenian fleet of a few triremes in Cyprus during the decade following Athens's surrender to Sparta, and was ultimately chosen by Artaxerxes II to command a Persian-Athenian fleet against the Spartans. After his great victory off Cnidus in 394 B.C., Conon returned to Athens with enough Persian gold to rebuild the city's naval base. He was imprisoned by the satrap Tissaphernes during a diplomatic mission and died without ever returning to Athens. His son Timotheus proved a worthy successor in leading the Athenian navy to new victories.

Croesus (r. c. 560 B.C.–546 B.C.): Last king of the wealthy kingdom of Lydia and so rich that his name became proverbial. He ruled from the city of Sardis on the Hermon River. Croesus brought the Greek cities of the Asiatic coast under his dominion but respected their religion and consulted their oracles. His military strength depended upon the famous Lydian cavalry, as well as Greek mercenary hoplites. The Delphic Oracle told Croesus that if he crossed the river Halys he would destroy a great kingdom; he did cross the Halys River to confront Cyrus the Persian, but the great kingdom that he destroyed was Lydia itself.

Cyrus II, or Cyrus the Great (r. 557 B.C.–530 B.C.): This charismatic conqueror, the son of a Persian king and a Median princess, elevated the previously obscure nation of Persia to the status of a world power through his conquests of Media, Lydia, Babylonia, and central Asia. His personal qualities of honor and uprightness made Cyrus a legendary figure among peoples as diverse as the Jews and the Greeks.

Cyrus the Prince (c. 435 B.C.–401 B.C.): This younger son of Darius II was sent west to oversee the satrapies of Asia Minor and administer the Persian efforts to secure the defeat of Athens. Prince Cyrus's close friendship with the Spartan commander Lysander resulted in continuous funding for the Spartan naval enterprises and, ultimately, the Spartan victory in the Peloponnesian War. After the death of his father and the accession of his older brother as Artaxerxes II, Prince Cyrus assembled a large army of mercenaries, including the famous Ten Thousand, to help seize the throne; he was killed, however, at the Battle of Cunaxa.

Darius I (r. 522 B.C.–486 B.C.): Though not a descendant of Cyrus, Darius I became Great King after a violent struggle with other claimants following the death of Cambyses. He commemorated his success on the cliff face at Behistun. Darius I established new capitals at Susa and Persepolis and set up the well-organized administrative system of the empire that was to endure through all subsequent reigns. He added the Indus River Valley, Thrace, and the Aegean islands to the empire but failed to conquer Greece after his army was defeated by the Athenians at the Battle of Marathon in 490 B.C.

Darius III (r. 336 B.C.–330 B.C.): The last of the line of Persian Great Kings, Darius III acceded to the throne in the same year that Alexander the Great became king of Macedon. His reign was dominated by his unsuccessful effort to preserve the empire from conquest by Alexander, whom Darius III faced personally at Issos and Gaugamela. He was assassinated by his own courtiers.

Datis the Mede (early 5th century B.C.): General appointed by Darius I to command the expedition against Athens and Eretria in 490 B.C. After crossing the Aegean and bringing many islands under Persian control, Datis succeeded in taking Eretria but was defeated by the Athenians during the Marathon campaign. It is not clear whether he was present at the famous battle or was in the process of transporting his cavalry around to Athens by ship at the time.

Democedes (late 6th century B.C.): A self-taught Greek physician, Democedes was born in Croton in southern Italy and held posts of honor as a medical expert in Aegina, Athens, and Samos before being captured by the Persians. He gained the trust of both Darius I and his wife, Atossa, and was appointed by Darius to lead a Persian reconnaissance mission around the seas and coasts of Greek territories in about 515 B.C.

Herodotus (c. 490 B.C.–425 B.C.): Famous as the "father of history," Herodotus left his home in Halicarnassus as a young man and spent many years traveling throughout the lands around the Mediterranean. He assembled the *Histories*, a history of the Greek and Persian wars, from accounts of eyewitnesses and local traditions woven into a larger narrative about the rise of Persia and the longstanding conflicts between East and West. Part raconteur, part geographer, and part ethnographer, Herodotus found a wide audience for his narrative at such sites as Athens and Olympia. He deplored the Peloponnesian War that pitted Greek against Greek and, at the end of his life, was a citizen of the new Panhellenic colony of Thuriae in Italy.

Isocrates (436 B.C.–338 B.C.): Extraordinarily long-lived Athenian teacher of rhetoric, who was still writing remarkable orations at the age of 99. He was a pupil of Socrates, a friend of the general Timotheus, and a supporter of Philip II of Macedon's claims to leadership in the Greek world. In the political arena, Isocrates is most important for his championship of the vision of Panhellenic unity and a Greek crusade against the Persian Empire.

Leonidas (r. c. 490 B.C.–480 B.C.): A king of Sparta famous for commanding the contingent of 300 Spartans and several thousand other Greeks who held the pass at Thermopylae in 480 B.C. against the gigantic army of Xerxes. Leonidas rose to heroic stature when he refused to surrender, even though he and his men were surrounded. He roused his men to fight to the death, thus creating inspiring martyrs at a time when the Greek cause desperately needed such a unifying example.

Leotychidas (r. 491 B.C.–469 B.C.): A king of Sparta whose reign overlapped that of the more famous Leonidas (there were two royal lineages in Sparta and, therefore, a double kingship). Leotychidas was put in command of the allied Greek fleet in 479 B.C. and succeeded in destroying the remnant of Xerxes's armada at the Battle of Mycale in Asia Minor. His reluctance to defend the newly liberated Ionian Greeks was the first step in turning them toward a strong allegiance to Athens rather than Sparta.

Lysander (c. 440 B.C.–395 B.C.): Spartan admiral (*navarchos*) and victor in the naval battles of Notion and Aegospotami. Perhaps the greatest strategist that Sparta ever produced, Lysander was also successful as a diplomat, and his friendship with the Persian prince Cyrus ensured the continued flow of the Persian gold that funded the Spartan naval effort. He took credit for the Spartan victory over Athens in the Peloponnesian War, but his unbridled ambition eventually became intolerable to the Spartans at home and the oppressed allies abroad.

Mardonius (early 5th century B.C.): Persian general under Darius I and Xerxes who urged a policy of aggression against Greece in the hope of becoming satrap of the Hellenic lands once the conquest was achieved. In about 492 B.C., he successfully invaded Thrace on behalf of Darius I. Mardonius is best known, however, as the general left behind by Xerxes with orders to complete the conquest of Greece after the naval disaster at Salamis. He was killed during the Battle of Plataea in 479 B.C.

Miltiades (c. 554 B.C.–489 B.C.): Athenian military leader famous for his successful generalship at the Battle of Marathon in 490 B.C. against a Persian expeditionary force. Earlier in his career, Miltiades had ruled the Gallipoli Peninsula as a sort of personal fiefdom; he then became a vassal of the Great King and participated in Darius I's campaign to Scythia. Miltiades's standing was so high in the Aegean world that he was able to marry a Thracian princess; their son Cimon inherited his father's abilities as a commander.

Olympias (mid-4th century B.C.): A daughter of the Molossian king from a mountainous realm in northern Greece, Olympias met Philip II of Macedon at Samothrace and subsequently married him. She bore Philip II's first male heir, Alexander, and exerted a powerful influence on the young conqueror's early years. Olympias outlived both her husband and her son but died during the struggles between Alexander's successors.

Pausanias the Regent (late 6th century B.C.–early 5th century B.C.): A nephew of King Leonidas, Pausanias became regent with royal powers after Leonidas's death at Thermopylae (Leonidas's own son was still too young to rule). Pausanias achieved glory when he led the Greek army to victory at Plataea in 479 B.C., thus ending Xerxes's hopes of conquering the Greek mainland. His high-handed behavior toward the Ionian Greeks at Byzantium the following year drove them into an alliance with Athens and created the Delian League.

Pericles (c. 494 B.C.–429 B.C.): Athenian general, statesman, and visionary architect of Athens's Golden Age. Pericles was the son of Xanthippus (the Athenian general at Mycale) and Agariste (a member of the powerful and wealthy Alcmaeonid clan). Pericles first came to prominence in his early 20s when he sponsored the production of Aeschylus's *Persians*. As general, he led naval expeditions into former Persian waters when he took Athenian fleets into the eastern Mediterranean and the Black Sea. After the Peace of Callias, Pericles devoted himself to beautifying Athens with the wealth of the maritime empire.

Pharnabazus (late 5th century B.C.–early 4th century B.C.): A Persian noble who served as satrap of the satrapy in northern Asia Minor that stretched along the Hellespont, the Sea of Marmara, and the Bosphorus (with a capital at Dascylium). Pharnabazus strove to help the Spartans overcome the Athenians in the closing years of the Peloponnesian War. Within a decade, he was aiding the Athenian Conon in an effort at sea to destroy Spartan hegemony. Most Greeks found him to be the very pattern of Persian honor and nobility.

Philip II (382 B.C.–336 B.C.): King of Macedon and father of Alexander the Great. Philip II's ambition was to transform the mountainous and forested kingdom of Macedon into a world power. He created a new type of phalanx armed with long pikes (sarissas), coordinated the movements of infantry and cavalry, and kept his men in training through a professionalized military service. At the end of his life, the adept diplomat became the hegemon of the Greek city-states and planned an invasion of Persia but was assassinated before he could carry it out.

Themistocles (c. 523 B.C.–459 B.C.): Athenian statesman and master strategist who guided the Greeks to victory in 480 B.C. during the invasion of Xerxes. He believed that Athens's future lay with the sea and was responsible for persuading the Athenians to fortify the Piraeus and to use the proceeds from a silver strike to build a fleet of 200 triremes. In the end, however, the Athenians turned against him and he had to seek protection from the Great King. He died in Persian territory, still in disgrace with the Athenians.

Thucydides (c. 454 B.C.–c. 404 B.C.): A wealthy Athenian general in the early years of the Peloponnesian War, Thucydides was banished for failure to carry out a mission. He took advantage of his exile to write the *Histories*: an account of the war and the world's first work of true analytical historical composition. His work is unfinished, but it is clear in the final sections (dealing with the years after 413 B.C.) that he began to perceive the important role that would be played by Persia in settling the affairs of the Greek city-states.

Tissaphernes (late 5th century B.C.–early 4th century B.C.): Satrap of western Asia Minor (which he governed from the provincial capital at Sardis), Tissaphernes was a cunning diplomat and schemer, useful at times as an ally to both Spartans and Athenians. He was a friend of Alcibiades during the latter's stay in Asia Minor. Later, Tissaphernes became embroiled in the dynastic struggle between Prince Cyrus and Artaxerxes II and was ultimately executed on the orders of the Great King.

Xenophon (c. 428 B.C.–354 B.C.): A noble Athenian and pupil of Socrates, most famous for writing the *Anabasis* (*Going Up,* a.k.a., *The Persian Expedition*), an account of his adventures in marching with the Ten Thousand in 401 B.C. He is a vital source for information about Persian life, customs, and administration in the late 5th century B.C. He put some of his idealistic thoughts on the Persians into his book *Cyropaedia* (*The Education of Cyrus*). He accompanied Prince Cyrus into the heart of the Persian Empire in Cyrus's attempt to gain the throne. In later life, Xenophon campaigned with the Spartans, whom he found more admirable than his fellow Athenians.

Xerxes (r. 486 B.C.–465 B.C.): A king of Persia and the son of Darius I and Atossa, Xerxes is best known through the pages of Herodotus's *Histories* as the king who led the largest army and fleet ever assembled in an unsuccessful attempt to conquer Greece (481 B.C.–479 B.C.). He was assassinated 14 years later, having spent most of the rest of his reign with his harem. He was probably the Persian king who appears in the Book of Esther.

Bibliography

Adcock, F. E. *The Greek and Macedonian Art of War.* Berkeley: University of California Press, 1957. Still a classic after half a century, this slim volume encapsulates the author's many insights and observations on military strategy, tactics, equipment, personnel, and the place of the army and navy in the Greek city-state.

Aeschylus. *Prometheus Bound and Other Plays: Prometheus Bound, The Suppliants, Seven Against Thebes, The Persians.* Philip Vellacott, trans. London: Penguin, 1961. An accessible introduction to *Persians*, the world's oldest surviving play, which includes an invaluable description of the Battle of Salamis by a man who fought in the great naval engagement himself. Vellacott's translation is very free, intended more as an acting text than as a word-for-word translation.

Allen, Lindsay. *The Persian Empire.* Chicago: University of Chicago Press, 2005. Do not be deceived by the beautiful cover or the extraordinary array of colorful photos—this is a hard-hitting scholarly overview of Achaemenid history that manages to provide a coherent narrative of the events, combined with careful assessments of the sources on which the historical reconstruction is based. An essential book.

Andronikos, Manolis, et. al., eds. *The Search for Alexander: An Exhibition.* Boston: New York Graphic Society, 1980. This extensively illustrated exhibition catalog presents an extraordinary array of portrait busts, coins, weapons, royal treasures, and other artifacts associated with Alexander the Great, but its greatest value perhaps derives from the thoughtful essays, such as the one by Andronikos on the discovery of the royal Macedonian tombs at Vergina.

Bengtson, Hermann. *The Greeks and the Persians: From the Sixth to the Fourth Centuries.* New York: Delacorte, 1968. A straightforward narrative history of the material covered in this course, written by a distinguished scholar of ancient history at the University of Munich, with contributions by other specialists on various regions of the Persian Empire.

Blamire, A. *Plutarch: Life of Kimon.* London: Institute of Classical Studies, 1989. The author provides the Greek text and an English translation of Plutarch's biography of the great Athenian naval commander (one of the best of his *Lives*), along with a detailed commentary covering the entire period of the Delian League and its campaigns against the Persian Empire.

Briant, Pierre. *From Cyrus to Alexander: A History of the Persian Empire.* Winona Lake, IN: Eisenbraun, 2002. Valuable for its comprehensive assembling of texts and ancient references to Persian history, religion, and culture. Not really a "history," as the title claims, but a gigantic historiographical essay about the author's evaluation of the various sources. Difficult to use because of the idiosyncratic ordering of material and the skimpy index.

Broad, William. *The Oracle: The Lost Secrets and Hidden Message of Ancient Delphi.* New York: Penguin, 2006. A study of the geology and history of Delphi and its famous oracle, including an account of interdisciplinary work conducted at the site by geologist Jelle de Boer and archaeologist John Hale.

Burn, A. R. *Persia and the Greeks: The Defense of the West, c. 546–478 B.C.* New York: St. Martin's Press, 1962. The best history of the early stages of the Greek and Persian wars, written by a scholar who fought in Greece during World War II and, thus, could view such sites as Thermopylae with a soldier's eye. Eminently clear and practical throughout, with handy maps and diagrams of battlefields. Burn's working out of the day-by-day diary of Xerxes's fleet and army from August to September 480 B.C. is alone worth the price of the book.

Camp, John, and Elizabeth Fisher. *The World of the Ancient Greeks.* New York: Thames and Hudson, 2002. An excellent introduction to archaeological sites and discoveries in Greece. The authors combine their account of sites and artifacts with a historical survey. Copiously illustrated.

Cartledge, Paul. *Thermopylae: The Battle That Changed the World.* New York: Vintage, 2006. An enthusiastic retelling of the Spartan stand at the "Hot Gates" under King Leonidas, written by a prominent scholar and champion of the Spartan military ethos.

De Sélincourt, Aubrey. *The World of Herodotus.* Boston: Little, Brown and Co., 1963. Written by a distinguished translator of Herodotus's histories, this book includes substantial sections on Herodotus's life, Greece before the Greek and Persian wars, the campaigns of Darius and Xerxes, Greek literature, and the city-state.

De Souza, Philip. *The Greek and Persian Wars, 499–386 B.C.* London: Routledge, 2003. A well-illustrated introduction to the events and issues in the period from the Ionian revolt to the King's Peace.

Farrokh, Kaveh. *Shadows in the Desert: Ancient Persia at War.* Oxford: Osprey, 2007. Fascinating, well organized, and beautifully illustrated, with maps as well as photographs of important sites and artifacts. The first third of the book covers Achaemenid Persia and the period of the Greek and Persian wars; the remainder carries the story down to the Islamic conquest.

Fitzhardinge, L. F. *The Spartans*. London: Thames and Hudson, 1980. An excellent introduction to Spartan civilization, art, and religion, offering a corrective to the stereotypical view of the Spartans as either noble heroes or single-minded killing machines. As the title page states: "150 illustrations"!

Gorman, Vanessa. *Miletos: The Ornament of Ionia*. Ann Arbor: University of Michigan Press, 2001. A scholarly monograph that assembles historical and archaeological information about the greatest Greek city in Asia Minor.

Green, Peter. *Alexander of Macedon*. London: Pelican, 1974. A vivid retelling of Alexander's life and adventures.

———. *The Year of Salamis, 480–479 B.C*. London: Weidenfeld & Nicholson, 1970. A well-known scholar presents a compelling reconstruction of Xerxes's doomed invasion of Greece.

Hanson, Victor Davis. *The Western Way of War: Infantry Battle in Classical Greece*. New York: Knopf, 1989. A compact but revolutionary book by the foremost American scholar of ancient Greek military history.

Harper, Prudence O., et. al., eds. *The Royal City of Susa: Ancient Near Eastern Treasures in the Louvre*. New York: Harry Abrams, 1992. A lavishly illustrated exhibition catalog, with an excellent introductory essay and spectacular coverage of early Elamite Susa, as well as Susa during its years as a royal Persian capital city.

Heckel, Waldemar, and Ryan Jones. *Macedonian Warrior: Alexander's Elite Infantryman*. Westminster: Osprey, 2006. A short but lavishly illustrated study, with many modern reconstructions of battlefield scenes and armed soldiers. This title is included as an example of one of the many handbooks published by Osprey on military history, a number of which also provide specialist studies related to the Greek and Persian wars.

Herodotus. *The Histories*. Aubrey de Sélincourt, trans. New York: Penguin, 2003. The primary source for the Greek and Persian wars from the beginning down to 479 B.C. This classic translation is revised and introduced by John M. Marincola.

Hignett, C. *Xerxes' Invasion of Greece*. Oxford: Clarendon, 1963. The great value of this work lies not in Hignett's narrative of Xerxes's expedition (as is the case with Peter Green's book) but in his obsessive quest for the original sources from which Herodotus may have drawn the details of his account. Good topographical discussions of the battlefields and the line of march are also included.

How, W. W., and J. Wells. *A Commentary on Herodotus*. Oxford: Clarendon Press, 1912. The granddaddy of all commentaries on Herodotus's account of the rise of Persia and the expedition of Xerxes. Incredibly, even after almost a century of additional scholarship and discoveries, no one has published a book that supersedes this one.

Isocrates. *Orations*. George Norlin, trans. London: Heinemann, 1928. This is the Loeb Classical Library three-volume edition of Isocrates's orations, including the great "Panegyricus," in which he urged Panhellenic unity and a Greek invasion of Persia led by Athens. Contains the Greek text with the English translation on the facing pages.

Kagan, Donald. *The Fall of the Athenian Empire*. Ithaca: Cornell University Press, 1987. A detailed reconstruction of the years from 413 B.C. to 404 B.C., including reconstructions of Cyzicus and other battles in which the Persians attempted to aid the Spartan effort to destroy Athens. In addition to the narrative account, the author includes an analysis of the ancient sources (Thucydides, Xenophon, Diodorus Siculus, Plutarch, and others) and a review of modern scholarship and opinions.

Kuhrt, Amélie. *The Persian Empire: A Corpus of Sources from the Achaemenid Period*. New York: Routledge, 2007. This pioneering work in two volumes is the source book that historians have been waiting for: vast in scope, clear in organization, and beautifully (if minimally) illustrated. The texts, translated from a number of ancient languages, are grouped so as to provide a chronological survey of Persian history, followed by thematic chapters on such topics as kingship, religion, and the economy; the only failing is an unhelpful index. Take out a second mortgage and order your copy today!

Lazenby, J. F. *The Defence of Greece, 490–479 BC*. Warminster: Aris & Phillips, 1993. A military history of the years from the Marathon campaign to the battles of Plataea and Mycale.

Lenardon, Robert J. *The Saga of Themistocles*. London: Thames & Hudson, 1978. The best introduction to the visionary statesman, general, and strategist who engineered the Greek victory at Salamis and the transformation of Athens into a dominant naval power.

Lyle, Evelyn. *The Search for the Royal Road*. London: Vision Press, 1966. An illuminating personal account of a journey overland from Sardis to Susa, illustrated by the author's own photographs.

Miller, Helen Hill. *Bridge to Asia: The Greeks in the Eastern Mediterranean.* New York: Scribner, 1967. Not a scholarly history but a perceptive travelogue of Asia Minor and the eastern Aegean islands. Engagingly written, with photographs of the modern ruins and excellent maps.

Morrison, John, J. F. Coates, and N. B. Rankov. *The Athenian Trireme: The History and Reconstruction of an Ancient Greek Warship.* Cambridge: Cambridge University Press, 2000. An account of the Athenian trireme and its history, including sections on individual battles, by the team behind the designing and sea trials of the replica trireme *Olympias*.

Moscati, Sabatino, ed. *The Phoenicians.* New York: Rizzoli, 1999. A rich collection of papers that introduce the Phoenicians: master mariners of antiquity and the chief providers of ships to the navies of the Great Kings of Persia.

Myres, John Linton. *Herodotus: Father of History.* Oxford: Clarendon Press, 1953. An indispensable reconstruction of Herodotus's life, travels, purpose, achievement, and critics. Such over-imaginative passages as Myres's account of Salamis (one of the few pieces of serious scholarship that merits the epithet "zany") are more than balanced by the exhaustive approach, the intriguing analysis of the structure of *Histories*, and the author's love of his subject.

Olmstead, A. T. *History of the Persian Empire: Achaemenid Period.* Chicago: University of Chicago Press, 1948. A narrative of the Achaemenid kings and their realm, from Cyrus to Alexander the Great.

Plutarch. *The Age of Alexander: Nine Greek Lives.* Ian Scott-Kilvert, trans. Harmondsworth: Penguin, 1973. This handy compendium brings together Ian Scott-Kilvert's translations of the lives of Alexander, Agesilaus, Demosthenes, and other leaders.

———. *Plutarch on Sparta*, rev. ed. Richard Talbert, trans. London: Penguin, 2005. Before Richard Talbert tackled the Herculean task of mapping the classical world for the *Barrington Atlas*, he translated a number of biographies and essays by Plutarch that create a composite portrait of the ancient Spartans, both men and women. An essay attributed to Xenophon, with a description of Spartan society and military organization, is included as an appendix.

———. *The Rise and Fall of Athens: Nine Greek Lives.* Ian Scott-Kilvert, trans. Harmondsworth: Penguin, 1960. Ian Scott-Kilvert's translations make